Guide to Housing Be
and Council Tax Ber

JOHN ZEBEDEE, MARTIN WARD AND SAM LISTER

Shelter

CHARTERED INSTITUTE OF HOUSING

The Chartered Institute of Housing is the only professional organisation representing all those working in housing. Its purpose is to maximise the contribution that housing professionals make to the well-being of communities. The Institute merged with the Institute of Rent Officers and Rental Valuers in February 1999. The Chartered Institute has over 18,000 members working for local authorities, housing associations, the Rent Service, educational establishments and the private sector.

For further information, please write to:

Chartered Institute of Housing
Octavia House
Westwood Way
Coventry
CV4 8JP

Telephone: 024 7685 1700
Fax: 024 7669 5110
E-mail: *customer.services@cih.org*
Web site: *www.cih.org*

SHELTER

Shelter is Britain's largest homelessness charity, with a network of 59 housing aid centres and projects providing advocacy and assistance at a local level for people in housing need. Shelter believes that everyone should be able to live in a decent and secure home that they can afford within a mixed neighbourhood where people feel safe, can work and fulfil their potential.

For further information about Shelter, please write to:

Shelter
88 Old Street
London
EC1V 9HU

Telephone: 0845 458 4590
E-mail: *info@shelter.org.uk*
Web site: *www.shelter.org.uk*

For help with your housing problems any time, day or night,
freephone Shelterline: 0808 800 4444.

Guide to Housing Benefit, Peter McGurk and Nick Raynsford, 1982-88 (1st to 9th editions); Martin Ward and John Zebedee, 1988-90 (10th to 12th editions).

Guide to Housing Benefit and Community Charge Benefit, Martin Ward and John Zebedee, 1990-93 (13th to 15th editions).

Guide to Housing Benefit and Council Tax Benefit, John Zebedee and Martin Ward, 1993-2003 (16th to 25th editions: 1st to 10th of this title).

Guide to Housing Benefit and Council Tax Benefit, John Zebedee, Martin Ward and Sam Lister with additional material by Colin Hull, 2003-05 (26th to 27th editions: 11th to 12th of this title).

John Zebedee is an independent benefits trainer and writer. He has taught more than 1,600 courses for local authorities, housing associations, advice and law centres and others.

Martin Ward is an independent benefits consultant and trainer (e-mail *mward@info-training.co.uk*). He jointly maintains a web-site which gives convenient access to relevant legislation and other useful sources – *www.info-training.co.uk*

Sam Lister is policy officer at the Chartered Institute of Housing and a trustee of the Worcester Housing and Benefits Advice Centre.

John Zebedee and Martin Ward have specialised in housing benefit since the introduction of the 1982-83 scheme and in council tax benefit since it was introduced in 1993.

ISBN 1 903208 70 X

Production by Davies Communications (020 7482 8844)

Printed by Antony Rowe Ltd

Cover photography: Nick David

Preface

This is the twenty-seventh in our series of guides. This edition covers the rules about housing benefit and council tax benefit as they apply from April 2004, using the information available on 1st April 2004. HB and CTB are currently in no danger of ossifying as there are numerous changes this year.

We welcome comments and criticisms on the contents of our guide and make every effort to ensure it is accurate. However, the only statement of the law is found in the relevant Acts, regulations, orders and rules (chapter 1).

This guide has been written with the help and encouragement of many other people. Early editions were written by Nick Raynsford and Peter McGurk, and much is owed to them. Colin Hull wrote chapter 11 (Help with rates in Northern Ireland), and we are very grateful for his work.

This year we wish to thank the following in particular:

Stephen Bryant, Jill Charman, Mary Connolly, Ann Goslyn, Claire Horsfield, Ryan James, Claire Jenkins, Maxine Lawrence, Penny Matthews, Spencer May, Marleen McKittrick, Phillip J. Miall, Ian Nisbet, Nick Price, Jim Read, Julie Ryan, Lesley Sopor, Mark Tindley, Imogen Wilson, Leicestershire Welfare Rights, Linda Davies and Peter Singer (editing and production) as well as staff from the Department for Work and Pensions and the technical advice and guidance section of The Rent Service. Their help has been essential to the production of this guide.

John Zebedee, Martin Ward and Sam Lister

April 2004

Contents

Abbreviations

The principal abbreviations used in the guide are given below. A key to the marginal references can be found at the end of chapter 1 in table 1.2.

CTB	Council tax benefit
CTC	Child tax credit
DSD	The Department for Social Development in Northern Ireland
DWP	The Department for Work and Pensions
EP	Extended payment
GB	England, Scotland and Wales only
GLHA	DWP Guidance Local Housing Allowance
GM	The Housing Benefit and Council Tax Benefit Guidance Manual, DWP, April 2002, with supplements to February 2004
HB	Housing benefit (including in Northern Ireland help with rates)
HRA	Housing revenue account
IB	Incapacity benefit
IS	Income support
JSA	Jobseeker's allowance (including JSA (Cont) & JSA(IB))
JSA(Cont)	Contribution-based jobseeker's allowance
JSA(IB)	Income-based jobseeker's allowance
NI	Northern Ireland
NIHE	The Northern Ireland Housing Executive
RCA	The Rate Collection Agency in Northern Ireland
SDA	Severe disablement allowance
SI	Statutory instrument
SR	Statutory rules (Northern Ireland)
UK	England, Scotland, Wales and Northern Ireland
WTC	Working tax credit

1 Introduction

1.1 Welcome to this guide, which this year celebrates the 21st anniversary of the housing benefit (HB) scheme and the 11th of the council tax benefit (CTB) scheme. HB and CTB are important schemes providing people with help towards paying their rent and council tax and in Northern Ireland rates. Our guide is for use by anyone who is interested in the schemes, including administrators, advisers, claimants and landlords.

1.2 The guide describes the HB and CTB schemes administered throughout the United Kingdom from April 2004 and, where there are variations in the scheme between England, Scotland, Wales and Northern Ireland, these are explained. This chapter summarises the HB and CTB schemes and explains:

- the basic conditions for benefit;
- the terminology, references and benefit rates;
- which authorities are responsible for administering the schemes;
- how they should go about making their decisions on claims, etc;
- the legal and other sources of information; and
- how the marginal references work.

Overview and basic conditions for benefit

1.3 HB and CTB are national welfare benefits administered principally by local councils in Great Britain and in Northern Ireland by executive agencies of the NI government. The purpose of the HB scheme is to help people on low incomes pay their rent and, in Northern Ireland, rent and rates. In Great Britain the CTB scheme provides assistance with council tax and takes two forms. 'Main CTB' is by far the more common. It helps people on low incomes pay their council tax. 'Second adult rebate' (also known as 'alternative maximum CTB') is not based on the claimant's needs or resources but on the income of certain adults in the claimant's household. Claimants eligible for both main CTB and second adult rebate are awarded whichever is the most valuable.

AA 1(1),(1A),(1B)
CBA 130(1)(4), 134(1)(4)
NIAA 1(1),(1A),(1B)
NICBA 126(1), 130(1),(3)

1.4 The Social Security Acts (paras 1.39-40) set out the basic conditions of entitlement. To be entitled all these conditions must be satisfied in every case. The circumstances in which a claimant satisfies these conditions are set out in detailed regulations which it is the purpose of this guide to describe.

1.5 The basic conditions for HB and CTB are:

(a) a valid claim has been made which includes details of any national insurance number(s) (chapter 5); and

(b) the claimant is liable to pay rent and/or council tax for their home (paras 2.33-67 and 9.7-12) or, in Northern Ireland they are liable for rent and/or rates (chapter 11); and

(c) they are occupying that home (chapter 3 and para. 9.7); and

(d) they are not a member of an excluded group, (para 1.11) and;

(e) their capital does not exceed the maximum amount (para 13.13); and

(f) either:

- their income is not too high as defined by the needs of their household (para. 1.7); or
- (in the case of CTB only) they are entitled to a second adult rebate on the basis of the income of other adults who live with them (chapter 8).

1.6 The conditions for CTB are similar to HB, but with some subtle differences. For example, liability for rent mainly depends on the landlord and tenant having agreed a genuine contract, whereas liability for council tax is imposed (chapters 2 and 9). These are dealt with in the guide as they arise.

1.7 Whether or not a claimant's income is low enough depends on five factors, which also determine the amount of benefit payable. These are:

- the amount of rent, council tax or, in Northern Ireland, rates which is 'eligible' for benefit (chapters 10, 9 and 11 respectively)
- the size of the claimant's family (para. 4.5, chapters 4 and 12); and
- the personal circumstances of the family members, principally: their age; whether they have a disability or any caring responsibilities (chapter 12);
- the claimant's income, including the income of their family members, (chapters 13-15) when compared to their family size and personal circumstances of its members (chapters 7 and 12); and
- whether any other adults who are not part of the claimant's family live with the claimant as part of their household (paras. 4.3 and 4.21-22) and, if they do, any assumed contribution they make towards the rent (paras. 7.4 and 7.17-38).

1.8 Except in the 'Pathfinder' authority areas (Table 22.1) the maximum amount of HB is 100% of the claimant's eligible rent, or in Northern Ireland 100% of their eligible rent and rates. The maximum amount of CTB is 100% of the claimant's eligible council tax. As the claimant's net income increases above his or her applicable amount, HB and main CTB are withdrawn by a percentage of that excess income. The percentage or taper for HB (in Northern Ireland HB for rent), is 65% and for main CTB (in Northern Ireland HB for rates) is 20%. In the Pathfinder areas the maximum amount of HB for most claimants who rent their home from a private landlord (but not other types of accommodation) is based on flat rate allowance which varies according to the household's size (table 22.2) regardless of whether this is more or less than the actual rent.

1.9 The level of rent which is eligible for benefit for claimants who rent their home from a private landlord (and in certain circumstances other types of landlord) is set by the rent officer (in Northern Ireland the NIHE), (chapter 10). The circumstances in which the rent is referred to the rent officer (or NIHE) for an assessment are described in chapter 6. In the Pathfinder areas (table 22.1) the rate of the flat rate allowance for each household type (para. 1.8) is also set by the rent officer.

1.10 From the start of the current HB scheme in 1988 until 1999 the calculation of HB and CTB followed a similar structure to other income-related benefits such as income support and, until its abolition, family credit. However, these common rules began to diverge when family credit was replaced by working families' tax credit in October 1999. In 2003 this link with other benefits was further weakened, first by the introduction of child tax credit and working tax credit and second by the introduction of the pension credit in 2003. These new benefits are assessed on a different basis. For example, working and child tax credits use gross income calculated over the year (rather than net weekly income for HB and CTB) while pension credits do not have a maximum savings limit. From April 2004, the common basis for assessing household requirements (the applicable amount) will diverge still further when the child allowances will be removed from the calculation of income support and income-based jobseeker's allowance; instead any child elements will be paid as child tax credits (existing claims will be converted to the new system gradually during 2004-05). The introduction of pension credit from October 2003 has meant that in effect there are now two different ways of calculating HB/CTB (and consequently two different sets of regulations) one for claimants aged under 60 and one for those aged 60 or over. In the longer-term the divergence of the HB/CTB rules from other benefits and tax credits may result in inconsistencies which prove unsustainable as different methods of assessing entitlement result in new anomalies (known as benefit traps) as claimants' circumstances change and/or they move between benefits. Ultimately this may lead to the re-introduction of a new common basis of assessment at some later date, perhaps based on the new tax and pension credits.

1.11 Nearly everyone with low enough income and capital can get HB and/or CTB. However, there are some exceptions. For reasons of policy the Government has legislated to exclude some groups from benefit altogether, for example, many full-time students and people who have only come to live in the UK recently cannot get HB or CTB. For those two groups, see chapters 20 and 21 respectively.

Other exceptions apply, notably young people who have recently left care. Chapter 2 outlines these rules about entitlement and details of further exceptions.

1.12 HB and CTB cannot be awarded unless a claim is made, and there are numerous procedural rules involved in claiming (chapter 5). There are specific rules about what claimants must be told and when and how benefit is awarded (chapter 16). Starting in April 2004, once an award has been made it will continue to be paid indefinitely until the claimant's circumstances change so that either: they are no longer entitled at all (para. 1.5) or the amount of benefit they are entitled to is different and the authority replaces it with a new award (chapter 17). With the exception of claimants in receipt of the pension credit, claimants are expected to keep the council informed about changes in their circumstances (chapter 17). Failure to do so is one of the principal causes of underpayments (paras. 17.37-39) and overpayments (chapter 18) – though councils do themselves make mistakes too. Disagreements about the correct award often result in appeals (chapter 19).

AA 1,5
NIAA 1, 5

1.13 HB and CTB are a significant source of help for many claimants. DWP statistics for Great Britain in August 2003 show 3.81 million people were in receipt of HB, 4.66 million were in receipt of main CTB. Some 70% of HB and 68% of CTB recipients respectively were also getting income support or income-based jobseeker's allowance. The average weekly amounts of HB and CTB were £55.85 and £12.09 respectively (all figures taken from HB and CTB *Quarterly Summary Statistics* August 2003, DWP, Information and Analysis Directorate). This is equivalent to £13.99 billion expenditure annually. The DWP no longer publishes separates statistics for second adult rebates but the last published figure, for May 2002, showed that some 128,000 were in receipt of second adult rebate, 37,000 of whom were non-income support cases. DSD statistics for Northern Ireland in August 2003 show that there were 126,800 in receipt of Housing Benefit as administered by the NIHE (excluding claims administered by the RCA). The average weekly entitlement was £51.02 which is equivalent to £336 million annually (DSD Statistics and Research Agency). There are no separate statistics for rate rebates except the yearly planned expenditure of the Northern Ireland Office. In March 1999 the expected annual expenditure for Northern Ireland during 2001-02 was £306 million on rent rebates and allowances and £50 million on rate rebates (£16 million of which was on owner occupiers). This is equivalent to around 2.5% of the total for HB/CTB in Great Britain.

1.14 Responsibility for running the HB and CTB schemes gives administering authorities a prime role in maintaining the incomes of disadvantaged groups and can reduce rent, council tax and, in Northern Ireland, rates arrears. In Great Britain authorities are reimbursed for their expenditure through central government subsidy payments, and this is a very significant proportion of authorities' revenue income. Chapter 23 gives more detail about subsidy payments to councils in Great Britain.

AA 134, 139, 191
NIAA 126, 167

1.15 HB was first introduced throughout the UK in 1982-83 and was replaced with a new HB scheme in 1988. CTB came in because of the introduction of council tax in Great Britain in 1993. Table 1.1 summarises changes to the HB and CTB scheme over the past year. Earlier editions of this guide give similar lists (in table 2.1 in most editions).

Table 1.1: Summary of changes after April 2003

SI 2003 No. 1050 NISR 2003 No 224	5th May 2003	Clarification of rules about supersessions
SI 2003 No. 1195 NISR 2003 No 261	21st and 26th May 2003	Hospital down-rating applies after 52 weeks, not after 6 weeks
SI 2003 No. 973	1st June 2003	Rent officers in Wales are responsible to the Welsh National Assembly
SI 2003 No. 1338 NISR 2003 No 294	16th June 2003	Benefit periods can be extended for people aged 60+
SI 2003 No. 1632 NISR 2003 No 317	21st July 2003	Claims by people aged 60+ may be made to a 'nominated office'
SI 2003 No. 1701 SI 2003 No. 1914 NISR 2003 No 329 NISR 2003 No 351	1st August to 1st September 2003	Student up-rating; minor additional disregards from student income
SI 2003 No. 1731 NISR 2003 No 338	8th August 2003	Disabled child premium continues for up to 8 weeks following the death of the child
NISR 2003 No. 274	15th September 2003	Attending a work focused interview ceases to be a condition for getting HB in Northern Ireland (the case in Great Britain since 30th September 2002)
SI 2003 No. 2279 NISR 2003 No 417	1st October 2003	Income and capital disregards introduced for the Employment Retention and Advancement scheme; clarification of other income and capital disregards and carer premium
	4th October 2003	The 21st birthday of the 'partial start' of the original HB scheme
SI 2003 No. 325 SI 2003 No. 1338 SI 2003 No. 2275 SI 2003 No. 2526 NISR 2003 No 197 NISR 2003 No 294 NISR 2003 No 418 NISR 2003 No 432	6th October 2003	Introduction of state pension credit; abolition of benefit periods for people aged 60+; awards of HB/CTB continue indefinitely; consequential amendments to rules about referrals to the rent officer, extended payments and continuing payments; automatic retrospective awards of HB/CTB during the

	first year; new rules for assessing income and capital of people aged 60+	
6th October 2003	Clarification of rules about revisions and supersessions when another state benefit is awarded	SI 2003 No. 2275 SI 2003 No. 2526 NISR 2003 No 418 NISR 2003 No 432
17th October and 17th November 2003 onwards	Introduction of Local Housing Allowance pilots	SI 2003 No. 2398 SI 2003 No. 2399
27th October 2003	Disregards introduced for the Return to Work Credit scheme	SI 2003 No. 2439
5th March 2004	Clarification of rules about the date changes of circumstances take effect; clarification of up-rating dates for savings credit cases	SI 2004 No. 290 NISR 2004 No 46
1st April 2004	Abolition of CTB restrictions for dwellings in bands F, G and H	SI 2004 No. 154
1st April 2004	The Children (Leaving Care) Act 2000 comes into force in Scotland, excluding certain young care leavers from HB entitlement, in whose case support should be provided by the local authority. This mirrors the rules already in force in England and Wales since October 2001	SI 2004 No. 747
1st and 5th April 2004	Main annual up-rating of HB/CTB figures	SI 2004 No. 552 NISR 2004 No 82
1st and 6th April 2004	Tidying up of income disregards of payments on training schemes and of rules about income from working tax credit and child tax credit	SI 2004 No. 565 NISR 2004 No 143
4th April 2004	The 21st birthday of housing benefit	
5th April 2004	Abolition of benefit periods for all; awards of HB/CTB continue indefinitely; consequential amendments to rules about referrals to the rent officer, extended payments and continuing payments	SI 2004 No. 14 NISR 2004 No 144
5th April 2004	Extended payments introduced for people who have been on incapacity benefit or severe disability allowance for 28 weeks, etc	SI 2004 No. 319 SI 2004 No. 574 NISR 2004 No 145
9th April 2004	Rent officer referrals rules amended to work properly when someone moves	SI 2004 No. 781

Reference	Date	Change
SI 2003 No. 2634 NISR 2004 No 47	12th April 2004	The 30 hours per week earned income disregard becomes the 16 hours per week earned income disregard in many cases; other minor adjustments to rules about assessing income
SI 2004 No 1232 NISR 2004 No 197	1st May 2004	Amendments to Habitual Residence test following enlargement of the European Union
SI 2003 No. 325 NISR 2003 No 197	6th October 2004	Automatic retrospective awards of HB/CTB for people aged 60+ cease (but the DWP is thought to be planning to continue them)
		Exclusion from HB/CTB for children leaving care expected to be brought into force in Northern Ireland
SI 2003 No. 1589 NISR 2003 No 367	25th October 2004	Abolition of 'lone parent run-on'
SI 2000 No 2239 NISR 2000 No 260	28th January 2006	Demise of bereavement premium

Using this guide

TERMS USED IN THIS GUIDE

AA 134(1),(1A),(1B), (2), 139(1),(2), 191 NIAA 126(2),(3)

1.16 A number of different public authorities are involved in the administration of HB/CTB. The term 'authority' is used in this guide to cover them all, including the equivalent institutions in Northern Ireland. In Great Britain the public bodies which administer HB are only those local councils listed in paragraphs 1.20-21. The term 'tenant' is used to describe any kind of rent-payer including, for example, licensees. Across the UK the term 'housing benefit' (HB) covers two types of payment which may be made under the scheme in respect of help with rent payments, otherwise described as rent rebates and rent allowances. In Northern Ireland only the term 'housing benefit' also includes help with rates in the form of rate rebates. A rent rebate is an award of HB to a tenant of the authority administering the HB scheme (which takes the form of a reduced liability for rent). A rent allowance is an award of HB in the form of a cash payment to any other rent-payer which is paid either to that claimant or to his or her landlord, as described later in this guide, and can be used by the claimant towards their full rental liability. This distinction is important since only rent allowances (and not rebates) can be referred to the rent officer for a rent determination (in Northern Ireland a rent decision by the NIHE) which restricts the amount of benefit payable (chapter 6). This guide uses housing benefit as the general term, and rent rebate or rent allowance or rate rebate when this is more appropriate. The term 'CTB' is used to refer to both forms of CTB. One of these – 'alternative maximum council tax benefit' – is referred to in this guide, as in DWP guidance and most local authority forms, as 'second adult rebate'. Where it is more appropriate, the specific term 'main CTB' or 'second adult rebate' is used.

REFERENCES AND ABBREVIATIONS

1.17 A list of abbreviations used in the text is given at the front of this guide following the contents page. Paragraphs 1.62-65 and table 1.2 explain how to use the references in the margins throughout the guide.

Benefits and tax credits rates

1.18 In the case of all CTB claims and HB claims the amounts quoted are those which apply from 5th April 2004 for HB for rent paid weekly or in weekly multiples, and from 1st April 2004 for HB for rent in all other cases, and in all cases for CTB and, in Northern Ireland, for HB for rates. Other benefit rates are increased during the week commencing 12th April 2004 but must be taken into account for HB and CTB purposes from 1st/5th April 2004. This includes the working tax credit (WTC) and child tax credit (CTC). Student figures (chapter 21) apply from September 2003. A summary of the benefit rates for 2004-05 is printed at the back of the guide (appendix 5). The tax and national insurance rates quoted are those which apply from 6th April 2004 to 5th March 2005. HBR 68(3)(a)

Administration

1.19 Different arrangements apply in England and Wales, in Scotland, and in Northern Ireland. In any individual authority in Great Britain HB/CTB may be administered by one or more departments, usually the housing or treasurer's/finance department or by an external contractor acting on behalf of the council. For Northern Ireland, see paragraphs 1.22-24.

ENGLAND AND WALES

1.20 In some areas of England there are two tiers of local government. The authority responsible for administering the scheme is the 'housing authority'. The 'housing authority' means the council of a district, London borough or unitary authority or the Common Council of the City of London, but not a county council (unless it is a unitary authority). Tenants of a housing authority claim housing benefit from their landlord and are paid by rent rebate. All other tenants, including tenants of county councils, claim both HB and CTB from their local council which is also their housing authority and will be paid their HB by rent allowance.

Throughout Wales there is only one tier of local government so claimants should apply to their county or county borough council for both HB and CTB. Therefore all local authority tenants in Wales will be paid HB by rent rebate. In both England and Wales agency arrangements may exist for the administration of HB but not CTB (para. 1.25).

SCOTLAND

1.21 As in Wales, there is only one tier of local government so all tenants of Scottish local authorities (councils) claim HB and CTB from their landlord and will be paid HB in the form of a rent rebate. All other tenants of housing associations or other landlords (whether public or private) receive rent allowances and CTB from the local council. Since April 2002 this includes all remaining tenants and former tenants of Scottish Homes (now part of Communities Scotland) who previously received their HB from their landlord as a rent rebate (see Housing (Scotland) Act 2001, schedule 10 paragraph 17). As in England and Wales agency arrangements may exist for the administration of HB but not CTB (para. 1.25).

NORTHERN IRELAND

1.22 Northern Ireland has a social security system which is separate from, but generally mirrors, that in the rest of the United Kingdom. As described in the next two paragraphs, there are two main areas of housing benefit policy which are unique to Northern Ireland. Further details of variations between the legal systems may be found in paragraphs 1.40 and 1.43.

1.23 There is no council tax in Northern Ireland. Occupiers of domestic property are liable for rates instead (explained fully in chapter 11 of this guide). Help with domestic rates is provided through HB. As a general rule tenants (as opposed to owner occupiers) make their claim from the Northern Ireland Housing Executive (NIHE) although there are some exceptions, see chapter 11 for details. Owner occupiers make their claim for HB from the Rate Collection Agency (RCA), but again see chapter 11 for exceptions. The RCA is an Executive Agency of the Department of Finance and Personnel and is responsible for the collection of rates due to the 26 district councils and the regional rate. It receives payment from the Northern Ireland Housing Executive for properties in the public sector.

1.24 Decisions about the appropriate level of rent for rent allowance claimants are carried out by the Northern Ireland Housing Executive which is also responsible for administering housing benefit for tenants. In effect, the Executive carries out the same function as rent officers in England, Wales and Scotland.

AGENCY ARRANGEMENTS FOR HB

AA 134(5), 191 **1.25** Authorities in Great Britain (but not Northern Ireland) may make arrangements for housing benefit (but not council tax benefit) by which:

- one carries out the functions of the other; or
- functions are carried out jointly or by a joint committee.

Agency arrangements sometimes apply to local authority tenants living in property situated outside the landlord authority's boundaries, for example properties that the local authority has leased to house its homeless applicants. In such a case, they may receive a rent rebate from their landlord authority as opposed to the authority in which they live if agency arrangements have been agreed.

CONTRACTING OUT ADMINISTRATION

1.26 Authorities can contract out the administration of HB and CTB to private companies and a number have done so. The Local Government Act 1999 replaced compulsory competitive tendering (CCT) in England and Wales with a duty of obtaining best value for the taxpayer from April 2000. A similar agenda operates in Scotland.

1.27 Prior to July 2002 an authority which contracted out its administration remained responsible for making the decisions to award benefit on each individual claim. In authorities where the administration had been contracted out this resulted in a considerable duplication of work and was not conducive to efficient administration.

1.28 From 25th July 2002 authorities which contract out their benefit work are no longer required to make the decision on each claim. Under the new arrangements contractors are authorised to make decisions subject to the requirement that they provide the authority with a daily 10% random sample of claims on which decisions have been made for checking. SI 2002 No. 1888

1.29 The Deregulation and Contracting Out Act 1994 permits contractors to communicate directly with the DWP. The contracting out of HB/CTB administration does not affect an individual's entitlement or his or her right of appeal to an independent appeal tribunal.

BEST VALUE

1.30 The Local Government Act 1999 places the duty of 'Best Value' upon authorities in England and Wales, requiring them to make arrangements to secure continuous improvement in the way in which they carry out their functions. Authorities have to conduct performance reviews and publish annual local performance plans. The Government or, in Wales, the National Assembly, have devised performance indicators and national standards for local government activities including benefit administration.

1.31 Section 4(1) of the Act confers a power on the Secretary of State to specify by order Best Value performance indicators and standards. The indicators target the priorities of speed; accuracy; security of the benefit delivery; and also value for money and customer-focus.

BEST VALUE PERFORMANCE INDICATORS – ENGLISH AND WELSH AUTHORITIES

1.32 For English and Welsh authorities the indicators for 2003-04 are set out in ODPM/Welsh Assembly Government's Performance Standards Order 2003 (SI 2003 No. 530) as amended by SI 2004 No. 589. The indicators are as follows:

- claim security judged in relation to the number of claimants visited, fraud investigators in post, investigations undertaken, and convictions or sanctions imposed;
- average time for processing new claims;
- average time for processing notifications of changes of circumstance;
- percentage of cases for which the calculation of the amount of benefit due was correct on the basis of the information available for the decision for a sample of cases checked post-decision;
- the percentage of recoverable overpayments (excluding Council Tax Benefit) that were recovered in the year.

The detail of these is set out in ODPM/Welsh Assembly Guidance.

Proper decision-making

1.33 The authority's primary duty is one of proper decision-making. It has to apply the rules of the HB/CTB schemes to the facts of the individual case with the aim of arriving at sound decisions regarding benefit entitlement. The necessary steps in the decision-making process are:

- identifying the relevant facts in the case;
- proper consideration of the available evidence where the facts are in doubt or in dispute;
- establishing facts 'on the balance of probability' where necessary;
- correct interpretation of the law and its application to the facts of the case; and
- arriving at decisions that can be understood in terms of the relevant law and facts.

DISPUTED FACTS

1.34 The only facts which are relevant to the authority are those which have a bearing in relation to the application of the specific rules of the HB/CTB schemes. Where there is a disagreement about the facts between the authority and the claimant or other person affected, the authority must consider the available evidence to decide what the true position is. A factual dispute may also be the trigger for a request for revision, supersession or an appeal to an independent appeal tribunal (chapters 17 and 19).

1.35 The requirement of proof means that a disputed fact must be established to the satisfaction of the authority and, on appeal, the appeal tribunal. This does not, however, mean that the fact must be established with absolute certainty. In civil cases, such as matters involving HB/CTB, the appropriate test is 'on the balance of probability'. In other words, if the greater weight of evidence supports for example the claimant's view of the disputed fact then the claimant has proved the matter on the balance of probability.

1.36 In the first instance the burden of proof is on the claimant to support his or her claim by supplying the authority with all the evidence it reasonably requires (para. 5.33). The DWP's Verification Framework seeks to set out the minimum standards for collecting evidence when a claim is made (para. 5.40). However, where the authority asserts a particular proposition, for example, that a recoverable overpayment has occurred, the authority must have evidence to support its assertion. AA 5(1) HBR 73

1.37 The burden of proof is only decisive, however, where:

- there is no evidence – consequently where the authority asserts a disputed fact it must have evidence to support that assertion; or
- the evidence is exactly balanced – in which case the party on whom the burden of proof lies should not succeed.

ISSUES OF LAW

1.38 The rules of the HB/CTB schemes in Great Britain are set out in legislation passed by the UK parliament. (For Northern Ireland variations see paragraphs 1.22-24, 1.40 and 1.43.) Issues of law involve the application and interpretation of that legislation. For example, the question of whether or not the claimant's son counts as a non-dependant for HB/CTB purposes could only be answered by consideration of the definition of 'non-dependant' in the regulations as well as the relevant facts of the case. A dispute over the correct interpretation and application of the legislation may be the trigger for a request for revision or supersession or an appeal to an independent appeal tribunal (chapters 17 and 19). While legal disputes do not fall within the Local Government Ombudsman's remit, negligent reading of the benefit regulations by the authority may constitute maladministration (see for example complaint 91/B/3223 against Newbury District Council, 26th August 1993).

THE ACTS

1.39 In England, Wales and Scotland, the Acts of Parliament are as follows. The outline rules relating to HB and CTB entitlement are contained in the Social Security Contributions and Benefits Act 1992 (as amended), and the Social Security Administration Act 1992 (as amended) which sets the conditions for a valid claim. Section 115 of the Immigration and Asylum Act 1999 (which applies to GB and NI) provides the outline framework excluding certain persons subject to immigration control from HB and CTB entitlement. The outline rules on the administration of the HB/CTB schemes are contained in the Social Security Administration Act 1992 (as amended). The resulting repeals of earlier legislation and consequential amendments of related legislation are contained in the Social Security (Consequential Provisions) Act 1992. This Act also provides that the substitution of the consolidating Acts for the repealed enactments does not affect the continuity of the law. The Child Support, Pensions and Social Security Act 2000 contains the outline framework for decision-making and appeal arrangements as well as the separate discretionary housing payments scheme.

1.40 Though the social security system in Northern Ireland is separate from that in England, Wales and Scotland, the legislation generally mirrors Great Britain's so as to maintain a UK-wide social security system. For each GB Act there is a Northern Ireland equivalent which is (as far as possible) laid out in a similar manner. Thus there are the Social Security Contributions and Benefits (Northern Ireland) Act 1992 and the Social Security Administration (Northern Ireland) Act 1992. However, the form of primary legislation in Northern Ireland depends on the system of governance in place at the time it was made. During periods of direct rule from Westminster primary legislation is mainly made by orders in council or, occasionally, (usually in the case of consolidating legislation) an Act of the UK parliament. During periods of devolved government primary legislation is made by the Northern Ireland Assembly. However, the Assembly's powers are heavily circumscribed because it is under a duty to maintain a UK wide social security system (s87 Northern Ireland Act 1998). In effect this means it is obliged to continue to mirror the legislation in Great Britain.

REGULATIONS, ORDERS AND RULES

1.41 The Acts enable the government, normally following consultation with the local authority associations, to formulate delegated legislation – 'regulations', 'orders' and 'rules'– which contain and amend the details of the schemes (appendix 1, which lists both those relating to England, Wales and Scotland and those relating to Northern Ireland).

CBA 123(3),(4) NICBA 122(3) **1.42** In England, Wales and Scotland, the main rules of the HB scheme are contained in SI 1987 No. 1971, the Housing Benefit (General) Regulations as amended by subsequent regulations. The main rules of the CTB scheme are contained in SI 1992 No. 1814, the Council Tax Benefit (General) Regulations as amended. The DWP's intention is that the CTB regulations should maintain common provisions with the HB regulations. The details of the HB/CTB decision-making and appeal arrangements are contained in SI 2001 No. 1002, The Housing Benefit and Council Tax Benefit (Decisions and Appeals) Regulations.

1.43 In Northern Ireland, the legislation generally mirrors that in Great Britain. For each GB statutory instrument there is a Northern Ireland equivalent which is (as far as possible) laid out in a similar manner; though note that while in Great Britain the delegated legislation is made by statutory instrument (SI) in Northern Ireland secondary legislation is in the form of 'statutory rules' (SR). For example, the Housing Benefit (General) Regulations, SI 1987 No. 1971 (as amended) in GB are mirrored by Housing Benefit (General) Regulations (Northern Ireland) 1987, SR 1987 No. 461 (as amended).

OBTAINING THE LEGISLATION

1.44 Members of the public have a right to see copies of the relevant legal material together with the details of any local scheme (para. 22.10) at an authority's principal office. For information on Commissioners' decisions, see paragraphs 1.51-52.

1.45 The many and frequent amendments to the relevant legislation, and the government's decision to date not to produce a consolidation of the HB and CTB regulations, mean that it can be quite difficult to keep track of the current rules of the schemes. For those with internet access, all the relevant legislation as originally enacted (rather than as amended) may be accessed at *www.legislation.hmso.gov.uk*. For Northern Ireland go to *www.northernireland-legislation.hmso.gov.uk*. The current provisions relating to social security in Great Britain are also set out in the loose leaf work entitled *The Law Relating to Social Security* which is kept up to date with regular supplements. Volume 8 (Parts 1 and 2) contains relevant sections of the Acts and statutory instruments relating to HB/CTB. The advantage of this work is that, with the exception of the most recent changes it shows the law as amended and helpfully distinguishes those regulations concerning the calculation of benefit which apply only to claimants aged 60 or over (paras 1.10, 12.3 and 13.7) by the use of a bold typeface. This work can now also be accessed online at *www.dwp.gov.uk/advisers/docs/lawvols/bluevol/index.asp* for Great Britain and *www.dsdni.gov.uk/benefitlaw/lawrelating-socialsec.asp* for Northern Ireland. Many main public reference libraries hold hard copies of this publication and are also likely to provide free online access. Overall now for those with internet access it is relatively easy to piece together the current state of the law by using this work together with the HMSO site to track recent amendments.

1.46 The Child Poverty Action Group's *Housing Benefit and Council Tax Benefit Legislation* also contains all the law relevant in Great Britain at the point of publication plus detailed commentary which readers may find useful as a secondary source where they require expansion on a particular point raised in this guide.

OTHER RELEVANT LEGISLATION

1.47 In addition to the Acts and regulations, other pieces of legislation circumscribe the manner in which authorities may administer the schemes. The Local Government Act 1972 or the Local Government (Scotland) Act 1973 contain most of the law relating to the powers and duties of local authorities and the way in which they must carry out their business. The Local Government Finance Act 1982 and Audit Commission Act 1998 cover the auditing of, and public rights of access to, local authority accounts. They also place upon local authorities a duty to secure economy, efficiency and effectiveness in their administration of HB/CTB. The Sex Discrimination Act 1975 and Race Relations Act 1976 make it illegal to discriminate (either directly or indirectly) against someone, or victimise someone, on the grounds of their colour, race, nationality, sex or marital status. The Data Protection Act 1998 controls the use of, and access to, information about an individual held on a computer or recorded as part of a 'relevant filing system' i.e. any paper based system where the information held about an individual can be easily traced.

1.48 The Audit Commission Act 1998 enables the Secretary of State to request the Commission to conduct or assist the Secretary of State in conducting studies designed to improve economy, efficiency, effectiveness and quality of performance in the discharge by authorities of functions relating to HB/CTB administration.

STATUTORY INTERPRETATION AND CASE LAW

1.49 In the first instance, where there is no ambiguity, legislation should be taken to mean exactly what it says. The general rule is that the authority may not look beyond the relevant legislation itself to determine its meaning. However, certain forms of assistance are permissible, or must be considered, such as the precedents contained within case law on the meaning of a word or phrase. For example, where in the past a matter in dispute has been considered in the High Court, (Court of Session in Scotland), the interpretation made by a judge in the course of deciding such a case will in particular instances be binding upon all authorities. Relevant cases are identified in the appropriate paragraphs of this guide and are fully referenced, together with any published report, in appendix 2.

1.50 Decisions in HB cases are often highly persuasive though not binding with regard to CTB and *vice versa* (and a similar principle applies as between English and Welsh, Scottish, and Northern Ireland cases). Equally, many of the words and phrases which were brought forward into the HB/CTB schemes from the old supplementary benefit (SB) scheme, or other parts of social security law, have a body of case law attached. Again, as an aid to interpretation such decisions are of persuasive value though not binding upon authorities.

COMMISSIONERS' DECISIONS

1.51 Social Security Commissioners are appointed to decide appeals brought by individuals, the Secretary of State for Work and Pensions and authorities on questions of law from the decision of appeal tribunals.

1.52 Commissioners' decisions constitute a body of case law. Prior to July 2001, this was not binding upon an authority. It could, however, be considered persuasive where it related to exactly the same wording in the HB/CTB legislation. However, the Commissioners themselves may decide that a certain body of case law, although not strictly HB/CTB decisions, is binding – for example decisions relating to good cause and backdating (para. 5.78). Since July 2001, relevant Commissioners' decisions are binding on authorities, which in effect gives them the same status as High Court decisions (para. 1.50). They will become increasingly significant as the number of decided HB/CTB cases increases. This should help clarify some previously unclear parts of the legislation. The most significant Commissioners' decisions are available on-line at *www.osscsc.gov.uk* for Great Britain. Northern Ireland decisions can also be accessed on-line at *www.dsdni.gov.uk/benefitlaw/benefitlaw.asp* but as at April 2004 no HB decisions were listed on this site. Further details about accessing Commissioners' decisions can be found in appendix 2 and para. 19.75.

THE HUMAN RIGHTS ACT 1998

1.53 The Human Rights Act 1998 came into force on 2nd October 2000. It gives effect in the UK to the rights and freedoms guaranteed under the European Convention for the Protection of Human Rights and Fundamental Freedoms ('the Convention'). Authorities and appeal tribunals are under a duty to act compatibly with the Convention rights and all legislation must be read compatibly with the Convention rights as far as it is possible to do so. Also, courts and tribunals must have regard to the jurisprudence of the European Court of Human Rights and decisions and opinions of the Commission and Committee of Ministers. It is unlawful for the authority to act (or fail to act) in a way which is incompatible with a Convention right.

1.54 An authority does not act unlawfully if it could not have acted differently as a result of a provision of primary legislation. Nor does the authority act unlawfully where:

- it acts under a provision of secondary legislation;
- that legislation is made under a provision of primary legislation;
- that provision cannot be read compatibly with the Convention rights; and
- the authority is acting so as to enforce or give effect to that provision.

However, secondary legislation can be declared invalid by the courts where the primary legislation under which it is made is not directly in conflict with the Convention.

JUDGMENT

1.55 There are numerous occasions in the regulations where a decision must be made on the basis of what is 'reasonable' or 'appropriate'. For example, where the claimant has left the home through fear of violence then in specific instances the authority must treat the claimant as occupying two dwelling and consequently potentially entitled to HB on both dwellings 'if it is reasonable' that housing benefit should be paid in respect of both dwellings. There is no single right or wrong answer. In such cases the authority must exercise judgment in the light of the facts of the individual case. For example, if the claimant had brought the threats of violence upon him or herself by engaging in criminal activities it might be considered inappropriate to use public funds to meet the cost of two homes.

DISCRETION

1.56 Where an authority has a choice under the regulations to do or not do something, e.g. to make payments of a rent allowance to the claimant's landlord where there is no mandatory requirement to do so, this is a discretionary power. Such powers make the application of the regulations flexible and adaptable to the individual circumstances of the case.

CONTROLS ON EXERCISE OF JUDGMENT OR DISCRETION

1.57 In exercising judgment or discretion, authorities are bound by the established principles of administrative law that the courts have steadily evolved. If they are not in accordance with these principles, decisions may be open to legal challenge by way of judicial review (see *Judicial Review Proceedings,* Jonathan Manning, 2nd edition (2004), the Legal Action Group, ISBN 1903307171; or for Scotland see *Judicial Review in Scotland,* Tom Mullen and Tony Prosser, Wiley, ISBN 0471966142). For example, an authority must consider its discretionary powers in individual cases. It must not fetter its discretion by applying predetermined rules rigidly without giving genuine consideration to the merits of the individual case. The authority cannot decide, for example, that it will never use its power to make direct payments to landlords where it has the discretionary power to do so.

1.58 A power must be exercised reasonably. An authority will be considered to have acted unreasonably if, having regard to the nature of the subject matter:

- it takes into account matters which it ought not to consider; or
- it refuses or neglects to consider matters which it ought to take into account.

An authority will also have acted unreasonably if it comes to a conclusion that no reasonable authority could have come to.

DWP GUIDANCE MANUAL

1.59 The Department for Work and Pensions (DWP) is the central government department responsible for housing benefit and council tax benefit policy. It produces the *Housing Benefit and Council Tax Benefit Guidance Manual* (GM). The manual advises authorities on how to interpret the regulations and on administrative arrangements. Interesting or contentious parts of the manual are identified in this guide. The DWP also issues guidance on: the subsidy arrangements *(Subsidy Guidance Manual);* DWP policy on overpayments, *(HB/CTB Overpayments Guide);* Discretionary Housing Payments; and other aspects of HB/CTB administration which together with the Guidance Manual are now available on-line at: *www.dwp.gov.uk/housingbenefit/manuals/index.asp.* Print versions of most of these manuals can also be obtained from Corporate Document Services, 7 Eastgate, Leeds LS2 7LY (tel: 0113 399 4040).

DWP CIRCULARS

1.60 In addition to the GM, the DWP also issues regular circulars to authorities advising them of recent or forthcoming changes and other important matters. Until April 1994 these were denoted by the initials HB/CTB, followed by the year and the number, e.g. HB/CTB (93)3. In April 1994 the department revised the contents and presentation of its circulars. There are now three types of circular distinguished by a prefix – A for adjudication and operations, S for statistics and subsidy and F for fraud. Each type has its own number series and starts from 1/94. Recent circulars are listed in appendix 3. 'A' circulars from A2/2000 onwards and 'S' circulars from S1/2001 are available on-line at: *www.dwp.gov.uk/hbctb/index.asp.* While these circulars do not apply to Northern Ireland, the authorities there generally accept the validity of 'A' circulars (unless the law in Northern Ireland is different) and are happy to be referred to them where relevant. No separate series of circulars have been issued by the DSD for Northern Ireland. In practice the authorities copy and adapt the DWP circulars for their own use.

STATUS OF DWP ADVICE

1.61 While the Acts and regulations are binding upon authorities and appeal tribunals, the GM and DWP circulars are for information and guidance only and do not have the force of law (see the introduction to the GM), and this has been confirmed by the Commissioners (CH/3853/2001). Authorities do, however, often cite DWP advice in support of their decisions. The courts sometimes rehearse the advice contained within the GM with approval while recognising that it is not an aid to legal interpretation (see for example *R v Maidstone BC ex parte Bunce*).

How to use the marginal references

1.62 The following paragraphs illustrate how to use the commonest references found on the inside margins of this guide. The sections, regulations, paragraphs, etc, shown in marginal references have in many cases been amended by subsequent law. The sources mentioned in paragraphs 1.39-43 set out the law as so amended. Table 1.2 at the end of this chapter provides a key to the marginal references used in this guide.

MARGINAL REFERENCES FOR ENGLAND, WALES AND SCOTLAND

1.63 The following are examples of how the marginal references apply in England, Wales and Scotland. The reader may also find it helpful to look at the key to marginal references (Table 1.2) at the end of this chapter.

CBA 131(9)

This means section 131(9) of the Social Security Contributions and Benefits Act 1992 – in other words, sub-section 9 of section 131. (This gives the law about the 'better buy' calculation: para. 7.13.)

HBR 31(9)
CTBR 22(9)

These mean regulation 31(9) of the Housing Benefit (General) Regulations 1987 and regulation 22(9) of the Council Tax Benefits (General) Regulations 1992 – in other words, paragraph 9 of each of those regulations. (These give the law about assessing the income of self-employed childminders: para. 15.26.)

HBR sch 2 para 14
CTBR sch 1 para 15

These mean paragraph 14 of schedule 2 to the Housing Benefit (General) Regulations 1987 and paragraph 15 of schedule 1 to the Council Tax Benefits (General) Regulations 1992. (These give the law about the disabled child premium: para. 12.19.)

HBR 16(a),(b),
sch 2 paras 1,2
HBR 60+ 16(a),(b)
sch 2A paras 1,2
CTBR 8(a),(b)
sch 1 paras 1,2
CTBR 60+ 8(a),(b)
sch 1A paras 1,2

These mean regulation 16(a) and (b) and schedule 2 paragraphs 1 and 2 of the Housing Benefit (General) Regulations 1987 and regulation 16(a) and (b) and schedule 2A paragraphs 1 and 2 of the Housing Benefit (General) Regulations 1987 as amended by the Housing Benefit and Council Tax Benefit (State Pension Credit) Regulations 2003 (SI 2003 No.325). The equivalent rules for CTB follow. (These give the law about assessing the applicable amount of the claimant. A separate reference is required for claims where the claimant or their partner is aged at least 60 and those claims where the claimant (and their partner) are aged under 60 because there are two different ways of calculating benefit depending on the claimant's age (paras. 1.10, 12.3 and 13.x).

MARGINAL REFERENCES FOR NORTHERN IRELAND

1.64 The following are examples of how the marginal references apply in Northern Ireland. The reader may also find it helpful to look at the list of abbreviations following the Contents page of this guide. The legislation in Northern Ireland generally mirrors that in Great Britain. Therefore the references for Northern Ireland, except where explicitly stated, are covered by the Great Britain equivalent. The following examples illustrate this (and see also paragraph 1.65 and table 1.2):

- Nearly always, the reference within the equivalent regulations is identical and so there is no separate reference. (See the first example below.)
- Occasionally the references are similar but not identical in which case the specific Northern Ireland reference is placed immediately below. (See the second example below.)
- Occasionally part of the GB legislation is identical but diverges for some of the references only. In this case there is a UK-wide reference for the part that is identical, and a further GB reference for the part that diverges, immediately followed by a Northern Ireland reference for the divergent rules only. (See the third example below.)
- There is no council tax in Northern Ireland so these references only ever apply to Great Britain. (See the third example below.)

HBR 64(2)

In Great Britain this refers to Regulation 64(2) of the Housing Benefit (General) Regulations 1987, SI 1987 No. 1971 (as amended). For Northern Ireland it refers to Regulation 64(2) of the Housing Benefit (General) Regulations (Northern Ireland) 1987, SR 1987 No. 461 (as amended). (This gives the law about the minimum amount of HB payable: para. 7.12.)

CBA 130(1)(a)
NICBA 129(1)(a)

In Great Britain this refers to section 130(1)(a) of the Social Security Contributions and Benefits Act 1992. The equivalent Act for Northern Ireland is the Social Security Contributions and Benefits (Northern Ireland) Act 1992. The equivalent reference within the Northern Ireland Act is section 129(1)(a). (These give the law about who may be entitled to HB: para. 3.3.)

HBRGB sch 4 para 30
NIHBR sch 4 para 32
HBR sch 5 para 19
HBR 60+ 25(1)(h)
NIHBR 60+ 25(1)(f)
CTBR sch 4 para 32, sch 5 para 19
CTBR 60+ 175(1)(h)

The reference to schedule 5 paragraph 19 is identical in the GB and Northern Ireland regulations. However the equivalent references to sch 4 are slightly different in the Northern Ireland legislation. Therefore separate references are given for HB regulations in Great Britain (HBRGB) and Northern Ireland (NIHBR). In Great Britain a reference is additionally required for CTB. (These give the law about treatment of payments from the social fund as income and capital: para. 13.35.)

1.65 The regulations which relate to rent officer functions in Great Britain are broadly reflected in the main Northern Ireland housing benefit regulations (with some differences). Where the rules are similar, an equivalent Northern Ireland reference is included in the marginal references. Some parts of the text relating to rent restrictions apply to Great Britain only and where possible this is indicated in the title heading and opening text.

Table 1.2: Key to marginal references

AA	In Great Britain, The Social Security Administration Act 1992, and except in the case where a separate reference is given for Northern Ireland (i.e. NIAA), The Social Security Administration (Northern Ireland) Act 1992. In both cases followed by the section number.
CBA	The Social Security Contributions and Benefits Act 1992, and except in the case where a separate reference is given for Northern Ireland (i.e. NICBA), The Social Security Contributions and Benefits (Northern Ireland) Act 1992. In both cases followed by section number.
CPR	In Great Britain, The Social Security Commissioners (Procedure) Regulations 1999, SI No. 1495 (as amended); In Northern Ireland, The Social Security Commissioners (Procedure) Regulations (Northern Ireland) 1999, SR No. 225 (as amended), in both cases followed by the regulation number.
CTBR	The Council Tax Benefit (General) Regulations 1992, SI No. 1814 (as amended), followed by regulation number.
CPSA	The Child Support, Pensions and Social Security Act, and except in the case where a separate reference is given for Northern Ireland (i.e. NICSPSSA), The Child Support, Pensions and Social Security Act (Northern Ireland) 2000. In both cases followed by the section number.
DAR	In Great Britain, The Housing Benefit and Council Tax Benefit (Decisions and Appeals) Regulations 2001 SI No. 1002 (as amended); In Northern Ireland, The Housing Benefit (Decisions and Appeals) Regulations (Northern Ireland) 2001 SR No.

	213 (as amended), in both cases followed by the regulation number.
DARGB	The Housing Benefit and Council Tax Benefit (Decisions and Appeals) Regulations 2001 SI No. 1002 (as amended), followed by the regulation number. Reference applies to GB only.
DAR99	In Great Britain, The Social Security and Child Support (Decisions and Appeals) Regulations 1999 SI No. 991 (as amended); In Northern Ireland, The Social Security and Child Support (Decisions and Appeals) Regulations (Northern Ireland) 1999 SR No. 162 (as amended), in both cases followed by the regulation number.
DAR99GB	The Social Security and Child Support (Decisions and Appeals) Regulations 1999 SI No. 991 (as amended), followed by the regulation number. Reference applies to GB only.
HBR	In Great Britain, The Housing Benefit (General) Regulations 1987, SI No. 1971 (as amended); In Northern Ireland The Housing Benefit (General) Regulations (Northern Ireland) SR No. 487 (as amended), in both cases followed by the regulation number.
HBR 60+	In Great Britain, The Housing Benefit (General) Regulations 1987, SI No. 1971 as amended by The Housing Benefit and Council Tax Benefit (State Pension Credit) Regulations 2003, SI No. 325 (as subsequently amended); In Northern Ireland The Housing Benefit (General) Regulations (Northern Ireland), SR No. 487 as amended by The Housing Benefit (State Pension Credit) Regulations (Northern Ireland) 2003, SR No. 197 (as subsequently amended), in both cases followed by the regulation number. (These regulations describe rules for the calculation of income, capital and the applicable amount where the claimant or their partner is aged 60 or over).
HBRGB	The Housing Benefit (General) Regulations 1987, SI No. 1971 (as amended), followed by the regulation number. Reference applies to GB only.
NIAA	The Social Security Administration (Northern Ireland) Act 1992, followed by the section number.

NICBA	The Social Security Contributions and Benefits (Northern Ireland) Act 1992, followed by the section number.
NICPSA	The Child Support, Pensions and Social Security Act (Northern Ireland) 2000, followed by the section number.
NIDAR	The Housing Benefit (Decisions and Appeals) Regulations (Northern Ireland) 2001 SR No. 213 (as amended), followed by regulation number.
NIDAR99	The Social Security and Child Support (Decisions and Appeals) Regulations (Northern Ireland) 1999 SR No. 162 (as amended), followed by regulation number.
NIHBR	The Housing Benefit (General) Regulations (Northern Ireland) 1987 SR No. 487 (as amended), followed by regulation number.
NIHBR 60+	In Northern Ireland, The Housing Benefit (General) Regulations (Northern Ireland) SR No. 487 as amended by The Housing Benefit (State Pension Credit) Regulations (Northern Ireland) 2003, SR No. 197 (as subsequently amended), in both cases followed by the regulation number. (These regulations describe rules for the calculation of income, capital and the applicable amount where the claimant or their partner is aged 60 or over).
NISR	Statutory Rules of Northern Ireland (equivalent to Statutory Instruments in GB).
Reg	Regulation, followed by regulation number.
ROO	In England and Wales, The Rent Officers (Housing Benefit Functions) Order 1997, SI 1984; In Scotland, The Rent Officers (Housing Benefit Functions) (Scotland) Order 1997, SI 1985; in both cases followed by article number or schedule and paragraph number. GB only reference.
sch	schedule
SI	statutory instrument, followed by year and reference number
SR	statutory rules (apply to NI)

2 Who is eligible for HB/CTB?

2.1 This chapter explains the basic rules about who can get HB and/or CTB. It describes:

- who is eligible for CTB;
- who is eligible for HB;
- what payments HB can meet; and
- 'contrived' and other lettings where HB cannot be paid.

2.2 The conditions in this chapter usually come first in the order of things an authority is likely to consider when deciding a claim. But there are other conditions – for example, the claimant must occupy the dwelling as his or her home (chapter 3), and not have too much income or capital (chapter 7).

WHO IS ELIGIBLE FOR CTB?

CBA 131(3) **2.3** To be eligible for main CTB, or second adult rebate, the claimant must be:

- liable to pay the council tax in respect of a dwelling (para. 9.7); and
- a resident of that dwelling (para. 9.7).

2.4 Straightforward examples of who can get CTB are in table 2.1. Typical examples (and all would be awarded their CTB as a rebate) would be home owners, tenants, and so on.

EXCLUSIONS FROM CTB

2.5 The following are the main categories of people who cannot get CTB:

- owners (and other landlords) of unoccupied dwellings (para. 9.8);
- owners (and other landlords) of houses in multiple occupation (para. 9.8);
- all under-18-year-olds (para. 9.11);
- people who are severely mentally impaired (unless they are liable for council tax, which is unusual: para. 9.10-11);
- full-time students who are not liable for council tax (para. 9.10-11);
- most other full-time students (para. 21.24 – and see para. 2.7 about second adult rebate);
- certain people who are subject to immigration control or do not have habitual residence (chapter 20).

2.6 In the first case above, the exclusion is because they are not resident in the dwelling; in the next four cases it is because they are not liable for council tax on their dwelling; and in the last two it is because CTB law specifically excludes them from eligibility.

2.7 The rules for second adult rebate differ for students. In general, students are eligible for second adult rebate even if they are not eligible for main CTB.

Table 2.1: Straightforward examples of who can get HB/CTB

People who own their home	Not eligible for HB (because not liable for rent) Eligible for CTB
People in shared ownership schemes	Eligible for HB (on their rent) Eligible for CTB
People renting self-contained accommodation	Eligible for HB Eligible for CTB
People renting non-self-contained accommodation	Eligible for HB Not eligible for CTB (because not liable for council tax)

WHO IS ELIGIBLE FOR HB?

2.8 To be eligible for HB, the claimant must be: CBA 130(1)(a) NICBA 129(1)(a)

- liable to make payments (of rent or certain other items) in respect of a dwelling in the UK (para. 2.33); and
- living there as his or her normal home (chapter 3).

2.9 Straightforward examples of who can get HB are in table 2.1. In the public sector, HB can be awarded (as a rent rebate) to people renting from a council, a new town, Communities Scotland, the Northern Ireland Housing Executive, and people placed by housing authorities in 'bed and breakfast' establishments and hostels. In the private sector, HB can be awarded (as a rent allowance) to people renting from a private landlord, housing association, co-op or hostel.

2.10 However, unlike CTB, there are numerous further rules about which payments count for the purposes of the first rule above, which do not, how a person can be treated as liable to make payments even if he or she is not so liable (and *vice versa*), and so on. The remainder of this chapter describes these.

EXCLUSIONS FROM HB

2.11 The following groups of claimant cannot get HB – because HB law specifically excludes them from eligibility:

- certain people who are subject to immigration control or do not have habitual residence (chapter 20);
- most full-time students (para. 21.24);
- many under-18-year-old care leavers (see below); and
- many members of religious orders (see below).

ENGLISH AND WELSH CARE LEAVERS UNDER 18

SI 2001 No 3070
SI 2001 No 2874
SI 2001 No 2189
SI 2004 No 747

2.12 The following rules apply, under section 6 of the Children (Leaving Care) Act 2000, to 16-year-olds and 17-year-olds who have left local authority care in England and Wales, and from 1 April 2004, in Scotland to any care leaver who left care on or after 1 April 2004. The reason why most such care leavers cannot get HB is simply that the responsibility for their housing costs falls with social services. The reason why there are no equivalent rules for CTB is simply that under-18-year-olds cannot be liable for council tax.

2.13 A person is not eligible for HB if he or she is aged 16 or 17 and:

- in England and Wales has been looked after by a local authority for a period or periods amounting to at least 13 weeks beginning after they reached the age of 14 and ending after they reached the age of 16; or
- in England and Wales only was not subject to a care order at the time they became 16 because of being in hospital or being detained in a remand centre, a young offenders institution or a secure training centre or any other institution as the result of a court order; and immediately beforehand they had been looked after by a local authority for a period or periods amounting to at least 13 weeks which began after they reached the age of 14; or
- in Scotland only, has been looked after and accommodated by a local authority for a period or periods amounting to at least 13 weeks beginning after they reached the age of 14 and ending after they reached the age of 16. Whether a person has been 'accommodated' includes instances where the person has been placed under a supervision requirement following a children's hearing.

2.14 In calculating the 13 weeks periods, in England and Scotland no account should be taken of any time during which the child was looked after by a local authority in a pre-planned series of short-term placements (respite care), none of which individually exceeded four weeks, so long as at the end of each such placement the child was returned to the care of his or her parent, or someone who had parental responsibility. In Wales the 13 week period includes any period of respite care.

2.15 The above exclusion from HB does not apply, however, if the following circumstances apply:

- In England and Wales to anyone who lived with someone under a family placement for a continuous period of six months or more unless the family placement broke down and the child ceased to live with the person concerned. This rule applies whether the period of six months commenced before or after the child ceased to be looked after by the local authority.
- in Scotland the authorities have placed the young person with their family. Family in this instance includes any person aged at least 18 or who was looking after them before they went into care; or
- in Scotland a care leaver who left care before the 1 April 2004. These persons will still be entitled to benefit in the normal way.

NORTHERN IRELAND CARE LEAVERS UNDER 18

2.16 Because of delays in changing the law, 16 and 17-year-olds leaving care in Northern Ireland are not currently excluded from HB entitlement but such an exclusion is expected to be brought into effect from October 2004 under the provisions of the Children (Leaving Care) Act (Northern Ireland) 2002. The arrangements are likely to be similar, but not identical to those which currently apply to Great Britain.

MEMBERS OF CERTAIN RELIGIOUS ORDERS

2.17 Members of a religious order are not eligible for HB if they are maintained fully by that order. Monks and nuns in enclosed orders are excluded under this provision. The DWP (GM A3.42) points out that members of religious communities (as opposed to religious orders) are often eligible for HB since they frequently do paid work or retain their own possessions. The reason there is no similar exclusion from CTB is that the council tax bill goes to the owner in such cases. HBR 7(1)(j)

Which housing costs can HB meet?

PRIVATE AND VOLUNTARY CARE HOMES

2.18 Most residents of private or voluntary 'care homes' (as defined under the Care Standards Act 2000) are not eligible for HB except as follows: HBR 3(a),(d), 7(1)(k HBRGB 7(2)-(12) NIHBR 7(2)-(14)

- People who were eligible for HB on 29th October 1990 remain eligible for HB whilst resident in any type of care home, including if they move between homes.
- People in remunerative work (paras. 7.29-34) who were eligible for HB on 31st March 1993 remain eligible for HB until they move (other than temporarily) or until HB ceases for any reason.

- People paying a commercial rent to a close relative (para. 2.40) who were eligible for HB in respect of a care home on 31st March 1993 remain eligible for HB until they move (other than temporarily or until HB ceases for any reason.
- Except in Scotland, claimants are eligible for HB if they are in a small home not required to register under the Care Standards Act 2000 or that has been refused registration.
- Claimants are eligible for HB while resident in a care home which does not have to be registered because it is managed or provided by a body created by an Act of Parliament or incorporated by Royal Charter – such as the Salvation Army or Royal British Legion (GM A4.104). In such cases the residents can choose to remain on HB or choose to switch to JSA(IB)/IS, in which case those benefits can cover their housing costs (GM A4.106).

LOCAL AUTHORITY 'PART III' RESIDENTIAL ACCOMMODATION

HBR 8(2)(b)
HBRGB 8(2ZA),(2ZB)

2.19 The following rules apply to people provided with residential accommodation by social services, under sections 21-24 and 26 in 'Part III' of the National Assistance Act 1948 in England and Wales, section 59 of the Social Work (Scotland) Act 1968 and article 15 of the Health and Personal Social Services (Northern Ireland) Order 1972. Residents of such 'Part III' accommodation are not eligible for HB unless:

- the accommodation is neither owned or managed by social services, nor registered under the Care Standard Act 2000; or
- the accommodation is owned or managed by social services but the resident does not pay an inclusive charge for accommodation and board (i.e. cooked or prepared food). DWP guidance (GM A4.81) points out that the intention is to exclude from HB anyone to whom social services has a statutory obligation to provide accommodation with board under section 21(5) of the National Assistance Act 1948. The guidance also makes clear that 'if the provision of board [...] is unnecessary and is no longer made available to the resident concerned, entitlement to HB may arise [...]' (GM A4.81).

2.20 However, in England, Wales and Scotland, even where one of the above two exceptions applies, a claimant who was occupying 'part III' accommodation on 31st March 1993 (or was temporarily absent) is nevertheless excluded from HB for as long as he or she remains resident in it.

THE FOUR WEEKS' EXTRA HB IN THE ABOVE CASES

2.21 Where a claimant is in a care home and is in receipt of HB as described above, but becomes entitled to JSA(IB)/IS for the first time (for example because his or her capital has dropped below the JSA(IB)/IS limit), then the claimant is awarded four weeks' further HB. The same applies for claimants who choose to switch to JSA(IB)/IS as described above. In both cases the extra HB paid during the overlap can be deducted from the JSA(IB)/IS payable.

HOUSING COSTS MET THROUGH INCOME SUPPORT/INCOME-BASED JSA

2.22 Claimants whose accommodation costs are included in their income JSA(IB)/IS are excluded from help through the HB scheme. The main examples are home owners (para. 2.23) and the care home residents described above. HBR 8(2)(a),(3)

OWNER-OCCUPIERS AND LONG LEASEHOLDERS

2.23 Owner occupiers and long leaseholders (leaseholders whose lease was for more than 21 years) are not eligible for HB (though mortgage repayments, ground rent and service charges can be met through JSA(IB)/IS). This also applies to those who have the right to sell the freehold only with the consent of other joint owners. HBR 2(1) HBRGB 10(2)(a),(c) NIHBR 10(2)(a)

SHARED OWNERSHIP

2.24 Equity sharers buying part of their home from a housing association or housing authority and renting the other part under a shared ownership scheme are eligible for HB on the rental element (and their mortgage interest payments can be met through JSA(IB)/IS). HBR 10(2)(a)

HIRE PURCHASE, CREDIT SALE AND CONDITIONAL SALE AGREEMENTS

2.25 The following payments are not eligible for help under the HB scheme: HBRGB 10(2)(d) NIHBR 10(2)(b)

- a hire purchase agreement (for example to buy a mobile home);
- a credit sale agreement; or
- a conditional sale agreement unless it is for land. Conditional sale agreements are agreements for the sale of goods or land under which the purchase price is payable by instalments and the goods or land remain the seller's until the instalments are paid.

RENTAL PURCHASE SCHEMES

2.26 Payments under a rental purchase scheme are eligible for HB. In a rental purchase scheme all or part of the purchase price is paid in more than one instal- HBR 10(1) ment and the purchase is deferred until a specified part of the purchase price has been paid.

CO-OWNERSHIP SCHEMES

HBRGB 10(2)(e) NIHBR 10(2)(c) **2.27** People in housing association co-ownership schemes who will be entitled, on ceasing to be a member of the association, to a sum related to the value of the building are not eligible for HB *(R v Birmingham CC HBRB ex parte Ellery and Weir).*

CO-OP TENANTS

HBR 10(1) **2.28** Co-operative tenants are eligible for HB for their rent provided they have no more than a nominal equity share in the property.

CROWN TENANTS

HBRGB 10(2)(e) NIHBR 10(2)(c) **2.29** In England, Wales and Scotland all Crown tenants are excluded from eligibility for HB. In Northern Ireland this applies only to tenants of Ministry of Defence property. A Crown tenant is normally a person renting his or her home from someone managing the property for the Crown or whose landlord is a government department. Crown tenants are excluded from HB even if a government tenant uses a housing association as its managing agent. Guidance on this and other relevant matters is in DWP circulars HB/CTB (93)27 and A26/99.

2.30 Crown tenants can get JSA(IB)/IS towards their rent. If they do not qualify for JSA(IB)/IS), they can get rent rebates under voluntary schemes established by their landlords. Authorities often administer these schemes, but the schemes are quite separate from HB itself (GM chapter A8).

FORMER CROWN TENANTS

HBR 10(1) **2.31** Former Crown tenants and licensees whose agreement to occupy a Crown property has been terminated are eligible for HB if they are liable to pay mesne or violent profits (GM A8.91).

THE CROWN ESTATE COMMISSIONERS AND THE DUCHIES OF CORNWALL AND LANCASTER

HBR 10(1) **2.32** Tenants and licensees of properties managed by the Crown Estate Commissioners, and tenants and licensees of the Duchies of Cornwall and Lancaster are eligible for HB (GM A8.95-96).

Liability to pay rent

CBA 130(1)(a) NICBA 129(1)(a) HBR 6(1)(a) **2.33** The general rule is that a claimant is eligible for HB only if he or she is liable (has a legal obligation or duty) to pay rent for the home.

THE NATURE OF LIABILITY FOR RENT

2.34 Liability for rent can arise whether or not there is a written agreement: it can arise by word of mouth alone *(R v Poole Borough Council ex p Ross)*. The landlord must have the right to grant the tenancy in the first place, and must have the intention of repossessing the property if the claimant does not pay rent. It is not possible in law to grant a tenancy to oneself, nor can liability arise under a tenancy 'granted' to someone who already has the right to occupy the property in question. In the second case, for example, if a couple are joint owners of a property and one leaves, the other has the right to occupy all of it, so the absent one cannot 'grant' a tenancy to the present one. Several further points are mentioned in the following paragraphs.

2.35 Certain people, such as those with learning difficulties, may appear unable to enter into a liability. Nonetheless, someone formally appointed to act for them, such as a receiver appointed by the Court of Protection, can enter into a liability on that individual's behalf and thus he or she is eligible for HB (DWP circular HB/CTB A30/95 para. 12). The question of a child's or young person's liability to pay rent – particularly when assisted by a social services department – is examined in detail in DWP circular HB/CTB A16/96.

TREATING A CLAIMANT AS LIABLE EVEN WHEN HE OR SHE IS NOT

2.36 Any of the following, even if not liable to pay rent, are treated by law as liable, and are therefore eligible for HB: HBR 6(1)(b)-(e),(2)

- the partner of the liable person (including the partner of a full-time student who is not eligible for HB: para. 21.16);
- a former partner of the liable person who has to make the payments in order to continue to live in the home because the liable person is not doing so;
- anyone who has to make the payments if he or she is to continue to live in the home because the liable person is not making the payments and the authority considers it reasonable to treat him or her as liable to make those payments;
- a person whose liability is waived by the landlord as reasonable compensation for repairs or redecoration work actually carried out by the tenant – but only up to a maximum of eight benefit weeks in respect of any one waiver;
- someone who has actually met his or her liability before claiming.

2.37 Where the rent is varied either during an award or retrospectively, the claimant is treated as liable for the revised amount due.

'CONTRIVED' LETTINGS AND OTHER EXCLUSIONS FROM HB

2.38 The remainder of this chapter describes the circumstances in which a claimant cannot get HB, even though he or she is in fact liable for rent. The law does this by saying the claimant is treated as not liable to make the payments.

Examples: Treated as liable to pay rent

A claimant has been deserted by her partner. Although she is not the tenant the landlord will allow her to remain in the property if she continues to pay the rent. She should be treated as liable if her former partner is not paying the rent.

A claimant is the son of a council tenant. He takes over responsibility for paying rent while his father is working abroad for two years. The son should be treated as liable if it is reasonable to do so.

LANDLORD A CLOSE RELATIVE RESIDING IN THE DWELLING

HBR 7(1)(b) **2.39** Where the claimant's landlord is a 'close relative' (para. 2.40) of the claimant, or of the claimant's partner, and the landlord also resides in the dwelling (para. 2.42), the claimant is not eligible for HB.

WHO COUNTS AS A CLOSE RELATIVE?

HBR (1) **2.40** A 'close relative' is:

- a parent, step-parent or parent-in-law; or
- brother or sister; or
- son, son-in-law, daughter, daughter-in-law, step-son, step-daughter; or
- the partner of any of the above.

2.41 Arguably the term 'brother' and 'sister' should be taken to include 'half-brothers' and 'half-sisters' (GM A3.33-34 (following Commissioner's decision R(SB) 22/87)). 'Step-brothers' and 'step-sisters' are not treated as close relatives for HB purposes (HB/CTB A27/97 para. 4).

WHAT DOES 'RESIDES IN' MEAN?

2.42 Before January 1999 (when the law changed) this rule referred to a claimant who 'resided with' the landlord, intentionally making this the same as the definition used in relation to non-dependants (para. 4.22). The rule now refers to the landlord 'residing in' the dwelling. The DWP did not intend this apparent drafting error (Circular A1/99, para. 13), and it seems safe to assume that the definition of 'resides with' (para. 4.22) also applies here.

NON-COMMERCIAL AGREEMENTS

2.43 A claimant is not eligible for HB if the agreement under which he or she occupies the dwelling is not on a commercial basis. What constitutes a 'commercial basis' is not defined in the regulations but the authority must have regard to whether the agreement contains terms which are not enforceable at law in determining whether or not it is a commercial one. HBR 7(1)(a),(1A)

2.44 In *R v Sheffield CC HBRB ex parte Smith and others,* it was held that the authority must not only consider the amount payable for the accommodation but also the other terms of the agreement. The important factor is whether the arrangements are at 'arm's length' or more akin to the arrangements that would exist between close relatives who generally only make contributions to their keep or household running costs. Similarly, in *R v Sutton London Borough Council ex parte Partridge,* it was held that what is 'commercial' is not necessarily confined to the financial relationship. And in *R v Poole Borough Council ex parte Ross,* it was held that absence of a written tenancy agreement does not itself mean there is no liability to make payments, and that an element of friendship between the parties does not itself make it non-commercial

FORMER FOSTER CHILDREN

2.45 More specifically the DWP has advised that an arrangement that involves a former foster child remaining in his or her foster accommodation and paying rent once the fostering allowance ceases, for example where the foster child reaches the age of 18, should not normally be treated as a non-commercial arrangement (HB/CTB A 30/95 para. 17 iv).

CONTRIVED LIABILITIES

2.46 A claimant is not eligible for HB if the authority is satisfied that his or her liability was created to take advantage of the HB scheme. This is commonly referred to as a 'contrived' letting. General DWP guidance on this is in GM paragraphs A3.81-92. HBR 7(1)(l)

2.47 In *R v Solihull MBC HBRB ex parte Simpson* the Court considered that while the ability to attract HB could never realistically be the sole purpose of a tenancy, equally, and importantly, anyone eligible for HB must, by definition, have entered into an agreement to pay a rent which he could not afford. The mere fact of having done so could not of itself, except perhaps in extreme cases, be evidence of an arrangement entered in order to take advantage of the scheme. A similar point was made in *R v Sutton LBC HBRB ex parte Keegan.* The judge quashed the review board's decision not to award HB because 'it had attached a wholly disproportionate weight to the fact that the claimant could not meet her liability to pay rent'.

2.48 In the Sutton case the judge considered that before an agreement could be said to be 'contrived' the means, circumstances and intentions of the claimant and the landlord must be considered. In particular, consideration should be given to the consequences if HB is not to be paid. If it seems likely that the landlord will have to ask the claimant to leave the dwelling so that it can be re-let or sold, this is evidence that the liability has not been created to take advantage of the scheme.

2.49 In the Solihull case it was held that 'an arrangement whereby persons, who would in any event be eligible for HB, were provided with accommodation by a parent or relation who was then to receive rent generated from HB was not of itself an arrangement created to take advantage of the HB scheme'.

2.50 *R v Manchester CC ex parte Baragrove Properties* provides an example of the sort of extreme case envisaged in the Solihull judgment. In this case the authority was found to have acted correctly in interpreting the rule as permitting exclusion from HB entitlement cases where landlords were specifically charging higher rents to vulnerable tenants and where the authority could not use its powers to restrict the eligible rent (para. 10.58).

2.51 In *CSHB/718/2002,* the Commissioner emphasised the need for clarity in deciding why someone is not eligible for HB. There is a difference between not being liable for rent at all (paras. 2.33-34) and being liable in a way that was created to take advantage of the scheme. The claimant rented from his mother who was for all or part of the time in a nursing home. He did not pay any of the HB he received to his mother. The council said his tenancy was created to take advantage of the scheme. The Commissioner quashed this decision and directed a rehearing because the authority had failed to consider whether the claimant was disentitled by not being liable in the first place, and also failed to look at whether the intention to abuse the scheme existed at the time the agreement was created (he did not claim HB for the first three years of the tenancy).

MORTGAGE RESCUE SCHEMES

2.52 The DWP has advised authorities that mortgage rescue schemes developed by mortgage lenders to enable owner-occupiers in arrears with mortgage payments and facing repossession to convert the mortgage agreement into a tenancy for rent should not be regarded as contrived to take advantage of the scheme (circular HB/CTB(92)6).

RENTING A FORMER JOINT HOME FROM AN EX-PARTNER

HBR 7(1)(c) **2.53** Where a married or unmarried couple separate and the one remaining in the home, or a new partner, makes payments to the one who has left, the person making the payments is not eligible for HB.

2.54 In *R (on the application of Painter) v Carmarthenshire CC HBRB,* Mr Painter had originally been a lodger renting a bedroom and with the right to use the common parts. He subsequently formed a relationship with his landlady and moved into her room and jointly occupied the accommodation. The relationship ended and Mr Painter reverted back to a tenant and was liable to make payments of rent. The authority decided that Mr Painter was not eligible for HB because he was renting a former joint home from an ex-partner. It was argued that this rule only applied if the dwelling in respect of which the payments were due was the same dwelling which had been occupied during the relationship. Mr Painter submitted that the dwelling was in fact different. It no longer included the landlady's room. Additionally it was argued that if the regulation was applicable, it was incompatible with the Human Rights Act 1998. The Court held that the informal arrangements to occupy separate rooms did not affect the reality of the situation that the dwelling remained the same. It also held that there had been no breach of the Convention rights. Any discrimination was justifiable as a precaution against potential abuse of the housing benefit scheme.

RESPONSIBILITY FOR THE LANDLORD'S CHILD

2.55 A claimant is not eligible for HB if he or she is responsible, or a partner is responsible, for the landlord's child (i.e. someone under the age of 16). The DWP (GM A3.54) emphasises that 'responsibility for a child' means more than 'cares for'. HBR 7(1)(d)

2.56 This is a difficult rule to interpret as it blurs certain established concepts so far as means-tested benefits are concerned. It would appear to apply where the 'landlord' is the biological mother or father of a child, or has adopted a child, but where the child is nevertheless considered to be part of the claimant's family for JSA(IB), IS or HB purposes. The legality of this rule and the argument that it offended the Human Rights Convention was argued in *R v Secretary of State for Social Security, ex parte Tucker*. The Court held that the rule was not *ultra vires* nor contrary to the European Convention on Human Rights.

TRUSTS

2.57 A trust is an arrangement under which property is transferred to one or more people known as trustees. Trustees are required to look after the property or deal with it for the benefit of someone else, 'the beneficiary', or for some other purpose such as that of a charity.

RENTING FROM A TRUST OF WHICH ONE IS A TRUSTEE OR BENEFICIARY

2.58 A claimant is not eligible for HB if his or her landlord is a trustee of a trust of which one of the following is a trustee or a beneficiary: HBR 7(1)(e),(1B)

- the claimant or partner; or
- the claimant's or partner's close relative (para. 3.31) if the close relative 'resides with' (para. 4.22) the claimant; or

- the claimant's, or partner's, former partner,

unless in each case the claimant satisfies the authority that the liability was not intended to take advantage of the HB scheme.

RENTING FROM A TRUST OF WHICH ONE'S CHILD IS A BENEFICIARY

HBR 7(1)(f) **2.59** A claimant is not eligible for HB if his or her landlord is a trustee of a trust of which the claimant's or partner's child is a beneficiary. Unlike in the previous paragraph, this rule has no exception.

RENTING FROM A COMPANY OF WHICH ONE IS A DIRECTOR OR AN EMPLOYEE

HBR 7(1)(e),(1B) **2.60** A claimant is not eligible for HB if his or her landlord is a company of which one of the following is a director or an employee:

- the claimant or partner; or
- the claimant's or partner's close relative (para. 2.40) if the close relative 'resides with' (para. 2.42) the claimant; or
- the claimant's, or partner's, former partner,

unless in each case the claimant satisfies the authority that the liability was not intended to take advantage of the HB scheme. Note also that this rule does not apply if a claimant is employed by a company and rents from a director of the company (since a director is not the company itself).

2.61 The DWP advises (GM para. A3.56) that a 'company' means a registered company. This can be checked with Companies House and, if the company is registered in England and Wales, this can be done on-line at *www.companies-house.gov.uk*

FORMER NON-DEPENDANTS

HBR 7(1)(g),(1B) **2.62** A claimant is not eligible for HB if:

- he or she was, at any time prior to the creation of the rent liability, a non-dependant of someone who resided in the dwelling; and
- that person continues to reside in the dwelling,

unless the claimant satisfies the authority that the liability was not intended to take advantage of the HB scheme.

FORMER OWNERS

HBR 7(1)(h) **2.63** A claimant is not eligible for HB if:

- he or she, or a partner, previously owned the dwelling; and
- owned it within the last five years,

unless the claimant is able to satisfy the authority that he or she or a partner could not have continued to live in the dwelling without letting go of ownership.

2.64 This could be the case, for example, if a claimant is able to provide evidence that a mortgage lender would have sought possession unless the liable person had agreed to the transfer of the property and the establishment of a rental agreement; or if a housing association agrees to take over ownership of a property and take on the ex-owner as a tenant. In each case the authority will need to obtain from the former owner an explanation of his or her reasons for giving up ownership of the property (GM A3.67-71).

TIED ACCOMMODATION

2.65 A claimant is not eligible for HB if his or her, or a partner's, occupation of the dwelling is a condition of employment by the landlord. HBR 7(1)(i)

2.66 The DWP advises (GM A3.76) that this test should not be taken to mean 'as a result of the employment'. A retired employee, for example, may continue to live in previously tied accommodation but this would no longer be as a condition of employment by the landlord, and so this rule would not prevent eligibility for HB.

ILLEGAL AND UNLAWFUL TENANCIES

2.67 Sub-tenancies which are created in breach of a clause in the head lease not to sublet or assign the tenancy do not prevent the assignment or sub-letting from being valid between the head tenant and sub-tenant: *Governors of Peabody Donation Fund v Higgins* (not a HB case). Such lettings are unlawful rather than illegal and expose the head tenant to eviction for breach of the agreement. Given that there is a legal liability for rent it seems that these lettings are eligible for HB, unless it is also a letting to which paragraphs 2.36-66 above apply.

2.68 An illegal letting is one in which its creation would necessarily involve committing a criminal offence. An example would be where a landlord lets a dwelling which he or she knows is in contravention of a Housing Act closing order. In contrast to unlawful contracts, illegal contracts are generally not binding (see *A Casebook on Contract,* Ninth Edition, J.C. Smith) and so would not be eligible for HB. Where a letting was not illegal at the time it was created (e.g. prior to a closing order) it seems likely it would remain binding until the end of the next rental period, or if let on a fixed term at the end of the fixed term.

3 Occupying the home, absences and moves

3.1 One of the main conditions for getting HB is that the claimant must occupy the accommodation in question as his or her home. This chapter explains this, and covers

- what it means to occupy somewhere as a home for HB purposes;
- when HB can be awarded on two homes;
- when a claimant can get HB before moving in;
- how HB and CTB work when the claimant is temporarily absent.

3.2 This chapter does not apply to CTB – except for the rules about temporary absence (paras. 3.31 onwards). Instead, the equivalent condition for getting CTB is that the claimant must be resident in his or her dwelling (para. 2.3). In practice this usually means the same thing as the HB condition mentioned above. There are no rules about two homes and moving home in CTB. CTB can be awarded on only one home at a time.

HB: occupation as a home

CBA 130(1)(a)
NICBA 129(1)(a)
HBR 5(1)

3.3 HB can only be awarded on accommodation that is occupied (has been moved into) by the claimant, and only if it is occupied as a home. Accommodation occupied only for a holiday or business purposes is not a home and therefore is not eligible. Except as described later in this chapter, HB is only payable on one home – which is the home the claimant 'normally occupies' with any family he or she has (CH/2521/2002). The rules in this section do not apply to CTB (para. 3.2).

3.4 'Occupying' a home means more than simply being liable for rent: it means being physically present. Doubts about the claimant's occupation of the dwelling can often arise as a result of residency checks by an authority's visiting/fraud officers. If there is any doubt as to whether or not the claimant occupies the dwelling, the authority should consider all the relevant evidence before determining this matter.

HBR 5(2)

3.5 In considering which home the claimant normally occupies, the authority must have regard to any other dwelling occupied by the claimant or family, no matter whether it is here or abroad. The DWP advises that this requirement is not intended to exclude from eligibility someone who has set up home in this country but whose family, no longer being part of his or her household, remain abroad. Further specific rules are given in the remainder of this chapter.

HB: moving home and having two homes

3.6 There are several different rules about what happens when someone moves home or has two homes, in only some of which cases is the claimant eligible for HB on two homes at a time. The rules are very specific. If a claimant does not with fit within one of the rules then (often to the deep chagrin of his or her landlord) there is no possibility of stretching the law. This section does not apply at all to CTB (para. 3.2). It is never possible to get CTB on more than one dwelling at a time.

CLAIMANTS WHO HAVE MOVED BUT REMAIN LIABLE FOR RENT AT THEIR OLD HOME

3.7 This rule is commonly known as the overlapping HB rule. A claimant moving from one rented dwelling to another is eligible for HB on both of them only if all three of the following conditions are met: HBR 5(5)(d)

- only for the period after he or she has moved into the new dwelling;
- only if his or her liability for rent on both dwellings could not reasonably have been avoided; and
- only for up to four weeks.

3.8 To find out how HB is calculated in such cases, see paragraph 3.29. There is no legal requirement for a separate claim to be made for HB for this overlapping period. Note that the rule does not apply when a claimant moves out for repairs to be done (para. 3.23).

3.9 The DWP (GM A3.201) suggests that the rule should only be used in 'exceptional circumstances' but there is no such test in the law. If the conditions set out above are met then the authority must treat the claimant as occupying the two dwellings as a home. The authority does, however, need information and evidence that will enable it to identify an overlapping liability and determine whether or not it could reasonably have been avoided.

3.10 This rule applies, for example, where a claimant in housing need is offered at short notice an appropriate new tenancy and is obliged to take up liability for the new tenancy before the period of notice required by the landlord of the old home has expired. HB is only payable on both properties during this period, however, if the claimant has a liability for and has actually moved into the new property whilst having a liability to make payments on the old home. If the claimant is still in fact occupying and liable to make payments on the old home then the fact that he or she has a liability on the new home and may have transferred some items of furniture does not mean that he or she has met the test of having 'moved into' the new home. In such instances HB is only payable on the old home, not the new home.

CBA 130, HBR 5(5)(d), 7 **3.11** It used to be said that for this rule to operate both liabilities need to be eligible for HB, preventing it from applying if the claimant is moving into non-rented accommodation, owner-occupied accommodation or a care home. However, a Commissioner has recently held (CH/4546/2002) that as long as there is a liability for some sort of housing costs (albeit costs such as a miortgage or payments on a care home which HB cannot meet) then HB can be paid on the old home subject to the other conditions of this rule.

CLAIMANTS WHO HAVE MOVED BECAUSE OF FEAR OF VIOLENCE

HBR 5(5)(a) **3.12** A claimant is eligible for HB on two rented homes for up to 52 weeks if he or she:

- has left and remains absent from the former home through fear of violence
  - in the home, or
  - by a person who was formerly a member of the claimant's family; and
- has no intention to return to it; and
- is liable for rent on both that home and where he or she is now living; and
- it is reasonable to meet the rent on both homes.

3.13 For how HB is calculated in such cases see paragraph 3.29. If the claimant does not intend to return to the old dwelling, the previous rule applies instead (allowing HB to be paid on both for only four weeks: para. 3.7). If he or she is liable for rent on the old dwelling but not the new one, the rule about absences from home – described later – applies instead.

3.14 Actual violence need not have occurred for the rule to apply. The claimant has only to be afraid of violence occurring. If the authority considers, however, that the fear of violence is one that is not reasonably held or that the claimant brought it upon himself or herself, for example as a result of criminal activity, it may consider it unreasonable that HB should be paid in respect of both homes.

3.15 The feared violence in the home need not be related to a family or former family member. It could be related to anyone, e.g. a neighbour, so long as it is feared that violence could occur in the home. Where the fear is of violence outside the home it must be a former member of the claimant's family who poses the threat of violence. This would include not only an ex-partner but also an adult child. On the other hand, it is of course the case that someone who is afraid of violence outside the home may well be afraid of it coming into the home.

3.16 Authorities are advised to check regularly that the claimant intends to return to the previous home (GM A3.193). If the claimant subsequently decides not to return, HB on the former home stops. The HB paid on the former home while the claimant had the intention to return will have been properly paid and is not an overpayment.

CLAIMANTS WAITING FOR ADAPTATIONS FOR A DISABILITY

3.17 If a claimant becomes liable for rent on a new dwelling, but does not move into it straight away because they are necessarily waiting for it to be adapted to meet their disablement needs or those of a family member (para. 4.5), the claimant is eligible for HB for up to four weeks before moving in, so long as the delay in moving is reasonable. HBR 5(5)(e)

3.18 In this case, if the claimant is also liable for rent on their old home, they are eligible for HB on both homes during those four weeks. For how HB is calculated in such cases, see paragraph 3.29. Whether in the case of HB for one home or two, HB can be awarded only after the claimant has moved in and the claim must be made promptly: paragraph 3.30. HBR 5(6)(c)(i)

CLAIMANTS WAITING FOR A SOCIAL FUND PAYMENT

HBR 5(6)(c)(ii)

3.19 If a claimant becomes liable for rent on a new dwelling, but does not move into it straight away because he or she:

- has applied for a social fund payment to help with the move or with setting up home; and
- is aged 60 or more, or has a child aged under 6, or someone in the family is disabled in one of the ways relevant to a disability premium or disabled child premium,

the claimant is eligible for HB for up to four weeks before moving in, so long as the delay in moving is reasonable.

3.20 In this case, the claimant is not eligible for HB on his or her old home as well – a feature of the rule that has been criticized frequently over the years as discriminating against someone moving from a furnished rented home to his or her first unfurnished rented home. HB can be awarded only after the claimant has moved in and the claim must be made promptly: paragraph 3.30.

HBR 5(6)(c)(iii)

CLAIMANTS WAITING TO LEAVE HOSPITAL OR A CARE HOME

3.21 If a claimant becomes liable for rent on a new dwelling, but does not move into it straight away because they are waiting to leave a hospital or a care home, they are eligible for HB for up to four weeks before moving in, so long as the delay in moving is reasonable

3.22 This might well arise if someone's discharge from hospital is delayed, or someone cannot immediately manage to leave a care home. HB can be awarded only after the claimant has moved in and the claim must be made promptly: paragraph 3.30.

MOVING OUT FOR REPAIRS TO BE DONE

HBR 5(4) **3.23** A claimant who has had to leave his or her normal home while it is having essential repairs, and who has to make payments (rent or mortgage payments) on one but not both the normal home and the temporary accommodation, is treated as occupying the home for which payments made. If the payments due on that home are mortgage payments, the claimant is not eligible for HB. The other rules about moving home (above) and absences from home (below) do not apply to such claimants.

LARGE FAMILIES

HBR 5(5)(c) **3.24** Where the claimant's family (para. 4.5) is so large they have been housed by a housing authority in two separate dwellings, the claimant is eligible for HB on both homes. The DWP (GM para. A3.198) advises that both homes should be provided, but not necessarily owned, by the local authority. There is no time limit in this case.

3.25 Independently of the above rule, however, the Court of Appeal has held that a claimant (in what were fairly uncommon circumstances) can occupy two nearby houses as 'one home' for JSA(IB) purposes and this is strongly persuasive for HB (but not CTB): *Secretary of State for Work and Pensions v Miah.*

SINGLE AND LONE PARENT STUDENTS AND TRAINEES

HBR 5(3) **3.26** A single claimant or lone parent who is a student or on a government training course, and who has two homes but pays rent on only one, is treated as normally occupying that one (and is thus eligible for HB on it), even if he or she normally lives in the other one.

HBR 5(9) **3.27** The training courses referred to are those provided by, or under arrangements made with or approved by, a government department, any Secretary of State, Scottish Enterprise, or Highlands and Islands Enterprise. This definition includes training courses arranged by a local authority on behalf of one of these entities. The training course may be provided by the local authority itself or the local authority may contract with an external organisation to provide the course.

Example: Occupation as a home

The claimant normally lives with her parents but rents accommodation whilst on a government training course. In such circumstances she should be considered as normally occupying the rented accommodation during the period she is liable to pay housing costs.

STUDENT COUPLES

3.28 A couple is eligible for HB on two homes if one is a student who personally fulfils the criteria for student eligibility for HB and the other is not a student, or if both are students each of whom personally fulfils the criteria for student eligibility for HB (table 21.1). But occupying two homes must be unavoidable and it must be reasonable to pay HB on two homes (table 21.2). There is no time limit in this case. HBR 5(5)(b)

CALCULATION OF BENEFIT ON TWO HOMES

3.29 In the cases above in which HB is awarded on two homes (paras. 3.17, 3.19 and 3.21), a question that is not addressed in either the law or DWP guidance is that of how HB should be assessed. It appears that in these cases there is one benefit calculation based on the aggregated eligible rent of the two properties. Where the dwellings are in different areas, authorities will need to liaise and/or establish agency arrangements (para. 1.25).

ENTITLEMENT PRIOR TO MOVING IN: PROMPT CLAIMS

3.30 In the cases above in which HB is awarded before someone moves in (paras. 3.18, 3.20 and 3.30), it is necessary to claim promptly (i.e. before or in the first week of the new liability for rent – unless the claimant requests and is awarded backdated benefit). If the claim is then refused (perhaps because at that time the authority is not sure that the claimant will in fact move in), and the claimant reapplies within four weeks, the reapplication will be treated as having been made at the same time as the refused claim. And the award of HB cannot start until the claimant actually does move in. For more detail, see paragraphs 5.76-77. HBR 5(7)

HB and CTB: temporary absence

3.31 Claimants can, in the circumstances described in the remainder of this chapter, get HB and/or CTB even while temporarily absent from their home. The rules for HB and CTB are the same, though the wording does not sit well in the CTB scheme, the rules being couched in terms of 'occupation as a home' which is not one of the conditions of entitlement to CTB (para. 3.2).

ABSENCES: THE THREE RULES

3.32 During an absence from their home, a claimant remains eligible for HB and/or CTB: HBR 5(7A)-(9) CTBR 4C

- for up to 13 weeks during a trial period in a care home – so long as the claimant intends to return to their normal home if the care home is unsuitable (but if the claimant was absent from home for another reason before this, their total absence from home must not exceed 52 weeks); or

- for up to 52 weeks if they are absent (in the UK or abroad) for one of the reasons in table 3.1 – so long as the claimant intends to return to their normal home within 52 weeks or, in exceptional circumstances, not substantially later; or
- for up to 13 weeks during an absence (in the UK or abroad) for any other reason – so long as the claimant intends to return to their normal home within a strict 13 weeks.

HBR 5(9) CTBR 4(6) **3.33** Many of the reasons in table 3.1 refer to an absence being 'medically approved'. This means certified by a medical practitioner. The DWP advises (circular HB/CTB A8/95 para. 18) that a medical practitioner could, for example, be a GP or nurse, and that the approval need not necessarily be in the form of a certificate.

Example: Trying out a care home and then deciding to stay there

A woman who owns her home has been on CTB for a while. She then goes into a care home for a six-week trial period to see if it suits her.

- She remains eligible for CTB.

In the third week of her trial period, she decides she likes the care home. In the fourth week she tells her family and the managers of the home that this is the case. In the fifth week the managers make her an offer of permanent accommodation in the care home and she accepts this. She tells the authority straight away.

- Her eligibility for CTB ceases once it is clear that she will stay there permanently, because this is a change in her circumstances. So she is not eligible for CTB from her sixth week in the care home onwards. (But the CTB she was awarded for her first five weeks there was nonetheless correctly paid.)

ABSENCES: ADDITIONAL CONDITIONS

HBR 5(7A)-(9) CTBR 4C **3.34** In each of the above three cases (para. 3.33), there are three further conditions which must be met in order for HB/CTB to be granted during the absence:

- the claimant must still be liable for rent/council tax on their normal home; and
- the part of the home the claimant normally occupies must not be let or sub-let; and
- the claimant must provide the authority with the information and evidence needed for the claim to continue (chapter 17).

Table 3.1: People who can get HB/CTB during an absence of up to 52 weeks

Claimants in prison etc, who have not yet been sentenced (e.g. claimants on remand or in a bail hostel).

Claimants in a residential care or nursing home who are not just trying it out (e.g. during periods of respite care).

Claimants in hospital, or receiving medically approved* care.

Claimants undergoing medical treatment or medically approved* convalescence or who are absent because their partner or child is undergoing this.

Claimants undertaking medically approved* care of someone else.

Claimants caring for a child whose parent or guardian is absent from home in order to receive medical treatment or medically approved* care.

Claimants following a government training course (as defined in para. 3.27).

Students who are eligible for HB (e.g. if they have to study abroad for part of their course).

Claimants absent because of fear of violence in their normal home (regardless of who it would be from) or fear of violence from a former member of their family (whether this would occur in the normal home or elsewhere). This would apply to people other than those mentioned in paragraph 3.12 because, for example, they are staying with relatives and are not liable to pay rent on two homes but intend to return to occupy their original homes.

* For 'medically approved' see paragraph 3.33.

COUNTING THE LENGTH OF THE ABSENCE

3.35 In *R v Penwith DC HBRB ex parte Burt* it was held that the 13-week and 52-week time limits refer to absences which are continuous. So if the claimant (with the exception of prisoners on temporary leave: para. 3.40) returns to, and occupies the dwelling as a home, even for a short time, the allowable period of temporary absence starts again. The DWP suggests (GM para. A3.141) that a stay at home lasting, for example, only a few hours may not break the absence but one that lasts at least 24 hours may do so.

3.36 Depending upon the facts of the case, however, the authority may decide that the claimant's normal home is elsewhere for HB purposes (paras. 3.3-5). If another person occupying the dwelling starts paying rent in the absence of the claimant, the authority should consider treating that other person as liable and therefore eligible for HB (para. 2.36).

3.37 Once it becomes clear that the claimant is going to be away for more than 13 or 52 weeks, HB/CTB entitlement ends. The one exception is in the case of the absences in table 3.1. If such an absence is unlikely to substantially exceed the 52-week period, and if there are exceptional circumstances, the authority must pay up to the end of the 52nd week of absence. DWP guidance (GM para. A3.161) suggests that the term 'substantially exceed' relates to periods of absence greater than 15 months. It is, however, for the individual authority to interpret the term. The GM illustrates the concept of exceptional circumstances with the examples of someone prevented from returning home by an unanticipated event, and a discharge from hospital being delayed by a relapse. Other circumstances may also be considered.

ABSENCES IN PRISON, ETC

3.38 As indicated in table 3.1, until they are sentenced, a claimant in prison etc can get HB/CTB for up to 52 weeks. This means that (almost) all prisoners on remand can get HB/CTB.

Example: Remand and conviction

A man has been receiving HB for a while. He is then arrested and detained on remand pending his trial.

- The authority should assume that he will be absent for no more than 52 weeks. He therefore remains eligible for HB.

Fifteen weeks later he is tried, found guilty, and sentenced to a term of one year's imprisonment.

- Although he may well serve only six months in prison (after remission), and although the 15 weeks he has been on remand will count towards this, his total absence from home will now exceed 13 weeks. So his eligibility for HB ceases, because the fact that he has been sentenced is a change in his circumstances (chapter 17). (But the HB he was awarded for his 15 weeks on remand was nonetheless correctly paid.)

3.39 If and when the claimant is sentenced to prison etc, this counts as a change of circumstances. The relevant question is then: 'Will they return home within 13 weeks of when they left home?' In deciding the answer, it is assumed that the prisoner will get remission for good behaviour. Only if the answer is 'yes' can the claimant continue to get HB/CTB.

PRISONERS ON TEMPORARY LEAVE

3.40 Prisoners on temporary leave (to prepare for release) are counted as still being in prison. For further guidance on this, on the Home Detention Curfew Scheme, and prisoners generally, see GM A3.150-158.

HBR 5(8A)
CTBR 4B

4 The claimant's household

4.1 This chapter describes:

- the different types of claimant, and different categories of people who may live in the claimant's household;
- the circumstances in which the claimant is considered to be responsible for a child or young person for HB and main CTB;
- the circumstances in which partners and children or young people are treated as members of the claimant's household; and
- other people who may reside with the claimant or live in the same dwelling.

4.2 Authorities need to identify and define the people who live with the claimant to work out HB/CTB entitlement since:

- only one member of what counts as the claimant's family for benefit purposes can claim HB/CTB;
- in the case of second adult rebate, partners and/or jointly liable persons can affect entitlement;
- in the case of HB/main CTB fix ed deductions are made in certain cases for other people who live in the claimant's household who are classified as 'non-dependants';
- second adult rebate is worked out on the basis of the gross income of certain people who reside with the claimant known as 'second adults';
- the amount of HB/main CTB a non-income support/income-based JSA claimant receives is worked out with reference to the combined needs (in the form of the applicable amount) and the income and capital of the claimant's family;
- money from (sub-)tenants and boarders is taken into account in the case of a non-income support/income-based JSA claimant's income for HB/main CTB.

Household composition

4.3 The term 'household' is not defined in legislation. It should be given its normal everyday meaning, that is a domestic establishment containing the essentials of home life. People living in one dwelling (for example a house or flat) do not necessarily live together in the same household. The claimant's household may consist of:

- the claimant;
- the claimant's family;
- any other person who lives in the dwelling and who is classified as a 'non-dependant' for HB/main CTB.

In addition to the above, certain other people such as joint occupiers, (sub-)tenants, boarders and carers may live in the same dwelling as the claimant. Those 'non-dependants' and carers aged 18 or over who are not disregarded for the purpose of the council tax (appendix 6) count as 'second adults' for the purpose of second adult rebate.

CLAIMANT

4.4 The claimant may be: HBR 2(1) CTBR 2(1)

- single – i.e. a claimant who does not have a partner and is not responsible for a child/young person; or
- a lone parent – i.e. someone who does not have a partner but who is responsible for and is a member of the same household as a child/young person; or
- a member of a married or unmarried couple or polygamous marriage.

THE FAMILY

4.5 The claimant's family for benefit purposes consists of: CBA 137(1) NICBA 133(1)

- the claimant's partner(s), if a member of the same household; and
- any children or young persons the claimant is responsible for and who are members of the household (not just sons and daughters).

PARTNER

4.6 A partner is included in all instances where he or she is married or polygamously married or, in the case of a couple, unmarried but living together as husband and wife. The partner must be a member of the same household and, except in polygamous marriages, must be of the opposite sex to the claimant (though the DWP plans at some point to include same-sex partners). CBA 137(1) NICBA 133(1) HBR 2(1) CTBR 2(1)

LIVING TOGETHER AS HUSBAND AND WIFE

4.7 A married couple are treated as one unit as long as they are members of the same household. Either but not both may claim benefit. The same rules apply to an unmarried couple who are 'living together as husband and wife'.

4.8 Neither the Act nor regulations define the phrase 'living together as husband and wife'. The administration of this particular rule can give rise to serious financial and relationship problems. For example, if a man who has a high income starts living with a woman with a low income and the authority determines that they are 'living together as husband and wife' the woman may lose the whole of her benefit entitlement under this rule though she receives no money from the man. The High Court decision in *Crake and Butterworth v the Supplementary Benefit Commission* held that the first consideration when a man and woman appear to be living together as husband and wife is that of the purpose of the parties in living together. The HB/CTB schemes recognise many different ways in which a man and woman could live together in the same household, e.g. joint occupiers, landlady/lodger, etc.

4.9 If the purpose of the parties is unclear, the question of whether a couple are living together as husband and wife can only be decided by looking at their relationship and living arrangements and asking whether they can reasonably be said to be that of a married couple. Whilst the phrase 'living together as husband and wife' existed in the former HB scheme, it attracted most attention with the former supplementary benefit scheme as the 'co-habitation rule'. A body of case law developed. This is considered in vol. 3, chapter 11, paras. 11039-11069 of the DWP *Decision Maker's Guide* (*www.dwp.gov.uk/publications/dwp/dmg/index.asp*). The case law (see *Crake* para. 4.8) suggests that the following factors need to be considered before deciding that a couple are 'living together as husband and wife':

- whether or not they share the same household;
- the stability of the relationship;
- the financial arrangements;
- the presence or absence of a sexual relationship;
- shared responsibility for a child;
- public acknowledgment that they are a couple.

While all these factors should be considered, none individually is conclusive: what matters is the general relationship as a whole (Commissioners' decision R (SB) 17/81). If the DWP has awarded IS/JSA or pension credit as a couple, then the authority should accept this *(R v Penwith DC HBRB ex parte Menear)* unless it is clear that the claim for IS/JSA is based on a fraud *(R v South Ribble BC HBRB ex parte Hamilton).*

POLYGAMOUS MARRIAGE

HBR 2(1) CTBR 2(1) **4.10** A polygamous marriage is any marriage where there is more than one spouse. No marriage that takes place in the UK is valid if one of the partners is already married. Some other countries allow such marriages and these should be taken into account for HB/CTB purposes where they took place under the law of such a country.

PARTNER'S MEMBERSHIP OF THE SAME HOUSEHOLD

4.11 Any partner is normally treated as a member of the same household even when they are temporarily living away from the other members of the family. Temporary absence is not defined for the purpose of CTB but for the purpose of HB the partner is no longer counted as a member of the household where they are living away from the other members of the family and: HBR 15(1),(2) CTBR 7(1)

- do not intend to resume living with them; or
- the absence is likely to exceed 52 weeks, unless there are exceptional circumstances where the person has no control over the length of the absence such as hospitalisation and the absence is unlikely to be substantially more than 52 weeks.

CHILDREN AND YOUNG PERSONS

4.12 A child is defined as someone under the age of 16. A young person is someone aged 16 or over but under 19, not on income support or income-based JSA, nor in advanced education, nor a person aged 16 or 17 who would be excluded from HB if they made a claim as a result of the Children Leaving Care Act (paras. 2.12-16) and who is treated as a child for child benefit purposes. Child Benefit entitlement continues for eight weeks after the death of a child/young person. HBR 2(1), 13 CTBR 2(1), 5

4.13 To be treated as a child for child benefit the young person must receive 'relevant education', i.e. over 12 hours per week supervised study not above 'A' level, (G)NVQ level 3, OND, Scottish Higher Certificate or equivalent, at a recognised educational establishment or at some other place that the Secretary of State agrees to (the latter circumstance being confirmed by receipt of child benefit). Though child benefit is not payable for any week the young person is in full-time work, they are still treated as a child for child benefit purposes after leaving 'relevant education' up to and including the week of the appropriate terminal date or the first Monday before their 19th birthday, whichever comes first (see GM C1.76). The terminal date is:

- the first Monday in January; or
- the first Monday after Easter Monday; or
- the first Monday in September. (From 1998, this has been the terminal date for all 16-year-old school leavers: circular HB/CTB A45/97.)

4.14 Child benefit can be paid for an extended period beyond the terminal date where:

- the young person is registered for work/training under Work Based Training;
- the young person has not started Work Based Training;
- the young person has not reached the age of 18;

- the young person is not in remunerative work (paras. 7.33-36);
- child benefit was payable immediately before the extension period; and
- payment during the extension period has been requested in writing.

The child benefit extension period begins at the terminal date. If the terminal date is in September the extension period ends the week before the first Monday in January. For other terminal dates the extension period ends 12 weeks later.

4.15 Once the young person is no longer counted as a child for child benefit purposes they become a non-dependant for HB/main CTB purposes and HB and CTB claims should be re-assessed to exclude the young person's personal allowance and, where appropriate, the family premiums as well as any income the young person had. In the case of HB/main CTB no non-dependant deduction is made for anyone under 18 (table 7.2). Non-dependants, aged 18 or over, who are not disregarded for the purpose of council tax discounts (appendix 6) count as second adults for second adult rebate.

RESPONSIBILITY FOR A CHILD OR YOUNG PERSON

HBR 14(1), 2(a) CTBR 6(1), (2)(a) **4.16** The claimant is considered responsible for any child or young person they normally live with. This is usually straightforward but where the child or young person spends equal amounts of time in different households (e.g. where the parents have separated), or where there is doubt over which household they are living in, the child or young person is treated as normally living with the person who gets the child benefit. If no-one gets child benefit, the child or young person is considered the responsibility of:

HBR 14(2)(b) CTBR 6(2)(b)
- the person who has claimed child benefit; or
- the person the authority considers has 'primary responsibility' if more than one person has made a claim for the child benefit or no claim has been made.

HBR 14(3) CTBR 6(3) A child or young person can only be the responsibility of one person in any one benefit week (GM C1.91). If the claimant has a child or young person who lives with them and that child or young person in turn has a child, for example, the claimant's daughter and the daughter's baby, the authority must decide whether the daughter is dependent on the claimant or forms a family of her own. If the daughter receives income support (or income-based JSA) for herself and her baby she should not be considered part of the claimant's family (GM C1.69).

CHILD/YOUNG PERSON'S MEMBERSHIP OF THE SAME HOUSEHOLD

HBR 15(1),(2) CTBR 7(1) **4.17** Where the claimant is treated as responsible for a child or young person, that child or young person is counted as a member of the claimant's family even where they are temporarily living away from the other members of the family. Temporary absence is not defined for the purposes of CTB, but for the purposes of HB the child/young person is no longer counted as a member of the household where they are living away from the other members of the family and:

- does not intend to resume living with them; or
- the absence is likely to exceed 52 weeks, unless there are exceptional circumstances where the person has no control over the length of the absence such as hospitalisation and the absence is unlikely to be substantially more than 52 weeks.

4.18 The child/young person is also not counted where they are:

- absent from the claimant's home and being looked after by a local authority, or in Scotland or Northern Ireland are in the care of a local authority or the Department; HBR 15(4)(a) CTBR 7(3)(a)
- placed with the claimant or partner by a local authority or voluntary organisation, or in Scotland and Northern Ireland boarded out with the claimant or partner; or HBR 15(3)(a),(4)(b) CTBR 7(2)(a),(3)(b)
- placed for adoption or custodianship with the claimant or partner or elsewhere (though once adopted, they become a member of the household). HBR 15(3)(c),(4)(c) CTBR 7(2)(c),(3)(c)

4.19 A child or young person in local authority care who lives with the claimant under supervision must be treated as a member of the household. So must a child or young person in care who returns to live with the claimant for part or all of a benefit week if, given the nature and frequency of the visits, it is reasonable to do so. HBR 15(5) CTBR 7(4)

4.20 A child or young person who is absent in any other circumstance, e.g. attending boarding school, should be regarded as temporarily absent and treated as a member of the family (GM C1.140).

Non-dependants

4.21 A non-dependant is someone who normally resides with the claimant such as an adult son or daughter, or other relative, or a person treated as not liable to make payments in respect of the dwelling for HB (para. 2.38) and related provisions for CTB (para. 2.6) but specifically excludes: HBR 3(1),(2) CTBR 2(1)

- members of the claimant's benefit family (para. 4.5);
- a child or young person who lives with the claimant but who is not a member of the claimant's household (paras. 4.17-20), e.g. foster children;
- the persons identified in paras. 4.23-26.

Non-dependants cannot claim HB/CTB for any payments they make for their keep. Such payments are disregarded from the claimant's income (table 13.4) – instead a fixed deduction is usually made from the claimant's HB/main CTB where a non-dependant is present (para. 7.17). If a claimant resides with their landlord, neither the landlord nor a member of the landlord's family, e.g. a landlady's adult daughter, are treated as non-dependants of the claimant.

HBR 3(4) sch 1 para 7

4.22 For HB purposes a person does not count as normally residing with the claimant if that person:

- only shares a bathroom, lavatory and/or communal area (e.g. halls, passageways and rooms in common use in sheltered accommodation); or
- is visiting the claimant and normally resides elsewhere.

Thus people in self-contained accommodation within the same building as the claimant, e.g. a granny annex, do not count as non-dependants even if they share a bathroom and lavatory with the claimant. There is no definition of 'residing with' in the CTB rules.

Other people who may live in the claimant's dwelling

BOARDERS

HBRGB sch 4 para 42 NIHBR sch 4 para 45 CTBR sch 4 para 21

4.23 A boarder is someone who is liable to pay the claimant an accommodation charge which includes payment for at least some cooked or prepared meals made and consumed in that accommodation or associated premises. A person whose payment does not include an element for some cooked or prepared meals should be treated as a tenant or sub-tenant (para. 4.25). Income from a boarder is taken into account in the assessment of a non-income support/income-based JSA claimant's income in a different way from that of a tenant or sub-tenant (table 13.4). Boarders can claim HB but not CTB in their own right.

JOINT OCCUPIERS

HBR 3(2)(d) CTBR 3(2)(d)

4.24 A joint occupier is someone other than the claimant's partner who is jointly and severally liable with the claimant to pay council tax in respect of the dwelling for CTB purposes; and/or is jointly liable with the claimant to make payments in order to occupy the dwelling for HB purposes, e.g. joint tenants. Joint occupiers may be eligible for the appropriate benefit in their own right. For the purpose of calculating benefit the total council tax and/or rent will be apportioned between them (paras. 9.26-29, 10.6).

TENANTS AND SUB-TENANTS

HBRGB sch 4 para 20 NIHBR sch 4 para 22 CTBR sch 4 para 20

4.25 A tenant or sub-tenant is someone who is contractually liable to pay the claimant for the right to occupy part of the claimant's accommodation, but who is not:

- a member of the claimant's family;

- a non-dependant;
- a joint occupier;
- a boarder.

Where the payment includes something for meals, the person should be treated as a boarder (para. 4.23). A formal tenancy or sub-tenancy does not have to exist for someone to be treated as a tenant or sub-tenant for HB/CTB purposes, nor does this treatment create or imply the existence of a legal tenancy or sub-tenancy. In this respect the HB/CTB regulations and the landlord/tenant provisions of the Housing and Rent Acts do not accord precisely. A tenant or sub-tenant is able to claim HB in their own right. However, where the authority thinks the tenancy or sub-tenancy is contrived, HB is not awarded and instead the tenant or sub-tenant is treated as a non-dependant. For the treatment of the claimant's income from a tenant or sub-tenant, see table 13.4.

A CARER

4.26 A carer does not count as a non-dependant (or boarder) if he or she is looking after the claimant or partner and engaged by a charitable or voluntary organisation (not a public or local authority) which makes a charge for the service provided, even if the charge is paid by someone else. HBR 3(2) CTBR 3(2)

SECOND ADULTS

4.27 Non-dependants and carers, if they are aged 18 or over and are not disregarded for the purpose of council tax discounts (para. 9.16-17), count as second adults for the purpose of second adult rebate (chapter 8).

5 Making a claim

5.1 This chapter describes how to claim HB and CTB and when awards of benefit start. It covers:

- how and where to make a claim;
- what constitutes an effective claim;
- the information and evidence needed;
- how to remedy a defective claim;
- the date of claim;
- the first day of entitlement; and
- backdating.

The main change in the rules this year is that 'benefit periods' have been abolished and instead awards of HB/CTB (with certain exceptions) continue indefinitely (paras. 5.74-75).

General rules

CLAIMING HB OR CTB OR BOTH

5.2 Although HB and CTB are legally distinct benefits, it is usually possible to make a combined claim for both. There are, however, categories of claimant who are eligible to claim only one of these benefits (e.g. CTB only in the case of a home owner). It is also perfectly possible for someone who is eligible for both benefits to claim only one if that is what he or she wishes.

CLAIMING MAIN CTB OR SECOND ADULT REBATE OR BOTH

5.3 CTB is a single benefit. As the DWP points out (GM para. B2.63), a claim for CTB is therefore a claim for both main CTB and second adult rebate. An authority receiving a claim for CTB has a duty to consider entitlement to both. Some claimants qualify for only one: for example, a claimant with no second adults can only qualify for main CTB. Also, some claimants may wish to be considered for second adult rebate only: for example a wealthy claimant with a second adult who has low income. In such cases, the claimant is making a claim for CTB which nonetheless covers both types.

COUPLES

5.4 In the case of a couple (or polygamous marriage) one partner makes the claim on behalf of both. They may choose between them which partner this is to be. If they cannot agree, the authority must choose. Some authorities ask both partners to sign their claim forms. HBR 71(1) CTBR 61(1)

5.5 In some cases a couple may be better off if one partner rather than the other is the claimant. These are identified in this guide as they arise. In general, if the 'wrong' partner claims, the authority ought, as good practice, to return the claim form (having kept a copy or record) inviting the 'right' partner to sign it instead.

APPOINTEES

5.6 A claim may be made by a third party, known as an 'appointee', if the claimant is unable, for the time being, to act. In such cases, the appointee takes over all rights and responsibilities in relation to the HB/CTB claim. HBR 71(2)-(6) CTBR 61(2)-(6)

5.7 The authority may accept a claim from:

- a receiver appointed by the Court of Protection;
- an attorney;
- in Scotland, a tutor, judicial factor, curator or other guardian;
- in Northern Ireland, a controller appointed by the High Court; or
- a person appointed by the DWP to act on the claimant's behalf in connection with some other benefit.

In any other case, the authority may accept a written request from anyone over 18 to be an appointee, for example, a friend, a social worker or a solicitor.

5.8 Either the authority or the appointee can terminate the appointment by giving four weeks' written notice. It has become more common for landlords to request to act as appointees for their tenants. In these and all other cases it is appropriate for the authority to consider any potential conflict of interests before agreeing to the request.

Terminology

'BENEFIT WEEKS'

5.9 Many of the rules in this Guide refer to a 'benefit week'. For both HB and CTB, benefits weeks are defined as beginning on a Monday and ending on the following Sunday. HBR 2(1) CTBR 2(1)

'PASSPORT BENEFITS'

5.10 In this chapter, the term 'passport benefit' is used to mean the three benefits that qualify a claimant for maximum HB/CTB, namely:

- income-based jobseeker's allowance (JSA(IB));
- income support (IS); and
- guarantee credit.

'DWP', 'JOBCENTRE PLUS', 'PENSIONS SERVICE'

5.11 References below to a 'DWP office' mean the Pensions Service, Jobcentre or Jobcentre Plus office as appropriate. Pensions Service offices deal with claims for state pension credit. Jobcentre and Jobcentre Plus offices deal with claims for JSA(IB), IS and incapacity benefit.

How and where to make a claim

5.12 There are two ways of claiming HB/CTB, dealt with in turn below:

- people making a claim for a passport benefit (para. 5.10) or savings credit, or in certain cases incapacity benefit, may make their HB/CTB claim at the same time via the DWP;
- in all cases people may make their HB/CTB claim direct to the authority.

Claims via the DWP

METHOD OF CLAIM

HBR 72(4)(a) CTBR 62(4)(a) **5.13** Everyone who makes a claim for a passport benefit or savings credit is invited to claim HB and CTB at the same time. The law exists for this to happen with incapacity benefit claims too, but the DWP has not at the time of writing implemented this in practice. Detailed administrative arrangements are in GM paras. C12.60-549 and circular HB/CTB A14/2003, with samples of the official forms in GM chapter C12 annex A. The rules are given below.

HBR 72(4)(a) CTBR 62(4)(a) **5.14** If a person claims a passport benefit or savings credit (or in due course incapacity benefit: para. 5.13), the DWP gives him or her a form to claim that benefit and also form HCTB1 to claim HB/CTB. The claimant should return the HCTB1 direct to the authority. Here and below, references to form HCTB1 include form HCTB1(PC), the version used if the claimant or any partner is aged 60 or over.

5.15 Other forms may be used in place of form HCTB1, but the same procedures and other points apply in the same way as they do to form HCTB1:

- In some areas, instead of the national HCTB1 form, people may be asked to complete a local version designed by the authority.
- If a person reclaims a passport benefit or savings credit (or in due course incapacity benefit: para. 5.13) within 12 weeks of last receiving the same

benefit, then the DWP should give him or her form HBRR1 (a 'rapid reclaim form') instead of form HCTB1.

- In some areas where there are pilot projects, people may be asked to complete a single form covering both HB/CTB and JSA(IB)/IS. In this case only, the combined form is forwarded to the authority electronically.

5.16 On receipt of form HCTB1 direct from a claimant (para. 5.14) the authority may or may not need further information, evidence, etc (para. 5.33), and may or may not have to refer details to the rent officer (chapter 6). In the case of a claimant on savings credit, it will also need the DWP to provide its 'assessed income figure' (para. 13.152). If form HCTB1 is returned to the DWP instead of the authority, the DWP should forward it to the authority within two days of its decision about entitlement to the passport benefit.

HBR 2(1), 72(3), (4)(c), (5)(aa)
SI 1988 No. 662
NISR 1988 No. 118
CTBR 2(1), 62(3), (4(c), (5)(aa), 92

5.17 The DWP should usually be aware that someone has claimed HB/CTB on form HCTB1. In the case of the passport benefits (but not savings credit), the DWP sends the authority a decision form – form NHB(JSA), NHB(IS) or NHB(PC).

5.18 Form NHB(JSA) or NHB(IS) includes:

- the name and address of the claimant and any partner;
- National Insurance numbers when known;
- the date of the claim for the passport benefit and whether the claimant is entitled to it;
- if the claimant is entitled to the passport benefit, the date entitlement begins (and, if known, the date it ends); and
- in some cases, if the claimant is not entitled to the passport benefit, the reason why not.

5.19 If the claimant has been awarded a passport benefit, information included on form NHB(JSA) or NHB(IS) is binding on the authority in two respects:

- as proof of the claimant's entitlement to the passport benefit at the date shown;
- as proof that (at the date shown) the claimant therefore fulfils the income-related conditions for receiving maximum HB and/or maximum CTB (chapter 7): *R v Penwith District Council ex parte Menear.*

5.20 In other respects the authority must make its own decision about entitlement to HB/CTB. For example, the claimant still has to fulfil the other conditions of entitlement (such as being liable for rent or council tax, etc).

FOLLOW-UP PROCEDURES

5.21 To avoid a breach of confidentiality, the authority should notify the DWP if the claimant is not entitled to HB/CTB at the outset of the claim, or later ceases entitlement.

SI 1988 No. 662
NISR 1988 No. 11
CTBR 93

5.22 When the DWP hears of a change of circumstances likely to affect entitlement to HB or CTB, including cases when entitlement to a passport benefit ends, it sends details to the authority using form NHB(JSA) or NHB(IS) (para. 5.17). A claimant on state pension credit has no duty to notify the authority separately about changes already notified to the DWP (para. 13.151 and table 17.3). But a claimant on JSA(IB) or IS does have a separate duty to do so, and will very likely be overpaid if he or she does not.

CLAIMS DIRECT TO THE AUTHORITY

5.23 Anyone may claim HB or CTB or both direct from the authority. This is the only method available to claimants who are not also making a claim for a passport benefit (or in due course incapacity benefit: para. 5.13). A claim may be made on a form supplied by the authority or in some other format acceptable to the authority. The authority may or may not need further information, evidence, etc (para. 5.33) and may or may not have to refer details to the rent officer (chapter 6). In the case of a claimant on savings credit, the authority also needs the DWP to provide its 'assessed income figure' (para. 13.152).

APPLICATION FORMS

5.24 Authorities are responsible for designing their own application forms, though various organisations have made recommendations. Long forms may put people off claiming. The print should be reasonably large, the language clear and simple, and the design and layout comprehensible. Special forms may be used for various groups of claimants such as linguistic minority groups, students, council tenants, private tenants, those who are eligible only for CTB (e.g. home owners), and so on. Forms should include a question about whether the person has claimed a passport benefit. However, even if the authority considers the claimant may be entitled to a passport benefit, it has no power to require him or her to claim it (though it is good practice to let him or her know).

WHERE TO CLAIM: DESIGNATED OFFICES

HBR 2(1) CTBR 2(1) **5.25** The authority must have at least one 'designated office' and optionally more. This is the place to which claims should be sent and changes of circumstances notified. Designating additional offices, such as the authority's homeless persons unit or a hostel, is often advantageous, since the day a claim is received by these is then the official 'date of claim' (para. 5.53).

HBR 2(1) CTBR 2(1) **5.26** The authority must ensure that a person can find out its designated office by including the address on or with the claim form. It may additionally (but not instead) do this by explaining on or with the claim form how to contact the designated office electronically.

WHERE TO CLAIM: NOMINATED OFFICES

5.27 Any person aged 60 or more, or whose partner is, may also claim at a 'nominated office' – an office nominated by both the DWP and the authority. This may happen in places where the DWP and authorities are trying out pilots. HBRGB 72(4)(f) NIHBR &2(4)(c) CTBR 62(4)(f)

Is the claim effective?

5.28 This section explains what constitutes an 'effective claim' for HB/CTB – i.e. a claim which the authority must decide. The rules apply to all claims.

5.29 The two conditions for an effective HB/CTB claim are about:

- how the claim is made; and
- the provision of information and evidence.

If both the conditions are fulfilled, the claim is effective from the day it is received. This may either be because both conditions are fulfilled at the outset; or because they are later fulfilled, as described below (paras. 5.45 onwards).

HOW THE CLAIM IS MADE

5.30 The first condition for an effective claim is that it must be made in writing. Furthermore it must be: AA 1, 5, 6 HBR 72(1),(9) CTBR 62(1),(9)

- on a form approved by the authority and completed in accordance with the instructions on the form; or
- in some other written form which the authority accepts as sufficient in the circumstances of a particular case or a class of cases.

5.31 Authorities' own application forms clearly fall into the first category. Authorities may also regard the DWP's form HCTB1 (para. 5.14) as doing so. An example of the second category is a letter including a statement that the writer wishes to claim.

5.32 It is good practice for an authority receiving a claim which is not in writing (e.g. over the telephone) to issue or send out an application form for completion. In this case the claim is not effective before the written application arrives.

INFORMATION AND EVIDENCE

5.33 The second condition for an effective claim is that the authority may require from the claimant 'certificates, documents, information and evidence' so long as these are 'reasonably required... in order to determine... entitlement'. AA 1, 5, 6 HBG 72(1), 73(1), CTBR 62(1), 63(1),(3)

5.34 The exception is that it may not require any information whatsoever about the following types of payment, whether they are made to a claimant, partner, child, young person, non-dependant or second adult. These payments are in any case always disregarded in the assessment of HB and CTB:

- payments from the Macfarlane Trusts, the Eileen Trust or the Fund, and in certain cases payments of money which originally derived from those sources (para. 13.60);
- payments in kind (i.e. goods not money) of capital from a charity or from the above sources;
- payments in kind of income from any source.

AA 1
HBR 2B
CTBR 2B
NISR 1999 No. 372
SI 1999 No. 920

5.35 A further rule relating to National Insurance numbers applies in all cases except for claims for HB made in respect of a hostel (as defined in para. 6.10). It is that (in order for a claim to be effective) the claimant must either provide their National Insurance number and the National Insurance number of their partner (but not that of anyone else), along with information or evidence establishing these; or provide information or evidence enabling it to be ascertained; or make an application for a National Insurance number and give information or evidence to assist with this. In the case of a claimant on a passport benefit (para. 5.10) or savings credit, authorities have been advised (circular A28/3002) that verification by the DWP can be accepted as verification by the authority.

5.36 Though an authority may require the information, evidence, etc, by writing to the claimant for this, it may not require the claimant to attend an interview, though it may request this: *R v Liverpool CC ex parte Johnson No. 2*. An authority has no duty to decide a claim if a relevant document has been forged, even if the statements in the forged document are true: *R v Winston*.

5.37 Apart from the points made earlier in this chapter and in relation to extended payments (chapter 17), the law does not specify what type of proof the authority should require about any particular matter (though see below for DWP guidance under the Verification Framework). The authority must not seek unnecessary proof. For example, a self-employed claimant should not normally be expected to have accounts prepared by someone else. Some information may require detailed proof, for example, if a claimant's capital is close to £16,000.

5.38 In some cases, the authority may wish to check or confirm information with a third party. For example, authorities normally ask claimants to get their landlord to confirm details of rent.

5.39 If it is necessary for an authority to approach a third party direct, the DWP points out (GM para. C8.230) that such enquiries should be made only 'with the claimant's written agreement'. (In practice, this is commonly done by making acceptance of contact with third parties part of the declaration on a claim form.) The one exception is that no permission is required to contact a pension provider about notional income from a pension scheme (para. 13.143).

THE VERIFICATION FRAMEWORK

5.40 The DWP's Verification Framework ('VF') for HB and CTB suggests the types of evidence authorities may seek about the claimant and any family. This is advice, not law, and its main objective is to prevent fraud. Many but not all authorities have decided to adopt the VF. Those that do get additional subsidy from the DWP.

5.41 The VF does not apply in the case of hostel claims (para. 6.10) for the first 13 weeks of a claim, and the DSS has also warned local authorities that over-zealous application of the VF can endanger hostels' work (DWP circular HB/CTB A48/99).

5.42 The legal test for what information and evidence authorities may require in order to determine a claim for HB or CTB is, in broad terms, that this must be 'reasonably required… in order to determine… entitlement' (para. 5.33). The DWP has taken the view that, with appropriate exceptions, the requirements of the VF meet this test, and this has been broadly accepted by the commissioners (CH/999/2002) though they have emphasised that the VF does not apply to themselves or to tribunals (CH/5088/2002). An authority which adopts the VF must inevitably have taken the same view.

5.43 There may, however, be circumstances in which the requirements of the VF conflict with this legal test (for example, if an authority applies the requirements of the VF as a blanket rule in an inappropriate case). In particular, commissioners have been critical of authorities which adopt the VF unthinkingly in individual cases: CH/2323/2002; and have emphasised that it does not apply to tribunals or to the commissioners themselves: CH/5088/2002.

5.44 The DWP's current VF instructions are in *The Verification Framework: Manual,* DWP, April 2002 (issued with DWP circular HB/CTB F5/2002, and supplemented by circular A38/2003). At the time of writing no more up-to-date version has been issued.

REMEDYING DEFECTIVE CLAIMS

5.45 Specific rules apply to a 'defective claim' – which simply means a written claim which does not comply with one or both of the conditions in paragraph 5.29:

HBR 72(6)-(8),73(2
CTBR 62(6)-(8),
63(2)

- if it is not on an approved form (and the authority does not accept the form it is in as sufficient), the authority should send the claimant an approved form for completion;
- if it is on an approved form, but is incomplete, the authority should return the form to the claimant for completion (and it is good practice to keep a copy or record of the returned form);

- if reasonably required information, evidence, etc, is not given or included with the form, the authority must request the claimant to provide this. At the same time, it must also inform the claimant of the duty to notify relevant changes of circumstances which occur, and say what these are likely to be.

HBR 72(8),73(1)
CTBR 62(8), 63(1)

5.46 In all three cases, the authority must allow at least four weeks for the claimant to comply with the request, and should allow longer if reasonable to do so. Some authorities send a reminder, allowing a further period for the reply. If the claimant complies within four weeks (or longer if reasonable) the claim is effective from the original date. Furthermore, the three cases may apply one after the other (as illustrated in the example) or one of the cases may apply more than once (most commonly, a need for yet further information, evidence, etc). Each time, the authority should allow the claimant four weeks to comply (or longer if reasonable).

HBR 76(2),77(1)
CTBR 66(2), 67(1)

5.47 In any of the above cases, the authority has no duty to decide a claim if the claimant takes so much longer than four weeks to comply that the delay becomes unreasonable. This often arises when a claimant does not provide the information, evidence, etc, reasonably required by the authority.

Example: Remedying a defective claim

Claimant action	A claimant sends the authority a letter saying 'I wish to claim...'
Authority action	The letter does not contain sufficient details for the authority to assess the claim. The authority sends the claimant its ordinary application form for completion.
Claimant action	The claimant returns the form within four weeks, having omitted to answer some of the questions.
Authority action	The claim is now on an approved form, but is incomplete. The authority returns the form to the claimant for completion.
Claimant action	The claimant completes the form, and returns it after five weeks, with a note explaining he has been in hospital.
Authority action	The authority accepts that five weeks is reasonable, but needs evidence of income. The authority writes to the claimant requesting this.
Claimant action	The claimant returns the evidence within four weeks.
Authority action	The authority decides the claim. The claim is effective from the date when the letter was received.

APPEALS ABOUT WHETHER A CLAIM IS EFFECTIVE

5.48 In the past, it was widely accepted that if the authority considers it has no duty to decide a claim, there is nothing about which the claimant can appeal (para. 19.16) – since there has been no decision.

5.49 However, the commissioners reversed this in January 2003 in relation to income support and related incapacity benefit claims (CH/540/2002), stating that the exclusion of appeal rights on whether and when an effective claim for benefit has been made is invalid and has been since 2nd October 2002 (when the Human Rights Act 1998 came in). The Secretary of State withdrew his further appeal against this in July 2003. This case is highly persuasive in HB/CTB because of the similar arrangement of appeal rights and exclusions and the Human Rights principles involved.

AMENDING A CLAIM

5.50 A claimant may write amending a claim at any time before a decision is made on it. The amendment is treated as having been made from the outset of the claim. Once a decision is made, the equivalent of amending a claim is notifying a change of circumstances (para. 17.8) or requesting a reconsideration (para. 17.55).

HBR 74(1)
CTBR 64(1)

WITHDRAWING A CLAIM

5.51 A claimant may write withdrawing a claim at any time before a decision is made on it. The authority is then under no duty to decide the claim. Once a decision is made, there is no provision for withdrawing a claim.

HBR 74(2), 76(2)
CTBR 64(2), 66(2)

Date of claim

5.52 This section describes what counts as the 'date of claim' for HB and CTB. The general rule is given first, then the exceptions which can apply. Table 5.1 summarises the main rules.

5.53 The 'date of claim' is an important concept: it affects the date on which entitlement to HB/CTB actually begins (which may be before, on, or after the date of claim, depending on the other circumstances of the case, as described later in this chapter).

Table 5.1: Date of claim for HB/CTB

RULE	DATE OF CLAIM
General rule	
◆ all claims other than those mentioned below	The date the HB/CTB claim is received by the authority
Claimants also claiming a passport benefit	
◆ if the passport benefit is awarded, and an HB/CTB claim is received by the authority or DWP within four weeks of the passport benefit claim	The first day of entitlement to the passport benefit
◆ if the passport benefit is awarded but the above time limit is not met	The date the HB/CTB claim is received by the authority
◆ if the passport benefit is not awarded	The date the HB/CTB claim is received by the authority or DWP, whichever is earlier
Claimants becoming liable for rent or council tax for the first time while on a passport benefit	
◆ if a claim for HB/CTB is received by the authority within four weeks of the start of that new liability	The first day of that new liability (and for further rules about people moving home, see paras. 17.26-28)
◆ otherwise	The date the HB/CTB claim is received by the authority
Claimants or partners aged 60-plus	
◆ if they claim HB/CTB at a nominated office (para. 5.27)	The date the HB/CTB claim is received by the nominated office
◆ but until 5th October 2004	Their date of claim is often earlier (para. 5.67)

Note: 'Passport benefit' means JSA(IB), IS or guarantee credit (para. 5.10).

GENERAL RULE

5.54 The general rule is that the date of claim is the day a claim is received at the authority's 'designated office' (paras. 5.25-26). This includes cases where a claim is delivered on a day when the authority's offices are not open. HBR 72(5)(c) CTBR 62(5)(d)

5.55 So claims which are 'on the mat' after a weekend or a bank holiday should, if appropriate, be regarded as having been received on the Saturday, Sunday or bank holiday. Otherwise, the claimant may lose up to two weeks' HB/CTB (paras. 5.72-73).

SUCCESSFUL PASSPORT BENEFIT CLAIMANTS WHO CLAIM HB/CTB WITHIN FOUR WEEKS

5.56 This rule applies if: HBR 72(5)(e) HBR 60+ 72(5)(a) CTBR 62(5)(e) CTBR 60+ 72(5)(a)

- a person claims and is awarded a passport benefit (JSA(IB), IS or guarantee credit); and
- the person's or any partner's HB/CTB claim (whether or not on the HCTB1 form) is received by the authority or the DWP no more than four weeks after the passport benefit claim was received by the DWP.

5.57 In this case, the date of claim for HB/CTB is:

- the date of first entitlement to the passport benefit (and in the case of JSA(IB) this means the first 'waiting day'); or
- if earlier, the date the HB/CTB claim was received by the DWP or the authority.

This rule applies regardless of delays by the DWP in providing the details to the authority.

5.58 The four weeks limit (para. 5.56) may not be extended. However it applies independently from the time limits allowed for the remedying of defective claims (e.g. if the HCTB1 form is incomplete, or further information or evidence is required).

SUCCESSFUL PASSPORT BENEFIT CLAIMANTS WHO CLAIM HB/CTB AFTER FOUR WEEKS

5.59 If a person claims and is awarded a passport benefit (JSA(IB), IS or guarantee credit) but fails to claim HB/CTB within four weeks of making that claim, the date of claim for HB/CTB is the day the claim is received by the authority. HBR 72(5)(c) CTBR 62(5)(d)

UNSUCCESSFUL PASSPORT BENEFIT CLAIMANTS

5.60 If a person claims a passport benefit (JSA(IB), IS or guarantee credit) but is not awarded it, the date of claim for HB/CTB is the day the HB/CTB claim is received by the DWP or the authority, whichever is earlier. HBR 72(5)(b) HBR 60+ 72(5)(aa) CTBR 62(5)(b) CTBR 60+ 62(5)(aaa)

Examples: Date of claim

SUCCESSFUL INCOME SUPPORT CLAIMANT

A claimant applies for income support. The DWP receives her application on Wednesday 8th September 2004, and later assesses her as entitled to income support from that date.

The date of claim for HB/CTB is also Wednesday 8th September so long as the DWP or the authority receives a claim for HB/CTB (whether on form HCTB1 or not) within four weeks of the date of claim for income support (i.e. on or before Wednesday 6th October 2004).

UNSUCCESSFUL JSA(IB) CLAIMANT

A claimant applies for income-based jobseeker's allowance and sends form HCTB1 with it. The DWP receives his application on Wednesday 8th September 2004, and the DWP later assesses him as not entitled to JSA(IB).

The date of claim for HB/CTB is Wednesday 8th September.

JSA(CONT) OR SAVINGS CREDIT CLAIMANTS

HBR 72(5)(b)
HBR 60+ 72(5)(aaa)
CTBR 62(5)(b)
CTBR 60+ 62(5)(aaa)

5.61 If a person claims JSA and is awarded only JSA(Cont), or claims pension credit and is awarded only savings credit, the date of claim for HB/CTB is the day the HB/CTB claim is received by the DWP or the authority, whichever is earlier.

PASSPORT BENEFIT CLAIMANTS BECOMING LIABLE FOR RENT OR COUNCIL TAX

HBR 72(5)(bb)
HBR 60+ 72(5)(bb)
CTBR 62(5)(c)
CTBR 60+ 62(5)(bb)

5.62 This rule makes it easier for a person on a passport benefit (JSA(IB), IS or guarantee credit) to get HB/CTB from when they first become liable for rent and/or council tax.

5.63 It applies if:

- a person is receiving a passport benefit; and
- they become liable for rent or council tax for the first time; and
- the person's or any partner's HB/CTB claim is received by the DWP or the authority no more than four weeks after the new liability begins.

5.64 In this case, the date of claim for HB is the first day of their new liability for rent; the date of claim for CTB is the first day of their new liability for council tax. Generally speaking this means that the person's HB/CTB will start straight away (paras. 5.72-73). Note that, so long as the claimant (or partner) is receiving a passport benefit immediately before the event in question, the rule applies regardless of whether they continue to receive the passport benefit afterwards.

5.65 This rule applies, for example, when a claimant on a passport benefit:

- inherits the tenancy of their home;
- becomes liable for council tax because of the death of someone in their home or some other change in circumstances;
- becomes liable for council tax on a dwelling which has been exempt.

It is not a rule about moving home while on a passport benefit. For that change of circumstances, see paragraph 17.29.

CLAIMS VIA A NOMINATED OFFICE

5.66 In the case of a person aged 60 or more, or whose partner is, who has claimed HB/CTB at a nominated office (para. 5.27), the date of claim for HB/CTB is the date the HB/CTB claim is received at the nominated office.

HBR 72(5)(c),(d)
CTBR 62(5)(c),(d)

CLAIMS BY PEOPLE AGED 60+

5.67 During the first year of state pension credit (which was introduced on 6th October 2003) the following rule applies to any claimant (not just those on state pension credit). It applies if:

Reg 29 of
SI 2003 No 325
Reg 21 of NISR
2003 No 197

- the claimant's or any partner's 60th birthday occurs or occurred on or before 5th October 2004; and
- the claim for HB/CTB is made on or after 7th October 2003 but no later than 5th October 2004; and
- the claimant has satisfied the conditions for HB/CTB continuously from the date of claim as worked out below to the date the claim was actually received.

In such cases the date of claim for HB/CTB is 6th October 2003 or, if later, the claimant's or partner's 60th birthday. The claimant does not have to ask for back-dating or have 'good cause' (para. 5.76) for this rule to apply: it applies automatically if its conditions are met.

Examples: Claims by people aged 60+

CLAIMANT WHO QUALIFIES UNDER THE RULE

A claimant in her 70s submits her first claim for HB/CTB in September 2004. She has met the conditions for HB/CTB continuously since 6th October 2003.

Because she has met the conditions for HB/CTB continuously since 6th October 2003, her date of claim for HB/CTB is 6th October 2003.

CLAIMANT WHO DOES NOT QUALIFY UNDER THE RULE

A claimant reaches 60 on 1st January 2004, but has too much capital to meet the conditions for HB/CTB until 1st April 2004. He submits his first claim for HB/CTB on 1st July 2004.

Because he has not met the conditions for HB/CTB continuously since his 60th birthday, that cannot be his date of claim. Unless he applies for and is awarded backdated HB/CTB, his date of claim is 1st July 2004.

ADVANCE CLAIMS

HBR 5(7), 72(11)
HBR 60+ 72(11A)
NIHBR 72(10)
NIHBR 60+ 72(10A)
CTBR 62(1), (12), 66(2)
CTBR 60+ 62(12A)
NHBR 72(5A)

5.68 A person may claim:

- HB or CTB up to 17 weeks in advance of their 60th birthday; or
- HB or CTB up to 13 weeks in advance of some other event which will mean they will become entitled to HB/CTB; or
- CTB, or HB for rates in Northern Ireland, up to eight weeks before they will become liable for council tax/rates;
- HB for a period of up to four weeks before moving into their home if they meet the conditions in paragraph 3.30.

5.69 In each case the date of claim is:

- in the first two cases above, any date in the week before the benefit week (para. 5.9) containing the birthday or event in question;
- in the third case above, the date of first liability for council tax/rates;
- in the fourth case above, the date of claim under the general rule (para. 5.54), or if later, the date the claimant actually moves in.

DELAYS IN SETTING COUNCIL TAXES

CTBR 62(11)

5.70 If an authority delays setting its council taxes until after 31st March in any year, and if a CTB claim is received within four weeks after the setting of the council taxes, the date of claim is set so that the claimant's entitlement begins on 1st April in that year (or the benefit week in which the person's entitlement begins if this falls between 1st April and the date the claim is received).

First day of entitlement

GENERAL RULE

5.71 The general rule is that: HBR 65(1) CTBR 56(1)

- HB and CTB are awarded from the Monday following the 'date of claim' (as described earlier), even if the date of claim is a Monday.

Exceptions to the general rule are given below.

WHEN LIABILITY FOR RENT BEGINS

5.72 If the date of claim is in the same benefit week as the claimant or partner becomes liable for rent (or before then), HB is awarded from the benefit week in which the date of claim falls: HBR 65(2) 69(4)(a),(5),(6) 70(2),(4)

- if rent is expressed on a weekly basis (or in multiples of weeks), the full weekly amount of HB is awarded in that week (regardless of when liability began);
- if rent is expressed on a non-weekly basis (e.g. daily or calendar-monthly), entitlement for that week is assessed on a daily basis: divide the ordinary weekly entitlement by seven, then multiply the result by the number of days of liability.

These rules have been confirmed in *Secretary of State for Work and Pensions v. Robinson and Another.* They also apply to HB for rates in Northern Ireland if the rates are included in the rent.

WHEN LIABILITY FOR COUNCIL TAX BEGINS

5.73 If the date of claim is in the same benefit week as the claimant or partner becomes liable for council tax (or before then), CTB is awarded from the benefit week in which the date of claim falls: CTBR 51(1), 56(2)

- entitlement for that week is assessed on a daily basis: divide the ordinary weekly entitlement by seven, then multiply the result by the number of days of liability.

The award of benefit

5.74 An award of HB/CTB lasts indefinitely. As described in chapter 17, it stops only if the claimant:

- stops qualifying for HB/CTB such that they no longer satisfy all the conditions for benefit (para.1.5) (e.g. the claimant becomes an ineligible student, dies, acquires too much capital or income, etc);
- fulfils the conditions for an extended payment, thus requiring an end to the award of HB/CTB.

Examples: First day of entitlement

GENERAL CASE

A man claims HB and CTB because his income has reduced. His date of claim is Thursday 15th July 2004. His rent is payable to his landlord each calendar month. He is liable for council tax.

HB and CTB are awarded from the benefit week commencing with the Monday following his date of claim. So Monday 19th July is the claimant's first day of entitlement. From that week onwards, he is entitled to his normal weekly amount of HB and CTB.

There would be no difference if his rent was due weekly or on any other basis.

CLAIMANT MOVING TO NEW HOME

A woman moves into her flat on Sunday 1st August 2004. Her date of claim is Sunday 1st August. Her rent is payable to her landlord each calendar month, and is due from 1st August. She is liable for council tax from 1st August.

HB and CTB are awarded from the benefit week commencing with the Monday in which her date of claim falls, i.e. Monday 26th July. But she is not liable for rent or council tax until the Sunday, so Sunday 1st August is her first day of entitlement. In that first week, entitlement to HB and CTB is one-seventh of her normal amount (for the Sunday only).

If her rent was due weekly (or in multiples of weeks), there would be a difference in HB (only). Her first day of entitlement to HB would be Monday 28th July. From that week onwards she would be entitled to her normal weekly amount of HB. (But she would still only qualify for one-seventh of the normal amount of CTB.)

ABOLITION OF BENEFIT PERIODS

5.75 HB and CTB used to be awarded for a fixed 'benefit period', requiring a regular 'renewal' claim to be made (sometimes as often as once every six months). This was abolished for most people aged 60+ from 6th October 2003 (or as early as 16th June 2003 in some cases) and for everyone else from 5th April 2004. Details of how the rules worked before the abolition are in the 2003-04 edition of this guide.

Backdating

HBR 72(15)
NIHBR 72(14)
CTBR 62(16)

5.76 HB and CTB must be backdated for up to 52 weeks if the claimant requests this in writing, and 'had continuous good cause for [his or her] failure to make a claim'. It is possible for there to be 'good cause' for backdating HB but not CTB, or vice versa. Technically, it is the date of claim which is backdated. So HB/CTB can be backdated even if the claimant is not currently entitled to any HB/CTB. For example, a claimant whose capital has recently increased to over £16,000 could have his or her claim backdated for the period when it was less than £16,000. Benefit during any backdated period must be calculated according to the rules which applied at that time. Many authorities now include a question on their claim forms about whether the claimant wishes to make a claim for backdating.

'GOOD CAUSE'

5.77 Backdating is not discretionary. It is obligatory once the authority determines:

- that the claimant had good cause for failure to make the claim earlier; and
- that his or her good cause lasted throughout the period until the written request for backdating was actually made (whether for the same reason throughout, or for a combination of successive reasons).

5.78 However, the question remains of judging just what constitutes 'good cause'. It is clear that authorities should not have an immutable list of what does and does not constitute good cause, but should consider any relevant factor. The commissioners have held that case law from other social security benefits about backdating (which goes back to the 1940s) is binding on the analysis of 'good cause' in HB/CTB: CH 5221/2001. This case law is summarised in the DWP's *Adjudication Officers' Guide* (reproduced in GM chapter A2, annex A), which many authorities follow, at least in a general sense.

5.79 Some examples of when claimants may have 'good cause' are listed below.

- If the claimant was ill and had no-one to make the claim on their behalf.
- If the claimant could not reasonably have been expected to know their rights, e.g. if there have been detailed changes in the law.
- If the claimant did not understand that they could claim, perhaps because of age, inexperience, language difficulties, difficulty in understanding technical documents or some other reason.
- If the claimant was wrongly advised that they were not entitled to HB/CTB.
- If the claimant was unable to manage their affairs and did not have an 'appointee'.

WHAT IS, AND IS NOT, 'BACKDATING'?

5.80 'Backdating' only arises when benefit is awarded for a past period for which the claimant has not already claimed HB/CTB. The following do not count as 'backdating' in this sense:

- awarding HB/CTB for a past period because other rules require it to be done (for example the rule for claimants aged 60+: para. 5.67);
- basing a claim on an application form which was (on the balance of probability) received by the authority or the DWP but was then mislaid;
- basing a claim on an application form which the authority originally (and wrongly) regarded as demonstrating that the claimant was not entitled to HB/CTB;
- basing a claim on an application which the authority originally treated as defective but which the authority no longer regards as such because the claimant has now provided relevant information, evidence, etc, within a timescale which the authority now accepts is reasonable;
- increasing entitlement retrospectively for someone who was awarded too little HB/CTB in a past period (e.g. as in para. 17.47);
- allowing a claimant to keep underlying entitlement when an overpayment is calculated (para. 18.16).

LIMIT ON BACKDATING

HBRGB 72(15)
NIHBR 72(14)

5.81 HB and CTB cannot be backdated more than 52 weeks before the date on which the authority received the claimant's written request for backdating (even if this is later than when the claimant made his or her claim for HB/CTB). This does not prevent an authority from revising to correct an official error, nor does it prevent a claimant from seeking compensation from the authority for earlier periods if the authority itself was at fault.

6 Referrals to the rent officer, etc

6.1 In Great Britain, authorities must refer details of many HB cases to the rent officer following a claim for HB and then at certain times during an award of HB. This does not apply to certasin claims in the pathfinder areas with local housing allowances (para. 22.22 and table 22.1), but for all other areas this chapter explains the rules and covers:

- which cases must be referred to the rent officer, and when and how they are referred;
- the rent officer's determinations and how they are made;
- how errors and appeals are dealt with; and
- the rules about pre-tenancy determinations.

Rent officers are independent of the authority. In England, they are employed by the Rent Service, an executive agency of the DWP; in Wales, by the Rent Officer Service, an executive agency of the Welsh Assembly; and in Scotland by the Rent Registration Service, an executive agency of the Scottish Executive.

6.2 In Northern Ireland, there is no requirement to refer to the rent officer (and no rent officer). Instead, the Northern Ireland Housing Executive (NIHE) makes all decisions on HB claims including rent restriction. However, such decisions are required in exactly the same circumstances as referrals are required to be made to the rent officer in Great Britain, and the NIHE makes its decisions on the same basis that the rent officer makes his or her determinations in Great Britain (paras. 6.23-34) – with some exceptions mentioned in the chapter as they arise.

6.3 Rent officer referrals can be required in many kinds of rent allowance cases (including claims from private tenants or licensees, hostel residents, people renting a houseboat, mooring, mobile home or caravan site, people with a rental purchase agreement, and – in certain circumstances – housing association tenants). They are never required in rent rebate cases (claims from tenants of the authority administering HB). They relate only to HB for rent (not CTB or HB for rates in Northern Ireland).

WHY ARE REFERRALS MADE TO THE RENT OFFICER?

6.4 As described in this chapter, in Great Britain the rent officer provides the authority with various figures in respect of the cases referred to him or her – and in Northern Ireland similar rental valuations are made by the NIHE. In both cases, these figures are used in different ways depending on whether the HB case in question is an 'Old Scheme' or 'New Scheme' case (as defined in para. 10.7).

- In Old Scheme cases in Great Britain, the rent officer's figures are used to establish whether the authority might receive reduced HB subsidy on any part of the claimant's HB (chapter 22). In such cases in Northern Ireland, those subsidy implications do not apply. However, in either case, in assessing the HB claim, the authority must make its own determination of eligible rent based on the HB regulations (paras. 10.51 onwards).
- In New Scheme cases, the authority uses the rent officer's figures in calculating the claimant's 'eligible rent' (paras. 10.31 onwards): they are binding on the authority for this purpose.

6.5 The rent officer does not distinguish (in making his or her determinations) between the above types of case: it is the authority that decides which cases fall within which scheme. This is an important duty for the authority, since it can make a substantial difference to the amount of HB a claimant qualifies for.

Which cases are referred and when?

GENERAL RULES AND EXCEPTIONS

6.6 The authority must refer all HB cases to the rent officer, and the Executive in Northern Ireland must make a rent decision in all HB cases, except those falling in the list of exceptions in table 6.1. The referral or decision must be made at the following times: HBRGB 12A(1)-(3),(8) NIHBR 10A(1)

(a) whenever it receives a new HB claim – unless less than 52 weeks have passed since it last made a referral for the dwelling and there has been no 'relevant change of circumstances'; and

(b) whenever it receives notification of a 'relevant change of circumstances' relating to an award of HB – even if less than 52 weeks have passed since it last made a referral for the dwelling; and

(c) whenever 52 weeks have passed since it last made a referral for the dwelling.

What counts as a 'relevant change of circumstances' is defined in paragraph 6.11 (and see also para. 6.7). Table 6.2 shows what date the rent officer's figures are implemented from.

6.7 The effect of point (a) in paragraph 6.6 is that if, say, a couple with no children claim HB and the case is referred to the rent officer, and six months later the couple move out and a claim for the dwelling is received from another couple with no children, then there is no referral because less than 52 weeks have passed

Table 6.1: Cases which are never referred to the rent officer

HBRGB 12A(1),(2)(b) sch 1A paras 3-11A NIHBR 10A(3) sch 1B paras 3-6

- Rent rebate cases (i.e. council tenants renting from the authority administering their HB, or in Northern Ireland tenants of the NI Housing Executive).
- Tenancies in England and Wales entered into before 15th January 1989 and tenancies in Scotland entered into before 2nd January 1989 (in other words, 'regulated tenancies': the dates just mentioned are those when the 1988 Housing Acts came into force).
- In Northern Ireland any controlled letting subject to the Rent (Northern Ireland) Order 1978, SI 1978 No. 1050.
- Any other 'regulated tenancies' which continue to fall within the Rent Act 1977 or the Rent (Agriculture) Act 1976 (these applied before the 1988 Housing Acts came into force). For example, a tenant whose tenancy began in 1988, but who was later transferred by the landlord to alternative accommodation, may still have a 'regulated tenancy'.
- Housing Action Trust lettings.
- Bail hostels.
- Lettings of former local authority or new towns housing stock which has been transferred to a new owner (for example, a housing association) under the Housing Act 1985 (or equivalent new towns provisions) or the tenants choice provisions of the Housing Act 1988 – unless there has been a rent increase since the date of the transfer and the authority states in the referral that the rent is unreasonably expensive or (for transfers which took place before 7th October 2002 only) that the accommodation is unreasonably large.
- Lettings where the landlord is a registered housing association or other registered social landlord – unless the authority considers that the accommodation is unreasonably large or the rent is unreasonably expensive, in which case the authority must make a referral and must state in making the referral that the rent is unreasonably expensive or that the accommodation is unreasonably large. In such cases, the authority should take into account all relevant factors: for example, in considering whether the accommodation is unreasonably large, the authority must not simply adopt the rent officer's size criteria (paras. 6.24-26).

and there has been no 'relevant change of circumstances' (since a change in identity is not sufficient: table 6.3). More detail is given in the example below.

6.8 The rules have been partially simplified this year. The 52-weeks time limit (para. 6.6) is particularly clear compared with last year's rules. As illustrated in the following example, it is also clear that the 52 weeks counts from the date the authority made the last referral (not, say, the date of the determination by the rent officer). Unfortunately there remains an apparent error in the law, in that it does not appear to allow a referral to be made 52 weeks after a referral has been made for a pre-tenancy determination (para. 6.52). It is also unusual that some changes are implemented on a day other than a Monday (table 6.2).

Table 6.2: When rent office figures are implemented

DAR 7(2ZA), 8(6A),(6B)

REASON TRIGGERING THE REFERRAL	DATE RENT OFFICER FIGURE IS IMPLEMENTED FROM
A claim	The start of the award of HB
A 'relevant change of circumstances'	The date the change itself takes effect (typically the following Monday: chapter 17)
52 weeks have passed	If the rent officer's new determination means that the claimant qualifies for: *more HB or the same amount, and the claimant's rent is payable weekly or in multiples of weeks:* the day immediately after the last day of the 52 week period in question, unless that is not a Monday, in which case from the Monday immediately before that day *more HB or the same amount, and the claimant's rent is payable otherwise than above:* the day (which could be any day of the week) immediately after the last day of the 52 week period in question *less HB (regardless of when rent is payable):* the Monday following the date the rent officer determination 'was received' by the authority.

Example: Rent officer referrals, time limits and implementation dates

The claimant's first ever claim for HB is received by the authority on Tuesday 11th May 2004 and the authority refers the details to the rent officer that very day. The authority awards HB from Monday 17th May 2004.

Even if it takes the rent officer some weeks to respond, his or her figures apply from Monday 17th May 2004.

There are no changes in the claimant's circumstances.

The next referral to the rent officer is therefore due 52 weeks after the last one, which is Tuesday 10th May 2005. The referral is made. The rent officer's reply is received by the authority on Thursday 20th May 2005.

- if the rent officer's new figures mean the claimant is entitled to more HB (or the same amount) and the claimant's rent is due weekly or in multiples of weeks, then they apply to her case from Monday 9th May 2005;
- if the rent officer's new figures mean the claimant is entitled to more HB (or the same amount) and the claimant's rent is due calendar monthly or daily, then they apply to her case from Tuesday 10th May 2005 (i.e. on a daily basis);
- if the rent officer's new figures mean the claimant is entitled to less HB, then they apply to her case from Monday 24th May 2005 (the Monday after the authority received them).

There are no changes in the claimant's circumstances.

The next referral to the rent officer is therefore due 52 weeks after the last one, which is Tuesday 9th May 2006. The above rules apply again.

The claimant's non-dependant (who has been there all along so far) moves out on Saturday 13th May 2006.

Because this is a relevant change of circumstances, a further referral is required on Saturday 13th May 2006 and can be made up to three days after that date. It is in fact made on Monday 15th May 2006. The resulting new figures (whether higher, lower or the same) apply to the claimant's case from the Monday after the change of circumstances, namely Monday 22nd May 2006.

There are no further changes in the claimant's circumstances.

The next referral to the rent officer is therefore due 52 weeks after the last one, which is Monday 14th May 2007... and so on.

REPRESENTATIVE REFERRALS FOR HOSTEL CASES

6.9 For hostel cases in Great Britain (para. 6.10), no referral is required if a rent officer determination has been made for similar accommodation within the hostel during the previous 12 months, unless there is a 'relevant change of circumstances' (para. 6.11). For these purposes, accommodation must be treated as similar if it provides the same number of bed spaces. It may also be treated as similar in other appropriate cases. The earlier referral applies to any such similar accommodation within the hostel. In Northern Ireland the NIHE decides whether a fresh decision is required in hostel cases on the same basis.

WHAT IS A 'HOSTEL'?

6.10 A 'hostel' is defined for these purposes as any building (other than a residential care home or nursing home: paras. 2.18-20) to which both the following apply:

- it provides domestic accommodation which is not self-contained together with meals or adequate facilities for preparing food; and
- it is:
    - managed or run by a registered housing association or registered social landlord, or
    - run on a non-commercial basis, and wholly or partly funded by a government department or agency or local authority, or
    - managed by a registered charity or non-profit-making voluntary organisation which provides care, support or supervision with a view to assisting the rehabilitation of the residents or their resettlement into the community.

WHAT IS A 'RELEVANT CHANGE OF CIRCUMSTANCES'?

6.11 Table 6.3 lists all the changes which count as a 'relevant change of circumstances' for the purposes of the rules described earlier. If there has been a 'relevant change of circumstances' since an HB case was last referred to the rent officer, a further referral must be made to the rent officer as a result of that change. If the authority does not become aware of such a change straightaway, a referral must be made when it does become aware of it.

HBRGB 12A(1)(b),8
sch 1A para 2(3)
NIHBR 10A(1)(a)
12A(2)(a)
sch 1B para 2(3)

Table 6.3: 'Relevant changes of circumstances'

- Except in hostel cases (para. 6.10), there has been a change in the number of occupiers.
- Any child or young person in the household has reached the age of 10 or 16 – but only if, at the last referral, the rent officer gave a size-related rent determination (para. 6.24).
- There has been a change in the composition of the household – but only if, at the last referral, the rent officer gave a size-related rent determination (para. 6.24). (One example is when two people have ceased to be a couple.)
- There has been a substantial change or improvement in the condition of the dwelling – regardless of whether there has been an associated change in the rent. (For example, central heating has been installed.)
- The claimant has moved to a new dwelling.
- There has been a substantial change in the terms of the letting agreement (excluding a change in a term relating to rent alone) – regardless of whether there has been an associated change in the rent. (For example, the landlord has taken over the responsibility for internal decorations from the tenant or *vice versa.*)
- There has been a rent increase and:
  - the rent increase was made under a term of the letting agreement (which need not be in writing) and that term is the same (or substantially the same) as at the previous referral to the rent officer; and
  - at the previous referral, the rent officer did not make any of the following determinations: a 'significantly high rent determination', a 'size-related rent determination' or an 'exceptionally high rent determination' (paras. 6.23-27).
- At the previous referral to the rent officer, the claimant was not a 'young individual' (para. 6.12), but the claimant in the current case is a 'young individual'.

DEFINITION OF 'YOUNG INDIVIDUAL'

6.12 Every claimant who is a 'single claimant' (para. 4.4) and is under the age of 25 is a 'young individual' (see also para. 6.14) unless he or she: HBR 2(1), 11(3B)

(a) rents his or her home from the authority, or in Northern Ireland the Housing Executive, itself;

(b) rents his or her home from a registered housing association or registered social landlord;

(c) is under the age of 22 and was formerly in social services care under a court order (under section 31(1)(a) of the Children Act 1989 in England and Wales, or equivalent provisions in Scotland and Northern Ireland) which applied (or continued to apply) after his or her 16th birthday;

(d) is under the age of 22 and was formerly provided with accommodation by social services (under section 20 of the Children Act 1989 in England and Wales, or equivalent provisions in Scotland and Northern Ireland) but is no longer in that accommodation or remains in it but the accommodation is no longer provided by social services;

(e) has one or more non-dependant(s);

(f) qualifies for a severe disability premium in the assessment of his or her HB (para. 12.23), income support or JSA(IB);

(g) lives in a care home (paras. 2.18-20);

(h) lives in certain types of hostel (as defined in para. 6.10).

6.13 As described in Chapter 10, the rules applying to young individuals take account of the rent officer's 'single room rent determination'. It is the authority (not the rent officer) which decides whether someone is a 'young individual'. Note that (e) above applies only to non-dependants: having a sub-tenant, boarder or joint occupier does not stop someone being a 'young individual'. Technically, it is also worth noting that the law works in a peculiar way in the following cases:

- for claimants who fall in case (a) above, the law defines them as 'young individuals' but then says that no referral may be made to the rent officer in their case: this is the same as saying that they are not 'young individuals';
- for claimants who fall in cases (e) or (f) above, the law defines them as 'young individuals' but then says that the authority must ignore any single room rent determination made by the rent officer in their cases: this is the same as saying that they are not 'young individuals';
- for claimants who fall in cases (g) or (h) above, the law defines them as 'young individuals' but then says that the rent officer may not make a

single room rent determination in their cases: this is the same as saying that they are not 'young individuals' (except that it is the rent officer who determines whether they live in the accommodation described in those cases, not the authority).

Making the referral

TIME LIMITS AND METHOD OF REFERRAL

HBRGB 12A(3),(4) **6.14** The referral must be made within three working days of the event triggering it (table 6.2) or as soon as practicable thereafter. Days when the authority's offices are closed for receiving or determining claims do not count as 'working days' for this purpose. The DWP recommends authorities use a standard form (HBR1). Authorities and rent officers may agree to communicate by electronic means (e.g. by fax) rather than in writing.

INFORMATION REQUIRED BY THE RENT OFFICER

HBRGB 12A(1A), (1ZA), (1B), (7A), 106 **6.15** Table 6.4 lists the information the authority should give when making a referral to the rent officer. It gives the rules as they apply from 1st or 7th April 2003. The law specifically requires certain information to be included (this is indicated in the table) and also generally requires the authority to provide any other information required by the rent officer. This other information can sometimes vary from rent officer to rent officer: the table shows what information is normally required.

Table 6.4: Information required by the rent officer

IDENTIFICATION AND GENERAL INFORMATION

- A case reference number.
- The claimant's name.
- The address of the property.
- The number of occupiers there.
- The age and sex of those occupiers and their relationship to the claimant (e.g. 'son', 'sub-tenant').
- The date the claimant commenced occupation (which may be approximate if necessary).
- Whether the landlord is a registered housing association or other registered social landlord.

- The details of the letting agreement, including the period of the letting.
- The type of accommodation (e.g. house, bedsit, room).
- In the case of a room, its location within the property (e.g. 'first floor, front').
- Details of all the rooms in the property, the ones the claimant has sole use of, and the ones the claimant has shared use of.

RENT, SERVICES, ETC

- Whether the claimant is a 'young individual' (para. 6.12) *.
- If the rent includes a charge for cleaning of rooms or windows (except so far as this is eligible for HB: para. 10.98); emergency alarms; medical, nursing or personal care; or general counselling or support:
  - the fact that it does*; and
  - the authority's valuation of the total value of these ineligible items*.
- The gross actual rent on the property after deducting the above valuation (if applicable)*.
- Whether the rent includes any amount for water charges, fuel or meals (but no valuation of any of these is required)*.
- Details of all other eligible and ineligible services included in the rent, and details of any variable service charges.
- Whether central heating is provided.
- Whether a garage is provided.
- Whether the accommodation is furnished fully, partly or minimally, or is unfurnished.
- Who is responsible for internal decorations (landlord or claimant).
- If the claimant is a joint occupier (para. 6.35) the figures for rent and services mentioned above should be those for the whole property*.
- In the case of combined domestic and business premises, the figures for rent and services mentioned above should relate only to the domestic part.
- The figures for rent and services mentioned above should be given for the period for which rent is due. For example, if the claimant's rent is due calendar monthly, they should be given as calendar monthly figures.

* NOTE:
Items marked with an asterisk are those specifically mentioned in the law (para. 6.15).

The rent officer's determinations

ROO sch 1 paras 1-7
NIHBR sch 1A
paras 1-5

6.16 The rent officer (in Northern Ireland the Housing Executive) may provide one or more of the following determinations. More information on each is given in the next few paragraphs:

- a claim-related rent determination;
- a local reference rent determination;
- a single room rent determination;
- certain determinations relating to service charges.

The rent officer does not make any determinations if the referral is withdrawn by the authority. The rent officer is not required to visit the dwelling but does so in many cases.

GENERAL RULES AND ASSUMPTIONS ABOUT DETERMINATIONS

HBRGB 12A(6)
ROO sch 1 paras 7-8
NIHBR 10A(2)(f)
sch 1A paras 6-7

6.17 In making the determinations described below (paras. 6.22-34), the rent officer (in Northern Ireland the Housing Executive):

- must base these on the facts as they stood on the date on which the authority made the referral, unless the claimant had left the accommodation by that date, in which case they are based on the facts as they stood at the end of the claimant's letting;
- provides these for the same period (e.g. weekly, calendar monthly) as that for which the authority supplied the information to the rent officer (table 6.4);
- must 'assume that no one who would have been entitled to housing benefit had sought or is seeking the tenancy';
- must ignore all rents payable to housing associations, other registered social landlords and registered charities;
- must include the value of any meals provided to the claimant (except that, in the case of the exceptionally high rent determination, the rent officer may choose whether to include meals or not);
- must exclude the value of all other service charges which are ineligible for HB (para. 10.75 onwards).

'LOCALITY', 'NEIGHBOURHOOD' AND 'VICINITY'

ROO sch 1
paras 1(4),3(5),4(6)
NIHBR sch 1A
paras 1(3),3(4),
4(2),4A(2)

6.18 In the past, the rent officer made all his or her determinations by reference to the 'locality', a concept which was not defined, but which was held in the Court of Appeal *(Regina (Saadat and Others) v the Rent Service)* to mean a relatively limited area. The law was amended as a result on 6th November 2001, eleven days after the judgment. Since then, the rent officer makes his or her determinations by reference to the 'locality', the 'neighbourhood' or the 'vicinity', as defined below. (In all the following, 'area' is not defined in the law and takes its ordinary English meaning.) No amending rules have yet been introduced for Northern Ireland and so the term 'locality' is still in use for all Northern Irish rent decisions.

6.19 In Great Britain, 'locality' (used in determining local reference rents: para. 6.28; and single room rents: para. 6.31) means an area: ROO sch 1 para 4(6)

- which comprises two or more neighbourhoods (as defined below), one of which must be the neighbourhood where the dwelling is, and each of which must adjoin at least one other; AND
- where a tenant of the dwelling 'could reasonably be expected to live having regard to facilities and services for the purposes of health, education, recreation, personal banking and shopping which are in or accessible from the neighbourhood of the dwelling, taking account of the distance of travel, by public and private transport, to and from facilities of the same type and similar standard'; AND
- which contains 'residential premises of a variety of types' including ones held on a 'variety of tenancies'.

6.20 'Neighbourhood' (used in determining exceptionally high rents: para. 6.27; and in part of the definition of locality: para. 6.19) means: ROO sch 1 para 3(5)

- in the case of dwelling in a town or city, 'that part of that town or city where the dwelling is located which is a distinct area of residential accommodation';
- in the case of a dwelling not in a town or city, 'the area surrounding the dwelling which is a distinct area of residential accommodation' and where there are dwellings satisfying the size criteria (table 6.5).

6.21 'Vicinity' (used in determining significantly high rents: para. 6.23; and size-related rents: para. 6.24) means: ROO sch 1 para 1(4

- 'the area immediately surrounding the dwelling'
- however, for size-related rents only (not significantly high rents), if 'the area immediately surrounding the dwelling' contains no dwellings matching the size criteria (table 6.5), 'vicinity' instead means 'the area nearest to the [claimant's] dwelling where there is such a dwelling'.

CLAIM-RELATED RENT DETERMINATIONS

6.22 In all cases, the rent officer must make a 'claim-related rent determination.' This is the only, lower or lowest of the following (the latter three are described in the following paragraphs): ROO sch 1 para 6 NIHBR sch 1A para

- the referred rent, adjusted (as regards service charges) in accordance with the general rules and assumptions (para. 6.17);
- the significantly high rent;
- the size-related rent;
- the exceptionally high rent.

SIGNIFICANTLY HIGH RENT DETERMINATIONS

ROO sch 1 para 1
IHBR sch 1A para 1

6.23 The rent officer determines whether the referred rent for the dwelling is 'significantly higher than the rent which the landlord might reasonably have been expected to obtain'. If it is, he or she makes a significantly high rent determination: this is the amount 'the landlord might reasonably have been expected to obtain' for the dwelling, having regard to 'the level of rent under similar tenancies [or licences] of similar dwellings in the vicinity (or as similar as regards tenancy [or licence], dwelling and vicinity as reasonably practicable'. 'Vicinity' is defined in para. 6.21. Also, the general rules and assumptions apply (para. 6.17). In Northern Ireland 'locality' is still used instead of 'vicinity'.

SIZE-RELATED RENT DETERMINATIONS

ROO sch 1 para 2
IHBR sch 1A para 2

6.24 Except in the case of site rents for caravans or mobile homes and mooring charges for houseboats, the rent officer also determines whether the dwelling exceeds the size criteria given in paragraph 6.25 and table 6.5. If it does, he or she makes a size-related rent determination: this is the amount 'the landlord might reasonably have been expected to obtain' on a dwelling which:

- is in 'the same vicinity' (in Northern Ireland 'locality'); and
- is let under a similar tenancy under the same terms as the tenancy of the dwelling in question; and
- matches those size criteria; and
- is in a reasonable state of repair; and
- in other respects, matches the claimant's dwelling 'as closely as reasonably practicable'.

'Vicinity' is defined in para. 6.21. Also, the general rules and assumptions apply (para. 6.17).

6.25 The size criteria (para. 6.24 and table 6.5) allow for every 'occupier' – which is defined for this purpose as 'a person (whether or not identified by name) who is stated [by the authority], in the application [to the rent officer] for the determination, to occupy the dwelling'. There is no further definition, but the term appears intended to have a degree of flexibility. Note that (as circular HB/CTB A18/97 points out), the authority (not the rent officer) determines whether or not someone is an 'occupier'; and the term is not expressly limited to those

Table 6.5: The rent officer's size criteria

These are relevant for size-related rent determinations (para. 6.24), exceptionally high rent determinations (para. 6.27) and local reference rent determinations (para. 6.28). For who counts as an occupier for these purposes, see paragraphs 6.25-26.

ROO sch 2 NIHBR sch 1A para 9

- One room is allowed as a bedroom for each of the following occupiers, each occupier coming only within the first category which applies to him or her:
  - a married or unmarried couple (paras. 4.4, 4.6);
  - a single person aged 16 or more;
  - two children of the same sex under the age of 16;
  - two children (of the same or opposite sexes) under the age of 10;
  - a child under the age of 16.
- One, two or three living rooms ('rooms suitable for living in') are allowed as follows:
  - one if there are one to three occupiers;
  - two if there are four to six occupiers;
  - three if there are seven or more occupiers.
- The size criteria relate to the total number of rooms allowed (under either of the above headings). It is irrelevant whether the claimant actually uses those rooms as bedrooms or living rooms.

Example: The rent officer's size criteria

A couple have two children aged 6 and 8. No-one else lives with them. Their dwelling has three bedrooms, one living room, a kitchen, a bathroom, a toilet and several uninhabitable cupboards.

The rent officer's size criteria ignore the kitchen, bathroom and toilet. The criteria allow them four bedrooms/living rooms in all, as follows:

- one room as a bedroom for the couple;
- one room as a bedroom for the two children;
- two rooms as living rooms – because there are four occupiers.

Their four rooms (three bedrooms and one living room) do not exceed the size criteria because bedrooms and living rooms are interchangeable for these purposes.

whose circumstances are taken into account in the calculation of the claimant's entitlement to HB (though see below). It is clear that all the following should be included as 'occupiers' for this purpose:

- the claimant and members of his or her family (paras. 4.4-20); and
- everyone else who normally lives in the dwelling, such as non-dependants, (sub-)tenants, boarders, joint occupiers, certain carers (para. 4.26) and certain other children and young persons who do not count as a member of the family (para. 4.19).

6.26 The Court of Appeal in *R v Swale BC HBRB ex p Marchant* has held that a child who spends time in the homes of each of his or her parents (who live apart) counts as an 'occupier' only in the home of the parent who is 'responsible' for him or her (para. 4.16 – typically the one who receives child benefit). This case does not apply in other difficult situations. One example is that of a grown-up child who lives away from home for part(s) of the year (perhaps as a student) but returns home from time to time (perhaps in the holidays). It is clear that he or she counts as an 'occupier' in weeks in which he or she is treated as a non-dependant. In other weeks (if any), it can be argued that he or she counts as an 'occupier' (since the definition of 'occupier' appears flexible and is unaffected in this situation by the Marchant case), but it is unlikely that all local authorities will agree with this. Matters such as this are open to appeal.

EXCEPTIONALLY HIGH RENT DETERMINATIONS

ROO sch 1 para 3
HBR sch 1A para 3

6.27 Except in the case of hostels (para. 6.10) or care homes (para. 2.18-20), the rent officer also determines whether either of the figures described above (paras. 6.23-26), or (if he or she has not made a determination in either of those cases) the referred rent for the dwelling, is 'exceptionally high'. If it is, he or she makes an exceptionally high rent determination: this is 'the highest rent, which is not an exceptionally high rent and which a landlord might reasonably have been expected to obtain' on a dwelling which:

- is in 'the same neighbourhood'(in Northern Ireland 'locality'); and
- matches the size criteria (table 6.4); and
- is in a reasonable state of repair.

'Neighbourhood' is defined in para. 6.20. Also the general rules and assumptions apply (para. 6.17).

LOCAL REFERENCE RENT DETERMINATIONS

ROO sch 1 para 4
HBR sch 1A para 4

6.28 Except in the case of hostels (para. 6.10) or residential care homes or nursing homes (para. 3.12-14), the rent officer also determines whether any of the figures described above (paras. 6.23-27), or (if he or she has not made a determination in any of those cases) the referred rent for the dwelling, is greater than the 'local reference rent' described below. If it is, he or she makes a local reference rent determination (in other words, notifies the authority of the local reference rent). If it is not, he or she notifies the authority that it is not.

6.29 In determining the 'local reference rent', the rent officer takes account of the range of rents 'which a landlord might reasonably have been expected to obtain' on dwellings which:

- are in 'the same locality'; and
- match the size criteria (table 6.5) or have the same number of rooms as the claimant's dwelling, if less; and
- in the case of one-room dwellings, are in the same category as the claimant's dwelling (see below); and
- are let on an assured tenancy (or a similar tenancy or licence); and
- are in a reasonable state of repair.

'Locality' is defined in para. 6.19 (except for Northern Ireland: para. 6.18). Also the general rules and assumptions apply (para. 6.17).

The categories (mentioned above) of one-room dwellings are:

- one-room dwellings where a 'substantial' part of the rent is 'fairly attributable' to 'board and attendance' included within the rent;
- other one-room dwellings where the tenant shares a kitchen, toilet, bathroom and living room ('room suitable for living in') with someone who is not a member of his or her household (paras. 4.3 and 6.26); and
- other one-room dwellings.

For the purposes of deciding whether it is a one-room dwelling in the first place, the definition of a 'room' is the same as in the note to table 6.6.

6.30 The 'local reference rent' is then the figure which is half-way between:

- the lowest such rent which is not an 'exceptionally low rent'; and
- the highest such rent which is not an 'exceptionally high rent'.

SINGLE ROOM RENT DETERMINATIONS

6.31 Except in the case of hostels (para. 6.10) or care homes (paras. 2.18-20), and only if the authority states in the referral that the claimant is a 'young individual' (para. 6.12), the rent officer also determines whether the claimant's rent is greater than the 'single room rent' described below. If it is, he or she makes a single room rent determination (in other words, notifies the authority of the single room rent). If it is not, he or she notifies the authority that it is not.

ROO sch 1 para 5
NIHBR sch 1A para 4A

6.32 In determining the 'single room rent', the rent officer takes account of the range of rents 'which a landlord might reasonably have been expected to obtain' on dwellings which:

- provide exclusive use of one bedroom;
- provide no other bedroom;
- provide shared use of a living room ('room suitable for living in');
- provide shared use of a toilet and bathroom;
- provide shared use of a kitchen (and no exclusive use of facilities for cooking food);
- do not provide board and attendance;
- are in 'the same locality';
- are let on an assured tenancy (or a similar tenancy or licence);
- are in a reasonable state of repair.

'Locality' is defined in para. 6.19 (para. 6.18 for Northern Ireland). Also the general rules and assumptions apply (para. 6.17).

6.33 The 'single room rent' is then the figure which is half-way between:

- the lowest such rent which is not an 'exceptionally low rent'; and
- the highest such rent which is not an 'exceptionally high rent'.

SERVICE CHARGES DETERMINATIONS

ROO sch 1 paras 6(3),7 NIHBR sch 1A para 5

6.34 Except in the case of a hostel (para. 6.10); the rent officer must determine the value of the ineligible service charges (apart from meals) he or she excluded in making the claim-related rent determination (unless the amount is negligible).

JOINT OCCUPIERS

ROO 2(1)(a) NIHBR sch 1A para 14

6.35 In the case of accommodation occupied by joint occupiers, the rent officer's determinations (apart from the single room rent determination) relate to the dwelling as a whole. It is for the authority to make any necessary apportionment (para. 10.6).

NOTIFICATION AND TIME LIMITS

ROO sch 1 para 9

6.36 In Great Britain only, the rent officer has a duty to notify the authority of the following:

- the claim-related rent (all cases);
- the local reference rent (if any);
- the single room rent (if any);

- except in the case of a hostel (para. 6.10), the value of the ineligible service charges (apart from meals and support charges) he or she has excluded in making his or her claim-related rent determination;
- whether the claim-related rent includes an amount for ineligible meals (as can be the case if it is an exceptionally high rent determination).

6.37 The rent officer should notify the authority of the above determinations within five working days or, if the rent officer intends to inspect the dwelling, within 25 working days (or, in either case, as soon as reasonably practicable after that). The period begins on the day the rent officer receives the referral from the authority or (if he or she has requested this) on the day he or she receives further information needed from the authority. ROO 2(1)(a),3(1)(a)

Table 6.6: Indicative rent levels: the rent officer's categories of dwelling

ROO sch 1 para 11(3),(5) NIHBR sch 1A para 8(3),(5)

(a) One-room dwellings where a 'substantial' part of the rent is 'fairly attributable' to 'board and attendance' included within the rent.

(b) Other one-room dwellings where the tenant shares a kitchen or toilet with someone who is not a member of his or her household (paras. 4.3 and 6.26).

(c) Other one-room dwellings.

(d) Two-room dwellings.

(e) Three-room dwellings.

(f) Four-room dwellings.

(g) Five-room dwellings.

(h) Six-room dwellings.

Note: Definition of 'room'

For these purposes, a 'room' is defined as a 'bedroom or room suitable for living in':

- including a room the claimant shares with any member of his or her household, including a non-dependant (para. 4.21), or with a boarder or (sub-)tenant (paras. 4.23, 4.25);
- but (in the case of one-room dwellings: categories (a) to (c)) excluding a room he or she shares with anyone else.

INDICATIVE RENT LEVELS

ROO sch 1 para 11
NIHBR sch 1A para 8

6.38 Separate from the provisions described above, the rent officer provides each authority, on the first working day of each month, with 'indicative rent levels' for its area. The law allows the authority to take these into account in estimating payments on account (para. 16.16), and the subsidy rules encourage this. Indicative rent levels do not apply to site rents for caravans or mobile homes, houseboat moorings or rental purchase agreements. (They also do not take account of the rent officer's size criteria: table 6.5.)

6.39 One 'indicative rent level' is provided for each category of dwelling shown in table 6.6. In determining the indicative rent level for each category, the rent officer takes account of the range of rents 'which a landlord might reasonably have been expected to obtain' on dwellings which:

- are in that category;
- are in the area of the authority (not 'the locality' of the dwelling);
- are let on an assured tenancy (or a similar tenancy or licence); and
- are in a reasonable state of repair;
- adjusted – as regards service charges only – in accordance with the general rules and assumptions (para. 6.17).

The 'indicative rent level' for each category is then:

- the lowest such rent which is not an 'exceptionally low rent'; plus
- one-quarter of the difference between that and the highest such rent which is not an 'exceptionally high rent'.

Appeals and errors

6.40 There is no right of appeal to a social security appeal tribunal against the rent determinations made by the rent officer (or in Northern Ireland against rent decisions made by the NIHE). Instead, the following procedures apply (paras. 6.41-50 for Great Britain; para. 6.51 for Northern Ireland). In England the courts have considered that these procedures are sufficiently independent to comply with the Human Rights Act: *R (on the application of Cumpsty) v The Rent Service.* This case is at least very strongly persuasive in Wales and Scotland.

APPEALS BY THE CLAIMANT

HBRGB 12CA

6.41 This section applies only in Great Britain. For Northern Ireland, see para. 6.51. If a claimant makes written representations to the authority relating wholly or partly to any determination by the rent officer (and does so within six weeks of notification of the HB decision based on that rent officer determination), the authority must, within seven days of receipt apply to the rent officer for a re-determination for the case in question. The authority must forward the claimant's representations at the same time. This must be done even if the representations are made by a later claimant at the same address. There are however limitations (in the next paragraph).

6.42 For any particular claimant and any particular dwelling, only one application to the rent officer may be made in respect of any particular determination (plus one in respect of any particular substitute determination: para. 6.49). This is the case regardless of whether the authority itself has previously chosen to make an application for a re-determination. HBRGB 12CA

6.43 However, a claimant who considers that a referral should or should not have been made in the first place (e.g. a claimant who disputes whether he or she falls within one of the exceptions described earlier in this chapter) has the right to use the ordinary HB appeals procedure (chapter 19) to challenge this. This is because the determination whether or not to refer a case to the rent officer is made by the authority.

Appeals by the authority

6.44 The authority (in Great Britain only) may itself choose to apply to the rent officer for a re-determination. For any particular claimant and any particular dwelling, it may do this only once in respect of any particular determination (plus once in respect of any particular substitute determination: para. 6.49); unless a re-determination is subsequently made as a result of an appeal by the claimant (para. 6.41), in which case the authority may do this once more.

RENT OFFICER RE-DETERMINATIONS

6.45 In each of the cases described above (paras. 6.41-44), the rent officer must make a complete re-determination. Even if the application for a re-determination relates only to one figure, the rent officer has to reconsider all matters pertaining to the case in question. All the assumptions, etc, applying to determinations (para. 6.17 onwards) apply equally to re-determinations. Re-determinations should be made within 20 working days or as soon as practicable after that. The period begins on the day the rent officer receives the application from the authority or (if he or she has requested this) on the day he or she receives further information needed from the authority. HBRGB 12B ROO 4, sch 3

6.46 The rent officer making the re-determination (called a 're-determination officer') must seek and have regard to the advice of one or two other rent officers. In England, the Rent Service (formerly the rent officer service) has set up independent re-determination units and advises that reasons for their re-determinations are always supplied to the claimant and the authority. Similar arrangements are in place in Wales and Scotland. It would certainly be open to challenge if reasons were not given (as happened fairly frequently in the past).

HOW THE RE-DETERMINATION AFFECTS HB

6.47 In broad terms, re-determinations affect HB in the same way as determinations (para. 6.4). However, in 'New Scheme' cases (para. 10.7), the following further rules apply:

- If the effect of the re-determination is that the 'maximum rent' increases, this applies from the date of the rent officer's original determination. So the claimant is awarded any resulting arrears of HB (but this applies only to the claimant in question, not to a previous claimant at the same address).
- If the effect of the re-determination is that the 'maximum rent' reduces, this applies from the date of the rent officer's re-determination following the appeal: the reduction is not applied retrospectively. So it does not mean (unless the authority delays applying it) that the claimant has been overpaid HB.

DEALING WITH ERRORS

ROO 7A **6.48** The rent officer has a duty to notify the authority, as soon as is practicable, upon discovering that he or she has made an error, other than one of professional judgment, in a determination or re-determination (including a substitute determination or substitute re-determination). This applies in Great Britain only.

ROO 4A(1) **6.49** In such cases the authority must apply to the rent officer for a substitute determination (or substitute re-determination). The authority must also do this if it discovers that it made an error in its application to the rent officer as regards the size of the dwelling, the number of occupiers, the composition of the household or the terms of the tenancy. In all such cases, the authority must state the nature of the error and withdraw any outstanding applications for rent officer determinations in that case.

ROO 4A(2) **6.50** All the assumptions, etc, applying to determinations (para. 6.17 onwards) also apply to substitute determinations/re-determinations. In broad terms, substitute determinations and substitute re-determinations affect HB in the same way as re-determinations (para. 6.47).

Appeals in Northern Ireland

NIDAR 4(1) sch para 1 **6.51** In Northern Ireland a decision to restrict the rent is made by the Executive so the decision can be revised or superseded in the normal way (para. 17.43). Application for a revision must be made wihin one month. However, a decision which restricts the rent cannot be appealed.

Pre-tenancy determinations

HOW TO GET A PRE-TENANCY DETERMINATION

6.52 People can find out whether their HB would be likely to be restricted if they claimed HB, by asking for a 'pre-tenancy determination' ('PTD'). Any 'prospective occupier' of any dwelling (other than a council letting) may apply to the authority requesting it to refer the rent to the rent officer. So may any current occupier of a dwelling whose current agreement commenced at least 11 months previously and who is contemplating entering a new agreement there (but see para. 6.55). Authorities have standard forms for people who require a PTD. HBRGB 12A(8) ROO 3(1) NIHBR 12A(5)

6.53 The main conditions for getting a PTD are that the person must: HBRGB 12A(1)(c) NIHBR 12A(1)

- indicate on the form that he or she would be likely to claim HB if he or she took up the letting (or took up the new agreement);
- sign the form; and
- obtain a signature on the form from the landlord consenting to a referral. The landlord will be expected to provide the rent officer with necessary information and allow access to the dwelling.

THE AUTHORITY'S DUTIES

6.54 With two exceptions (para. 6.55), whenever an authority receives a request for a PTD, it must refer the details to the rent officer within two working days of the date of the request for the PTD. The rent officer's duties in such cases are described in paragraph 6.56. HBRGB 12A(3)

6.55 First, if the request for the PTD is invalid (e.g. if the landlord has not consented), the authority must return it to the person along with a notification of why it is invalid. Secondly, if: HBRGB 12A(2A)

- the authority already has a rent officer determination which was made for the dwelling in question; and
- the conditions for making a further referral to the rent officer are not met (table 6.2),

the authority must, within four working days of the request for the PTD, supply details of that determination to the person along with a notification of why a current PTD referral cannot be made.

RENT OFFICER AND NIHE TIME LIMITS

6.56 When the rent officer receives a referral requesting a PTD, he or she makes the same determinations as in any other case referred to him or her. The rent officer notifies the result to the authority within five working days. In Northern Ireland where the Executive receives a PTD it should make a decision within seven days. ROO 2(1)(a), 3(1)(a) NIHBR 12A(3)

CLAIMS FOR HB FOLLOWING A PRE-TENANCY DETERMINATION

HBR 10(3), 11(1), 12A **6.57** With two exceptions (para. 6.58), when the authority receives an HB claim on a dwelling to which a PTD applies, the authority uses the PTD in the same way as if it had been a rent officer determination made following the claim (i.e. no additional referral is required).

6.58 The PTD does not apply, and a referral must be made to the rent officer, if:

- the PTD was made more than 12 months ago; or
- the circumstances indicated in the claim for HB are different from those indicated in the request for the PTD (i.e. there are differences between them which constitute a 'relevant change of circumstances': para. 6.11).

CALCULATING 'MAXIMUM RENTS' FROM PRE-TENANCY DETERMINATIONS

HBRGB 11(6A),(6B) NIHBR 11(7),(8) **6.59** With the exceptions described in the previous and following paragraphs, whenever the authority is required to calculate a 'maximum rent' in assessing a claimant's eligible rent (chapter 10), it uses the rent officer figures provided in the PTD.

6.60 If the claimant's actual rent at the date of his or her claim for HB is lower than the 'maximum rent' calculated from the rent officer figures provided in the PTD, similar points arise as in paragraph 10.45.

APPEALS

DAR 1(2), 3(1)(a) **6.61** There is no right of appeal relating to a pre-tenancy determination until and unless it is used in connection with the determination of a claim for HB (in which case the ordinary rules about appeals about rent officer determinations apply: paras. 6.4 onwards).

7 Calculating HB and main CTB

7.1 This chapter explains how to calculate HB and main CTB. These are dealt with together as they are calculated in a similar way to each other. The chapter covers:

- how to calculate HB and main CTB;
- who counts as a non-dependant, and how non-dependant deductions affect HB and main CTB; and
- how figures are converted to weekly amounts and when they are rounded.

Different rules apply to second adult rebate (chapter 8), 'extended payments' (para. 17.81) and 'continuing payments' (para. 17.94).

7.2 In broad terms, claimants with no income or low income (including all claimants on JSA(IB), IS or guarantee credit) qualify for maximum benefit – which may be reduced if there are non-dependants in their home. The more income claimants have, the less benefit they get, but there is no general upper limit. The level of income at which benefit entitlement runs out varies from claimant to claimant depending on a wide range of factors.

The calculation

7.3 The next few paragraphs explain with examples how to calculate entitlement to HB and main CTB on a weekly basis. Table 7.1 summarises the rules. It is also worth bearing in mind that the claimant's actual entitlement can be reduced for the following reasons:

- to recover a recoverable overpayment (para. 18.10);
- to recover an administrative penalty relating to an overpayment (para. 18.78); or
- to punish him or her for two or more convictions relating to fraud in the space of three years (vulgarly known as the 'two strikes' provisions). This can only be done on the instructions of the DWP and in practice it rarely if ever occurs. The details are in the 2003-04 edition of this guide.

MAXIMUM BENEFIT

7.4 The starting point for all calculations of HB and main CTB is the claimant's 'maximum benefit'. On a weekly basis, this is: CBA 130(1),(4), 131(1),(3) NICBA 129 (1),(4) HBR 61(4),(10) CTBR 51(1)

- in calculating HB:
  - the whole of the claimant's weekly eligible rent (chapter 10) and/or rates in Northern Ireland (chapter 11),
  - minus any non-dependant deductions which apply;
- in calculating main CTB:
  - the whole of the claimant's weekly eligible council tax (chapter 9),
  - minus any non-dependant deductions which apply.

CLAIMANTS ON JSA(IB), IS OR GUARANTEE CREDIT

7.5 A claimant qualifies for maximum benefit (para. 7.4) whilst he or she (or any partner) is: CBA 130(1),(3), 131(5),(6) NICBA 129(1),(3) HBR 2(3A)(d), sch 4 paras 4, 4A sch 5 paras 5, 5A CTBR 2(3A)(d), sch 4 paras 4, 4A sch 5 paras 5, 5A

- on income-based jobseeker's allowance (JSA(IB)); or
- on income support (IS); or
- on guarantee credit; or
- treated as receiving JSA(IB) or IS (para. 7.6).

CLAIMANTS TREATED AS BEING ON JSA(IB) OR IS

7.6 A claimant also qualifies for maximum benefit (para. 7.4) whilst he or she (or any partner) is: HBR 2(1), (3A) CTBR 2(1), (3A)

- entitled to JSA(IB) but not receiving it because of a sanction; or
- in the 'waiting days' before his or her JSA(IB) starts – or would start apart from a sanction; or
- subject to a restriction in his or her JSA(IB) or IS as a result of breaching a community order; or
- disqualified from getting JSA(IB) following certain convictions (para. 7.3).

In these cases, the law works by treating the claimant as though he or she was actually on JSA(IB) or IS.

CTB CLAIMANTS FORMERLY ON JSA(IB) OR IS

7.7 A claimant also qualifies for maximum benefit in CTB only (not HB), if he or she lost entitlement to JSA(IB) or IS on 1st April 2003, and the only reason for this was that the assessment of his or her JSA(IB) or IS no longer included support charges because they became payable by Supporting People (para. 10.103). This lasts without time limit and regardless of any future change CTBR sch 4 para 4B in the claimant's circumstances after that date. DWP circular HB/CTB A7/2003 gives details of the administrative arrangements for this small number of cases.

CLAIMANTS NOT ON JSA(IB), IS OR GUARANTEE CREDIT

7.8 In any case other than those described above (paras. 7.5-7), if the claimant's capital (valued as in chapters 13 to 15) is over £16,000, then he or she does not qualify for any HB or main CTB at all, and so the remainder of this chapter does not apply. Otherwise, the claimant's weekly income (chapters 13 to 15) is compared with his or her applicable amount (chapter 12).

CBA 130(1),(3), NICBA 129(1),(3) **7.9** If the claimant has no income, or has income which is less than (or equal to) his or her applicable amount, the claimant qualifies for maximum benefit (para. 7.4).

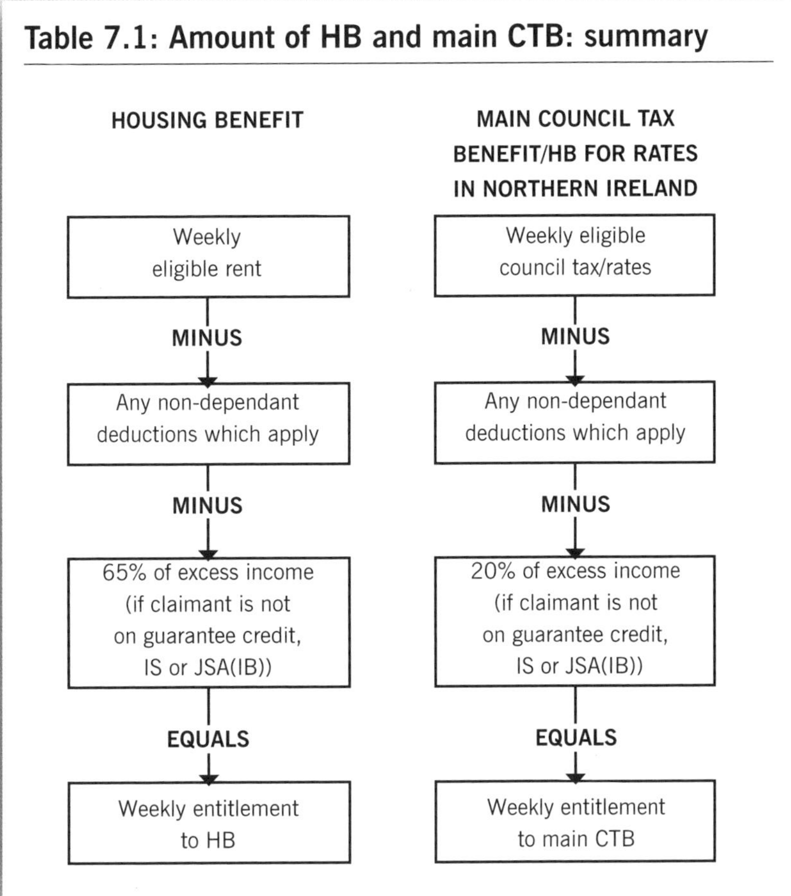

Table 7.1: Amount of HB and main CTB: summary

7.10 If the claimant's weekly income is more than his or her applicable amount, the difference between the two is known as 'excess income'. The claimant qualifies for: CBA 130(1),(3), 131(5),(8) NICBA 129(1),(3)

- maximum benefit (para. 7.4);
- minus a percentage of this excess income (para. 7.11).

7.11 The percentage, also known as a 'taper', is as follows: HBR 62 CTBR 53

- 65 per cent in calculating HB (for rent);
- 20 per cent in calculating main CTB;
- 20 per cent in calculating HB for rates in Northern Ireland.

Examples: Calculating HB and main CTB

CLAIMANT ON JSA(IB), IS OR GUARANTEE CREDIT

A claimant has no non-dependants: she lives alone. Her eligible rent is £85.00 per week. The council tax on her home would be £16.00 per week apart from the fact that she qualifies for a 25% council tax discount, which reduces her liability to £12.00 per week.

Claimants on JSA(IB), IS or guarantee credit get maximum benefit – which is based on their eligible rent and eligible council tax.

HB:	Eligible rent	
	equals weekly HB	£85.00
Main CTB:	Eligible council tax	
	equals weekly main CTB	£12.00

CLAIMANT NOT ON JSA(IB), IS OR GUARANTEE CREDIT

A couple have no non-dependants. They are not on JSA(IB), IS or guarantee credit. Their joint weekly income exceeds their applicable amount by £20.00. Their eligible rent is £90.00 per week. Their eligible council tax liability is £17.56 per week.

Claimants with excess income get maximum benefit minus a percentage of their excess income.

HB:	Eligible rent	£90.00
	minus 65% of excess income (65% x £20.00)	£13.00
	equals weekly HB	£77.00
Main CTB:	Eligible council tax	£17.56
	minus 20% of excess income (20% x £20.00)	£4.00
	equals weekly main CTB	£13.56

MINIMUM BENEFIT

HBR 64(2) **7.12** If the weekly amount of HB calculated as above is less than 50p, then it is not awarded. There is no equivalent rule in CTB, where an award can be as little as one penny.

MAIN CTB AND THE 'BETTER BUY'

CBA 131(9) **7.13** If the amount of a claimant's main CTB calculated as above is lower than his or her entitlement to second adult rebate, he or she will not get main CTB, but will get second adult rebate instead. This is because of the 'better buy' comparison, described in paragraphs 8.29 onwards. Examples are given at the end of chapter 8.

HB AND RENT-FREE PERIODS

HBR 70(1) **7.14** The following additional rules apply if a claimant has rent-free weeks or other rent-free periods. They do not apply in cases where a landlord has waived the rent in return for works carried out by the tenant (para. 2.36).

7.15 No HB is awarded during rent-free periods, including in Northern Ireland rate-free periods where rates are paid with the rent. HB is awarded only for periods in which rent is due.

HBR 70(2) **7.16** During the periods in which rent is due, the calculation factors (i.e. applicable amount, income and any non-dependant deductions) are adjusted as follows:

- if rent is expressed on a weekly basis: multiply the calculation factors by 52 or 53, then divide by the number of weeks when rent is due in that year;
- if rent is not expressed on a weekly basis: multiply the calculation factors by 365 or 366, then divide by the number of days when rent is due in that year.

Non-dependant deductions

7.17 HB and main CTB are normally reduced for each non-dependant living in the claimant's home. The next paragraphs explain when a deduction is or is not made, and the additional rules involved. There are some differences between HB (for rent), main CTB, and HB for rates in Northern Ireland. These are mentioned whenever they arise. There are also differences if the claimant or any partner is aged 65 or over. In their case the deductions are delayed, as described in paragraphs 7.37-38.

7.18 Non-dependants are usually adult sons, daughters, other relatives or friends who live in the claimant's household on a non-commercial basis (paras.

4.21-22). Some claimants receive money from their non-dependants to pay for their keep. This may include a contribution towards rent, council tax, food or household expenses. This money is not treated as the claimants' income (table 13.4). Instead deductions are made from the claimant's HB and main CTB. However, these deductions are not related to what the non-dependant actually pays. They are fixed sums which apply even if the non-dependant pays the claimant nothing at all. The level of deductions (table 7.3) is high in some cases, and may cause claimants hardship.

CASES IN WHICH NO DEDUCTION IS MADE

7.19 As described in paragraphs 7.20-22 and table 7.2, there are three types of case in which no non-dependant deduction is made. HBR 3(2) CTBR 3(2)

7.20 No deduction applies in respect of any of the following, because they are defined in the law as not being non-dependants (para. 4.21):

- children aged under 16 and young persons aged 16 to 18 inclusive (whether or not they are counted as a member of the family for HB/CTB purposes);
- boarders, (sub-)tenants and joint occupiers;
- carers provided by a charity or voluntary organisation for whom the claimant or partner are charged;
- the claimant's landlord and members of the landlord's household.

7.21 There are no non-dependant deductions in either HB or main CTB if the claimant or any partner: HBR 2(1), 63(6) CTBR 2(1), 52(6)

- is registered blind or has ceased to be registered blind within the past 28 weeks because of regaining sight (para. 12.13); or
- receives the care component of disability living allowance payable at any rate; or
- receives attendance allowance payable at any rate or any of the related benefits in entries (e) to (g) of paragraph 12.13.

In such cases, if the claimant has more than one non-dependant, no deduction applies for any of them. (Note that the second and third cases cease to apply when disability living allowance or attendance allowance themselves cease – for example, when the claimant or partner have been in hospital for four weeks.)

7.22 No deduction applies in respect of any non-dependant who falls within certain groups. The main groups are summarised in table 7.2. As indicated there, there are some differences between the groups applying for HB purposes and those applying for main CTB purposes. Appendix 6 defines all the relevant categories of people and gives the detailed rules about whether a non-dependant deduction applies in HB and main CTB. HBR 63(1),(7),(8) CTBR 52(1),(2),(7),

Table 7.2: Non-dependants for whom no deduction applies

HBR 2(1), 63(6)
HBR 60+ 63(7)(dd)
CTBR 2(1), 52(6)
CTBR 60+ 52(8)(c)

- Non-dependants aged under 18.
- Non-dependants aged under 25 who are on JSA(IB), IS or either kind of SPC.
- In CTB only, non-dependants aged 25+ who are on JSA(IB), IS or either kind of SPC. (In HB there is a deduction in such cases.)
- If the claimant is aged 65+ (or any partner is), non-dependants who are students (at all times of the year).
- If the claimant is aged under 65 (and any partner is too), non-dependants who are students (but in HB only there is a deduction in the summer vacation if they take up remunerative work).
- Non-dependants receiving a Work Based Training Allowance.
- Non-dependants in prison or similar forms of detention.
- Non-dependants who have been in hospital for 52 weeks or more.
- Non-dependants whose normal home is elsewhere.
- In CTB only, non-dependants who fall within any of the groups who are 'disregarded persons' for council tax purposes. (In HB there is a deduction in such cases unless they fall within any of the earlier entries in this table.)

Note:
Appendix 6 gives full information about all the above categories of people. It includes all the 'disregarded persons' mentioned above – such as (in various circumstances) education leavers, students, student nurses, apprentices, people who are severely mentally impaired, and carers.

CASES IN WHICH A DEDUCTION IS MADE

HBR 63(1),(2)
CTBR 52(1),(2)

7.23 In cases other than those described above, a non-dependant deduction is made. The amount depends upon whether the non-dependant is in 'remunerative work' (paras. 7.29-34) and, if so, on the level of his or her gross income. The amounts for HB and main CTB are different, and are listed in table 7.3. Additional rules for claimants who are joint occupiers and for non-dependant couples are in paragraphs 7.35-36.

Table 7.3: Summary of weekly non-dependant deductions

	Deduction in HB (for rent)	Deduction in main CTB (and HB for rates in Northern Ireland)
Non-dependants in remunerative work with gross income of:		
£308.00 per week or more	£47.75	£6.95
between £247.00 and £307.99 per week	£43.50	£5.80
between £186.00 and £246.99 per week	£38.20	£4.60
between £144.00 and £185.99 per week	£23.35	£4.60
between £97.00 and £143.99 per week	£17.00	£2.30
under £97.00 per week	£7.40	£2.30
Non-dependants not in remunerative work (regardless of income level)	£7.40	£2.30

Notes:

'Remunerative work' is defined in paras. 7.29 onwards.

Don't forget that there is no deduction at all in the cases in table 7.2.

NON-DEPENDANTS IN REMUNERATIVE WORK

7.24 For non-dependants in remunerative work, there are six possible levels of deduction in HB and four in main CTB (table 7.3), depending in either case on the level of the non-dependant's gross income (unless no deduction is appropriate at all: paras. 7.20-22). HBR 63(1),(2) CTBR 52(1),(2)

7.25 It is the non-dependant's gross income, not net income, which is relevant. So long as the non-dependant is in remunerative work, the rule relates to his or her income from all sources. The only exception is that the following types of income are always disregarded: HBR 63(9) CTBR 52(9)

- disability living allowance (either or both components);
- attendance allowance and the related benefits in entries (e) to (g) of paragraph 12.13;

- payments from the Macfarlane Trusts, the Eileen Trust, the Fund or the Independent Living Funds, including payments in kind from these sources and payments of money which originally derived from them (para. 13.60).

7.26 As regards any other source of income, there are no rules saying how the gross amount is to be assessed, though none of the disregards in chapter 14 applies. The DWP advises correctly that for non-dependants with savings, the gross actual interest received should be included here (GM para. A5.178). However the DWP also advises (GM para. A5.177) that if a non-dependant is self-employed, 'gross income' means before the deduction of expenses. This seems obviously wrong, since it must be plain in this context that 'gross income' means before the deduction of tax and national insurance (but after the deduction of expenses).

7.27 It is up to individual authorities to decide what level of evidence is required about the income of a non-dependant in remunerative work. If there is no evidence (and only if the claimant is in remunerative work), the highest deduction is made (table 7.3). In such cases, if the evidence is later provided, and reveals that a lower deduction should have been made, this means that the claimant has been awarded too little benefit: the claimant must be awarded the arrears – if he or she provides the evidence within one month of the notification of the decision on his or her claim (though the time limit can be extended in certain circumstances: para. 17.43).

NON-DEPENDANTS NOT IN REMUNERATIVE WORK

HBR 63(1)
CTBR 52(1)

7.28 For non-dependants not in remunerative work, the lowest level of deduction applies in both HB and main CTB (table 7.3) regardless of the amount – if any – of the non-dependant's income (unless no deduction is appropriate at all: paras. 7.19-22).

'REMUNERATIVE WORK'

HBR 4(1)
CTBR 4(1)

7.29 Remunerative work is work:

- for which payment is made, or expected to be made; and
- which averages 16 hours or more per week.

HBR 4(2)-(4)
CTBR 4(2)-(4)

7.30 In calculating a weekly average of income, authorities should take into account any recognisable cycle. If there is no such cycle, they should take into account the expected hours of work per week and also (except where the non-dependant is just starting work) the average during the period immediately prior to the claim. This period should be five weeks unless some other period would result in a more accurate estimation in an individual case.

7.31 Once it is established that a person is in remunerative work, he or she continues to count as being in remunerative work during any recognised, customary or other holiday, and also during any period of absence without good cause (but not during sick leave, maternity leave, paternity leave or adoption leave: para. 7.33). HBR 4(4) CTBR 4(4)

7.32 A further rule applies to people employed in schools, other educational establishments, or anywhere else where their recognisable cycle of work is one HBR 4(2A) CTBR 4(2A)

Examples: Calculating HB and main CTB

CLAIMANT ON INCOME SUPPORT WITH WORKING NON-DEPENDANT

A lone parent is on income support. Her eligible rent is £65.00 per week. Her eligible council tax liability is £15.00 per week. Her 26-year-old son lives with her. He earns £325 per week gross for a 35-hour week.

Claimants on income support get maximum benefit, which in this case involves a non-dependant deduction. The son is in remunerative work with gross income of at least £308 per week, so the highest level of deduction applies in both HB and main CTB (table 7.3).

HB:	Eligible rent	£65.00
	minus non-dependant deduction, which in this case is	£47.75
	equals weekly HB	£17.25
Main CTB:	Eligible council tax	£15.00
	minus non-dependant deduction, which in this case is	£6.95
	equals weekly main CTB	£8.05

CLAIMANT ON INCOME SUPPORT WITH NON-DEPENDANT ON INCOME SUPPORT

The son in the previous example loses his job and starts receiving income support.

The calculation is as above, except that now there is no non-dependant deduction in main CTB and the lowest deduction applies in HB (table 7.2).

HB:	Eligible rent£65.00	
	minus non-dependant deduction, which in this case is	£7.40
	equals weekly HB	£57.60
Main CTB:	Eligible council tax	£15.00
	no non-dependant deduction applies	
	equals weekly main CTB	£15.00

year. Their average weekly hours are found by considering only the periods when they work (e.g. school term-times). The result applies both during those periods and during the periods when they do not work (e.g. school holidays). (Note however that changes in income – e.g. between term-time and holidays – are taken into account.)

HBR 2(1), 4(5)-(7) CTBR 2(1), 4(5), (6), (7)

7.33 A non-dependant is treated as not being in remunerative work in any of the following cases:

- in any benefit week during which he or she receives JSA(IB), IS or pension credit for four days or more (regardless of his or her other circumstances);
- on any day on which he or she is on maternity, paternity or adoption leave, i.e. is absent from work for one of those reasons, and has a right to return to work under his or her contract or under employment law;
- on any day on which he or she is absent from work because he or she is ill (whether or not receiving statutory sick pay and regardless of whether the employer is making up his or her wages). However, an absence due to illness which falls wholly within a benefit week (Monday to Sunday) will not be taken into account, because of the rules on changes of circumstances (para. 17.18);
- on any day for which he or she has been or will be paid a Sports Council sports award, so long as he or she is not expected to receive any other payment for that day.

7.34 The following are also not remunerative work:

- education (since this is not 'work');
- training (since this is not 'work') including attendance on government training schemes and the New Deal (para. 13.63) (but those paid by their employer do not count as trainees);
- voluntary or other work for which the person is paid expenses only (since it is not 'remunerative');
- periods of lay-off (since this is absence with good cause).

NON-DEPENDANT COUPLES

HBR 63(3),(4) CTBR 52(3),(4)

7.35 In the case of a non-dependant couple (or a polygamous marriage), only one deduction applies, being the higher (or highest) of any that would have applied to the individuals if they were single claimants. In appropriate cases, there is no deduction (e.g. if they are both under 18). For the purpose of the various gross income limits in table 7.3, each non-dependant partner is treated as possessing the gross income of both of them.

NON-DEPENDANTS OF JOINT OCCUPIERS

7.36 The following rules apply when a claimant is jointly liable for the rent or council tax on his or her home with one or more other persons who are not his or her partner, and there is also a non-dependant living there. They would arise, for example, if a brother and sister are joint occupiers and have a non-dependant living with them. The law is slightly unclear in some of these cases but the key question is 'whose household is the non-dependant part of?' Having decided that, the rules work as follows: HBR 63(5) CTBR 52(35)

- If the non-dependant is part of the household of only one of them, then the whole non-dependant deduction is made in any claim for benefit made by that one, and no deduction is made in any claim for benefit made by the others.
- If the non-dependant is part of the household of more than one of them, the amount of the non-dependant deduction is shared between them. Any of them claiming benefit gets his or her resulting share of the non-dependant deduction. In main CTB, the share must be equal between the joint occupiers (but only between the ones who are jointly liable for the council tax on the home: para. 9.27). In HB, the share need not be equal: the authority should take into account the number of joint occupiers concerned and the proportion of rent each pays (para. 10.6).

DELAYED EFFECT OF NON-DEPENDANT CHANGES FOR PEOPLE AGED 65 OR MORE

7.37 A new rule (introduced on 6th October 2003) applies when: HBR 60+ 68(9)-(12) CTBR 60+ 59(10)-(13)

- the claimant or any partner is aged 65 or more; and
- a non-dependant moves in, or there is an increase in a non-dependant's income which causes an increase in the amount of the deduction.

7.38 In such cases the change in entitlement to HB or main CTB is not implemented until the day 26 weeks after the change actually occurred or, if that is not a Monday, the following Monday. At that point, the claimant's current circumstances are taken into account (not the ones applying 26 weeks or more ago, nor any applying in the intervening period): this is illustrated in the examples.

Examples: Non-dependant changes for people aged 65+

A non-dependant moves in on Wednesday 6th October 2004.

This takes effect 26 weeks and 5 days later – on Monday 11th April 2005.

A non-dependant moves in on Wednesday 6th October 2004, then her income increases on 1st January 2005.

Both things take effect on Monday 11th April 2005.

A non-dependant moves in on Wednesday 6th October 2004, then he moves out on Sunday 10th April 2005.

No deduction is ever made for him.

Conversion to weekly amounts and rounding

7.39 Although for technical reasons (to do with the council tax itself) some of the CTB regulations are expressed on a daily basis, most of the rules relate to a weekly amount and this is the approach adopted in this guide.

7.40 The following paragraphs explain the rules that apply whenever figures involved in the calculation of HB and CTB (including second adult rebate) have to be converted to weekly amounts. The final paragraph describes rounding. Further rules apply if the claimant has rent-free periods (paras. 7.14-16). For the equivalent rules for rates in Northern Ireland, see chapter 11.

RENT

HBR 69(1),(2) **7.41** Whenever a weekly figure is needed for rent, the following rules apply (and the same rules apply to service charges):

- for rent due in multiples of weeks, divide the rent by the number of weeks it covers;
- for rent due daily, multiply the daily amount by seven;
- for rent due calendar monthly (or at any other intervals which are not multiples of weeks), divide the rent by the number of days it covers to find the daily rent, then multiply the daily rent by seven. This means there are two possibilities for a calendar monthly tenant: 12 months' rent can be divided by 365 (or 366 in appropriate years) and then multiplied by seven, or a particular month's rent can (though this is in practice uncommon) be divided by 28, 29, 30 or 31 (as appropriate) and then multiplied by seven.

COUNCIL TAX

7.42 Whenever a weekly figure is needed for council tax liability, the following rules apply: CTBR 51(1)(b)

- for annual figures, divide the council tax by 365 (or 366 in financial years ending in a leap year) to find the daily figure, and then multiply the daily figure by seven;
- for figures which do not relate to a whole year, divide the council tax by the number of days it covers to find the daily figure, and then multiply the daily figure by seven.

INCOME

7.43 Whenever a weekly income figure is needed, the following rules apply:

- for an amount relating to a whole multiple of weeks, divide the amount by the number of weeks it covers;
- for an amount relating to a calendar month, multiply the amount by 12 to find the annual figure, then divide the annual figure by 52 or 53. In practice, authorities usually divide by 52 if there are 52 Mondays in the current financial year (as is the case in 2004-05) or by 53 if there are 53, though the law does not specifically require this;
- for an amount relating to a year (this typically applies only to self-employed income), divide the amount by 365 (or 366 as appropriate) to find the daily figure, and then multiply the daily figure by seven;
- for an amount relating to any other period, divide the amount by the number of days it covers to find the daily figure, then multiply the daily figure by seven.

ROUNDING

7.44 In HB, the authority may round any amount involved in the calculation to the nearest penny, halfpennies being rounded upwards. In CTB, there is no similar rule: indeed the DWP recommends that entitlement should be calculated to at least six decimal places (GM para. B3.300). This is to avoid reconciliation errors at the end of the financial year. Notifications sent to claimants about their entitlement may be rounded to the nearest penny. HBRGB 69(9) NIHBR 69(8)

8 Second adult rebate

8.1 This chapter applies only in England, Wales and Scotland. It explains the type of CTB known as 'second adult rebate' and covers:

- who is eligible for second adult rebate;
- the information needed to establish eligibility;
- how to calculate second adult rebate;
- the information needed to do the calculation; and
- the 'better buy' comparison.

8.2 In broad terms, second adult rebate is awarded when the claimant has a 'second adult' in his or her home who is on income support or income-based jobseeker's allowance or is on a low income. (It was designed to compensate for the loss of council tax discount caused by the presence of the 'second adult'.) Although the level of the claimant's own income and capital (and that of the claimant's partner) is irrelevant, certain other circumstances of the claimant and other household members may prevent entitlement to second adult rebate. Also, because of the 'better buy' comparison (para. 8.29), second adult rebate is only awarded if the claimant does not qualify for the other type of CTB known as 'main CTB', or qualifies for more second adult rebate than main CTB. Chapter 7 gives details of how main CTB is calculated.

8.3 This guide, in common with DWP guidance and most local authority forms and other documentation, uses the informal term 'second adult rebate' for what is known in the law as 'alternative maximum council tax benefit'.

Eligibility for second adult rebate

CBA 131(1),(3),(6),(7),(9)

8.4 Several pieces of information are needed to establish whether a claimant is eligible for second adult rebate and, if so, how much it is to be. These are summarised in the flow chart in table 8.1, and described in detail below.

PRESENCE OF SECOND ADULT

CBA 131(6)(b),7)(a),(11) CTBR 55(a),(c)

8.5 A claimant can only qualify for second adult rebate if there is at least one 'second adult' in his or her home. A person can only be a 'second adult' if he or she:

- is a non-dependant or in certain circumstances someone else (paras. 8.6-7); and

Table 8.1: Second adult rebate flow chart

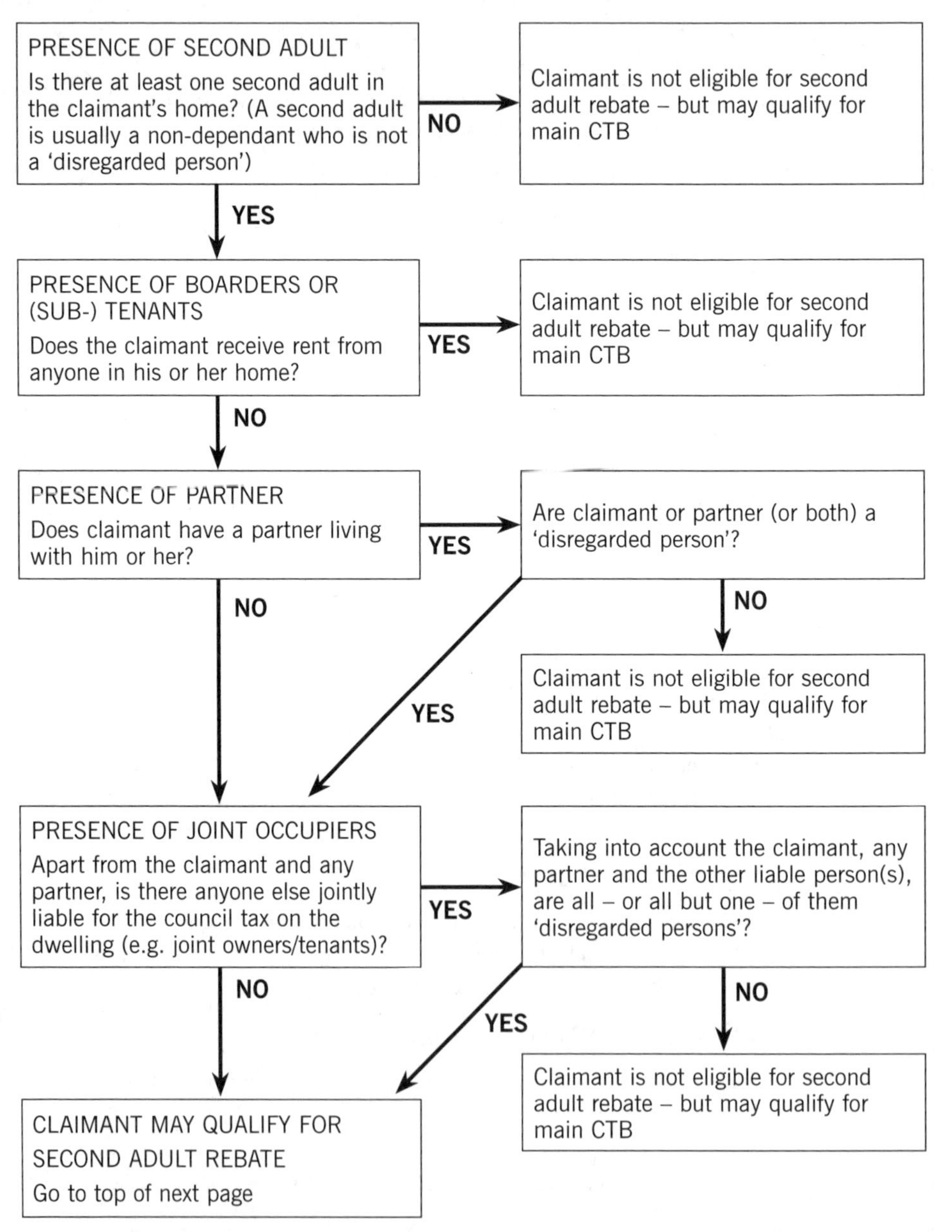

Table 8.1 continued

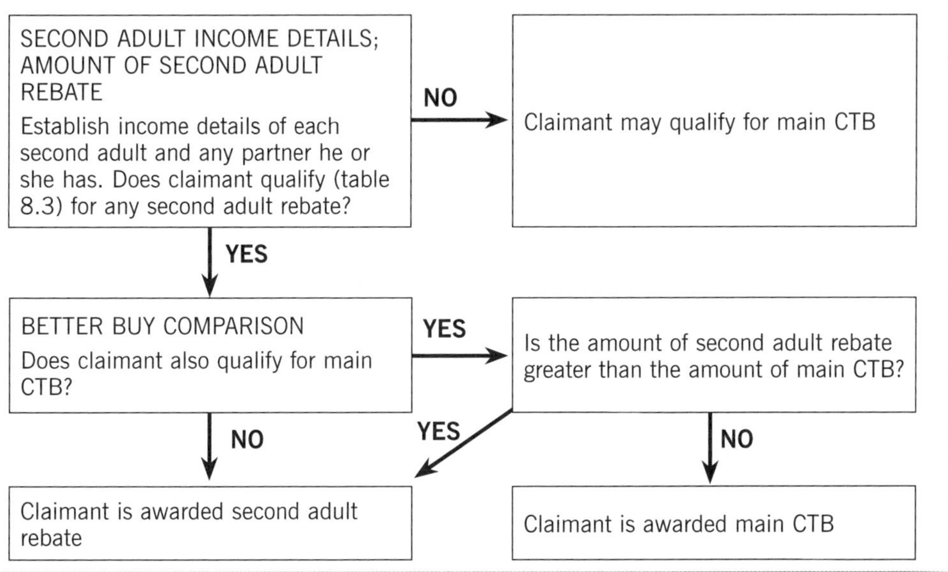

- is not a 'disregarded person' (para. 8.8).

There may be two or more 'second adults' in the claimant's home: the claimant can still qualify for second adult rebate.

8.6 A non-dependant is by far the most common kind of second adult so long as he or she is not a 'disregarded person'. Typical non-dependants are adult sons, daughters, other relatives or friends who live in the claimant's household on a non-commercial basis (para. 4.21).

8.7 A person can also be a second adult if he or she is the type of carer who is defined in law as not being a non-dependant (para. 4.26), so long as he or she is not a 'disregarded person'. This is not common because many carers are 'disregarded persons' (categories 14 to 17 in appendix 6). There may be other categories who count as a second adult, such as paid companions or live-in employees of the claimant or partner – so long as they are not a 'disregarded person' (and do not pay rent: para. 8.9).

8.8 A 'disregarded person' cannot be a second adult. This means a person who falls within any of the groups which are disregarded for council tax discount purposes (para. 9.17). The main groups are summarised in table 8.2. Appendix 6 defines all the relevant categories of people and gives the detailed rules about whether they are 'disregarded persons'.

Table 8.2: 'Disregarded Persons': simplified summary

- People under 18, or aged 18 if child benefit is payable.
- Education leavers under 20.
- Various students, foreign language assistants and student nurses.
- Youth Training trainees under 25.
- Apprentices on NCVQ/SVEC courses.
- People who are severely mentally impaired.
- Carers.
- People in prison or other forms of detention.
- People who normally live elsewhere.
- Members of religious communities.
- Diplomats and members of international bodies or of visiting forces.

PRESENCE OF BOARDERS OR (SUB-)TENANTS

8.9 A claimant who receives rent from any resident in his or her home is not eligible for second adult rebate (even if all the other conditions are fulfilled). Typically, this means that home-owner claimants with boarders or tenants, and tenant claimants with boarders or sub-tenants, cannot get second adult rebate.

CBA 131 (6)(a),(11
CTBR 2(1)

8.10 The exclusion from entitlement applies only if the person paying rent is 'resident' in the claimant's dwelling. A 'resident' means a person aged 18 or more who has 'sole or main residence' there. Therefore, rent received from an under-18-year-old or a holiday-maker does not prevent entitlement.

8.11 The exclusion appears in the Act of Parliament rather than the regulations. The Act does not, however, define 'rent'. The regulations give a definition of 'rent' for other purposes as being (in broad terms) a payment which could be met by HB, and this definition seems appropriate here.

8.12 The exclusion is worded in such a way that it applies only if someone is liable to pay rent to the claimant. It does not apply if someone is liable to pay rent to the claimant's partner (or any other resident).

Example: A couple who have a tenant

A couple are liable for council tax on their home. The only people living with them are their adult son and a tenant. The tenant's letting agreement was signed by the woman in the couple, who takes all the responsibility for the letting and receives all the income from it.

They should ensure that the man is the claimant. No-one is liable to pay rent to him. So he may qualify for second adult rebate, so long as all the other conditions apply (and there are several in a case like this: table 8.1).

CLAIMANT'S INCOME AND CAPITAL

8.13 None of the rules about eligibility for second adult rebate takes into account the amount of a claimant's (or partner's) income or capital in any way.

8.14 The £16,000 capital limit (which applies for HB and main CTB) does not apply when second adult rebate is being considered. Millionaires can get second adult rebate (so long as they fulfil the appropriate conditions).

CLAIMANT'S AND PARTNER'S OTHER CIRCUMSTANCES

CBA 131(7)(b) **8.15** If the conditions mentioned earlier are satisfied, the final condition about eligibility for second adult rebate depends on whether the claim is made by:

- a single claimant or a lone parent (with no joint occupiers);
- a couple (with no joint occupiers); or
- a claimant who has joint occupiers.

SINGLE CLAIMANTS AND LONE PARENTS

8.16 There is no further condition if the claimant is single or a lone parent. It does not matter whether he or she is or is not a 'disregarded person' (para. 8.8). But if the claimant is jointly liable for council tax, see paragraph 8.18.

COUPLES

CTBR 55(b) **8.17** There is a further condition if the claimant is in a couple. Couples are eligible for second adult rebate only if at least one partner is a 'disregarded person' (para. 8.8). It does not matter whether this is the claimant or the partner – and so long as one of them is a 'disregarded person' it does not matter whether the other one is or is not a 'disregarded person'. But if the couple are jointly liable for council tax with some other person, see paragraph 8.18. A polygamous marriage is eligible for second adult rebate if all – or all but one – of the partners are 'disregarded persons'.

JOINT OCCUPIERS

8.18 There is also a further condition if the claimant is jointly liable for the council tax on his or her home with at least one other person (other than just his or her partner if the claim is made by a couple). In such cases, information is needed about all of these joint occupiers. Each one who makes a claim is eligible for second adult rebate so long as either: CTBR 55(d)

- all the joint occupiers are 'disregarded persons'; or
- all but one of the joint occupiers are 'disregarded persons'.

8.19 This rule typically applies to joint owners and joint tenants. For example, if two sisters jointly own their home (and they have a second adult), each of them is eligible for second adult rebate so long as at least one of them is a 'disregarded person' (para. 8.8). Or if three single people jointly rent their home (and they have a second adult), each of them is eligible for second adult rebate so long as at least two of them are 'disregarded persons'.

8.20 In all such cases, each joint occupier who makes a claim qualifies for his or her share of the total amount of second adult rebate. This share must always be equal between all the joint occupiers, including any who are students. CTBR 54(2),(3)

Second adult rebate

8.21 Having established that the claimant is eligible for second adult rebate, the authority needs the following information in order to calculate the amount on a weekly basis:

- the claimant's weekly eligible council tax liability (para. 8.23); and
- details of the second adult's income or, if the claimant has more than one second adult, details of all the second adults' incomes (paras. 8.24 onwards).

8.22 As shown in table 8.3, the amount of second adult rebate may be 25 per cent, 15 per cent or 7½ per cent of the claimant's weekly eligible council tax – depending on the income of the second adult(s). No matter how many second adults a claimant has, the claimant can only get one amount of second adult rebate.

8.23 The amount of a claimant's eligible council tax liability is described in chapter 9. Paragraph 7.42 explains how to convert council tax figures to a weekly amount. Examples of the calculations follow. The last example illustrates how a 25 per cent discount is dealt with in calculations. The example at the end of this chapter illustrates the calculation of second adult rebate for joint occupiers.

Table 8.3: The amount of second adult rebate

CTBR 2(3A), 54(1)
sch 2 para 1(1),(2)

FOR CLAIMANTS WITH ONE SECOND ADULT

If the second adult is on JSA(IB)*, IS or pension credit	25%
If the second adult is not on those benefits and his or her gross income ** is:	
under £144.00 per week	15%
between £144.00 and £185.99 per week	7½%
£186.00 per week or more	nil

FOR CLAIMANTS WITH TWO OR MORE SECOND ADULTS

If all the second adults are on JSA(IB)*, IS or pension credit	25%
If at least one of the second adults is not on those benefits and the combined gross income of all the second adults *** is:	
under £144.00 per week	15%
between £144.00 and £185.99 per week	7½%
£186.00 per week or more	nil

Notes

* For these purposes a person counts as receiving JSA(IB) if he or she is entitled to JSA(IB) but not receiving it because of a sanction, or in the 'waiting days' before JSA(IB) starts (or would start apart from a sanction).

** If the second adult has a partner, the partner's gross income is added in.

*** For each second adult who has a partner, the partner's gross income is added in. But if any of the second adults is on JSA(IB), IS or pension credit (or has a partner who is), then his or her income (and any partner's) is disregarded.

ASSESSING SECOND ADULTS' GROSS INCOME

8.24 To calculate the amount of second adult rebate (table 8.3), it is necessary to assess the gross income of any second adult who is not on JSA(IB), IS or pension credit (or treated as receiving JSA(IB): table 8.3). If the second adult has a partner, the partner's income is added in with the second adult's income (even if the partner is a 'disregarded person' and so could not be a second adult in his or her own right). If the gross income is £186.00 per week or more, the claimant does not qualify for second adult rebate. CTBR sch 2 paras 2,3

Examples: Calculating second adult rebate

SINGLE CLAIMANT WITH SECOND ADULT ON JSA(IB)

A single claimant is the only person liable for council tax on his home. The only person living with him is his adult daughter, who is on JSA(IB). Neither the claimant nor his daughter is a 'disregarded person'. His eligible council tax liability is £20.00 per week.

Eligible for second adult rebate?

As a single claimant, he is eligible for second adult rebate because:

- he has a second adult living with him (his daughter); and
- he does not receive rent from a boarder or (sub-)tenant.

Amount of second adult rebate

His daughter is on JSA(IB) so the weekly amount is:

25% of weekly eligible council tax (25% x £20.00)	£5.00

COUPLE WITH TWO SECOND ADULTS

A couple are the only people liable for council tax on their home. The only people living with them are their two adult sons. One son is on JSA(IB). The other son is working and his gross pay is £133 per week. He also has savings which generate a weekly gross interest of £5 per week. One partner in the couple is a full-time mature university student. The other partner and the sons are not 'disregarded persons'. The couple's eligible council tax liability is £24.00 per week.

Eligible for second adult rebate?

As a couple, they are eligible for second adult rebate because:

- they have at least one second adult living with them. In fact they have two second adults (the sons); and
- they do not receive rent from a boarder or (sub-)tenant; and
- at least one of the couple is a 'disregarded person' (the student).

Amount of second adult rebate

If there is more than one second adult, their gross incomes are combined. But in this case the income of the son on JSA(IB) is disregarded. So only the other son's income counts. That son's gross weekly income is £133 (from the job) plus £5 (interest), which amounts to £138, so the weekly amount of second adult rebate is:

15% of weekly eligible council tax (15% x £24.00) £3.60

DISCOUNT PLUS SECOND ADULT REBATE

A single woman is the only person liable for council tax on her home. The only other person living with her is her father, who is on income support. The woman is a carer who counts as a 'disregarded person'. Her father is not a 'disregarded person'. The council tax for the dwelling (before any discount is granted) is £730 per year – which is £14 per week.

Discount

When calculating council tax discounts, 'disregarded persons' are ignored (appendix 6). So for discount purposes, this dwelling has one resident. The woman qualifies for a 25% discount which, on a weekly basis, is:

25% of the weekly amount for the dwelling (25% x £14.00) £3.50

Eligible for second adult rebate?

As a single claimant her own circumstances are immaterial. She is eligible for second adult rebate because:

- she has a second adult living with her (her father); and
- she does not receive rent from a boarder or (sub-)tenant.

Amount of second adult rebate

Her father is on income support so she qualifies for second adult rebate of 25% of her weekly eligible council tax. This means 25% of liability for council tax before the discount is subtracted, which is:

25% of weekly eligible council tax (25% x £14.00) £3.50

She qualifies for both the discount and the second adult rebate, the total of the two being £7.00 per week.

Better buy

It turns out in this particular case that, because of her own low income, the woman qualifies for main CTB of £4.00 per week. Since her main CTB is greater than her second adult rebate, she gets only her main CTB. The final result is that she qualifies for main CTB of £4.00 plus the discount of £3.50, so in total her council tax bill is reduced by £7.50 per week.

8.25 If a claimant has more than one second adult, it is necessary to combine the income of all of them, apart from any who are on income support or JSA(IB) (or treated as receiving JSA(IB): table 8.3) – adding in the income of the partner of each second adult. Once it is clear that the gross income of some of them has reached £186 per week, there is no need to go any further (because of course it is impossible that the gross income of all of them would be lower).

8.26 It is gross, not net, income which is relevant, and it is calculated in exactly the same way as a non-dependant's income is calculated for the purposes of main CTB, as outlined in paragraphs 7.26-27. However, the DWP points out (GM para. B3.101) that the authority may adopt a 'local scheme' (para. 22.10) whereby a second adult's income from a war disablement, war widow's or war widower's pension is wholly or partly disregarded. The authority is entitled to require the same level of evidence, proof, etc, as when it assesses a claimant's income (para. 5.37).

8.27 Providing details of second adults' income (and that of their partners) can pose several difficulties for claimants. They may not be able to obtain these details, or may not wish to ask. However, if the authority does not know how much the gross income is, it cannot award a second adult rebate.

DISCRETIONARY HOUSING PAYMENTS

8.28 If a claimant qualifies for second adult rebate no discretionary housing payment (para. 22.2) may be awarded.

The 'better buy'

8.29 A claimant cannot be awarded both main CTB and second adult rebate at the same time. Deciding which one the claimant is actually awarded is often called a 'better buy' comparison. As indicated in table 8.1: CBA 131(9)

- a claimant who only qualifies for main CTB is awarded that;
- a claimant who only qualifies for second adult rebate is awarded that;
- a claimant who qualifies for both is awarded whichever of the two is higher or, if the two are the same, main CTB. This is decided entirely according to the amounts themselves and entirely by the authority. A claimant cannot choose to have the lower figure.

Some examples of the better buy calculation are given below.

JOINT OCCUPIERS AND THE BETTER BUY

8.30 If a dwelling has two or more joint occupiers and one or more of them claims CTB, each joint occupier's entitlement to main CTB and second adult rebate is assessed separately, and the better buy comparison is done separately for each joint occupier. This can mean that one joint occupier is awarded main CTB, another second adult rebate. The second of the examples below illustrates this. CBA 131(9) CTBR 54(2),(3)

A RULE OF THUMB

8.31 If a claimant qualifies for a large amount of main CTB, it is unlikely that he or she will qualify for a larger amount of second adult rebate. As a rule of thumb, this is the case if the claimant's main CTB meets around 35 per cent or more of his or her council tax liability.

Example: Better buy

LONE PARENT WITH ONE NON-DEPENDANT/SECOND ADULT

A lone parent is the only person liable for the council tax on her home. She is not on income support and has excess income for main CTB purposes of £25.00. The only people living with her are her daughter of 15 and her son of 21. The son works 12 hours per week for a gross pay of £150 per week (and has no other income). Only the daughter (because of being under 18) is a 'disregarded person'. The lone parent's eligible council tax liability is £16.00 per week. Her circumstances means that she is eligible for second adult rebate (the son is her second adult) as well as main CTB (taking the son into account as a non-dependant).

Main CTB

Weekly eligible council tax	£16.00
minus non-dependant deduction for son (although the son's income is over £144 he is not in remunerative work, so the lowest deduction applies: table 7.3)	£2.30
minus 20% of excess income (20% x £25.00)	£5.00
equals weekly main CTB	£8.70

Second adult rebate

The level of the son's gross income means that the claimant qualifies for a 7½% second adult rebate:

weekly second adult rebate (7½% x £16.00)	£1.20

Better buy comparison

Her entitlement to main CTB is greater than her entitlement to second adult rebate, so she is awarded main CTB only.

Example: Better buy for joint occupiers

TWO JOINT HOME-OWNERS WITH ONE NON-DEPENDANT/SECOND ADULT

The only residents of a (d)well(ing) are three sisters, Elsie, Lacie and Tillie. Elsie and Lacie jointly own it, and are jointly liable for the council tax there. Tillie lives there rent-free. She is their non-dependant. The eligible council tax for the whole dwelling is £20.00 per week.

Elsie is a full-time university student (learning, as it happens, to draw) and is therefore a 'disregarded person'. She has capital of £20,000.

Lacie is working (as a treacle operative, in fact). She is not a 'disregarded person'. For main CTB purposes she has excess income of £30.00 (and capital under £3,000).

Tillie is on income support. She is not a 'disregarded person'. She is therefore a second adult.

Elsie's claim for CTB

Elsie is not eligible for main CTB – she has too much capital (and, in any case, most full-time students are not eligible for main CTB, though they are eligible for second adult rebate: para. 21.25).

Elsie is eligible for second adult rebate (para. 8.18). Tillie is on income support, so the second adult rebate for the whole dwelling is 25 per cent of the council tax. Because there are two joint occupiers, Elsie qualifies for half of this,

which is (½ of 25% x £20.00)	£2.50

Lacie's claim for CTB

Lacie is eligible for main CTB. Because there are two joint occupiers, it is worked out on half the council tax for the dwelling. Because Tillie is on income support, there is no non-dependant deduction for her.

Lacie's entitlement to main CTB is:

weekly eligible council tax (½ x £20.00)	£10.00
minus 20% of excess income (20% x £30.00)	£6.00
which is	£4.00

Lacie's entitlement to second adult rebate is the same as Elsie's,

which is (½ of 25% x £20.00)	£2.50

Better buy comparisons

Elsie: No better buy comparison is required.

She is awarded second adult rebate of	£2.50

Lacie: A better buy comparison is required.

Her main CTB (£4.00) is greater than her second adult rebate (£2.50).

She is awarded main CTB of	£4.00
The total weekly CTB awarded on the dwelling is therefore	£6.50

9 Eligible council tax

9.1 CTB is worked out by reference to the claimant's 'eligible council tax'. This chapter, which applies only in England, Wales and Scotland, explains this term, and gives the details of how to work out eligible council tax in all cases. It covers:

- the council tax itself, and who has to pay it;
- the exemptions, disability reductions, discounts, etc. which can reduce or eliminate council tax liability;
- eligible council tax for the both main CTB and second adult rebate purposes.

COUNCIL TAX OVERVIEW

9.2 The council tax is the means by which local people help meet the cost of local public services. It is a tax on residential properties known as dwellings. Local councils, known in England and Wales as billing authorities and in Scotland as local authorities, are responsible for the billing and collection of the tax. (Scottish authorities are also responsible for collecting the council water charge.) Table 9.1 lists the key considerations that arise when considering council tax liability, etc. Fuller details of the council tax are in Martin Ward's *Council Tax Handbook* (5th edition, updated by Alan Murdie, Child Poverty Action Group, 2002), which covers many matters not included in this Guide (such as billing, payment, penalties, appeals, and so on).

Table 9.1: Council Tax: key considerations

- Which dwelling is being considered?
- What valuation band does it fall into?
- How much is the council tax for that band?
- Who is liable to pay the council tax there?
- Is the dwelling exempt from council tax altogether?
- Do they qualify for a disability reduction?
- Do they qualify for a discount?
- Do they qualify for main CTB or second adult rebate?
- Should the council use its power to reduce liability?

DWELLINGS AND VALUATION BANDS

9.3 One council tax bill is issued per dwelling, unless the dwelling is exempt (para. 9.11). A dwelling means a house, a flat, etc. whether lived in or not, and also houseboats and mobile homes that are used for domestic purposes.

9.4 The amount of tax depends first on which valuation band a dwelling has been allocated to, and this is shown on the bill. The lower the valuation band, the lower the tax. An amount for each band is fixed each year by the billing or local authority, and often includes amounts for other bodies (such as a county council, a parish council, the police, etc).

9.5 Dwellings are currently valued as at 1st April 1991, and there are currently eight valuation bands – band A to band H. In Wales a further valuation takes place as at 1st April 2005, and an additional band (band I) is added then. In England a further valuation takes place as at 1st April 2007, and the power exists for additional bands to be added then. Details for further valuations in Scotland are not known at the time of writing.

9.6 The valuation list holds current details of which band dwellings are in. In England and Wales it can be seen at either the local valuation office or the billing authority's main office or viewed on-line at the Valuation Office Agency's site, *www.voa.gov.uk*. In Scotland it may be seen at the local authority's main office.

WHO IS LIABLE TO PAY COUNCIL TAX?

9.7 Council tax is normally payable by someone resident in the dwelling (but there are also exceptions described in the next paragraph). A 'resident' is someone aged 18 or over, solely or mainly resident in the dwelling. Where there is more than one resident the liable person is the one with the greatest legal interest in the dwelling. So if a resident home-owner has a lodger, the home-owner is liable, not the lodger. If a resident council, housing association or private tenant has a lodger, the tenant is liable, not the lodger.

9.8 The most common exceptions to the above rule are that the owner (or other landlord) is liable for council tax on:

- a 'house in multiple occupation'. This means a house which was originally constructed or subsequently adapted for occupation by more than one household;
- many hostels and care homes; and
- unoccupied dwellings (unless they are exempt).

In other words, the residents (in the first two cases) are not liable, but many owners pass on the cost of paying the council tax (along with any other overheads) when fixing the rent.

JOINT LIABILITY

9.9 There are two ways in which joint liability (or 'joint and several liability') arises:

- if there is more than one resident with the greatest (or only) legal interest in the dwelling they are jointly liable for the council tax. For example two sisters who jointly own their home, or three friends who jointly rent their home, are jointly liable;
- if the liable person has a partner living with him or her, then the partner is jointly liable (even if he or she has no legal interest in the property). This applies to married and unmarried couples of opposite sexes and married and unmarried polygamous arrangements.

For exceptions see the next paragraph. For how jointly liable residents are dealt with in CTB, see paragraphs 9.26-30. There are further rules (not in this Guide) about joint liability for unoccupied properties.

STUDENTS AND PEOPLE WITH SEVERE MENTAL IMPAIRMENT

9.10 The exceptions to these rules on joint liability relate to severely mentally impaired persons and (since 1st April 2004) students. A person counts as 'severely mentally impaired' as described in category 13 in appendix 6; and as a student (for these purposes) as described in categories 5, 6 or 7 of that appendix. Such a person is not jointly liable if there is another resident with the same legal interest in the dwelling who is neither severely mentally impaired nor a student. See the next paragraph if they are all severely mentally impaired, or all students.

EXEMPTIONS

9.11 The following occupied dwellings are exempt from council tax:

- dwellings where all the residents are students, including in England and Wales where that dwelling is only occupied during term time;
- halls of residence mainly occupied by students;
- dwellings where all occupants who would otherwise be liable for the council tax are severely mentally impaired, including cases where the only other occupiers are students;
- dwellings occupied only by persons under 18 years of age;
- armed forces accommodation;
- in England and Wales only, annexes or similar self-contained parts of a property which are occupied by an elderly or disabled relative of the residents living in the rest of it; and
- in Scotland only, certain dwellings used as trial flats by registered housing associations for pensioners and disabled people.

Examples: Council tax liability, exemptions and discounts

Unless specifically stated none of the following are students, severely mentally impaired, etc.

A COUPLE WITH A LODGER

A couple live in a house which the man owns in his name only. They have children in their 20s living at home, and a lodger who rents a room and shares facilities.

The couple are jointly liable for the council tax, because the man is the resident with the greatest legal interest in the dwelling and the woman is jointly liable with him by being his partner. There is no reason to suppose they qualify for exemption, or a disability reduction or a discount.

A LONE PARENT

A lone parent owns her home and lives there with her three children, all under 18.

The lone parent is solely liable for the council tax, because she is the resident with the greatest legal interest in the dwelling. She is the only (adult) resident so she qualifies for a 25% discount.

THREE SHARERS

Three friends jointly rent a house (in other words all their names are on the tenancy agreement). No-one else lives with them.

They are all jointly liable for the council tax, because they all are residents with the greatest legal interest in the dwelling. There is no reason to suppose they qualify for exemption, or a disability reduction or a discount.

THE SHARERS' CIRCUMSTANCES CHANGE

One of the sharers leaves and is not replaced. One of the others becomes a full-time university student.

The remaining non-student resident is now the only liable person, and qualifies for a 25% discount because the student is disregarded when counting the residents.

9.12 Various unoccupied dwellings are also exempt. For example, an unoccupied dwelling which is substantially unfurnished is exempt for six months – and there are many other categories.

DISABILITY REDUCTIONS

9.13 The council tax bill is reduced if a dwelling has at least one resident and provides:

- an additional bathroom or kitchen for the use of the disabled person;
- a room, other than a bathroom, kitchen or toilet, used predominantly to meet the disabled person's special needs such as a downstairs room in a two storey house which has to be used as a bedroom by the disabled person; or
- sufficient floor space to enable the use of a wheelchair required by the disabled person within the dwelling.

9.14 In each case the authority must be satisfied that the facility in question is either essential, or of major importance, for the disabled person (who may be an adult or a child) in view of the nature and extent of the disability. Disability reductions are not limited to specially adapted properties.

9.15 The effect of the reduction is that the person is liable for the amount that would be due if his or her dwelling was in the next lowest valuation band (or in the case of a band A dwelling, one-sixth less than normal).

DISCOUNTS

9.16 The council tax bill is reduced if:

- there is only one resident in the dwelling. In this case the discount is always 25 per cent; or
- there are no residents in the dwelling (unless the dwelling is exempt). In this case the rules have changed from 1st April 2004. Depending on the circumstances, the discount can be 50% or any lower amount or even nil (in other words in some cases there is no discount).

9.17 When considering the number of people in the dwelling certain people including students, apprentices, carers, severely mentally impaired people and under-18-year-olds are disregarded. Appendix 6 describes the categories of person who are disregarded. A person can be disregarded for the purpose of awarding a discount but still liable to pay the tax.

OBTAINING AN EXEMPTION, DISABILITY REDUCTION OR DISCOUNT

9.18 An authority is expected to take reasonable steps to ascertain whether exemptions, disability reductions and discounts apply to the dwellings in its area. These can be awarded on the basis of information available to it, or someone can write requesting this. There is no time limit on obtaining exemptions, disability reductions or discounts, though the authority is entitled to seek appropriate evidence.

OTHER REASONS WHY LIABILITY MAY BE LOWER

9.19 In addition to the disability reductions and discounts mentioned above, some authorities offer a discount for prompt payment of the tax or the adoption of certain payment methods. In some areas council tax may be 'capped' by the government to a lower figure, and in a few areas there may be a 'transitional reduction' in liability because of recent re-organisation of authority boundaries. The following describes the final method of reducing liability in England only.

POWER TO REDUCE COUNCIL TAX LIABILITY

9.20 Since 18th November 2003, a new power has applied in England only enabling an authority to reduce any liability for council tax. This is a wide power (some would call it a discretion) which permits the authority to reduce liability 'to such extent as it thinks fit' and 'includes power to reduce an amount to nil'. This can be done 'in relation to particular cases or by determining a class of case in which liability is to be reduced to an extent provided by the determination.'

9.21 This power exists under section 13A of the Local Government Finance Act 1992, as inserted by section 76 of the Local Government Act 2003 (itself brought into force by section 128(2) of the 2003 Act). No further rules are given about how to get such a reduction, so a person could write in and ask, or an authority could design its own rules without any such request. Similarly, no mention is made of any kind of appeals mechanism, though presumably these matters could be judicially reviewed.

IMPACT ON DISCRETIONARY HOUSING PAYMENTS

9.22 The existence of the above new power is separate from the power to make discretionary housing payments (para. 22.2). The government contributes to awards of DHPs, which can be granted only to people on HB/CTB. Neither of those points apply to the above new power.

Eligible council tax

9.23 A claimant's 'eligible council tax' is the figure used in calculating his or her entitlement to main CTB (para. 7.4) and/or second adult rebate (para. 8.23). The eligible council tax figure used in calculating main CTB can differ from that used in calculating second adult rebate, as mentioned in the appropriate places below. An example is at the end of the chapter.

9.24 A claimant's weekly eligible council tax is calculated by working through the following steps: CTBR 51(1),(2), 54(1), sch 2 para 1(2)

1. Start with the council tax due on his or her home.
2. If the claimant is entitled to a disability reduction, use the council tax figure after that reduction has been made.

3. If the claimant is entitled to a discount, use the council tax figure after that discount has been made.
4. Apportion the result if the claimant is a joint occupier (see below).
5. Convert it to a weekly figure (as described in para. 7.39).

9.25 All the above steps apply when calculating eligible council tax for main CTB purposes. But steps 3 and 4 are omitted when calculating eligible council tax for second adult rebate purposes (see para. 9.30). See also paragraph 9.31 about other items which can affect a council tax bill.

APPORTIONMENT FOR JOINT OCCUPIERS

CTBR 51(3),(4) **9.26** A joint occupier is one of two or more people who are jointly liable to pay the council tax on a dwelling, other than just a couple or polygamous arrangement. In such cases, the figures used in calculating eligible council tax are apportioned between the joint occupiers for main CTB purposes (but not second adult rebate: para. 9.30).

9.27 This apportionment is found by dividing the total council tax liability by the number of people who are jointly liable.

9.28 If amongst several jointly liable people some are a couple or polygamous marriage, the law is unclear. The DWP advises (GM para. B2.36) that if there are three jointly liable people, two of whom are a couple, then the couple are eligible for main CTB on two-thirds of the council tax liability and the other person on one-third.

9.29 It is also worth noting here that, in most cases, students and people who are severely mentally impaired are not jointly liable for council tax (para. 9.10) so the apportionment ignores them.

VARIATIONS WHEN CALCULATING SECOND ADULT REBATE

CTBR 52(2),(3), 54(1), sch 2 para 1(2) **9.30** As mentioned earlier, there are two differences in the rules for calculating eligible council tax for second adult rebate purposes:

- Step 3 in paragraph 9.24 does not apply. In other words, a claimant's eligible council tax is calculated as though he or she did not qualify for any council tax discount. This is mainly for mathematical reasons. As illustrated in the following example, a claimant who qualifies for a discount does not lose it (and see also para. 8.23).
- Step 4 in paragraph 9.24 does not apply. In other words, there is no apportionment between joint occupiers. Instead, the apportionment will be done after the calculation of second adult rebate is otherwise complete (as described in para. 8.20).

OTHER ITEMS AFFECTING ELIGIBLE COUNCIL TAX

9.31 The following additional rules apply to main CTB and also to second adult rebate: CTBR 51(2)

- in the case of an authority which offers discounts against its council taxes for people who pay in a lump sum or by a method other than cash (e.g. direct debit), CTB is calculated on liability before those discounts are subtracted;
- if lower council taxes are set as a result of council tax 'capping' procedures, these apply from the beginning of the financial year, and CTB is worked out (throughout the financial year) on the lower amount;
- if a council tax bill is increased to recover an earlier overpayment of CTB or of community charge benefit, CTB is calculated before those amounts are added; and
- if a penalty is added to a council tax bill, CTB is calculated as if that penalty was not included.

ABOLITION OF CTB RESTRICTIONS

9.32 From 1st April 2004, there is no restriction on eligible CTB for people in higher band dwellings. In previous years, with exceptions, if a claimant's dwelling fell in valuation band F, G or H, his or her eligible council tax was restricted to the amount for a dwelling in band E. Details are in the 2003-04 edition of this Guide.

Example: Eligible council tax

THE CLAIMANT AND HIS HOUSEHOLD

A claimant's dwelling falls in band D, which in his area is £900 per year. With him lives only his cousin (as his non-dependant). The claimant is a full-time student with income from several sources, including a grant towards his disablement needs. His cousin is on income support. The claimant qualifies for:

- a disability reduction, because he has a large enough house to use his wheelchair indoors. This is worth £100 per year; and
- a 25% council tax discount, because he is a full-time student, so there is only one countable resident in his home, his daughter. This is worth £200 per year.

ELIGIBLE COUNCIL TAX FOR MAIN CTB

In calculating main CTB his eligible council tax is the figure obtained by deducting both the disability reduction and the discount from the amount for the dwelling. This is (£900 – £100 – £200 =) £600, the weekly equivalent of which is (to the nearest penny) £11.51.

It turns out, though, when the authority assesses his entitlement to main CTB, that he does not qualify because he has too much capital.

ELIGIBLE COUNCIL TAX FOR SECOND ADULT REBATE

In calculating second adult rebate his eligible council tax is the figure obtained by deducting the disability reduction from the amount for the dwelling but not the discount (para. 9.30). This is (£900 – £100 =) £800, the weekly equivalent of which is (to the nearest penny) £15.34.

Because his cousin is on income support, he qualifies for second adult rebate equal to 25% of the last figure (table 8.3). This is (to the nearest penny) £3.84. On an annual basis this is £200.

HIS RESULTING LIABILITY FOR COUNCIL TAX

The following are the annual figures:

The council tax for the dwelling is	£900
He is granted his disability reduction of	– £100
He is granted his discount of	– £200
He is granted second adult rebate of	– £200
So his resulting liability is	= £400

10 Eligible rent

10.1 HB is worked out by reference to the claimant's 'eligible rent'. This chapter explains this term, and gives the details of how to work out 'eligible rent' in all cases. It covers:

- what counts as 'rent' for HB purposes and how this differs from 'eligible rent';
- eligible rent for council (and in Northern Ireland, NIHE) tenants;
- eligible rent for housing association tenants;
- eligible rent for private tenants under the 'New Scheme' (also sometimes known as 'maximum rent' in these cases);
- eligible rent for private tenants under the 'Old Scheme';
- eligible rent for registered rent cases;
- eligible rent for other cases; and
- which service charges are eligible to be met through HB.

The chapter does not apply to certain claims in the pathfinder areas to which the local housing allowance applies (para. 22.22 and table 22.1).

MARGINAL REFERENCES IN THIS CHAPTER

SI 1995 No 1644
NISR 1996 No 111
SI 1996 No 965
NISR 1996 No 181

10.2 A general description of how marginal references work in this guide is in paragraphs 1.63-66 and table 1.2. Additionally, in this chapter only:

- 'HBR 10' and 'HBR 11' are to regulations 10 and 11 of the Housing Benefit (General) Regulations SI 1987 no. 1971 as they currently apply – i.e. as they apply to 'New Scheme' cases;
- 'HBR Old 10', 'HBR Old 11' and 'HBR Old 12' are to regulations 10 to 12 of those regulations as they stood immediately before 2nd January 1996 – i.e. as they continue to apply to 'Old Scheme' cases;
- in the section about service charges (paras. 10.75 onwards), references to 'HBR 10' and 'HBR 11' should be regarded as including references to 'HBR Old 10' and 'HBR Old 11'.

'Rent' and 'eligible rent'

'RENT'

HBR 8(1), 10(1)

10.3 The term 'rent' has various meanings in different branches of the law. As far as HB is concerned, all the types of payment shown in table 10.1 count as rent.

In this chapter, the term 'actual rent' is used to mean the total of all the payments shown in that table which a claimant is liable to pay on his or her normal home.

10.4 Charges for services are also included in the legal definition of 'rent' for HB purposes. This does not means that HB will necessarily pay for them (paras. 10.75 onwards). Note that certain categories of claimant and certain types of dwelling are not eligible for HB even where the claimant is liable for rent (paras. 2.11 onwards); that some housing costs which do not count as rent for HB purposes can be met through income support or income-based jobseeker's allowance (para. 2.22); and that further rules apply in relation to increases to cover arrears of rent; to garages and land; and to business premises (paras. 10.106-108).

Table 10.1: Payments counted as rent for HB purposes

- Rent in its ordinary sense, whether under a tenancy or licence, including board and lodging payments and payments for 'use and occupation'.
- 'Mesne profits' in England, Wales and Northern Ireland or 'violent profits' in Scotland (paid after a tenancy or right to occupy is terminated).
- Houseboat mooring charges and berthing fees and caravan and mobile home site charges (even if owned by the claimant, and in addition to rental if not owned).
- Payments made by residents of charitable almshouses.
- Payments under rental purchase agreements.
- Payments for crofts and croft land in Scotland.

'ELIGIBLE RENT'

10.5 A claimant's 'eligible rent' is the figure used in calculating his or her entitlement to HB (para. 7.4). It could be exactly equal to his or her actual rent (this happens in some council tenant cases, for example), but often it is different. The three main reasons for this are: HBR 10(3)

- many service charges cannot be met by HB: for example water charges, meals and most fuel (and, in Northern Ireland, any rates element included in the rent must be identified: chapter 11);
- in the case of much privately rented accommodation (and some housing association and similar accommodation), the rent officer's or NIHE's valuations are used to work out the eligible rent rather than the landlord's figures;

- in some cases the eligible rent may be restricted to a lower figure.

This chapter explains all the rules about working out 'eligible rent'. A summary of the main points may be found in tables 10.3 and 10.4.

APPORTIONMENT FOR JOINT OCCUPIERS

HBR 10(5) **10.6** In the case of a claimant who is a joint occupier (para. 4.24), many of the figures used in calculating eligible rent are apportioned between the joint occupiers. In doing this, the authority must determine how much of the actual rent on the dwelling is fairly attributable to each of the joint occupiers, taking into account the number of people paying towards the rent, the proportion of rent paid by each, and any relevant other circumstances – such as the size and number of rooms each occupies, and whether there is any written or other agreement between them. The authority must then apportion the figures used in calculating the claimant's eligible rent on the same basis. Unlike CTB (para. 9.29), the rent is apportioned amongst all of the joint occupiers even if one of them (or more than one) is a student, a rule confirmed by the Court of Appeal *(Naghshbandi v LB Camden and the Secretary of State for Work and Pensions)*.

In CH/3376/2002, the commissioner dealt with a case where there were two joint tenants, one of whom was absent. He held that the proportion of rent paid is not necessarily the predominant factor (though in appropriate cases it can be), and apportioned the whole of the rent to the tenant who was present, taking account of a wide range of personal factors including his age, health, sick mother, local connections, attempts to ameliorate the situation and lack of control over the other tenant's (his step-son's) failure to pay the rent and whether it was appropriate to expect the claimant to seek alternative accommodation. The example illustrates a similar situation.

Example: Joint occupiers

TOM, DICK AND HARRY

Three unrelated friends in their thirties, Tom, Dick and Harry, jointly rent a two-bedroom housing association house, where the rent for the whole house is £150 per week (and this does not include any service charges). Dick and Harry have a bedroom. Tom uses the living room as a bedroom. They share the kitchen and all other facilities. They have each contributed one-third of the rent in the past. Harry loses his job and claims HB, saying that his share remains one-third.

Harry's eligible rent is very likely to be regarded as £50 per week. It is possible that a fairer split would be something other than one-third each, but unlikely based on the information given.

TOM MOVES OUT

Tom moves out. He is not replaced. Dick and Harry keep their own bedrooms and begin to share the living room. They agree between them that they should contribute equally to the rent.

Harry's eligible rent is now very likely to be regarded as £75 per week – unless the authority considers that the new rent is unreasonable and has the power to restrict it (as described in later parts of this chapter).

Definitions

'OLD SCHEME' CASES *versus* 'NEW SCHEME' CASES

10.7 Especially in the private rented sector, the amount of a claimant's eligible rent depends very much on whether his or her case falls within the 'Old Scheme' or the 'New Scheme'. (Strictly speaking, the distinction applies to all types of HB case – including council tenants, NIHE tenants and housing association tenants – but the greatest impact is on private sector tenants.) 'Old Scheme' and 'New Scheme' are defined below. In broad terms, all claimants who have been on HB since before 2nd January 1996 (and some claimants who have more recently taken over an HB claim from someone who has been on HB since before then) fall within the 'Old Scheme'. So do claimants in certain kinds of accommodation where care, support or supervision is provided.

SI 1995 No. 1644 Reg 10
NISR 1996 No. 111 Reg 16

10.8 Terminology varies widely across the country. 'Old Scheme Cases' are also known as 'Old Regulation 11 Cases', 'Old Cases' or 'Exempt Cases' (because they were exempt from the January 1996 changes). 'New Scheme Cases' are also known as 'New Regulation 11 Cases', 'New Cases' or 'Non-exempt cases'.

10.9 As described below, a person falls within the Old Scheme if he or she:

- is (personally) an 'exempt claimant'; or
- has had exemption transferred to him or her; or
- is claiming HB in respect of 'exempt accommodation'.

Otherwise, he or she falls within the New Scheme.

'EXEMPT CLAIMANTS'

10.10 A claimant is an 'exempt claimant' (and therefore falls within the 'Old Scheme') if he or she:

SI 1995 No. 1644
NISR 1996 No. 111

- was 'entitled to' HB on Monday 1st January 1996 in Great Britain or Monday 1st April 1996 in Northern Ireland; and

- has remained 'entitled to and in receipt of' HB continuously since that date (disregarding breaks in HB entitlement/receipt of up to 52 weeks in the case of a 'welfare to work beneficiary': table 13.3; or in any case disregarding breaks of four weeks or less); and
- has not moved home since that date, or has moved only because a fire, flood, explosion or natural catastrophe made his or her former home uninhabitable.

10.11 Note that, without there being any apparent reason for it, the above rules are different from rules protecting people against other changes (e.g. para. 10.31).

TRANSFERRING EXEMPTION: DEATH, DEPARTURE AND DETENTION

SI 1995 No. 1644 Reg 10 NISR 1996 No. 111 Reg 16

10.12 Exemption is transferred in the following three ways from one claimant ('A') to another claimant ('B') (who therefore falls within the 'Old Scheme'). 'Partner' and 'member of the household' have their specific HB meanings (paras. 4.3 onwards):

- A dies; and B was (until then) his or her partner or any other member of the household;
- A leaves the dwelling; and B was (until then) his or her partner;
- A is 'detained in custody pending sentence upon conviction or under a sentence imposed by a court' (and is not entitled to HB under the rules about absences from home: chapter 3); and B is (or was until then) his or her partner.

10.13 Additionally, in all three cases:

- At the date of his or her death, departure or detention, A must be in receipt of HB (or a 'welfare to work beneficiary' – table 13.3 – who was in receipt of HB no more than 52 weeks previously);
- B must occupy the dwelling as a home on that date (or be treated as occupying it: para. 3.3 onwards);
- B's claim for HB must be made within four weeks of that date (or back-dated to fall within those four weeks: paras. 5.89 and 5.93);
- B's claim is then treated as having been made on that date;
- B then continues to be exempt for as long as he or she:
    - remains 'entitled to and in receipt of' HB continuously (disregarding breaks in HB entitlement/receipt of up to 52 weeks in the case of a 'welfare to work beneficiary': table 13.3; or in any case disregarding breaks of four weeks or less): this includes renewal claims so long

as they run continuously or are backdated to run continuously (disregarding breaks as just mentioned), and

- does not move to occupy a new dwelling as his or her home, or moves only because a fire, flood, explosion or natural catastrophe makes his or her home uninhabitable;

◆ B's exemption is then transferred to any other claimant in the same way as described above (para. 10.12). There is no limit to the number of transfers of exemption so long as the above conditions are complied with in each case.

Example: Old Scheme cases: exempt claimants and transferring exemption

(1) Mrs Sawable is a part-time magician's assistant. She is in receipt of HB, on behalf of herself and her husband, on 1st January 1996.

So she is an exempt claimant from 2nd January 1996.

(2) Her HB claim becomes due for renewal on various dates over the next few years. She renews it on time in each case, so there is no break in her entitlement to HB.

So she continues to be an exempt claimant.

(3) Mrs Sawable (still on HB) dies in May 2004, due to an accident at work. Mr Sawable makes a claim for HB within four weeks of her death.

So, because of the rules about 'transferred exemption', he is an exempt claimant.

'EXEMPT ACCOMMODATION'

10.14 Any claimant in 'exempt accommodation' falls within the 'Old Scheme', no matter when his or her claim for HB is made. 'Exempt accommodation' is: SI 1995 No. 1644 NISR 1996 No. 111

◆ any accommodation 'provided by':
  - a housing association, whether registered or unregistered,
  - a registered charity,
  - a non-profit-making voluntary organisation,
  - a non-metropolitan county council, or
  - any other registered social landlord,

where (in each of the cases) 'that body or a person acting on its behalf also provides the claimant with care, support or supervision'; or

- in Great Britain only, any resettlement place provided by a local authority or non-profit-making voluntary organisation.

10.15 For the purposes of the first type of exempt accommodation, there is no definition of 'care', 'support' or 'supervision': these terms take their ordinary English meanings and are open to appeal (chapter 19). Also, what it means for accommodation to be 'provided by' the body concerned is open to debate, though it is not restricted to cases where the claimant pays rent to that body. (For example, if a registered charity makes arrangements with a private landlord to use accommodation owned by him for its clients, and the landlord collects the rent but the charity retains the right to say who will live in the accommodation, it may be argued that the accommodation is 'provided by' the charity.)

'REGISTERED RENT CASE'

HBRGB sch 1A paras 5-9 NIHBR sch 1B, para 4

10.16 'Registered rent case' is not a term used in the law. It is used in this guide to mean all pre-January 1989 tenancies in Great Britain, and most pre-October 1978 tenancies in Northern Ireland, which are still subject to the Rent Acts whether or not the rent has been registered (i.e. fixed) by the rent officer. (The Rent Acts were the Acts that governed landlord and tenant law at that time and people who have had the same tenancy since then still fall within those Acts.)

'HOUSING ASSOCIATION' AND 'REGISTERED HOUSING ASSOCIATION'

HBR 2(1)

10.17 For HB purposes, a 'housing association' means the same as in section 1(1) of the Housing Associations Act 1985 or, in Northern Ireland, article 114 of the Housing (Northern Ireland) Order 1981 No.156 as amended by SI 1986 No.1035. These define a housing association as a society, body of trustees, or company:

- whose objects or powers include the power to provide, manage, construct or improve housing; and
- which does not trade for profit or, if it does, is limited by its constitution not to pay interest or dividends above a limit (currently 5%) set by the Treasury or, in Northern Ireland, the Department of Finance and Personnel.

A 'housing association' may (or may not) also be a charity, registered with the Charity Commissioners.

HBR 12A(8) NIHBR 12A(5)

10.18 For HB purposes, a 'registered housing association' means a housing association which is registered with the Housing Corporation (in England), Welsh Assembly (in Wales), Communities Scotland (in Scotland) or the Department for Social Development (in Northern Ireland). In Great Britain (but not Northern Ireland) associations so registered are also known as registered social landlords.

'HAMA' AND 'HAL' SCHEMES

10.19 Housing Associations sometimes act as managing agents for private landlords: these are known as 'HAMA' schemes (Housing Associations as Managing Agents). In these cases the Housing Association is not the landlord so claims from rent-payers in such accommodation count as private tenant cases (paras. 10.31 onwards).

HBR 11(3B)
HBRGB sch 1A para 3
NIHBR sch 1B para 3
SI 1995 No. 1644
NISR 1996 No. 111

10.20 Sometimes housing associations also lease accommodation from private landlords and in turn rent it out to tenants: these are known as 'HAL' schemes (Housing Association Leasing). In these cases the housing association is the tenant's landlord so claims from rent-payers in such accommodation count as housing association cases (paras. 10.25 onwards).

Eligible rent for council and NIHE tenants

10.21 The eligible rent of a council tenant (or in Northern Ireland a tenant of the NIHE) is simply:

HBR 10(3)

- the actual rent;
- minus amounts for service charges which are ineligible for HB (paras. 10.75 onwards).

10.22 This applies in all rent rebate cases (para. 1.11): it applies whether it is the claimant or a partner (or both) who rents from the council. (Different rules apply to people renting from county councils: paras. 10.71.)

10.23 In all these cases:

- non-weekly rents need to be converted to a weekly figure (para. 7.39);
- adjustments must be made in the case of joint occupiers (para. 10.6);
- it is always the authority (not, say, the rent officer) which determines how much the eligible rent is and deals with all matters relating to service charges.

10.24 In theory at least, it is possible for the authority to reduce the eligible rent below the figure described above, depending on whether the case falls within the Old Scheme or New Scheme (para. 10.7). For an Old Scheme case, the same rules and protections apply as for a private sector Old Scheme case (para. 10.51). For a New Scheme case, the general power in paragraph 10.48 applies. In practice, council tenants' eligible rents are rarely if ever restricted, though the Court of Appeal has recognised this as a possibility *(Burton v Camden London Borough Council)*.

HBR 10(6B)
HBR Old 11

> **Example: Eligible rent for a council tenant**
>
> A claimant rents a council flat. His actual rent is £50 per week. This figure includes £3 per week for the cleaning and lighting of communal areas and £1 per week for use of the communal TV aerial.
>
> His eligible rent is calculated as follows. The charge for the communal areas is eligible for HB. However, the TV aerial is not eligible, so this has to be deducted from his actual rent to find his eligible rent. His eligible rent is therefore £49 per week.

Eligible rent for housing association and stock transfer tenants

HBR 2(1) **10.25** The eligible rent of a housing association tenant, or former public sector tenant whose property has since been transferred to a new landlord, depends first on whether the claimant falls within the Old Scheme or the New Scheme (para. 10.7). This applies in all cases in which the landlord is a housing association (para. 10.17), whether or not the housing association is a registered housing association, or registered social landlord: it applies whether it is the claimant or a partner (or both) who rents from them. The rules on rent officer (or NIHE) referrals for New Scheme cases for stock transfer property are similar to but slightly more generous than the rules for referring registered housing association New Scheme cases (para. 10.29). The circumstances in which the rent is referred for both these types of landlord in New Scheme cases are dealt with in table 10.2, and further rules are then given in paragraphs 10.28-30. The rules for housing association and stock transfer property Old Scheme cases are given in paragraph 10.27. Note that property of both registered and unregistered housing associations, including transferred stock, counts as Old Scheme if 'care, support or supervision is provided' (paras. 10.14-15).

NIHBR sch 1B paras 1,3,5 **10.26** There are some drafting problems with the law in Northern Ireland which can be interpreted as meaning that all housing association tenants (without exception) should be treated as 'registered rent cases'. It is assumed that this is not the intention of those who drafted the law and that this error will if necessary be corrected.

OLD SCHEME CASES

HBR Old 11 **10.27** In Old Scheme cases (regardless of whether the landlord is a registered or unregistered housing association or stock transfer or not), the claimant's eligible rent is worked out in the same way as for a private sector Old Scheme case (para. 10.51). For example:

- the authority could restrict the eligible rent on grounds of unreasonableness (but must have comparables demonstrating this and cannot rely on figures provided by the rent officer);
- however, there are rules preventing all or part of such a restriction in the case of certain protected groups.

NEW SCHEME CASES

10.28 In New Scheme cases, everything depends on whether the authority refers the rent to the rent officer on the grounds that it considers the rent or size to be unreasonable (table 6.1). In Northern Ireland, if the Housing Executive considers the rent or size unreasonable it is obliged to apply the rent restriction rules in the same way that rent officers do in Great Britain. The circumstances in which the rent is referred for all New Scheme housing association and stock transfer cases are shown in table 10.2. Note that in Great Britain (and possibly Northern Ireland: para. 10.26) the concessions on automatic referrals in New Scheme cases only apply to stock transfer tenants and tenants of registered housing association, not unregistered housing associations (paras. 10.17-18).

HBR 2(1), 10(3), sch 1A para 3
NIHBR sch 1B para 3

10.29 If the authority docs make a referral to the rent officer, the claimant's eligible rent is worked out in the same way as for a private sector New Scheme case (para. 10.33). For example:

HBR 11(1)
HBRGB 12A
NIHBR 10A

- the rent officer's figures are binding and a 'maximum rent' will apply – which often results in the eligible rent being restricted;
- however, there are rules preventing all or part of such a restriction in the case of certain protected groups.

10.30 If the authority does not make a referral to the rent officer, the claimant's rent is worked out in the same way as for a council tenant (para. 10.21) – but the resulting eligible rent cannot be restricted in any way (because if the authority considers the rent to be unreasonable, it must refer the rent to the rent officer – table 6.1 – and the previous paragraph will then apply).

HBR 10(3)

Eligible rent for private tenants

10.31 There are two main ways of working out a private tenant's eligible rent, depending on whether the claimant falls within the New Scheme or the Old Scheme (as defined in paras. 10.7-15). Rules for those two types of cases are dealt with in turn below, and are followed by some further rules which apply in registered rent cases and other special cases.

10.32 This applies in all cases in which the landlord is a private individual or company: it applies whether it is the claimant or a partner (or both) who rents from them.

Eligible rent for New Scheme private sector cases

HBR 11(1)
HBRGB 12A
NIHBR sch 1A

10.33 In New Scheme private sector cases (para. 10.31), the claimant's eligible rent is always the 'maximum rent' applying in his or her case (as described in the following paragraphs), unless:

- the claimant and/or other occupiers could formerly afford the accommodation (para. 10.38); or
- the claimant has had a bereavement (para. 10.41); or
- the claimant's rent details change during his or her benefit period (para. 10.45); or
- the authority reduces the eligible rent to below the maximum rent in certain cases (para. 10.48); or
- the claimant has a registered rent (para. 10.67).

Table 10.2: Eligible rent: concessions for housing associations and stock transfer landlords

HBR 2(1), 11(3B)
HBRGB 12(8),
sch 1A paras 3, 11A
NIHBR 12(5),
sch 1B paras 3,6
SI 1995 No. 1644
NISR 1996 No. 111

NEW SCHEME CASES: STOCK TRANSFER LANDLORDS IN ENGLAND, WALES AND NORTHERN IRELAND

(a) All former local authority or NIHE stock where the transfer took place on or after 7 October 2002 (whether or not transferred to a housing association).

- These properties can only have their rents referred if there has been a rent increase since the transfer took place and the authority considers that the rent is unreasonably high (but not if it considers the property unreasonably large).

(b) All former local authority, new town or NIHE stock where the transfer took place before 7 October 2002 (whether or not transferred to a housing association).

- These properties can only have their rents referred if there has been a rent increase since the transfer took place and the authority considers that either: the rent is unreasonably high; or the accommodation is unreasonably large (table 6.1).

NEW SCHEME CASES: STOCK TRANSFER LANDLORDS AND SCOTTISH HOMES PROPERTY IN SCOTLAND

(c) All former local authority, new town stock regardless of transfer date.

- The rules do not appear to give any specific concessions to Scottish stock transfers equivalent to the rest of the UK, although this omission was probably unintended. If this is the case then concessions would only apply if the new landlord is a housing association.

(d) Scottish Homes Residuary Body stock and former Scottish Homes property.

- Since April 2002 Scottish Homes tenants are paid by rent allowance so, unless their home has transferred to a housing association, it appears that their rents must be referred to the rent officer. This result was probably never unintended.

ALL HOUSING ASSOCIATION PROPERTY INCLUDING TRANSFERRED STOCK

(e) All housing association stock in Great Britain & NI*.

- In New Scheme Cases, except where the home is also stock transfer property in which case the appropriate rule above applies, tenants of registered housing associations can only have their rents referred to the rent officer (in NI to the NIHE for a rent decision*), if the authority considers that either the rent is unreasonably high or the accommodation is unreasonably large.
- The single room rent does apply to tenants of registered housing associations (para 6.12).
- Special rules about the timing of referrals apply to hostels where the accommodation is owned or managed by a registered housing association (para 6.9-6.10).
- Housing association property where 'care support or supervision' is provided is 'exempt accommodation' and is dealt with as an Old Scheme case. This applies whether the housing association is registered or unregistered. (para 10.17-18).

* Tenants of housing associations in NI see para 10.26.

MAXIMUM RENT: THE GENERAL RULE

HBR 2(1), 11

10.34 The claimant's 'maximum rent' is the lowest of the figures provided by the rent officer (chapter 6) in his or her case (or the only figure if the rent officer provides only one). But before deciding which is lowest, the figures must be adjusted in certain cases. Table 10.3 describes the rent officer's figures and shows how to calculate maximum rent.

10.35 There are two exceptions: different rules can apply to claims continuing from before 6th October 1997 (para. 10.36), and to lettings begun in or before January 1989 (para. 10.67).

MAXIMUM RENT: THE '50% TOP-UP' FOR CERTAIN OLDER CLAIMS

SI 1997 No. 852
SI 1997 No. 1975
SI 1999 No. 2734
NISR 1997 No. 170
NISR 1997 No. 377
NISR 1998 No. 416

10.36 As described in the next paragraph, the calculation of a claimant's maximum rent is different in the case of any claimant who meets the following conditions:

- the claimant was 'entitled to and in receipt of' HB on Sunday 5th October 1997; and
- the claimant has remained 'entitled to and in receipt of' HB continuously since that date (disregarding breaks of up to 52 weeks in the case of a 'welfare to work beneficiary': table 13.3; but in any other case with no breaks whatsoever): this includes renewal claims so long as they run continuously or are backdated to run continuously (disregarding breaks as just mentioned); and
- the claimant has not moved to occupy a new dwelling as his or her home since that date (regardless of the reason for the move); and
- the claimant has qualified for a '50% top-up' continuously since his or her first renewal claim beginning after that date; and
- the rent officer has provided a local reference rent in the claimant's case.

10.37 If a claimant meets all the above conditions, he or she must be considered for a 50% top-up, calculated by working through the following steps:

- Start with the rent officer's figures and make all the adjustments exactly as in steps 1 and 2 in table 10.3.
- The claimant's maximum rent is then the average of (i.e. half-way between) the local reference rent and the claim-related rent; unless the single room rent is lower than that, in which case the maximum rent is that single room rent.

Table 10.3: Calculating 'maximum rent' for New Scheme cases

1. START WITH THE RENT OFFICER'S FIGURES

The authority needs all the figures provided by the rent officer, which could be one or more of the following:

- a claim-related rent determination;
- a local reference rent determination;
- a single room rent determination (only in the case of a 'young individual': para. 6.12).

Convert these to a weekly figure at this stage (para. 7.39). Work through Step 2 separately for each figure.

2. ADJUSTMENTS MADE BY THE AUTHORITY *

(a) Deduction for meals

Deduct an amount for meals – but only if the claimant's actual rent includes meals. Use the amounts shown in table 10.6. There are two exceptions:

- do not deduct anything for meals in the case of the single room rent;
- do not deduct anything for meals in the case of the claim-related rent if the rent officer has notified the authority that it does not include meals.

(b) Apportionment for joint occupiers

If the claimant is a joint occupier, apportion the resulting figures (para. 10.6). Do not, however, apportion the single room rent.

3. CALCULATE MAXIMUM RENT

The claimant's 'maximum rent' is the lowest of the resulting figures (or if there is only one figure, it is that one).

* Note: No adjustment is made for water charges, fuel or any service charges other than those in this table: if those are included in the claimant's actual rent, the rent officer takes this into account when fixing his or her figures (chapter 6).

Examples: Calculating maximum rent

EXAMPLE ONE: A STRAIGHTFORWARD CASE

A private tenant over the age of 25 makes a first claim for HB. Her actual rent is £80 per week including water charges and fuel charges. She is not a joint occupier. The rent officer has provided the following figures:

- a claim-related rent determination of £70 per week;
- a local reference rent determination of £65 per week;
- no single room rent determination (because the claimant is not a 'young individual')

Because none of the adjustments in table 10.3 apply in this case, her maximum rent is simply the lower of the above two figures, i.e. £65 per week.

EXAMPLE TWO: A JOINT OCCUPIER AGED UNDER 25

A private tenant under the age of 25 makes a first claim for HB. He is a joint occupier with two others: they share their rent equally. The actual rent for the whole property is £180 per week including water charges and fuel charges. The rent officer has provided the following figures:

- a claim-related rent determination of £150 per week;
- a local reference rent determination of £135 per week;
- a single room rent determination of £42 per week.

The only adjustment in table 10.3 which applies is the apportionment for joint occupiers:

- the adjusted claim-related rent is (£150 ÷ 3 =) £50 per week;
- the adjusted local reference rent is (£135 ÷ 3 =) £45 per week;
- the single room rent is not adjusted; it is £42 per week.

The claimant's maximum rent is the lowest of the resulting figures, i.e. £42 per week.

Note: In both cases, further rules apply if the claimant could afford the accommodation when he or she took on the rent commitment (para. 10.38).

Example: Maximum rent with a '50% top-up'

A private tenant over the age of 25 makes a renewal claim for HB. She was on HB on 5th October 1997. She has not moved since then and she meets all the other conditions to be considered for a 50% top-up. Her actual rent is £100 per week including water charges and fuel charges. She is not a joint occupier. The rent officer has provided the following figures:

- a claim-related rent determination of £90 per week;
- a local reference rent determination of £70 per week;
- no single room rent determination (because she is not a 'young individual).

Because she qualifies for a 50% top-up (paras. 10.36-37), and because none of the adjustments in table 10.3 applies, her maximum rent is the average of (i.e. half-way between) the local reference rent and the claim-related rent, which is £80 per week.

MAXIMUM RENT: PROTECTION FOR PEOPLE WHO COULD FORMERLY AFFORD THEIR ACCOMMODATION

10.38 This is the first of the two 'protected groups' – people who are protected against the effect of the rules about maximum rents (and various other rent restrictions: para. 10.58). A claimant falls within this protected group if: HBRGB 11(9),(10) NIHBR 11(12),(13)

- he or she or any combination of the occupiers of his or her home (para. 10.43) could afford the financial commitments there when the liability to pay rent was entered into (no matter how long ago that was); and
- the claimant has not received HB for any period in the 52 weeks prior to his or her current claim. Receipt of CTB during those weeks is ignored.

10.39 In such a case, the protection lasts for the first 13 weeks of his or her entitlement to HB. During those weeks, his or her eligible rent is worked out in the same way as for a council tenant (para. 10.21) – but the resulting eligible rent cannot be restricted in any way.

10.40 This protection gives the claimant time to move, without the additional pressure of having insufficient HB. In the case of a couple, so long as the claimant has not received HB during the past 52 weeks, it is immaterial whether his or her partner has. In some cases it therefore makes a substantial difference which person in a couple makes the claim for HB (para. 5.5).

MAXIMUM RENT: PROTECTION FOR PEOPLE WHO HAVE HAD A BEREAVEMENT

HBRGB 11(7),(8)
NIHBR 11(9),(10)

10.41 This is the second of the two 'protected groups' – people who are protected against the effect of the rules about maximum rents (and various other rent restrictions: para. 10.58). A claimant falls within this protected group if:

- any of the occupiers of his or her home (para. 10.43) has died within the last 12 months (including occupiers who were temporarily absent); and
- the claimant has not moved home since the date of that death.

10.42 In such a case, the protection lasts until 12 months after that death. During that period it works as follows. If the claimant was on HB at the date of the death, his or her eligible rent must not be reduced to below whatever was his or her eligible rent immediately before that date (it is, however, increased if any rule requires this). If the claimant was not on HB at the date of the death, his or her eligible rent is worked out in the same way as for a council tenant (para. 10.21) – but the resulting eligible rent cannot be restricted in any way.

Examples: The protected groups

EXAMPLE ONE: BEREAVEMENT

A claimant makes a claim for HB shortly after the death of her husband (and the council agrees to backdate the claim: para. 5.76). She has not moved since her husband's death. Her actual rent is rather high.

Because of the protection for people who have had a bereavement, her eligible rent must not be restricted in any way until the first anniversary of her husband's death. Until then, her eligible rent is her actual rent minus amounts for any ineligible services.

EXAMPLE TWO: REDUNDANCY

A claimant makes a claim for HB a few weeks after he is made redundant (and he does not request backdating). His actual rent is high. He moved to this address when he was in a well-paid job and could easily afford the rent and outgoings. He has not been on HB in the last year.

Because of the protection for people who could formerly afford their accommodation, his eligible rent must not be restricted in any way for the first 13 weeks of his entitlement to HB. During those weeks, his eligible rent is his actual rent minus amounts for any ineligible services.

DEFINITIONS: 'OCCUPIER' AND 'RELATIVE'

10.43 For the purposes of the above two protected groups, the only 'occupiers' taken into account are: HBRGB 11(11),(12) NIHBR 11(14),(15)

- the claimant;
- any member of his or her family (partner, child, young person: paras. 4.5-20);
- any 'relative' (para. 10.44) of the claimant or partner (including non-dependants, boarders, tenants, sub-tenants and joint occupiers) who has no separate right to occupy the dwelling.

10.44 A 'relative' is defined for the above (and all other HB) purposes as: HBR 2(1)

- a parent, parent-in-law, daughter, son, daughter/son-in-law, step-daughter/son, sister or brother; or
- a partner (married or unmarried: para. 4.6) of any of the above; or
- a grandparent, grandchild, aunt, uncle, niece or nephew.

MAXIMUM RENT IF THE CLAIMANT'S RENT CHANGES

10.45 Once a claimant's maximum rent has been calculated as above, it applies throughout his or her award of HB – except as described in the following two paragraphs. HBRGB 11(5),(6A),(6B),(13) NIHBR 11(5),(6A),(8),(16)

10.46 If the claimant's details have to be re-referred to the rent officer (paras. 6.6-11), a new maximum rent must be calculated as above and used for the remainder of his or her award of HB (whether it is higher or lower than – or the same as – the initial maximum rent). Not all rent increases (indeed very few) trigger a re-referral to the rent officer.

10.47 If the claimant's actual rent reduces to below the maximum rent, the law is a little unclear. It appears to mean that, over-riding all the above rules, the most a person's eligible rent can ever be is what he or she actually pays minus the authority's valuation of amounts for ineligible service charges. If this is not the effect of the law, it would seem reasonable for the authority to use its general power to restrict the eligible rent (para. 10.48) to that figure.

REDUCING MAXIMUM RENT IN CERTAIN CASES

10.48 In private sector New Scheme cases, the authority has a general power to reduce any claimant's eligible rent to below the 'maximum rent' calculated as above if 'it appears to the authority that in the particular circumstances of the case the eligible rent... is greater than it is reasonable to meet by way of housing benefit.' (The same power applies in council tenant New Scheme cases: para. 10.24, but not in housing association cases: para. 10.30.) In such a case, the eligible rent is reduced to 'such lesser sum as seems to that authority to be an appropriate HBR 10(6B) rent in that particular case' and authorities must have regard to factors such as personal circumstances: *R v HBRB of the City of Westminster ex parte Laali.*

10.49 In practice, reductions under this provision are uncommon. They can be made only if the authority makes a proper judgment about the above matters (para. 1.33). This means (as pointed out in circular HB/CTB A7/96) that the authority 'should have evidence and an objective justification' before making a reduction (see also GM para. A10.440-41).

INCREASING MAXIMUM RENT FOR EXCEPTIONAL HARDSHIP

10.50 Increases for exceptional hardship were abolished in July 2001 and replaced with discretionary housing payments (para. 22.2).

Eligible rent for Old Scheme private sector cases

HBR Old 10, 11, 12
SI 1996 No. 1644
SI 1997 No. 852
NISR 1996 No. 111
NISR 1997 No. 170

10.51 In Old Scheme private sector cases (para. 10.31), the claimant's eligible rent is worked out in the same way as for a council tenant (para. 10.21) unless:

- the authority restricts the eligible rent to a lower figure (paras. 10.52 onwards); or
- the claimant has a registered rent or other fixed rent (paras. 10.66-69).

ELIGIBLE RENT RESTRICTIONS

10.52 The rules about eligible rent restrictions in Old Scheme cases are summarised in table 10.4. In applying them, authorities:

- must not take a blanket approach (GM para. A4.277): each step must be considered in the individual circumstances of each case and each step is open to appeal;
- must not restrict a claimant's eligible rent just because of the subsidy rules. The requirements of the HB regulations (described below) are the only test that is relevant in deciding whether or not benefit should be restricted.

There has been much case law about these matters, well explained in *Housing Benefit and Council Tax Benefit Legislation,* by Lorna Findlay and others, published annually by the Child Poverty Action Group. The key points are referred to below.

Table 10.4: HB restrictions for Old Scheme cases: a simplified summary

STEP ONE: IS THE RENT OR SIZE UNREASONABLE?

The claimant's HB can be restricted only if, compared with suitable alternative accommodation:

- the rent is unreasonably high; or
- the dwelling is unreasonably large; or
- a rent increase is unreasonable.

STEP TWO: IS THE CLAIMANT IN A PROTECTED GROUP?

Protections against HB restrictions can apply for claimants:

- who could afford their accommodation when their letting began; or
- who have had a death in their home; or
- who have children or young persons, or are aged 60 or more, or are sick or disabled.

STEP THREE: SHOULD THE ELIGIBLE RENT BE RESTRICTED?

If the rent is unreasonable (step one) and none of the protections applies (step two), the authority must decide how much (if at all) the claimant's eligible rent should be reduced.

DECIDING WHAT IS 'UNREASONABLE' BY FINDING COMPARABLES

10.53 The first question is whether: HBR Old 11(2), 12

- the rent is unreasonably high, or
- the accommodation is unreasonably large for all the occupiers, or
- a rent increase is unreasonably high, or
- a rent increase is unreasonably soon after another increase during the previous year.

10.54 As regards size, the question of who counts as an occupier is open to interpretation (since 'occupier' is not further defined for these purposes) and appeal (chapter 19), but it is not limited to the groups listed in paragraph 10.38. Though the Swale and Marchant case (para. 6.26) may affect how some authorities interpret 'occupier' for these purposes, there is an argument that that case was about the definition of 'occupier' in a different context and so is not binding here.

10.55 In all the above cases, authorities:

- must make a comparison (as regards the rent, size or rent increase, as appropriate) with suitable alternative accommodation (paras. 10.56-57);
- may additionally take account of figures provided by the rent officer (if the case was referred to the rent officer: chapter 6) – and the DWP advises that they 'must' do this (GM para. A4.274), bearing in mind that the rent officer's function is different;
- must not, at this stage, take into account the impact of the subsidy rules on their own finances (para. 10.64).

10.56 Authorities should make the comparison by working through the following questions:

(a) what is the rent (including all eligible and ineligible services) for the claimant's dwelling?

(b) what type of alternative accommodation is suitable for the claimant? and, in order to determine this, what services are requisite in order to regard the alternative accommodation as suitable and what other factors need to be taken into account (para. 10.57)?

(c) what rent (including all eligible and ineligible services) would be payable for such accommodation?

(d) is the rent in (a) unreasonably high by comparison with the rent in (c)?

The above is based on *R v Beverley BC HBRB ex p Hare*. As regards (d) above, 'unreasonably high' means more than just 'higher': *Malcolm v Tweeddale DC HBRB*.

HBR Old 11(6)(a),(7),(8) **10.57** In deciding what alternative accommodation would be suitable for the claimant (question (b) above), authorities:

- must take account of the nature of the alternative accommodation and the exclusive and shared facilities provided, having regard to the age and state of health of all the occupiers (as defined in paras. 10.38-39). 'For example, a disabled or elderly person might have special needs and require more expensive or larger accommodation than would otherwise be the case' (GM para. A4.290);
- must only take into account alternative accommodation with security of tenure which is reasonably equivalent to what the claimant currently has (GM A4.289);
- 'must have a sufficiency of information to ensure that like is being compared with like… Unless that can be done, no safe assessment can

be made of the reasonableness of the rent in question or the proper level of value': *Malcolm v Tweeddale DC HBRB;*

- may take account of alternative accommodation outside the authority's own area if there is no comparable accommodation within it. But if this is necessary, it is unreasonable to 'make comparisons with other parts of the country where accommodation costs differ widely from those which apply locally' (GM para. A4.291).

PROTECTED GROUPS

10.58 Three groups of claimants are protected against the effect of the above rules about HB restrictions. The first two groups, and the rules applying to them, are the same as those described in paragraphs 10.33-37; the details of the third group, and the rules applying to it, are described below. HBR Old 11(3)-(5), 12(2),(3)

VULNERABLE PEOPLE

10.59 A claimant falls within this protected group if any of the occupiers of his or her home (as defined in paras. 10.43-44) is: HBR Old 11(3),(6)(b

- aged 60 or more; or
- responsible for a child or young person in the household (paras. 4.12-20); or
- incapable of work for social security purposes (though the person need not have claimed a relevant social security benefit).

In such a case, the authority must not reduce the claimant's eligible rent unless there is suitable alternative accommodation available (para. 10.60) and it is reasonable to expect the claimant to move (para. 10.61).

10.60 What counts as suitable alternative accommodation was described earlier (para. 10.57). The point here is that it must be available. For example, accommodation the claimant has recently left, or an offer of accommodation the claimant has refused, may be available – but only while it actually remains available to the claimant, and not after it has been let to someone else. In *R v East Devon DC HBRB ex p Gibson,* the judge emphasised that the authority was not an accommodation agency, and said: 'It is... quite sufficient if an active market rent is shown to exist in houses in an appropriate place at the appropriate level of rent to which the [eligible] rent is restricted. There must, however, be evidence at least of that... otherwise the recipient, if he had to move, would have nowhere to go. It is, however, sufficient, as I wish to stress, to point to a range of properties, or a bloc of property, which is available without specific identification of particular dwelling houses'. The DWP follows this and emphasises that 'authorities should regard accommodation as not available if, in practice, there is little or no possibility of the claimant being able to obtain it, for example because it could only be HBR Old 11(3) obtained on payment of a large deposit which the claimant does not have' (GM para. A4.299).

HBR Old 11(6)(b) **10.61** In deciding whether it is reasonable to expect the claimant to move, authorities must take into account:

- the claimant's prospects of retaining employment; and
- the effect on the education of a child or young person who would have to change school (this means any child or young person mentioned in para. 10.43).

In *R v Sefton MBC ex p Cunningham,* the judge emphasised the authority's duty to take individual circumstances into account when considering 'suitability', 'availability' and 'reasonableness'. In that case, the Review Board's decision was overturned because there was no evidence that it had considered the effect of a move on the claimant's eight-year-old child's education.

RESTRICTING THE ELIGIBLE RENT

3R Old 11(2), 12(1) SI 1999 No. 2734 NISR 2000 No. 74 **10.62** The final question (if it applies at all, considering the above points) is of how much to restrict the eligible rent. In considering this, the authority must work through the following questions:

(a) is it appropriate to make a reduction in the claimant's eligible rent? and if it is

(b) what is the appropriate amount for the reduction? and

(c) how was that appropriate amount arrived at?

The above is based on the judgments in *Mehanne v Westminster CC HBRB,* and *R v Beverley BC HBRB ex p Hare.* As regards (b) above, the authority must not reduce the claimant's eligible rent below the cost of comparable alternative accommodation: *R v Brent LBC ex p Connery.*

10.63 As regards all the above questions, authorities must consider what is appropriate in the individual circumstances of each case. There are cases in which no reduction is appropriate. There are also cases in which no reduction is appropriate for the time being but may become appropriate later on. In practice in such cases, some authorities still tend to restrict claimants' eligible rents to what the rent officer has recommended (in cases which have been referred to the rent officer: chapter 6). However, the rent officer's figures do not take into account personal circumstances at all, whereas the question of what is 'appropriate' places a duty on authorities to do so.

THE IMPACT OF SUBSIDY

10.64 In *R v Brent LBC ex p Connery,* it was held that: 'An authority was entitled, except when acting in those cases where an absolute duty was to be fulfilled, to take into account the implications for its own financial situation [e.g. subsidy] when exercising its discretion' (as quoted in *The Times*, 25.10.89). As described earlier, there are three main questions to be considered in applying the rules about HB restrictions:

- whether the rent, size or rent increase is unreasonable;
- whether people fall within the protected groups; and
- whether to reduce the eligible rent or disallow a rent increase and, if so, by how much.

10.65 The first two are questions of fact. Subsidy considerations cannot therefore play a part in answering them. The DWP's opinion is that the authority may take subsidy into account in answering the third question, though not as the only consideration (GM para. A4.292).

IF A RENT HAS BEEN FIXED AS BINDING ON THE LANDLORD

10.66 In addition to the other Old Scheme rules, if a claimant's rent has been fixed by a rent officer, rent tribunal or rent assessment committee (so that it is binding on the landlord), the claimant's eligible rent must not exceed that fixed figure. This applies for one year from the date on which the fixed figure takes effect. (If, however, the letting began in or before January 1989, see below.)

HBR Old 11(1), (1A)
HBRGB Old 11(1A)
NIHBR Old 11(1)

Eligible rent for registered rent cases

10.67 The following rules apply to:

- tenancies in England and Wales which were entered into before 15th January 1989;
- tenancies in Scotland which were entered into before 2nd January 1989;
- tenancies in Northern Ireland which are protected or statutory tenancies to which article 3 of the Housing (Northern Ireland) Order 1978 applies, i.e. their rent is fixed by a rent officer;
- tenancies granted on or after those dates in which the landlord is required to preserve the tenant's rights (typically because the landlord has moved a tenant whose tenancy began before those dates).

HBRGB 10(3)
HBRGB Old 11(1), (1A)
HBRGB sch 1A
NIHBR 10(3)
NIHBR Old 11(1)
NIHBR sch 1B

These are referred to in this Guide as 'registered rent cases'. They are sometimes also called protected tenancies, regulated tenancies, fair rent tenancies, Rent Act tenancies, and even the 'Old, Old Scheme'.

10.68 In registered rent cases, the claimant's eligible rent is worked out as follows (but see also the next paragraph):

- if the claimant's rent has been fixed by a rent officer, rent tribunal or rent assessment committee (so that it is binding on the landlord), the claimant's eligible rent equals that figure minus any ineligible service charges included within it;

- in any other case, it is worked out in the same way as for a council tenant (para. 10.21).

HBR 10(6B) HBR Old 11

10.69 In either of the above cases, it is possible for the authority to restrict the rent – though this is in practice rare. The rules are as follows:

- if the case falls within the 'Old Scheme' (para. 10.7), it is dealt with in the same way as any other Old Scheme private sector case (paras. 10.51 onwards);
- if the case falls within the 'New Scheme', then a maximum rent cannot apply (because the case is not referred to the rent officer: chapter 6). The only way in which the rent can be restricted is if the authority uses its general power described in para. 10.48.

Eligible rent for other cases

TENANTS OF CHARITIES AND VOLUNTARY ORGANISATIONS

10.70 The eligible rent of a claimant renting from a registered charity or a non-profit making voluntary organisation is worked out in the same way as for private sector cases (paras. 10.26 onwards); unless the charity or voluntary organisation is a registered housing association, in which case the rules for housing association tenants apply (paras. 10.25-30).

TENANTS OF ENGLISH COUNTY COUNCILS

AA 134(1B), 191 HBRGB 12A(1)

10.71 The eligible rent of a claimant renting from an English county council (a typical example would be when a claimant rents from a county council social services department) is worked out in the same way as for private tenant cases (para 10.31). This does not apply where the council is a unitary authority, in which case the landlord is the same body as pays HB and its tenants are treated in the same way as other council tenants (para. 10.21).

TENANTS OF PROBATION OR BAIL HOSTELS

HBRGB sch 1A para 10

10.72 In Great Britain only, tenants of probation hostels and bail hostels are treated in the same way as registered rent cases (paras. 10.67).

TENANTS IN RESETTLEMENT PLACES

10.73 The eligible rent of a claimant renting a resettlement place (defined as in para. 10.14) is worked out in the same way as for a private sector Old Scheme case (paras. 10.51 onwards) – unless it is a rent rebate case, in which case it is dealt with as such (para. 10.21).

TENANTS IN HOSTELS AND NIGHT SHELTERS

10.74 There are no rules specifically for hostels or night shelters. The various rules given in the rest of this chapter apply. For example, a hostel might also be a registered housing association, a registered charity, etc; in which case the rules for that type of accommodation apply.

Service charges

10.75 The remainder of this chapter deals with service charges (and related charges) which may be included in a claimant's actual rent, or payable as well as the rent. It applies to all HB claims and explains which charges are eligible for HB and which are not. The section covers: HBR 10, 11, sch 1

- which service charges are and are not eligible for HB; and
- whether the authority or the rent officer is responsible for valuing the various kinds of services.

This section is relevant only in the calculation of HB for rent (not CTB or HB for rates in Northern Ireland).

THE IMPORTANCE OF SERVICE CHARGES

10.76 Many tenants pay for services either in with their rent (in which case it is immaterial whether they are mentioned in their letting agreement) or separately. As illustrated in the examples, there are two main methods of showing service charges in letting agreements:

- a claimant's rent may be shown as so much per week (or month, etc) including certain services; or
- it may be shown as so much per week (or month, etc) with an amount for service charges being due on top of the rent.

10.77 Whether a service charge is eligible for HB affects the amount of a claimant's eligible rent (para. 10.5), which in turn affects the amount of his or her HB.

- If a charge is 'eligible for HB', this means that it is in principle a charge which can be included in a claimant's eligible rent. With certain exceptions (mentioned below as they arise), it does not need to be valued; and no deduction is made for it at any stage in deciding the amount of a claimant's eligible rent unless the charge for it is excessive (para. 10.86).
- If a charge is 'ineligible for HB', this means that it is in principle a charge which cannot be included in a claimant's eligible rent. With certain exceptions, it needs to be valued and deducted at some point in deciding the amount of a claimant's eligible rent (para. 10.78).

Councils, housing associations and many other landlords provide details of service charges to their tenants (and in many cases, tenants have a right to this information: for good information on this, see *Housing Rights Guide* by Geoffrey Randall, published by Shelter). It is in their interests as well as their tenants' to bear in mind the detailed rules when deciding what services to provide and how much to charge for them.

Examples: Service charges

1. A council tenant claimant's rent is expressed as being £100 per fortnight including £20 per fortnight for fuel for the claimant's own room and £10 per fortnight for heating, lighting, cleaning and maintaining communal areas. In this case the eligible rent is £80 per fortnight (£40 per week). The ineligible charge for fuel for the claimant's own room is deducted.
2. A housing association claimant's rent is expressed as being £70 per fortnight plus £20 per fortnight for fuel for the claimant's own room and £10 per fortnight for heating, lighting, cleaning and maintaining communal areas. In this case the eligible rent is £80 per fortnight (£40 per week). The eligible charge for the communal areas is added.

Notes

- The facts in the two examples are the same but are expressed differently.
- Information about the service charges illustrated is given later in this chapter.
- The terms 'net rent' and 'gross rent' are sometimes used to distinguish between different methods of expressing a rent figure. But they are used in different ways nationally and are best avoided for HB purposes.

WHO DEALS WITH SERVICE CHARGES

10.78 In Great Britain, service charges may be dealt with by the authority or the rent officer (or both of them) in assessing a claimant's eligible rent. In Northern Ireland, service charges are always dealt with by the NIHE. Fuller details are given in the remainder of this chapter, but in general terms:

- when a 'maximum rent' applies in assessing the claimant's eligible rent (as in many private tenant cases, for example), the rent officer provides the council with figures which are already adjusted to take account of most service charges: in effect, the rent officer values them;
- when a 'maximum rent' does not apply (as in all council, most housing association and some private tenant cases), it is the authority which assesses all matters relating to service charges.

'Maximum rent' is explained in paragaph 10.34. Details of which rules apply for various service charges are given at the relevant places throughout this chapter.

DEFINITION OF 'SERVICES'

10.79 The law defines 'services' as 'services performed or facilities... provided for, or rights made available to, the occupier...' and 'service charge' as any periodical charge for any such service. HBR 10(7)

Which service charges are eligible?

10.80 Service charges are eligible for HB, so long as they: HBR 10(1),(3),(7)

- have to be paid as a condition of occupying the dwelling as a home; and
- are not listed in the regulations as ineligible (as described in the following paragraphs); and
- are not excessive in relation to the service provided (para. 10.86).

The rules about individual service charges, and whether they are eligible for HB, are in paragraphs 10.87 onwards.

10.81 The first of these conditions need not have applied from the date the letting agreement began. A service charge is eligible for HB (subject to the other conditions) whenever the claimant agreed to pay it, if the only alternative would have been to lose his or her home. (Note also that a different rule applies in the case of charges for garages, land etc: para. 10.107.)

10.82 Details of which service charges are eligible for HB (subject to the above points) follow, and are summarised in table 10.5. Helpful advice on services is given by the DWP (GM paras. A4.170-192).

10.83 Sometimes services are provided free to a claimant. The DWP points out in relation to hostel residents (thought the point is relevant to all claims) that 'HB should be based only on items included in the resident's charge. [Authorities] must confirm which services are included in the hostel charge.' (GM para. A4.129).

VALUING INELIGIBLE SERVICE CHARGES

10.84 When the authority has the duty of valuing ineligible service charges (para. 10.78), this is done as follows: HBR 10(3), sch 1 para 2

- if the amount can be identified from the letting agreement or in some other way, the authority uses the amount so identified as the value;
- but if this identified amount is unrealistically low for the service provided, or if the amount cannot be identified, the authority must decide what amount is fairly attributable to the value;

- however, different rules can apply for water charges, fuel and meals (paras. 10.87-96).

VALUING ELIGIBLE SERVICE CHARGES

HBR 10, sch 1
HBRGB sch 1B
NIHBR sch 1C

10.85 It is not usually necessary to value eligible service charges. The main exception is support charges. In general terms the authority values them as follows:

- if the amount can be identified from the letting agreement or in some other way, the authority uses the amount so identified as the value;
- but if this identified amount is excessive, or if the amount cannot be identified, the authority must decide what amount is fairly attributable to the value.

EXCESSIVE ELIGIBLE SERVICE CHARGES

HBR 10(6B), sch 1 para 3

10.86 In deciding whether an eligible service charge is excessive, the authority must take account of the cost of comparable services. If it is excessive, the authority must decide how much would be reasonable for that service and disallow the excess.

WATER CHARGES

HBR 10(3),(6)
HBRGB 2(1)

10.87 In Great Britain, water charges (including any sewerage or environmental charges) are not eligible for HB. So if such charges are included in a claimant's rent, an amount must be deducted for them. (No deduction is made at any stage if the claimant pays water charges direct to the water company, since in such a case the water charges are not included in the claimant's rent.) In Northern Ireland water charges are eligible for HB through the rates element of HB (though they are not separately identifiable). However the rates element is deducted from the rent as in Great Britain (paras. 11.11-15).

10.88 In cases in which a maximum rent applies, the rent officer deducts an amount for such charges (table 10.3). In other cases, the authority decides the value as follows:

- if the water charge varies according to consumption, either the actual amount or an estimate;
- otherwise, if the claimant's accommodation is a self-contained unit, the actual amount of the water charge;
- otherwise, a proportion of the water charge for the self-contained unit. The proportion should equal the floor area of the claimant's accommodation divided by the floor area of the self-contained unit (but in practice, authorities sometimes use different, simpler methods).

Table 10.5: Service charges summary

As described throughout this chapter, further details apply in many of the following cases.

TYPE OF SERVICE CHARGE	ELIGIBLE FOR HB?
Water charges	NO
Provision of a heating system	YES
Fuel for communal areas	YES
Other fuel	NO
Meals	NO
Furniture/household equipment	YES
Communal window cleaning	YES
Other exterior window cleaning which the occupier(s) cannot do	YES
Other window cleaning	NO
Communal cleaning	YES
Other cleaning	NO
Emergency alarm systems	NO
Counselling and support	NO
Medical/nursing/personal care	NO
Day-to-day living expenses	NO
Most communal services relating to the provision of adequate accommodation	YES

FUEL, ETC

10.89 Charges for fuel (such as gas, electricity, etc. and also any standing charges or other supply costs) are not eligible for HB. So if such charges are included in a claimant's rent, an amount must be deducted for them. (No deduction is made at any stage if the claimant pays fuel charges direct to the fuel company, since in such a case the fuel charges are not included in the claimant's rent.)

HBR 10(3)
HBRGB sch 1 paras 4, 5, 7
NIHBR sch 1 paras 4, 5, 8

10.90 There are two exceptions to the above:

- a charge for the provision of a heating system is eligible for HB, but only if it is separate from the fuel charge;
- a fuel charge for communal areas is eligible for HB, but only if is it separate from the fuel charge for the claimant's own accommodation. Communal areas are areas of common access (e.g. halls, stairways, passageways) and, in sheltered accommodation only, they also include common rooms (e.g. a dining room or lounge).

Table 10.6: Standard weekly fuel deductions

Amounts are added together if fuel is provided for more than one of the purposes shown.

IF THE CLAIMANT AND ANY FAMILY OCCUPY MORE THAN ONE ROOM	
Fuel for heating	£9.80
Fuel for hot water	£1.20
Fuel for lighting	£0.80
Fuel for cooking	£1.20
Fuel for any other purpose	NIL
Fuel for all the above	£13.00
IF THE CLAIMANT AND ANY FAMILY OCCUPY ONE ROOM ONLY	
Fuel for heating	£5.90
Fuel for hot water:	
if fuel for heating is also provided	NIL
if fuel for heating is not also provided	£1.20
Fuel for lighting:	
if fuel for heating is also provided	NIL
if fuel for heating is not also provided	£0.80
Fuel for cooking	£1.20
Fuel for any other purpose	NIL
Fuel for all the above: £5.90 for heating + £1.20 for cooking (+ NIL for hot water and lighting)	£7.10

10.91 In cases in which a maximum rent applies, the rent officer deducts an amount for such charges (table 10.3). In other cases, the rules depend on whether the amount of the fuel charge is known to the authority, as described below.

10.92 If the amount of a fuel charge is identifiable, the authority uses this figure as the value of the fuel charge. However, if this is unrealistically low or includes an element for communal areas which cannot readily be separated out, the fuel charge is treated as unidentifiable.

10.93 If the amount of a fuel charge is not identifiable (or not 'readily identifiable'), the authority decides its value by reference to standard amounts depending on what the fuel is for, as shown in table 10.6. As shown there, the standard amounts are lower for claimants who occupy one room only. If the authority uses these standard amounts, it must invite the claimant to provide evidence on which the 'actual or approximate' amount of the charge may be estimated; and, if reasonable evidence is provided, the authority must estimate the value of the fuel charge.

MEALS (INCLUDING FOOD)

10.94 Charges for meals are not eligible for HB. So if such charges are included in a claimant's rent, an amount must be deducted for them. HBR sch. 1 para 1(a), 1A

10.95 For these purposes, 'meals' includes the preparation of meals (e.g. where meals are prepared somewhere else and then delivered) and also the provision of unprepared food (e.g. cereal, bread still in its wrappings).

10.96 In cases in which a maximum rent applies, the rent officer (or NIHE) does not deduct an amount for such charges, though there are uncommon exceptions to this (table 10.3). So both in these cases and in all other cases, the authority decides the value by reference to standard amounts depending on what meals are provided, as shown in table 10.7. Those amounts cannot be varied; the actual amount the landlord charges for meals is never used. As shown in the table, one deduction applies for each person whose meals are paid for in the claimant's rent (whether this is the claimant, a member of the family or some other person such as a non-dependant). No deduction applies for anyone whose meals are not included (for example, a baby). When appropriate, deductions are calculated separately for each person (for example fewer meals may be provided for someone who goes out to work than for someone who does not).

FURNITURE AND HOUSEHOLD EQUIPMENT

10.97 Charges for the use of these are eligible for HB; unless there is an intention that they will become part of the claimant's personal property, in which case they are ineligible. Ineligible amounts are valued by the rent officer in maximum rent cases, otherwise by the authority. HBR 10(3), sch 1 para 1(b)

Table 10.7: Standard weekly meals deductions

A separate amount is assessed and deducted for each person whose meals are provided.

IF AT LEAST THREE MEALS ARE PROVIDED EVERY DAY	
For the claimant, and each other person from the first Monday in September following his or her 16th birthday	£19.85
For each other person	£10.05
IF BREAKFAST ONLY IS PROVIDED	
For the claimant, and each other person of any age	£2.45
ALL OTHER CASES	
For the claimant, and each other person from the first Monday in September following his or her 16th birthday	£13.20
For each other person	£6.65

CLEANING AND WINDOW CLEANING

HBR 10(3), sch 1 para 1(a)(iv)

10.98 Charges for the following are eligible for HB; unless the cost is met by Supporting People (para. 10.103) – in which case they are not eligible for HB:

- cleaning of communal areas;
- communal window cleaning; and
- cleaning the outsides of windows which no-one in the household can do.

Any other cleaning and window cleaning (such as cleaning the insides of windows and cleaning the claimant's own accommodation) is never eligible for HB (but may be met by Supporting People).

OTHER COMMUNAL SERVICES, ETC

HBR 10(3), sch 1 para 1(a)

10.99 Charges for the following are eligible for HB:

- children's play areas;
- TV and radio relay (though not normally of satellite or cable services);
- communal laundry facilities;
- other services which are related to the provision of adequate accommodation.

10.100 The DWP advises (GM para. A4.177, and see chapter A4 generally) that the last item includes:

- portering and refuse removal;
- lifts, communal telephones and entry phones.

OTHER DAY-TO-DAY LIVING EXPENSES, ETC

10.101 Charges for the following are not eligible for HB. So if charges for them are included in a claimant's rent, an amount must be deducted for them. The amount is valued by the rent officer in maximum rent cases, otherwise by the authority:

HBR 10(3), sch 1 para 1(g)

- laundry (e.g. washing sheets, etc, for the claimant);
- transport;
- sports facilities;
- TV and radio rental and licence and (in most cases) satellite service charges;
- any other leisure items or day-to-day living expenses; or
- any other services which 'are not related to the provision of adequate accommodation'.

SUPPORT CHARGES

10.102 Support charges are never eligible for HB. This includes charges for:

HBR 10(3), sch 1 para 1(f)

- cleaning and window cleaning over and above that mentioned in paragraph 10.98;
- emergency alarm systems;
- counselling and support; and
- medical, nursing and personal care.

10.103 Claimants who need such services may be able to have the cost met by Supporting People, a goverrnment programme for funding support services administered by local authorities (in Northern Ireland by the NIHE) and independent of HB/CTB. For the three years prior to 1st/7th April 2003, such charges could be met by HB for people in supported accommodation (subject to further conditions in some cases). The full details may be found in the 2002-03 edition of this guide.

10.104 In some situations there remain difficulties in distinguishing what constitutes a support charge as above (which is not eligible for HB) and what is merely part of the rent as any landlord would charge it (and which would therefore be eligible for HB: para. 10.105). Chasing rent arrears would usually be an example of the latter: most landlords would regard it as part and parcel of their day-to-day work. But it would become an example of the former if it formed a substantial part of the work of staff in a hostel for residents with difficulty budgeting.

OVERHEADS INCLUDING MANAGEMENT COSTS AND COUNCIL TAX

10.105 Whether the landlord's normal overheads (such as maintenance, insurance and repair costs) count as 'services' or simply as part of the claimant's rent is an arguable point. But in either case they are eligible for HB. In particular, this includes any part of the rent towards the landlord's liability for council tax (e.g. if the claimant has a resident landlord or lives in a house made up of bedsits). No amount is deducted for these items at any stage, so they do not normally need to be valued.

INCREASES TO COVER ARREARS OF RENT

HBR 8(2A) **10.106** If a claimant's rent has been increased in order to recover arrears of rent or other charges, that part of the rent is ineligible for HB. This rule applies only if an individual claimant's rent is increased to cover his or her own arrears on a current or former home. It does not apply when landlords increase rents on all their properties as a result of arrears generally.

GARAGES, LAND, ETC

HBR 2(4)(a) **10.107** The rent on a garage (or any other buildings, gardens or land included in the claimant's letting agreement) is eligible for HB, but only if:

- they are used for occupying the dwelling as a home; and
- the claimant acquired them at the same time as the dwelling; and
- the claimant has no option but to rent them at the same time.

Otherwise, they are eligible for HB only if the claimant has made or is making reasonable efforts to end liability for them.

BUSINESS PREMISES

HBR 10(4) **10.108** Rent on any part of a property which is used for business, commercial or other non-residential purposes is not eligible for HB. For example, if a claimant rents both a shop and the flat above it, only the rent relating to the flat is eligible for HB. If the rent on the business premises is not specified separately from the rent on the home, it is necessary for the authority to decide how much relates to each. For self-employed claimants who work from home, see paragraph 15.23.

11 Help with rates in Northern Ireland

11.1 This chapter deals with rate rebates, which, in Northern Ireland only, are still available as part of the HB scheme. Council tax and CTB do not exist in Northern Ireland and, while rate rebates appear similar to CTB there are, nevertheless, significant differences. Rate rebates can be paid by either the Northern Ireland Housing Executive (NIHE) or the Rate Collection Agency (RCA) although not by both simultaneously. The tenure of the property will, in the main, govern which of these organisations will deal with the claim but, as always, there are some exceptions to the general rules. This chapter covers:

- the background to this significant difference between the HB scheme in Northern Ireland compared to the rest of the UK;
- the legislative authority and administrative arrangements in place;
- who can get a rate rebate;
- which organisation will process the rate rebate application;
- what restrictions, if any, apply to the amount of eligible rates;
- conversion to weekly amounts (where necessary) and;
- how much rate rebate will be paid;
- payment of benefit by rebate or allowance.

Background

CURRENT POSITION

11.2 The arrangements for local government in Northern Ireland are very different from elsewhere in the UK. Although there are 26 district, borough and city councils they have comparatively few powers and many of the functions associated with local government in Great Britain are carried out by non-departmental public bodies and departments of the Northern Ireland Executive. Part of the funding of these services is by means of a domestic rate system, which comprises two elements. The first of these elements is the local rate, which is set by the local district council to fund the services it delivers, such as street cleansing and leisure facilities. The second element is the regional rate set by the Department of Finance and Personnel to fund other services, such as roads and water treatment. The property owner or occupier, however, receives only one rate demand and makes payment to the RCA, which passes the local element on to the local district council. If the property is tenanted the landlord will normally include rates charges in the overall amount payable by the tenant.

11.3 As there is no council tax in Northern Ireland it is clearly inappropriate that there should be a CTB. For this reason assistance with domestic rates charges is available, as part of the HB scheme, by means of a rate rebate processed either by the NIHE or RCA depending largely on the tenure of the property. Rate rebates, while bearing some comparison with CTB are, nevertheless, significantly different. Although the administrative arrangements are very different, the scheme which applies in Northern Ireland today is essentially the same as that which applied in Great Britain prior to the introduction of the community charge (poll tax) and its successor council tax.

THE FUTURE

11.4 Both the rating system itself and the administrative arrangements are currently under review by the Northern Ireland Executive. Among the possibilities are that Northern Ireland should adopt a council tax type system of funding local services which would mean the introduction of some form of council tax benefit. On 5th December 2003 the Northern Ireland Office Minister, Ian Pearson MP announced his intention to proceed with rating reform, the first stage of which would be to value homes on a capital value basis with 'the objective of having new valuations available to support the introduction of new arrangements during 2006' (Northern Ireland Executive Press Release 5/12/02). A decision as to whether the valuations should be individual or banded into ranges of different values (similar to the council tax) will be taken when analysis of work commissioned from the Valuations and Lands Agency (VLA) is complete. The Minister also confirmed that as part of the wider review of the rating system following further study a decision would also be taken on 'a reliefs scheme for those on modest means, but beyond the reach of the benefits system'. In the shorter term there is a possibility that the HB functions of the RCA and the NIHE could be merged to form a single HB agency. At this stage no definite conclusions have been reached but there is considerable pressure from the Treasury to make radical changes.

Legislative authority and administrative arrangements

11.5 The legislative authority to administer HB in Northern Ireland is derived from the Social Security Administration Act (Northern Ireland) 1992 which sets out the arrangements for the administration of the HB scheme in Northern Ireland. The NIHE is required by Section 126(3)(a) of the Act to administer all claims for HB from tenants. In carrying out its functions the NIHE can award rent allowances, rent rebates and rate rebates provided that the claimant is not an owner-occupier. If the claimant is an owner-occupier Section 126(3)(b) of the Act places a similar responsibility on the RCA but only in respect of rate rebates. Both organisations use the same framework of regulations, that is Housing Benefit (General) Regulations (Northern Ireland) 1987 SR 1987 No. 461 (as amended) and the Housing Benefit (Decisions and Appeals) (Northern Ireland) Regulations 2001 SR 2001 No. 213 (as amended).

RATE COLLECTION AGENCY (RCA)

11.6 The RCA is an executive agency within the Department of Finance and Personnel, a Department of the Northern Ireland Executive. As well as HB the RCA's other core function is to collect the rates levied on the owners and/or occupiers of all domestic and commercial properties in Northern Ireland. The RCA administers its HB service from one central location in Belfast although five local RCA offices (primarily dealing with receiving rates payments) will accept claim forms and documents from members of the public. Claim forms can be requested or downloaded from the RCA's website *(www.ratecollectionagencyni.gov.uk)*; alternatively the HB central unit can be contacted at Londonderry House, 21-27 Chichester Street, Belfast, BT1 4JJ (028 9025 2525).

11.7 Although the HB regulations apply equally to the RCA clearly any regulation dealing with the amount of rent eligible for HB will not be relevant when processing claims. This means that many of the more complex and controversial regulations, such as the post-April 1996 rules for assessing eligible rents and the provisions in which certain applicants are required to be treated as not liable to make payments (commonly known as the 'contrived tenancy' rules) can, effectively, be ignored by the RCA. Additionally the fact that all applicants have a rate liability and account considerably simplifies payment, as there is no necessity to issue cheques, the rate rebate is simply credited to the account; similarly overpayments are recovered by simply debiting the rate account.

Who can get a rate rebate

NICBA 129(1)(a)
NIHBR 8(1)(a), 9(1)

11.8 With very few exceptions, and subject to the usual rules on income and household circumstances, anyone with a rate liability (either directly or as part of an overall charge payable to a landlord) is potentially entitled to a rate rebate. Rate rebates are, therefore, payable to all of the following groups of claimants. (NB this list is not exhaustive):

- owner occupiers;
- tenants;
- boarders;
- lodgers;

- people living in houses in multiple occupation;
- people living in bed and breakfast accommodation;
- hostel residents.

11.9 There are, however, a few situations where a rate rebate cannot be paid even though the claimant has a rates liability. These are: NIHBR 7(1)(b),(c), 7A, 48A(1)

- The claimant is a full time student who does not fall within one of the groups who can qualify for HB (paras. 21.24-33).
- The claimant is deemed to be a 'person from abroad' (chapter 20).
- The rates liability is deemed to have been created to take advantage of the HB scheme (paras. 2.46-51). This is, however, more theoretical than actual as in practice it is difficult to see how this could occur.

In all these situations the NIHE/RCA is obliged to treat that person as not liable to make payments and consequently cannot pay a rate rebate.

11.10 There is one further situation in which the NIHE/RCA cannot pay a rate rebate: this is where the landlord is a registered charity and the property occupied is exempt from rates charges. Where this is the case there is simply no rates charge to rebate.

MUST THERE ALWAYS BE A RATES ELEMENT?

11.11 In some instances tenants (and also occasionally landlords) state that they are not being charged rates. Unless the tenant has to make rates payments directly to the RCA this is incorrect as, in the great majority of cases, rates form part of the overall charge payable by the tenant to the landlord. If the tenant has to pay rates directly the RCA will issue a rates demand, which will easily establish liability and the amount to be paid. This is the only situation where the NIHE should accept that the amount payable to a landlord is exclusive of rates. Otherwise it must assume that rates are included within the overall charge payable by the tenant to the landlord. This also applies to a new property where the rates have not yet been assessed. If this is the case a payment on account (based on the rates payable on a similar property) should be issued pending receipt of the actual amount of rates payable. NIHBR 9(2), 10(3)(a), (6)

11.12 If a rates element is not included the HB assessment could well be incorrect. This is particularly likely if non-dependant deductions have to be made or if the claimant has income in excess of his applicable amount. This is because different non-dependant deductions and excess income tapers apply to rates than those used for rent rebates and allowances.

CALCULATING THE RATES PAYABLE

11.13 Where the rates element is not separately identified the NIHE must calculate the amount of rates by reference to the Net Annual Valuation (NAV) of the dwelling and the amount of rates payable in the District Council area in which the dwelling is located. The NAV will, typically, not change unless there is an improvement to the property requiring it to be reassessed or if there is a general revaluation. In contrast, the amount of rates payable in a district council area will vary, usually upwards, each year.

11.14 Annual rates payable are calculated by multiplying the NAV by the rate in the pound for the district council area in which the dwelling is located. This is illustrated in the example below. The NAV can be obtained from the VLA's valuation list. NAVs for a particular property can now be accessed on-line at the VLA's website by searching on the address details *(http://vla2.nics.gov.uk)*. The current rate in the pound for each of the 26 districts (including the regional rate) can now be viewed on-line at the RCA site at *www.ratecollectionagencyni.gov.uk/poundages.htm*

Example – Calculation of annual rates payable

A property in Belfast district is listed on the VLA valuation list as having a NAV of £250.

1. NAV of dwelling	=	£250
2. Amount of rates per £1 of NAV in Belfast District for 2004-05	=	£3.0763
3. Annual rates (1 x 2) = £250 x £3.0763	=	£769.08

NIHBR 75(2)(b) DAR 7(2)(a),(3),8(2) **11.15** If, as is almost always the case, the rates payable change each year the NIHE must recalculate the rates element. If the overall charge has not been increased this will result in a reduction in the amount of the rent element. The NIHE should not wait either until the overall charge is increased or until it is advised by the tenant (or landlord). This is because there is no duty to notify changes in the amount of rates payable.

Which organisation processes the rate rebate application

GENERAL RULE

NIAA 126(3)(a),(b) NIHBR 2(2)(a)-(c) **11.16** In general rate rebate claims from tenants will be processed by the NIHE and those from owner-occupiers will be processed by the RCA. While there are some exceptions to this general rule relating to rent liability, for example, partners of tenants are treated as if they are liable for rent, in practice these present little difficulty, as they are clearly identifiable. There is sometimes a degree of confusion as to as to which agency should process the claim which largely arises because a person perceives that he or she is an owner occupier when this is not in fact the case. The exceptions and the areas of confusion are discussed in the following paragraphs.

PEOPLE WITH A LIFE INTEREST

11.17 This is probably the most common area of confusion and usually arises following the death of the former owner of a property. The terms of the will may leave ownership of the property to any other person (but usually a son or daughter) subject to the right of a named person to live in that property for as long as they wish or until they die. This is also known as 'having your day in the house'. NIAA 126(3)(b) NIHBR 2(1),(2)(a)

11.18 The person having a life interest is not an owner occupier despite the fact that the person may have lived in the property for many years and, indeed, may have been the partner of the former property owner. Although not an owner-occupier the person cannot be described as a tenant in the accepted sense. Indeed, even if this person was being charged a rent no rent allowance can be paid as the person has an absolute right to occupy the property without having to make payments of rent to do so. There is therefore no rent liability, but despite this there is still a rates liability and in these circumstances it falls on the NIHE to process the claim.

PARTICIPANTS IN CO-OWNERSHIP SCHEMES

11.19 The other main area of confusion relates to participants in an equity-sharing scheme operated by the Northern Ireland Co-ownership Housing Association. Such people are commonly considered to be owner-occupiers but despite this cannot claim a rate rebate from the RCA and should instead claim through the NIHE. This is because participants in the co-ownership scheme have to pay a mortgage (for whatever portion of the property they are purchasing) and a rent (for the remaining portion of the property) as well as rates. It is administratively convenient that participants in the co-ownership scheme should only have to deal with one agency processing both a rent allowance and a rate rebate. This is particularly so if that person qualifies for help with mortgage payments through income support as, otherwise, he or she would have to deal with three separate agencies all requiring similar information.

RENTAL PURCHASE SCHEMES

11.20 There is one further anomaly, which relates to people buying their homes through rental purchase schemes, i.e. where ownership does not transfer until the final instalment has been paid. Such people would also be commonly regarded as owner-occupiers but can receive assistance with both rental purchase instalments (as if they were rent) and with rates from the NIHE. NIHBR 8(1)(a), 10(1)(h)

EXCEPTIONS: PERSONS TREATED AS IF THEY ARE OWNER OCCUPIERS

NIHBR 6(1)(b),(c) **11.21** Although the tenure of the property largely governs which agency will deal with the rate rebate claim, it is important to note that this is not absolute. As well as the circumstances previously noted, the general provision, which allows the NIHE to accept a rent rebate or allowance claim from a person other than the liable person (para. 11.16), this rule applies equally to rate rebate only claims made to the RCA. Therefore it is possible for a rate rebate application to be accepted from and paid to the following persons:

- the partner of the person liable for rates (para. 2.36) including partners of full time students;
- a person whose liability has been waived by their landlord in return for doing repairs (para. 2.36);
- the former partner of the person liable for rates;
- some other person it is reasonable to treat as liable.

In the last two cases the conditions in paragraph 11.22 must also apply.

NIHBR 6(1)(c) **11.22** In order to treat a former partner or some other person as liable for rates it is also necessary to demonstrate that:

- the person left in occupation is required to make payments in order to continue to live there; and
- the person liable to make payments is not doing so; and
- it must also be 'reasonable to treat [that person] as liable'; in practice this means that that person must have been living in the home before the person liable for making rates payments stopped doing so.

11.23 This provision allows, for example, the RCA to accept and process a rate rebate claim from the partner of a sole owner who has had to move into residential care accommodation on medical grounds.

11.24 Table 11.1 summarises which agency will deal with rate rebate claims from particular types of occupiers.

Table 11.1: Which agency deals with claims

Owner occupier	RCA
Housing association tenant	NIHE
NIHE tenant	NIHE
Tenant of private landlord	NIHE
Co-ownership participant	NIHE
Buying through rental purchase	NIHE
Person with a life interest	NIHE
Partner of sole owner	RCA
Former partner of sole owner	RCA
Former non-dependant	RCA

What restrictions, if any, apply to the amount of eligible rates

GENERAL RULE: POWER TO RESTRICT ELIGIBLE RATES

11.25 Prior to April 1996 the amount of eligible rates could be restricted by the NIHE and RCA on the same grounds as those which applied to rents; that is, a restriction could be applied if the rates were deemed to be unreasonably high or if the property was over-large. In practice these cases were exceptionally rare and usually on the grounds that the property was over-large such as, for example, a single person (tenant or owner occupier) living alone in a five-bedroom house. NIHBR 9(1),(3) NISR 1996 No. 11

11.26 Since April 1996 however neither the NIHE nor the RCA have had any power to restrict the amount of eligible rates. With only a few exceptions the amount of rates eligible for HB is the full amount of rates charged on that property expressed on a weekly basis.

EXCEPTIONS TO GENERAL RULE

11.27 There are three exceptions to this rule. The first applies to both the NIHE and the RCA while the second and third will normally only apply to cases being dealt with by the NIHE. These are as follows: NIHBR 9(2), (4),(5

- If the rateable unit includes non-residential accommodation (such as a shop or commercial workshop) only that proportion of the rates which relates to residential accommodation is eligible.
- If the person occupies only part of a rateable unit (for example a boarder, lodger or someone living in a multi-occupied property) only the proportion of the total rates payable on the property which appears appropriate is eligible. For example if a person has exclusive occupancy of one room in an eight-bedroom house, sharing kitchen, bathroom and living room: then 1/8th of the total rates on the property as a whole would be eligible. Similarly, if that person had exclusive use of three of the eight rooms, the eligible rates would be 3/8th of the total rates on the property as a whole.
- If there is joint liability to pay rates (for example in a joint tenancy) eligible rates will normally be the total rates on the property divided by the number of people with a liability to pay. Exceptionally, however, unlike the GB rule relating to council tax benefit (paras. 9.26-29), if there is a difference in the proportions of the total rates paid this must be taken into account. This could mean, for example, that there would be a 2/3rd to 1/3rd split of the total rates payable.

Conversion to weekly amounts

NIHBR 69(2),(3) **11.28** HB is a weekly benefit and it is therefore necessary to convert the annual rates charge to a weekly figure before calculating entitlement. There are two alternative methods of conversion but the HB regulations stipulate the circumstances in which each method is to be used.

- The first method is used when a tenancy is on a weekly (or multiple of weekly) basis and the rates are included within the overall amount paid to the landlord by the tenant (where the tenant does not pay rates separately directly to the RCA). In these cases, except where the tenant has rent free weeks, the total rates charge is simply divided by number of weeks over which it is payable, which for a full year will be 52*. Benefit is then calculated in the normal way, deducting any non-dependant charges and any tapered excess income as appropriate (paras. 11.32-35). Where the tenancy has 'rent free' weeks an adjustment is necessary so that benefit is paid in the weeks in which they are charged rent (para 11.36).
- The second method is used where the claimant is an owner-occupier; a tenant who pays rates directly to the RCA or a tenant whose tenancy is other than on a weekly basis (such as calendar monthly or quarterly). In this method the total rates charge is divided by the number of days over the period to which it relates, which for a full year will be 365 (366 in a

leap year) and the resultant figure is multiplied by 7. Where the rates are paid as part of the rent and the tenant has rent free periods an adjustment is necessary so that benefit is only paid during the period in which rent is charged (paras. 11.35,37).

* In most years there will be 52 benefit weeks; occasionally, however, there will be 53.

11.29 It is important to note that due to the different methods of conversion there can be small differences in the weekly amounts calculated even though the annual charge is the same. Additionally, the weekly amounts totalled over a full year may also be slightly less than the annual figure depending on the method of conversion that must be used. It should also be noted that there is no discretion to use the method of conversion which results in a marginally higher amount of rate rebate. The method of conversion is determined solely by the status of the claimant as outlined above. In Great Britain a different method applies for the calculation of CTB (para. 7.42).

Example – Eligible rates based on annual rates bill of £650

METHOD A –WEEKLY TENANCY INCLUSIVE OF RATES

£650 divided by 52 = £12.50 weekly eligible rates

Annual amount of eligible rates	£650

METHOD B – ALL OTHER CASES

£650 divided by 365 = £1.78 per day

£1.78 multiplied by 7 = £12.46 weekly eligible rates

Annual amount of eligible rates	£647.92

ROUNDING

11.30 Any amount which as a result of the conversion to weekly amounts does not exactly equal a whole penny can be rounded down to the nearest whole penny if the remainder is less than half a penny, or up to the next whole penny if it is equal to or more than half a penny. NIHBR 69(8)

How much rate rebate will be paid?

11.31 As with rent rebates and allowances, the amount of rate rebate payable depends on the type and amount of the claimant's income as well as whether or not any non-dependants live in the household.

INCOME SUPPORT CASES

NICBA 129(3)(a)
NIHBR 3(2), 61(1)(b), sch 4 paras 4,4B, sch 5 para 5
NIHBR 60+ 22, 61(1)(b)

11.32 If the claimant receives income support, income-based jobseeker's allowance or the guarantee credit or treated as if they are (para. 7.6) he or she will receive the maximum rebate, which is the full amount of eligible rates expressed on a weekly basis less any non-dependant charges that apply (para. 11.34 and table 11.2). In addition, those claimants who lost all entitlement to IS/JSA(IB) as a result of the introduction of Supporting People (para. 10.103) (mainly long leaseholders) continue to be treated as entitled to the maximum rebate indefinitely (para. 7.7).

ALL OTHER CASES

NICBA 129(3)(b)
NIHBR 21(1), 61(1)(b), 62(a)
NIHBR 60+ 23, 24, 61(1)(b), 62(a)

11.33 If, however, the claimant does not receive income support, JSA(IB) or the guarantee credit then it is necessary to calculate entitlement. This is done on the same basis as claims for rent rebates and allowances (paras. 7.8-11) but note that there are two different methods depending on whether the claimant (or their partner if they have one) is aged at least 60 or younger (chapters 13 to 15). If they are aged at least 60 a further differentiation applies depending on whether or not they receive the savings credit (chapter 13). If the claimant's income is less than or equal to the applicable amount, the maximum rebate is awarded (paras. 7.4 and 11.32). If the claimant's income is greater than his or her applicable amount a taper of 20% of the excess income is applied. Once again this is expressed on a weekly basis, as illustrated in the example.

Example: Effect of taper where income exceeds applicable amount

A couple with one child aged 14, income of £160 per week (after disregards) and a weekly rate liability of £12.50.

1. Deduct applicable amount from income (after disregards) i.e.

Income	£160.00
Applicable amount	£145.52
Excess	£14.48

2. Take 20% of excess income and deduct from weekly eligible rates i.e.

Weekly eligible rates	£12.50
Less 20% of excess	£2.90
Weekly rate rebate	£9.60

Table 11.2: Weekly non-dependant deductions for rates

Non-dependant working 16 hours or more per week* with a gross income of:	
£308 per week or more	£6.95
between £247 and £307.99 per week	£5.80
between £144 and £246.99 per week	£4.60
under £144.00 per week	£2.30
Non-dependant not in work or working less than 16 hours* per week	
On income support or income-based jobseeker's allowance	NIL
All other cases (regardless of income level)	£2.30

* Strictly speaking what matters is whether the non-dependant is in remunerative work (see paras. 7.29-34).

Example: Effect of non-dependant deduction

Using the same example in paragraph 11.33 but this time with a non-dependant working over 16 hours with gross income of £195 per week

1. Deduct non-dependant charge from weekly eligible rates i.e.

Weekly Eligible Rates	£12.50
Less Non Dependant Charge	£4.60
Maximum Rate Rebate	£7.90

2. Deduct applicable amount from income (after disregards) i.e.

Income	£160.00
Applicable Amount	£145.52
Excess	£14.48

3. Take 20% of excess income and deduct from maximum Rate Rebate i.e.

Maximum Rate Rebate	£7.90
Less 20% of Excess	£2.90
Weekly Rate Rebate	£5.00

NON-DEPENDANT DEDUCTIONS

NIHBR 63 **11.34** As with rent rebates and allowances a non-dependant in the household can affect the amount of rate rebate payable. The normal rules concerning when a non dependant deduction is made to rent rebates/allowances apply equally to rate rebates (paras. 7.17-36 and table 7.2); in particular, no deduction is made if the claimant receives the care component of disability living allowance, attendance allowance or is registered blind (paras. 7.19-22). The rules as to the treatment of non-dependant couples and joint occupiers are the same as for rent allowances/rebates (paras. 7.35-36). Only the rate of deduction and the circumstances in which they apply are different. These are given in table 11.2.

ADJUSTMENT AND PAYMENT FOR RENT FREE PERIODS

11.35 In rare cases tenants who pay their rates as part of their gross rent may also have 'rent free' periods. If this is the case an adjustment is necessary so that benefit is paid only in the periods in which rent is charged. As with conversion to weekly amounts (paras. 11.28-29) there are two alternative methods of conversion but HB regulations stipulate the circumstances in which each method is to be used.

- The first method is used when a tenancy is on a weekly (or multiple of weekly) basis (para. 11.36).
- The second method is used where the tenant has a tenancy on other than a weekly basis (such as calendar monthly or quarterly)(para. 11.37).

METHOD 1: WEEKLY TENANTS WITH INCLUSIVE RENTS

NIHBR 70(2)(a) **11.36** The weekly benefit is calculated in the normal way (para.11.28) including any deductions which apply as a result of the taper or non-dependant charges (paras. 11.32-34) to give the 'true' weekly benefit. From this the total benefit for the whole period is calculated by multiplying the true weekly figure by the total number of weeks in the period to which it relates (including any rent free period), which unless liability commences part way through the year will be 52 or 53. This is then divided by the number of weeks in which the rent is charged (i.e. the whole period less any rent free weeks) and paid in equal instalments in each of those weeks together with any HB in respect of the rent. No HB is payable during any 'rent free' week.

METHOD 2: MONTHLY TENANTS ETC WITH INCLUSIVE RENTS

NIHBR 70(2)(b) **11.37** The true weekly benefit is calculated in the normal way (para.11.28) taking account of any deductions which apply as a result of the taper or non-dependant charges (paras. 11.32-34) and the resulting figure is divided by 7 to give the daily rate. A conversion factor is then applied by multiplying this daily rate by the total number of days in the period to which it relates including any rent free period (which unless liability commences part way through the year will be 365 or 366), and dividing by the number of days in the period when rent is chargeable. For example, if rent is charged monthly except March which is 'rent free' the division factor will be 334 (i.e. 365 – 31). The converted daily rate is then multiplied by the number of days in the rental period to which it relates in which rent is charged. For example, in a month with 30 days this will be 30 times the converted daily rate. No HB is payable during any 'rent free' period.

MINIMUM RATE REBATE

11.38 Unlike rent rebates and allowances, where no HB is payable if entitlement is less than 50p per week (since April 1991), there is no minimum rate rebate figure. Hence if a claimant is entitled to only 1p per week this has to be deducted from the rates account by the RCA, credited to the rent account or paid by the NIHE.

NISR 1991 No. 176

EXTENDED PAYMENTS OF RATE REBATE

11.39 These are dealt with in paragraphs 17.81-93 and table 17.7 of the Guide.

Payment of rate rebate as a rent allowance

11.40 In the vast majority of cases, HB for rates is paid as rebate. However, a rate rebate can be paid as if it was a rent allowance in the following circumstances:

NIHBR 88(2), 89, 90(3)

- the claimant is a tenant who is entitled to a rent allowance, or would be but for any non-dependant charges or the application of the taper; and
- the claimant pays rates to his or her landlord as part of the rent (whether or not the charge is separately identified) rather than directly to the RCA.

Note that this does not apply to owner-occupiers because they pay their rates directly to the RCA or NIHE tenants because they are paid by rebate. The decision to pay benefit as an allowance is at the discretion of the NIHE. Any allowance so payable can be paid to the tenant or directly to the landlord in accordance with the rules for rent allowances (paras. 16.12-40); in particular, where the total benefit is £2 per week or less payment can be four-weekly, or where it is less than £1 per week every six months.

12 Applicable amounts

12.1 An applicable amount is the figure used in calculating HB and main CTB to reflect the basic living needs of the claimant and family. This chapter covers:

- personal allowances;
- general rules about premiums;
- the detailed rules for each premium in turn; and
- further rules and special cases.

CBA 135
NICBA 131
HBR 16
HBR 60+ 16
CTBR 8
CTBR 60+ 8

12.2 A claimant's applicable amount is the same for both HB and main CTB purposes. It is the total of any personal allowances and premiums which apply in their case. All claimants have an applicable amount but for those in receipt of income support, income-based job seeker's allowance or the guarantee credit this is a technicality as they are treated as having no income and capital and are therefore entitled to maximum HB/CTB (para. 7.3). Consequently, this chapter does not apply to these claimants for the purpose of calculating HB/CTB.

SI 2003 No. 325
Reg 2, 12
NISR 2003 No. 197
Reg 2, 12

12.3 As described in the relevant places in this chapter, there are some differences in the law depending on whether:

- the claimant or any partner is aged 60 or over; and
- the claimant and any partner are both under the age of 60.

Personal allowances

HBR 16(a),(b),
sch 2 paras 1,2
HBR 60+ 16(a),(b)
sch 2A paras 1,2
CTBR 8(a),(b)
sch 1 paras 1,2
CTBR 60+ 8(a),(b)
sch 1A paras 1,2

12.4 Personal allowances are awarded for the claimant and any other family members (para. 4.5). There are different amounts for single claimants, couples and, if the claimant is under the age of 60, lone parents. Additions are made for children and young persons (sometimes known as dependants' allowances). The amounts, which vary with age, are given in table 12.1 and table 12.2.

Table 12.1: Weekly applicable amounts where the claimant and any partner are under the age of 60

PERSONAL ALLOWANCES

Single claimant	aged under 25	£44.05
	aged 25 or over	£55.65
Lone parent	aged under 18 (HB only)	£44.05
	aged 18 or over	£55.65
Couple	both aged under 18 (HB only)	£66.50
	at least one aged 18 or over	£87.30
Child/young person addition	regardless of age	£42.27

PREMIUMS

The claimant is awarded any of the following that apply:

Family premium *	'baby' rate	£26.45
	normal rate	£15.95
Disabled child premium	child/young person	£42.49
Enhanced disability premium	single claimant or lone parent	£11.60
	couple	£16.75
	child/young person	£17.08
Severe disability premium	single rate	£44.15
	double rate	£88.30
Carer premium	claimant or partner or each	£25.55

The claimant is awarded the highest of any of the following that apply:

Family premium (protected lone parent rate) *	'baby' rate	£32.70
	normal rate	£22.20
Disability premium	single claimant or lone parent	£23.70
	couple	£33.85
Bereavement premium	single claimant	£23.95

* The higher rate of family premium at the protected lone parent rate applies instead of the family premium in certain circumstances: paragraph 12.8.

Table 12.2 Weekly applicable amounts where the claimant or any partner are aged 60 or over

PERSONAL ALLOWANCES*		
Single claimant	aged 60-64	£105.45
	aged 65 or over	£121.00
Couple	both aged under 65	£160.95
	one or both aged 65 or over	£181.20
Child or young person		£42.27
PREMIUMS		
The claimant is awarded any of the following that apply:		
Severe disability premium	single rate	£44.15
	couple – one qualifies	£44.15
	couple – both qualify	£88.30
Enhanced disability premiums**	Child/young person only	£17.08
Disabled child premium		£42.49
Carer premium	claimant or partner or each	£25.55

* The DWP has acknowledged that the omission of personal allowances for lone parents aged 60 or over was unintended, and has advised that authorities should treat them as single claimants.

** The enhanced disability rate is only available for a child or young person – not the claimant or partner – where the claimant or any partner is aged 60 or over.

EXAMPLES: APPLICABLE AMOUNTS

Except for the lone parent in the fourth example, none of the following qualifies for any of the premiums for disability or for carers.

SINGLE CLAIMANT AGED 23

Personal allowance:

single claimant aged under 25	£44.05
No premiums apply	
Applicable amount	£44.05

COUPLE (BOTH UNDER AGE 60) WITH TWO CHILDREN AGED 13 AND 17

The older child is still at school so still counts as a dependant of the couple.

Personal allowances:

couple at least one over 18	£87.30
child aged 13	£42.27
child aged 17	£42.27
Premium: family premium (normal rate)	£15.95
Applicable amount	£187.79

COUPLE AGED 38 AND 65

Personal allowance:

Couple at least one aged 65	£181.20
Applicable amount	£181.20

DISABLED LONE PARENT UNDER 60 WITH BABY

The lone parent is in receipt of the highest rate of the care component disability living allowance and so qualifies for a disability premium and enhanced disability premium. Her baby is aged under one year.

Personal allowances:

Lone parent aged over 18	£55.65
Child	£42.27
Premiums:	
Family premium ('baby' rate)	£26.45
disability premium (single rate)	£23.70
enhanced disability premium (single rate)	£11.60
Applicable amount	£159.67

Premiums

HBR 16(c),(d)
sch 2 paras 3-6, 15
HBR 60+ 16(c)-(e)
sch 2A paras 3-4, 12
CTBR 8(c),(d)
sch 1 paras 3-6, 19
CTBR 60+ 8(c)-(e)
sch 1A paras 3-4, 12

12.5 Many claimants – but not all – qualify for one or more premiums. Tables 12.1 and 12.2 list the premiums available and give their amounts. A premium is awarded if its conditions of entitlement are satisfied. Some of the conditions are straightforward, some more complicated and less well known. Claimants may therefore miss entitlement unless authority staff are fully trained and claim forms are carefully designed. In particular, receipt of various state benefits triggers entitlement to many premiums, and general points about these are given in paragraphs 12.31-33 . The next few sections give the conditions for each premium.

HOW MANY PREMIUMS AT ONCE?

HBR sch 2 paras 5, 6
CTBR sch 1
paras 5, 6

12.6 Where the claimant or any partner is aged 60 or over they are entitled to all of the premiums identified in table 12.2 that they meet the conditions for. Where the claimant and any partner are under age 60 (table 12.1) they can only receive the highest of any of the following they qualify for: the family premium (protected lone parent rate), disability premium, or bereavement premium. They can also receive any other premiums they meet the conditions for in table 12.1. In this Guide, the premiums are described in such a way that all limitations are given as conditions for the premiums. The following examples illustrate how in certain circumstances there is a limit on the number of premiums that can be awarded at any one time.

EXAMPLES: OVERLAPPING PREMIUMS

OVER 60 WITH A DISABLED SON

A claimant is aged 63. He is not disabled in any way but his grandson aged 15 gets the highest rate of the care component of disability living allowance. No-one else lives with them.

The claimant gets a disabled child premium and an enhanced disability premium for his grandson. He also gets a family premium.

UNDER 60, DISABLED AND BEREAVED

A single claimant aged 58 has had a bereavement and fulfils the conditions for the bereavement premium. He also gets the highest rate of the care component of disability living allowance. He gets a disability premium and an enhanced disability premium. But he cannot get a bereavement premium (which is a lower amount than the disability premium) at the same time as the disability premium.

FAMILY PREMIUM

12.7 The condition for this premium is that there is at least one child or young person in the claimant's family – whether the claimant is in a couple or is a lone parent. The terms 'child', 'young person', 'family', 'couple' and 'lone parent' are used in the specific senses defined for HB and CTB (paras. 4.4-20). In particular, a child or young person need not be the natural child of the claimant but could, for example, be a grandchild living as part of the claimant's family.

HBR sch 2 para 3
HBR 60+ sch 2A para 3
CTBR sch 1 para 3
CTBR 60+ sch 1A para 3

12.8 There are two main rates of this premium (and see also para. 12.9):

- the 'baby' rate is awarded to couples and lone parents with at least one child aged under one year;
- the normal rate is awarded to other couples and lone parents (with at least one child or young person).

12.9 Where the claimant is under the age of 60, higher 'protected rates' of family premium apply to certain lone parents (never couples). They are £32.70 ('baby' protected rate) and £22.20 (normal protected rate). The conditions are in the next paragraph. There is no equivalent protected rate where the claimant is aged 60 or over.

HBR sch 2 para 3(2)-(4)
CTBR sch 1 para 3(2)-(4)

12.10 A lone parent under age 60 qualifies for the protected rates of the family premium if, and for as long as, all the following conditions apply:

- on 5th April 1998, they were entitled to HB or CTB and satisfied the conditions for the lone parent rate of the family premium or would have done so but for the fact that 5th April 1998 fell within a rent-free period;
- they have remained entitled to HB or CTB continuously since that date (ignoring breaks due only to rent-free periods);
- they have not ceased to be a lone parent at any time since that date;
- they have not become entitled to income support or to income-based jobseeker's allowance, or ceased to be entitled to both those benefits, at any time since that date; and
- they have not reached the age of 60 or become entitled to a disability premium at any time since that date.

As soon as any of the last four conditions ceases to apply, the person ceases permanently to qualify for the protected lone parent rate (but may still qualify for the basic rate).

PENSIONER PREMIUMS

12.11 Prior to October 2003, pensioner premiums were relevant to the calculation of the claimant's applicable amount if they or any partner were aged 60 or more (see paras. 12.12-18 of the 2003-04 edition of this Guide for the details).

HBR sch 2 paras 9, 9A, 10
CTBR sch 2 paras 9, 10, 11

While these premiums still exist in legislation, they are no longer relevant to the calculation of the claimant's applicable amount.

DISABILITY PREMIUM

12.12 A disability premium may be awarded where the claimant and any partner are under age 60. To receive this premium the claimant (or in the case of a couple, either partner) must count as 'disabled or long-term sick' in one of the ways described in paragraphs 12.13-14 (but note that it must be the claimant, not the partner, in the cases described in para. 12.15). In the case of a couple, the couple rate is awarded even if only one partner fulfils the conditions.

'DISABLED OR LONG-TERM SICK

HBR 2(1) sch 2 para 12(1),(2) CTBR 2(1) sch 1 para 13(1),(2)

12.13 The following are the ways of counting as 'disabled or long-term sick' in order to qualify for a disability premium (para. 12.12). They are that the claimant or any partner:

(a) is registered or certified blind (this means with the social services or social work department or in Northern Ireland with the Health and Social Services Board); or

(b) ceased to be registered or certified blind within the past 28 weeks because of regaining sight; or

(c) receives disability living allowance (either component payable at any rate); or

(d) receives the disability element or severe disability element of working tax credit; or

(e) receives any increase for attendance or mobility paid with an industrial disablement benefit or war disablement benefit (including constant attendance allowance, 'old cases' attendance payments, mobility supplement, severe disablement occupational allowance and exceptionally severe disablement allowance); or

(f) has part or all of their disability living allowance paid to the Motability fund; or

(g) has an invalid vehicle supplied by the NHS or gets DWP payments for car running costs; or

(h) is incapable of work and fulfils the further conditions in either of the next two paragraphs.

HBR sch 2 para 12(1),(4),(7) CTBR sch 1 para 13(1),(4),(6A) SI 1995 No 626 NISR 1995 No 129

PEOPLE WHO ARE INCAPABLE OF WORK: THE MAIN RULE

12.14 For the above purposes, the claimant or any partner counts as 'disabled or long-term sick' if they receive severe disablement allowance or incapacity benefit payable at the long-term rate (which starts after 52 weeks of incapacity for work), or are terminally ill and receive it at the short-term higher rate (which starts after 28 weeks of incapacity for work).

PEOPLE WHO ARE INCAPABLE OF WORK: THE '28/52-WEEK RULE'

12.15 Additionally, for the purposes of qualifying for a disability premium, the claimant (but not the claimant's partner) counts as disabled or long-term sick if they:

- are incapable of work; and
- have been incapable of work for a 'waiting period' (calculated as described below) of:
  - 28 weeks (196 days) if they are terminally ill, or
  - 52 weeks (364 days) in any other case.

After the waiting period is completed, there are further 'linking rules' (described below).

12.16 This way of qualifying for a disability premium 'fills the gap' for people who are incapable of work but do not get incapacity benefit. For couples, it must be the claimant – not their partner – who fulfils this rule. It can therefore be important which partner makes the claim (para. 5.5).

12.17 'Incapable of work' means the same here as it does for incapacity benefit purposes. Broadly, during the first 28 weeks the person must satisfy an 'own occupation test', and thereafter (or from the outset if they have no normal occupation) an 'all work test'. Broadly, a person is 'terminally ill' if their death can be expected within six months. The decision about whether a claimant is capable or incapable of work will always be made by a Decision Maker at the Jobcentre Plus office (DWP GM, para. C4.99).

THE 'WAITING PERIOD' AND THE 'LINKING RULES'

12.18 In the following, a 'gap' means a period during which the person either is capable of work or is disqualified from incapacity benefit. The waiting period (para. 12.15) need not be continuous. Any number of periods are added together so long as the gap between each is eight weeks or less.

Once a person has completed the waiting period, there are linking rules as follows:

- the claimant does not qualify for a disability premium during a gap;
- after a gap of eight weeks or less, the person qualifies for a disability premium straight away;
- after a gap of more than eight weeks, the person does not qualify for a disability premium until they have completed a fresh waiting period.

Breaks in entitlement to HB or CTB during the waiting period or after it have no effect on this rule.

DISABLED CHILD PREMIUM

HBR sch 2 para 14
HBR 60+ sch 2A para 8
CTBR sch 1 para 15
CTBR 60+ sch 1A para 8

12.19 The condition for this premium is that a child or young person in the family:

- is registered or certified blind (this means with the social services or social work department or in Northern Ireland with the Health and Social Services Board); or
- ceased to be registered or certified blind within the past 28 weeks because of regaining sight; or
- receives disability living allowance (either component payable at any rate).

A disabled child premium is awarded for each child or young person to whom this applies. If the child/young person dies the premium should continue for eight weeks following the death.

ENHANCED DISABILITY PREMIUM

HBR sch 2 paras 13A
HBR 60+ sch 2A para 7
CTBR sch 1 paras 14A
CTBR 60+ sch 1A para 7

12.20 Where the claimant and any partner are aged under 60 this premium can be awarded in respect of the claimant or partner and/or in respect of a child or young person in the family. Two or more of these premiums are awarded if appropriate – for example, if a claimant or partner qualifies and also one or more children or young persons. Where the claimant or any partner is aged 60 or over, this premium can only be awarded in respect of a child or young person in the family.

12.21 The condition in the case of the claimant or partner is that:

- the claimant is (or in the case of a couple, both partners are) aged under 60; and
- the claimant (or in the case of a couple, either partner) receives the highest rate of the care component of disability living allowance. (The mobility component of disability living allowance is not sufficient, nor are the lower or middle rates of the care component.)

In the case of a couple, the couple rate is awarded even if only one partner fulfils the second condition.

12.22 The condition in the case of a child or young person is that they receive the highest rate of the care component of disability living allowance. (The mobility component of disability living allowance is not sufficient, nor are the lower or middle rates of the care component.)

SEVERE DISABILITY PREMIUM

12.23 There are three conditions for this premium: HBR 2(1) sch 2 para 13 HBR 60+ sch 2A para 6 CTBR 2(1) sch 1 para 14 CTBR 60+ sch 1A para 6

- the person must be receiving:
  - the middle or highest rate of the care component of disability living allowance, or
  - attendance allowance, or
  - any increase for attendance or mobility paid with an industrial disablement benefit or war disablement benefit (including constant attendance allowance, 'old cases' attendance payments, mobility supplement, severe disablement occupational allowance and exceptionally severe disablement allowance);

  and
- the person must have no non-dependants (with the exceptions mentioned below);

  and
- no-one must be receiving carer's allowance to care for the person (though it does not count if carer's allowance is not awarded following certain benefit fraud convictions, nor does it count if it is not awarded because the person has been in hospital for four weeks or more). A back-dated award of carer's allowance is ignored for this purpose as regards any period before the award was made: in other words the backdated part does not cause an overpayment. (Until last year, carer's allowance was called invalid care allowance.)

12.24 A single claimant or lone parent who fulfils all three conditions gets the single rate of severe disability premium.

12.25 In the case of a couple, a severe disability premium is awarded as follows:

- if both partners fulfil all three conditions, they get the double rate;
- if both partners fulfil the first two conditions but only one fulfils the third condition, they get the single rate;
- if the claimant fulfils all three conditions, and their partner is registered or certified blind or ceased to be within the past 28 weeks, they get the single rate. In this case, if the 'wrong' partner makes the claim, they should be advised to 'swap the claimant role';
- if they have been getting the double rate, but one partner then ceases to fulfil the first condition because of having been in hospital for four weeks, they get the single rate from that point.

12.26 For the purposes of the above rule, the following non-dependants do not count (i.e. do not prevent the award of a severe disability premium):

- non-dependants under 18;
- non-dependants who are registered or certified blind or who ceased to be within the past 28 weeks;
- non-dependants receiving:
  - the middle or highest rate of the care component of disability living allowance, or
  - attendance allowance, or
  - any increase for attendance or mobility paid with an industrial disablement benefit or war disablement benefit (including constant attendance allowance, 'old cases' attendance payments, mobility supplement, severe disablement occupational allowance and exceptionally severe disablement allowance).

It should also be borne in mind that a number of categories of people are excluded from the definition of a non-dependant (para. 4.21).

Example: Severe disability premium, etc

A husband and wife are both under 60 and both receive the middle rate of the care component of disability living allowance. Neither of them is or has recently been registered or certified blind. Their daughter of 17 is in full-time employment and lives with them. Their son lives elsewhere and receives carer's allowance for caring for the husband. No-one receives carer's allowance for the wife.

Disability premium: Because of receiving disability living allowance, they are awarded the couple rate of disability premium.

Enhanced disability premium: Because they get the middle (not the highest) rate of the care component of disability living allowance, this cannot be awarded.

Severe disability premium:

- Both receive the appropriate type of disability living allowance.
- Although their daughter is a non-dependant, she is under 18.
- Someone receives carer's allowance for caring for only one of them.

So they are awarded the single rate of severe disability premium (for the second reason in para. 12.15).

CARER PREMIUM

12.27 The details relating to this premium changed on 28th October 2002 (and general guidance is in circular HB/CTB A10/2003). There are now two different ways to qualify for it. These are that the claimant (or, in the case of a couple, either partner):

HBR sch 2 paras 7(2), 14ZA HBR 60+ sch 2A paras 5(2), 9 CTBR sch 1 paras 7(2), 16 CTBR 60+ sch 1A paras 5(2), 9 SI 2002 No. 1457 NISR 2002 No. 321

- is entitled to, and is being paid, a carer's allowance (until last year called invalid care allowance), or was within the last eight weeks (whether carer's allowance stopped due to the death of the person being cared for or due to any other reason); or
- is entitled to carer's allowance, or was within the last eight weeks, but it is not being paid because of the rules about overlapping social security benefits (as illustrated in the examples), and the person they care for continues to receive attendance allowance or the middle or highest rate of the care component of disability living allowance. In Commissioners decision CIS/367/2003 it was held that since the rules state that the claimant only has to be 'entitled' and not 'in receipt of' carer's allowance there is no requirement for the carer to have made a claim for the allowance – it is sufficient that they would satisfy the conditions for it if they made a claim. This in fact has been the position since 3rd April 2000 when the regulations were amended. Although CIS/367/2003 is an income support decision the wording of the regulations are identical. (It is also worth noting that since 28th October 2002, many older people may qualify for this premium for the first time, whereas before that date the rules for carers allowance meant that no-one aged over 65 could qualify for carer's allowance and so get the premium.)

A single claimant who fulfils either condition gets one carer premium. A couple get one or two carer premiums, one if one of them fulfils either condition, two if both do.

12.28 It is worth noting that although entitlement to carer's allowance means the award of a carer premium for the carer, the person cared for may lose a severe disability premium (though not retrospectively: para. 12.23). However this happens only if the carer's allowance (or part of it) is actually being paid to the carer – and not in the situations illustrated in the examples. It is therefore not impossible for a couple who care for each other to qualify for a severe disability premium and also for two carer premiums.

HBR sch 2 para 14B HBR 60+ sch 2A para 11 CTBR sch 2 para 18 CTBR 60+ sch 2A para 11

Example: Carer premium and overlapping benefits

A claimant and her partner are both in receipt of retirement pension. She looks after her partner who receives attendance allowance. She is entitled to carer's allowance but has not claimed it. Even if she did make a claim for carer's allowance it could not be awarded because it would be overlapped by her retirement pension (in other words, payment of the latter prevents payment of the former).

Because she meets the necessary conditions for the carer premium, it should be awarded regardless of whether she makes a claim for carer's allowance. The award should be from the date her partner received attendance allowance (provided she was caring for him) or from 3rd April 2000, whichever occurred latest. If she subsequently stopped looking after her partner, she would no longer qualify for the carer premium because she would no longer be entitled to the carer's allowance.

BEREAVEMENT PREMIUM

HBR sch 2 para 8A
CTBR sch 1 para 8A
SI 2000 No. 2239

12.29 This premium is awarded to a claimant who meets all the following conditions:

- on 9th April 2001, the claimant was aged 55 or over but under 60 (in other words, their date of birth falls between 10th April 1941 and 9th April 1946, both dates included); and
- the claimant is still under 60; and
- the claimant does not qualify for a disability premium (or enhanced disability premium); and
- the claimant's spouse (i.e. husband or wife, not an unmarried partner) died on or after 9th April 2001; and
- the claimant has been receiving bereavement allowance in respect of that death but has ceased to do so; and
- the claimant is either on HB or CTB at the time bereavement allowance stops, or claims HB or CTB within eight weeks of the last day on which they were entitled to it; and

- at that date, the claimant is a single claimant (i.e. has neither a partner, married or unmarried, nor a child or young person in the family).

12.30 This premium ceases to exist on 10th April 2006 (by when all beneficiaries will have reached 60).

General rules

BEING 'IN RECEIPT' OF A BENEFIT

12.31 Receipt of a state benefit forms part of the condition for many of the premiums. For these purposes, a person is 'in receipt' of a benefit only if it is paid in respect of himself or herself, and only during the period for which it is awarded.

HBR sch 2 para 14B
HBR 60+
sch 2A para 11
CTBR sch 1 para 18
CTBR 60+
sch 1A para 11

DWP CONCESSIONARY PAYMENTS

12.32 For the purpose of entitlement to any premium, a DWP concessionary payment compensating for non-payment of any state benefit is treated as if it were that benefit.

HBR sch 2 para 14A
HBR 60+
sch 2A para 10
CTBR sch 1 para 17
CTBR 60+
sch1A para 10

OVERLAPPING SOCIAL SECURITY BENEFITS

12.33 Where a claimant is entitled to a qualifying benefit but does not receive it because of the rules about overlapping social security benefits (for example if widow's pension is payable instead of incapacity benefit) then the claimant will not normally be treated as being in receipt of the qualifying benefit except in the following circumstances:

HBR sch 2
paras 7, 14B
HBR 60+
sch 2A paras 5, 11
CTBR sch 1
para 7, 18
CTBR 60+
sch 1A paras 5, 11

- if they qualify for the carer's premium (paras. 12.27-28);
- if they qualified for that premium before the relevant qualifying benefit was overlapped then they will continue to be treated as in receipt of the qualifying benefit during any period in which they would be in receipt of that benefit but for the overlapping benefit rules. The purpose of this rule is that it protects claimants from a reduction in their benefit merely because they became entitled to an overlapping benefit at some later date;
- if the qualifying benefit is only partially overlapped (i.e. the overlapping benefit is paid at a rate which is less than the qualifying benefit).

Special cases

POLYGAMOUS MARRIAGES

HBR 17 sch 2
HBR 60+ sch 2A
CTBR 9 sch 1
CTBR 60+ sch 1A

12.34 The applicable amount for a claimant in a polygamous marriage (para. 4.10) is the sum of the following. If the following could combine to produce more than one result, the result which is most favourable to the claimant applies:

- where none of the partners in a polygamous marriage is aged 60 or over:
  - the personal allowance of £87.30, unless (in HB only) all the members of the polygamous marriage are under 18, in which case £66.50; and
  - £31.65 for each spouse in excess of two;
- where at least one of the partners in a polygamous marriage is aged 60 or over but none of the members of the marriage have attained the age of 65:
  - the personal allowance of £160.95; and
  - £55.50 for each spouse in excess of two;
- where at least one of the members of a polygamous marriage is aged 65 or over:
  - the personal allowance of £181.20; and
  - £60.20 for each spouse in excess of two;
- additions to the personal allowance for any child or young person as in any other case plus, if appropriate, disabled child premium and enhanced disability premium for them;
- family premium if there is at least one child or young person in their family;
- the double rate of severe disability premium if all members of the marriage fulfil all three conditions in paragraph 12.23; the single rate if all members of the marriage fulfil the first two of those conditions but someone receives an invalid care allowance for caring for at least one of them; and the single rate if the claimant fulfils all three conditions and all the other members of the marriage are registered or certified blind or ceased to be within the past 28 weeks;
- a carer premium in respect of each partner that satisfies the conditions (DWP HB/CTB *Pension Credit Handbook* – part 2, para. 145)
- the couple rate of any other premium if the ordinary conditions are satisfied.

CHILDREN AND YOUNG PERSONS WITH CAPITAL

12.35 Where the claimant and any partner are aged under 60 and in the claimant's family there is a child or young person with capital amounting to over £3,000 (assessed under the rules described in chapters 13-15): HBR 16(b) sch 2 paras 13A(2), 14(a) CTBR 8(b) sch 1 paras 14A(2), 15(a)

- no addition is made in the calculation of the claimant's personal allowance for that child or young person;
- no disabled child premium or enhanced disability premium is awarded for that child or young person; but
- the claimant's entitlement to a family premium (whether the basic rate or protected lone parent rate applies) is not affected (i.e. this is awarded regardless of any child's or young person's capital).

12.36 Where the claimant, or any partner, is aged 60 or over, these amounts are included in the claimant's applicable amount for each child or young person, irrespective of the amount of capital that dependent child or young person possesses.

Example: Child with capital of her own

A lone parent qualifies for the protected rate of the family premium (para. 12.10) and has a daughter of 13. Neither has any disability. The daughter has capital of over £3,000, so no addition is made for her in the personal allowances. Her capital does not affect the award of a family premium.

Personal allowance:	
lone parent aged over 18 (under 60)	£55.65
Premium:	
family premium (protected normal rate)	£22.20
Applicable amount	£77.85

PEOPLE ON TRAINING COURSES OR IN RECEIPT OF A TRAINING ALLOWANCE

HBR sch 2 para 7(1)(b), 12(5) HBR 60+ sch 2A para 5(1)(b) CTBR sch 1 para 7(1)(b), 13(5) CTBR 60+ sch 1A para 5(1)(b)

12.37 Once a person qualifies for any of the premiums for disability or for carers, if they go on a government-run or approved training course (para. 13.63), or for any period during which they receive a training allowance, the premium does not cease just because entitlement to a state benefit has ended or the person no longer fulfils the rule about being incapable of work. The objective of this rule is that otherwise there would be a disincentive to undertake such training.

PEOPLE IN HOSPITAL

12.38 The following rules apply only in the case of a stay in an NHS hospital (including an NHS trust hospital). They do not apply at all to those serving a custodial sentence, nor to private patients whose fees cover all their costs.

HBR sch 2 paras 12(1), 14 HBR 60+ sch 2A paras 6(7), 7 CTBR sch 1 paras 13(1), 15 CTBR 60+ sch 1A paras 6(7), 7

12.39 If a claimant or any member of the family goes into hospital, and disability living allowance or attendance allowance (or any of the items in entries (f) to (g) in para. 12.20) stops being paid as a result (which normally happens after four weeks in hospital), this by itself does not mean that the claimant loses entitlement to a disability premium or disabled child premium. However, the claimant's entitlement to a severe disability premium does stop after four weeks for this reason (except as described at the end of para. 12.25). And a carer's entitlement to a carer premium stops after the disabled person he or she is caring for has been in hospital for four weeks.

HBR 18 HBR 60+ 16 CTBR 10 CTBR 60+ 8

12.40 In most cases after a continuous period of 52 weeks in hospital, entitlement to HB/CTB ceases altogether (paras. 3.32 and 3.37). In such cases the calculation of the applicable amount is irrelevant. However, the applicable amount is reduced after the claimant or any partner has been in hospital for a total of 52 weeks or more (tables 12.3 and 12.4) which can be made up of any number of short periods added together. For the purposes of counting the 52 week period, two stays in hospital are added together if the break between them is four weeks or less. An income support commissioner's decision (CIS/571/1997) is persuasive for HB/CTB. It held that the day someone goes into hospital does not count as a day in hospital, whereas the day someone comes out does count as a day in hospital. There is no reduction under this rule if a child or young person goes into hospital.

12.41 If the claimant is in hospital for 52 continuous weeks or more, HB and CTB cease altogether (para. 3.81). If any partner, child or young person is in hospital for 52 continuous weeks or more, he or she ceases to count as part of the family (paras. 4.11, 4.17).

Table 12.3: Applicable amounts after hospital downrating (claimant and any partner under age 60)

HBR 18
CTBR 10

The downrating applies after 52 weeks in hospital.

(a) Single claimant	£19.90
(b) Lone parent	£19.90 plus: • additions for children/young persons • family premium • any disabled child premium • any enhanced disability premium
(c) Couple where one only has been in hospital for more than 52 weeks*	The applicable amount is reduced by £15.90
(d) Couple where both have been in hospital for more than 52 weeks**	The applicable amount is £39.80 plus any of the following which apply
(e) Polygamous marriage where not all have been in hospital for more than 52 weeks*	Applicable amount is the same as if none were in hospital minus £15.90 for each one who has been in hospital for more than 52 weeks
(f) Polygamous marriage where all have been in hospital for more than 52 weeks**	Applicable amount reduces to £19.90 for each member of the marriage plus any of the following which apply: • additions for children and young persons; • family premium; • any disabled child premium(s).

* In these cases entitlement to a premium remains even if the person in hospital fulfils the condition for it.

** For couples and polygamous marriages there may be two succeeding reductions in the applicable amount.

Table 12.4: Applicable amounts after hospital downrating (claimant or any partner aged 60 or over)

HBR 60+ 16(2),(3)
CTBR 60+ 8(2),(3)

The downrating applies after 52 weeks in hospital.

(a) Single claimant	£15.90
(b) Lone parent	£15.90 plus: • additions for children/young persons • family premium • any disabled child premium • any enhanced disability premium
(c) Couple where one only has been in hospital for more than 52 weeks	The applicable amount is reduced by £15.90
(d) Couple where both have been in hospital for more than 52 weeks	The applicable amount is reduced by £31.80
(e) Polygamous marriage where one or more members of the marriage have been in hospital for more than 52 weeks	The applicable amount is reduced by £15.90 multiplied by the number of the members of the marriage in hospital for more than 52 weeks

13 Income and capital

13.1 This and the following two chapters describe how income and capital are dealt with in the assessment of HB and main CTB. Chapters 14 and 15 give additional information relating to employed earners and the self-employed. This chapter covers:

- how different rules apply for different groups of claimants;
- general matters;
- benefits, pensions, and other state help;
- the home, property and possessions;
- savings and investments;
- trust funds and awards for personal injury;
- other items of income and capital;
- notional income and capital;
- children's and young persons' income and capital; and
- the separate rules used for claimants on savings credit.

There have been numerous changes this year, principally due to the different rules (introduced on 6th October 2003) for assessing income and capital for people aged 60+ (paras. 13.5 and 13.7-8).

13.2 Income and capital are assessed in the same way for HB and for main CTB purposes. The claimant is treated as having the income of any partner. All references in this chapter to the income or capital of a claimant should be read as also referring to the income and capital of a partner (para. 13.6). Income and capital are assessed differently for all purposes relevant to second adult rebate (para. 8.24) and to non-dependant deductions (paras. 7.24-27); this chapter does not apply in such cases.

The different rules for different groups of claimants

CLAIMANTS ON JSA(IB), IS OR GUARANTEE CREDIT

HBR sch 3 para 10, sch 4 para 5, sch 5 para 5
HBR 60+ 22
CTBR sch 3 para 10, sch 4 para 4, sch 5 para 5
CTBR 60+ 14

13.3 If a claimant is on JSA(IB), IS or guarantee credit (or his or her partner is), the whole of his or her (and any partner's) income and capital is fully disregarded. There are no exceptions whatsoever. The remainder of this chapter therefore does not apply in such cases. (Paras. 7.5-7 show how their entitlement to HB/main CTB is assessed.)

13.4 The same applies in CTB (but not HB), or in Northern Ireland HB in respect of rates only, to a person who lost JSA(IB) or IS on 1st April 2003 solely because Supporting People took over payments of certain support charges. This rule applies until the claimant or partner reaches the age of 60 (because no equivalent rule exists for 60+s: para. 13.7). CTBR sch 4 para 4B NIHBR sch 4 para 4B

CLAIMANTS ON SAVINGS CREDIT

13.5 If a claimant is on savings credit (or his or her partner is), there are special rules for assessing income and capital. The rules for people on savings credit are in paragraphs 13.150-159 and the other parts of this chapter do not apply.

OTHER CASES: WHOSE INCOME AND CAPITAL COUNTS

HBR 19, 39
HBR 60+ 21
CTBR 11, 30
CTBR 60+ 13

13.6 In all cases other than as above (paras. 13.3-5), for the purposes of assessing HB and main CTB, a claimant is treated as possessing any income and capital belonging to:

- the claimant himself or herself;
- any partner; and
- if the claimant and any partner are under 60, any children and young persons.

All references in this chapter to the income or capital of a claimant should be read as also referring to the income and capital of a partner. Paragraphs 13.144-147 describe how a child's or young person's income and capital is taken into account.

DIFFERENCES IN ASSESSMENT DEPENDING ON AGE

13.7 The law for people aged 60+ (or whose partner is) is different from those for people aged under 60 (and whose partner is). Whilst the two sets of regulations frequently produce the same effect, there is one clear-cut difference (the amount of disregard for income from (sub-)tenants: table 13.4). There are also several smaller differences, some acknowledged by the DWP to be unintended. The rules and differences are given at the relevant places in the remainder of this and the next two chapters. HBR 60+ 24 CTBR 60+ 16

13.8 In particular the approach to which types of income do and do not count in the assessment of HB/CTB is different for the two age groups: HBR 24(1) HBR 60+ 25(1) CTBR 16(1) CTBR 60+ 17(1)

- if the claimant or any partner is aged 60+, nothing counts as income unless the law says it does (an approach which suits computers);
- if the claimant and any partner are under 60, everything counts as income unless the law says it does not (an approach which makes it pointless to create imaginative new kinds of income).

WHEN A CLAIMANT IS TREATED AS HAVING A NON-DEPENDANT'S INCOME AND CAPITAL

HBR 20
CTBR 12
13.9 A special rule applies if:

- it appears to the authority that the claimant and non-dependant have entered into arrangements to take advantage of the HB or CTB scheme; and
- the non-dependant has both more income and more capital than the claimant; and
- the claimant is not on JSA(IB), IS or guarantee credit.

13.10 The rule in such cases is that:

- the claimant is treated as having the income and capital of the non-dependant; and
- the claimant's own income and capital is completely disregarded.

For the purposes of considering the amount (if any) of the non-dependant deduction, the non-dependant is treated as having his or her own income and capital (not the income and capital of the claimant).

Definitions and general matters

DISTINGUISHING CAPITAL FROM INCOME

13.11 HB and CTB law does not give a general definition of 'income' and 'capital'; though the regulations do define how certain types of payment should be treated: those rules are given as they arise in this and the next two chapters. Examples are given in table 13.1. The DWP gives good general advice (GM paras. C2.20-22):

> 'Capital can take a variety of forms. A payment of capital can normally be distinguished from income because it is:
>
> i. made without being tied to a period; and
>
> ii. made without being tied to any past payment; and
>
> iii. not intended to form part of a series of payments.
>
> As a general rule, capital includes all categories of holdings which have a clear monetary value...'

WHICH TYPES OF INCOME AND CAPITAL COUNT

13.12 As described in the later parts of this chapter, some types of income and capital are wholly disregarded; some are partly disregarded; and some are counted in full (table 13.1). Also, in some cases a claimant can be treated as having

Table 13.1: Examples of capital and income

CAPITAL WHICH IS (WHOLLY OR PARTLY) TAKEN INTO ACCOUNT FOR HB/MAIN CTB PURPOSES

- Savings in a bank, building society, etc.
- National Savings Certificates, stocks and shares
- Property (unless it falls within one of the numerous disregards)
- Redundancy pay (with some exceptions)
- Tax refunds

CAPITAL WHICH IS DISREGARDED FOR HB/MAIN CTB PURPOSES

- The home a claimant owns and lives in
- A self-employed claimant's business assets
- Arrears of certain state benefits
- Certain compensation payments
- A life insurance policy which has not been cashed in

INCOME WHICH IS (WHOLLY OR PARTLY) TAKEN INTO ACCOUNT FOR HB/MAIN CTB PURPOSES

- Earnings from a job or from self-employment
- Pensions
- Certain state benefits (e.g. contribution-based jobseeker's allowance, retirement pension)
- Rental received from a sub-tenant or boarder in the claimant's home
- Tariff income from capital

INCOME WHICH IS DISREGARDED FOR HB/MAIN CTB PURPOSES

- Reimbursement of expenses wholly incurred in the course of a job
- Certain state benefits (e.g. disability living allowance, attendance allowance)
- Certain charitable or voluntary payments
- Payments (e.g. 'keep') received from a non-dependant
- Fostering payments

These examples are simplified. In many cases further disregards apply. The detailed rules are given later in this chapter.

income or capital he or she does not in fact possess: this is known as 'notional' income or capital (para. 13.132).

WHY CAPITAL IS ASSESSED

HBR 37, 45
HBR 60+ 25(2),(5),(6), 38
CTBR 28, 37
CTBR 60+ 17(2),(5),(6), 30

13.13 A claimant's capital is first assessed under the rules in this chapter, then taken into account as follows:

- the first band (which is any amount up to the 'lower capital limit': para. 13.15) is completely ignored in the assessment of HB and main CTB;
- the next band (which is from the 'lower capital limit' to £16,000) is treated as generating 'tariff income' (para. 13.14);
- if it amounts to more than £16,000, the claimant is not entitled to HB or main CTB at all.

13.14 'Tariff income' is assessed as follows (and illustrated in the examples):

- deduct the appropriate 'lower capital limit' from the total amount of assessed capital;
- then divide the remainder by:
  - 250 if the claimant and any partner are aged under 60, but
  - 500 if the claimant or any partner is aged 60+;
- then, if the result is not an exact multiple of £1, round the result up to the next whole £1. This is the claimant's weekly tariff income.

13.15 The 'lower capital limit' (below which capital is ignored) is:

- £10,000 in some kinds of residential accommodation (para. 13.16: this applies in HB only);
- £6,000 in any other case if the claimant or any partner is aged 60+;
- £3,000 in all other cases.

13.16 The kinds of accommodation in which the £10,000 lower capital limit applies are:

- a residential care home or nursing home where the claimant has pre-1993 preserved rights (para. 2.18);
- local authority Part III accommodation (in Northern Ireland accommodation provided by the Health and Social Services Board) so long as board is not provided (para. 2.19);
- an unregistered Abbeyfield Home;
- accommodation which is not treated as a nursing home, but is provided together with both board and personal care under an Act of Parliament or Royal Charter. This can apply, for example, to accommodation provided by the Salvation Army (para. 2.18) or under the Polish Resettlement Act.

13.17 In CTB there is never a £10,000 lower capital limit (doubtless because a resident in the above types of accommodation cannot be liable for council tax). For HB for people aged 60+, the £10,000 lower capital limit continues regardless of absences of up to 52 weeks from such accommodation (or, in the case of Polish Resettlement Act accommodation, up to 13 weeks, so long as the person, with the consent of the manager, intends to return). For under-60s, there is no rule about absences.

Examples: Calculating tariff income

CLAIMANT UNDER 60

A single claimant aged 59 is a home owner and has capital, assessed under the rules in this chapter, of £8,085.93.

This first £3,000 is disregarded, leaving a remainder of £5,085.53. Divide the remainder by 250 and round the answer up to the next whole £1. The claimant has tariff income of £21.

CLAIMANT AGED 60+

A single claimant aged 61 is a council tenant and has capital, assessed under the rules in this chapter, of £8,085.93.

This first £6,000 is disregarded, leaving a remainder of £2,085.53. Divide the remainder by 500 and round the answer up to the next whole £1. The claimant has tariff income of £5.

HOW CAPITAL IS ASSESSED

13.18 The whole of a claimant's capital is taken into account, including certain types of income which are counted as capital, but excluding capital which is disregarded. The general rules about how capital is valued are given below. Other rules about this, about which types of income are counted as capital, and about which types of capital are disregarded, are mentioned in the relevant places in this chapter. Authorities may seek the assistance of the Valuation Office Agency in London in valuing capital items such as dwellings or other property. Forms authorities may use for this purpose appear in the Guidance Manual (chapter C2 annex E).

HBR 38
HBR 60+ 39
CTBR 29
CTBR 60+ 31

VALUING CAPITAL IN GENERAL

13.19 The following rule applies whenever a property, shares, or anything else (except for national savings certificates: para. 13.95) has to be valued for HB/ main CTB purposes. Other parts of this chapter mention considerations that also have to be taken into account for specific items. The rule has three steps:

HBR 41(a)
HBR 60+ 40(a)
CTBR 32(a)
CTBR 60+ 32(a)

- take the current market or surrender value of the capital item;
- then disregard 10% if selling it would involve costs;
- then disregard any mortgage or other 'incumbrance' (e.g. a loan) secured on it.

In practice, a claimant's capital is usually valued at his or her date of claim and revalued only if there is a reasonably large change. But it should be revalued whenever there is a change which affects tariff income.

VALUING JOINTLY HELD CAPITAL

HBR 44
HBR 60+ 44
CTBR 36
CTBR 60+ 36

13.20 The following rule applies when a capital item (e.g. a property) is held jointly by two or more people. An example is given below:

- first assume that all the joint owners own an equal share in the capital item;
- then value the person's resulting assumed share (as in para. 13.19) and count that as his or her capital.

It was held in an income support case, which is persuasive for HB and CTB purposes, that the above rule does not apply when an item is held in distinct, known shares (e.g. one person holds a one-third share and the other a two-thirds share) and that in such cases the actual share should be valued (as in para. 13.19) and counted as the person's capital *(Secretary of State for Work and Pensions v Hourigan)*.

Examples: Valuing capital

SHARES WHOLLY OWNED BY A CLAIMANT

A claimant owns 1,000 shares in a company. The sell price is currently £0.50 each.

For HB/main CTB purposes, from the current market value (1,000 x £0.50 = £500) deduct 10% (£50) giving £450. Assuming no loan or other incumbrance is secured on the shares, the value for HB/main CTB purposes is therefore £450.

A JOINTLY OWNED PROPERTY

A claimant and her sister inherit some land from their father. In his will, he stipulated that it was a joint inheritance. The land has recently been valued by the Valuation Office Agency, and the authority accepts their valuations, which are as follows:

- if the whole of the land was sold, it would fetch £10,000;
- if a half-share in the land was sold, the half-share would fetch only £4,000 (because of certain covenants which affect the use of the land).

The claimant has recently taken out a loan for £2,000 using the land as security (and none of the loan has yet been repaid).

For HB/main CTB purposes, the claimant's share of the capital in the land is valued as follows:

- first the claimant is treated as owning half of the land;
- then this half share is valued. Using the Valuation Office Agency's figure, the authority values the half share at £4,000;
- then 10% is deducted towards sales costs: £4,000 minus £400 leaves £3,600;
- then the claimant's loan is deducted: £3,600 minus £2,000 leaves £1,600.

So for HB/main CTB purposes, the claimant has capital of £1,600 (plus any other capital she may have).

WHY INCOME IS ASSESSED

13.21 A claimant's earned and unearned income, assessed under the rules described in this chapter and chapters 14 and 15, is compared with his or her applicable amount in calculating how much HB or main CTB he or she is entitled to (paras. 7.10-14).

HOW INCOME IS ASSESSED

13.22 The whole of a claimant's income is taken into account (though for people aged 60+, what counts as income in the first place is limited: paras. 13.7-8), including tariff income from capital (para. 13.14) and certain types of capital which are counted as income, but excluding income which is disregarded. General points about income are given below. Other rules about this, about which types of capital are counted as income, and about which types of income are disregarded in whole or in part, are mentioned in the relevant places in this chapter.

HBR 21, 24, 33
HBR 60+ 26
CTBR 13, 16, 24
CTB 60+ 18

13.23 The HB and main CTB rules distinguish earned income (i.e. earnings received by employed earners or by the self-employed) from unearned income (e.g. pensions, benefits, rent received by the claimant, and so on). Chapter 14 deals with earnings from a job, chapter 15 with self-employed earnings. The rules about unearned income are in this chapter.

DECIDING WHICH WEEKS INCOME BELONGS TO

13.24 The general objective for HB/main CTB purposes is '[calculating or] estimating the amount which is likely to be [the claimant's] average weekly income'. However, there are many specific rules and these are given in this and the next two

HBR 21(1)
HBR 60+ 26(1)
CTBR 13(1)
CTBR 60+ 8(1)

chapters as they arise. Where there is no specific rule, it is usually straightforward to decide according to the facts of the case which week or weeks a claimant's income belongs to for HB/main CTB purposes.

ARREARS OF INCOME

HBR 68
CTBR 59

13.25 In broad terms, it is usually the case that if a claimant receives arrears of income, then those arrears are treated as being income belonging to the week or weeks to which they relate (except to the extent that they are income which is disregarded). Exceptions to this and further specific rules are given in this and the next chapter as they arise.

INCOME TAX

HBR sch 4 para 1
HBR 60+ 28(11)
CTBR sch 4 para 1
CTBR 60+ 20(11)

13.26 The income tax payable on any kind of income, even income not listed elsewhere in this guide, is disregarded in the assessment of that income.

CONVERTING INCOME TO A WEEKLY FIGURE

13.27 For HB/main CTB purposes, income must be converted (if necessary) to a weekly figure. The details are given in paragraph 7.39.

Benefits, tax credits, pensions, etc

13.28 This section gives the rules about the assessment for HB/main CTB purposes of state benefits and tax credits, state and other pensions, and other payments from state, local authority and related sources. Paragraphs 13.29-34 give general rules, and paragraphs 13.35 onwards give specific rules for individual benefits.

STATE BENEFITS: GENERAL RULE FOR CURRENT PAYMENTS

HBR 23(1)
HBR 60+ 25(1)
CTBR 24(1)
CTBR 60+ 17(1)

13.29 Except when indicated in the following paragraphs, state benefits and pensions are counted in full as unearned income. For example, all the following are counted in full (as are many others):

- working tax credit;
- child tax credit;
- child benefit;
- contribution-based jobseeker's allowance;
- incapacity benefit;
- industrial injuries benefit;
- retirement pensions.

STATE BENEFITS: GENERAL RULE FOR ARREARS

13.30 Except when indicated in the following paragraphs (and there are many exceptions: see in particular para. 13.31), arrears of state benefits and pensions are counted as unearned income for the period they cover and there is no disregard of their capital value.

HBR 68(7)
HBR 60+ 28(6)
CTBR 59
CTBR 60+ 20(6)

Example: Arrears of incapacity benefit

A claimant, who has been receiving HB and main CTB for many years, has been receiving incapacity benefit since January 2003. It has been taken into account as her income for HB/main CTB purposes from that date. In June 2004, following a successful appeal, she is paid arrears of incapacity benefit for the period from September 2002 to January 2003.

The arrears are her income for the period from September 2002 to January 2003. The authority may therefore reassess her entitlement to HB/main CTB for that period, which may result in an overpayment (chapter 18).

STATE BENEFITS: LARGE ARREARS DUE TO OFFICIAL ERROR

13.31 In the case of several benefits (e.g. DLA: para 13.36), arrears are disregarded as capital for 52 weeks from the date of payment. In those cases (and they are identified throughout this section as they arise), there is a lengthened disregard if:

HBR sch 5 para 8
HBR 60+ sch 5ZA paras 18, 21, 21A
CTBR sch 5 para 8
CTBR 60+ sch 5ZA paras 18, 21, 21A

- the underpayment was due to official error; and
- the amount of the arrears is £5,000 or more; and
- the award of the arrears is made on or after 14th October 2002.

In such cases, the arrears are then disregarded (if this would be longer than the 52 weeks) for as long as the claimant or any partner remain continuously entitled to HB/CTB (including periods for which the partner remains continuously entitled after the claimant's death).

REDUCED STATE BENEFITS

13.32 If the amount of a state benefit received by a claimant has been reduced due to a Child Support Agency 'reduced benefit direction' (or if the claimant or any partner is aged 60+, due to a reduction for hospitalisation), the net amount (i.e. after the reduction) is counted as unearned income. Similarly, if it is reduced due to the overlapping social security benefit rules, the net amount is counted as unearned income (a rule which is laid down in the law only if the claimant or any partner is aged 60+, but must logically be true for all age groups).

HBR 33(3)
HBR 60+ 25(3),(4), 28(6)
CTBR 24(3)
CTBR 60+ 15(3),(4), 30(6)

13.33 However, if the amount of a state benefit received by a claimant has been reduced for any other reason (for example, in order to recover a previous overpayment), the gross amount (i.e. before the reduction) is counted as unearned income.

INCREASES IN STATE BENEFITS FOR DEPENDANTS

HBR sch 4 para 52
NIHBR sch 4 para 55
HBR 60+ 25(1)(h)(vii)
NIHBR 60+ 25(1)(f)(vi)
CTBR sch 4 para 51
CTBR 60+ 17(1)(h)(vii)

13.34 With some state benefits, an increase can be added for a dependent partner, or other dependent adult(s) or child(ren). These are dealt with as follows:

- If the claimant and any partner are under 60, count an increase as unearned income if the benefit it is paid with counts as unearned income – unless the dependant is not a member of the family (para. X.X), in which case disregard it.
- If the claimant or any partner is aged 60+, count the increase as unearned income if it is for a partner: no other increases are disregarded.

DISABILITY LIVING ALLOWANCE, OTHER BENEFITS FOR ATTENDANCE AND MOBILITY, AND GUARDIAN'S ALLOWANCE

HBRGB sch 4 pars 5-8, 50, sch 5 para 8
NIHBR sch 4, paras 5-8, 53, sch 5 para 8
HBR 60+ 25(1)(h)(i)-(vi),
NIHBR 60+ 25(1)(f)(i)-(vi) sch 5ZA paras 21, 21A
CTBR sch 4 paras 5-8, 49, sch 5 para 8
CTBR 60+ 18(1)(h)(i)-(vi), sch 5ZA paras 21, 21A

13.35 Current payments of the following are disregarded in full as unearned income:

- disability living allowance;
- attendance allowance and constant attendance allowance;
- exceptionally severe disablement allowance;
- severe disablement occupational allowance;
- payments compensating for non-receipt of the above;
- guardian's allowance.

13.36 Arrears of the above are disregarded in full as income. They are also disregarded as capital for 52 weeks from the date of payment, or longer for some large awards of arrears (para. 13.31).

'PRE-1973' WAR WIDOW'S AND WAR WIDOWER'S PENSIONS

HBRGB sch 4 para 43, sch 5 paras 8, 38
NIHBR sch 4 para 46
HBR 60+ 25(1), sch 5ZA paras 21, 21A
CTBR sch 4 para 42, sch 5 paras 8, 37
CTBR 60+ 17(1), sch 5ZA paras 21, 21A

13.37 There are special payments paid to 'pre-1973' war widows and widowers, the amount, from April 2004, being £62.68 per week. If the claimant or any partner is aged 60+, these payments are assessed in the same way as in paragraph 13.39. If the claimant and any partner are under 60:

- current payments are disregarded in full as unearned income;
- arrears of such payments are disregarded in full as income;
- arrears are also disregarded as capital for 52 weeks from the date of payment, or longer for some large overpayments (para. 13.31). The same applies to payments compensating for non-receipt of such pensions.

OTHER WAR WIDOW'S, WAR WIDOWER'S AND WAR DISABLEMENT PENSIONS

13.38 The following rules apply to:

(a) war widow's, war widower's and war disablement pensions;

(b) payments to compensate for non-payment of those;

(c) analogous payments from Governments outside the UK;

(d) Nazi persecution compensation payments.

HBRGB sch 4 paras 14, 53-55
NIHBR sch 4 paras 13, 56-58
HBR 60+ 25(1), sch 4A paras 1-6, sch 5ZA paras 21, 2
NIHBR 60+ sch 4A paras 1-7 sch 5ZA 21, 21A
CTBR sch 4 paras 14, 52-54
CTBR 60+ 17(1), sch 4A paras 1-6, sch 5ZA paras 21, 2

13.39 In Northern Ireland, current payments of items (a) to (c) are disregarded in full as income and from item (d) £10 per week. In England, Wales and Scotland, disregard as income:

- if the claimant or partner is aged 60+, all amounts granted for constant attendance or exceptionally severe disablement;
- regardless of age, any other amounts for attendance or mobility; and
- in all cases, £10.00 per week (subject to the rules on aggregation in para. 13.148; and see also para. 13.43).

13.40 In Northern Ireland, arrears of these payments are disregarded in full as unearned income. In England, Wales and Scotland, they are counted as unearned income for the period they cover apart from the £10.00 per week disregard.

13.41 If the claimant or any partner is aged 60+, arrears of amounts granted for constant attendance or exceptionally severe disablement are also disregarded as capital for 52 weeks from the date of payment, or longer for some large overpayments (para. 13.31). The same applies to payments compensating for non-receipt of such amounts.

13.42 In any case other than as described in paragraph 13.41, there is no disregard of the capital value of arrears.

13.43 It should be noted that many councils in England, Wales and Scotland operate a 'local scheme' whereby a larger amount or all of war widows', war widowers' and war disablement pensions (para. 13.38(a)) are disregarded currently and/or in arrears (para. 22.10). There is one exception: if the claimant or any partner is aged 60+, this does not apply to war disablement pensions – however the DWP accepts that this was a simple oversight in the drafting of the law. See also the rules for second world war payments, etc (para. 13.148).

WORKING TAX CREDIT AND CHILD TAX CREDIT

HBR 2(1), 21(1), (1ZA), 26(e)
HBRGB 40(9), sch 4 para 58, sch 5 para 8
NIHBR 40(8), sch 4 para 61, sch 5 para 8

13.44 The amount of working tax credit (WTC) and child tax credit (CTC) actually received in respect of any week is counted in full as unearned income for that week, but legislative changes in the amount of WTC/CTC (such as the April up-rating) may be disregarded for up to 30 benefit weeks. However, there are two circumstances in which an amount is disregarded from WTC:

HBR 60+ 25(1)(h), 39(3), sch 4A para 21 NIHBR 60+ 25(1)(f), 39(3) sch 4A para 21 CTBR 2(1), 13(1), (1ZA), 18(e), 24(2B), 31(9), sch 4 para 57, sch 5 para 8 CTBR 60+ 15(1)(h), 31(3), sch 4A para 21

- Certain recipients of WTC qualify for a disregard from their earnings of £12.32 per week (para. 14.36). If (uncommonly) their earnings are insufficient for this £12.32 disregard to be made in full from them (as described in para. 14.38), £12.32 is instead disregarded from their WTC.
- Certain claimants with child care costs qualify for a disregard from their earnings (para. 14.27). If (uncommonly) their earnings are insufficient for this disregard to be made in full from them, any balance of the disregard is made from their WTC.

13.45 Arrears of WTC and CTC (etc) are dealt with as in table 13.3. The general effect is that if, for example, there is a delay of six weeks in awarding someone WTC, it will not count as her income until the actual payments begin. Instead the arrears will be counted in a lump sum as her capital. Having said that, the practicalities for staff assessing HB and CTB are disproportionately complex, as the DWP have recently acknowledged (circular HB/CTB A18/2004).

Table 13.2: Arrears of working tax credit and child tax credit *

HBRGB 40(9), sch 5 para 8 NIHBR 40(8), sch 5 para 8 HBR 60+ 39(3) CTBR 31(9), sch 5 para 8 CTBR 60+ 31(3)

Arrears of working tax credit (WTC) and child tax credit (CTC) * are assessed for HB/CTB purposes by working through the following steps

(a) Treat the arrears as capital, not income. **

(b) If the claimant and any partner are under 60 and the arrears were awarded as a result of a change of circumstances:

Disregard the capital for 52 weeks from the date of payment, or longer for some large overpayments (para. 13.31).

(c) If the claimant or any partner is aged 60+ or the arrears were awarded for any other reason:

There is no disregard of the capital value of arrears.

Notes

* This table also applies to:

- predecessor benefits (working families' tax credit, disabled person's tax credit, family credit, disability working allowance, family income supplement and family allowance); and
- payments compensating for non-receipt of any of the items mentioned here,

but in these cases, if the claimant and any partner are under 60, step (b) applies even if the arrears were awarded for a reason other than a change of circumstances.

** But if the claimant or partner is aged 60+, do this only if the payment 'was made in respect of a period for the whole or part of which [HB/CTB] was [paid/allowed] before those arrears were paid'.

JSA(IB), IS, HB, CTB AND PENSION CREDIT

HBRGB sch 4 paras 4, 6, 35, 36, 48, 51, 61, 62, sch paras 5, 8, 28, 29, 42, 50, 51 NIHBR sch 4 paras 6, 38, 39, 43, 44, 51, sch 5 paras 5, 28, 29, 35, 42, 48 HBR 60+ 25(1)(h) 39(3), sch 5ZA paras 21, 21A NIHBR 60+ 25(1) 39(3), sch 5ZA paras 21, 21A CTBR sch 4 paras 36-38, 47, 50, 60, sch 5 paras 8, 28, 34, 35, 41, 44, 5 CTBR 60+ 17(1)(h), 31(3), sch 5ZA paras 21,

13.46 Current payments of:

- savings credit count in full as unearned income – but there are special rules for assessing HB/CTB from anyone on savings credit (paras. 13.150-159);
- guarantee credit, JSA(IB), IS, HB and CTB are all disregarded in full as income.

13.47 Arrears of all these benefits, and arrears of predecessor benefits (community charge benefit, housing benefit supplement and supplementary benefit), and arrears of payments compensating for non-receipt of any of these items, are:

- ignored as income (for slightly different legal reasons for each benefit); but
- disregarded as capital for 52 weeks from the date of payment in all cases, or longer for some large awards of arrears (para. 13.31).

The only exceptions are that the second point does not apply to HB or CTB at all, nor predecessor benefits if the claimant or any partner is aged 60+.

13.48 It is worth noting that the further rules about the date an award, change or end of entitlement to pension credit takes effect can also operate in a way that effectively causes payments of pension credit to be disregarded as income (para. 17.27 and table 17.5).

DISCRETIONARY HOUSING PAYMENTS

HBRGB sch 4 para 74, sch 5 para 8 NIHBR sch 4 para 73, sch 5 para 8 HBR 60+ 25(1) CTBR sch 4 para sch 5 para 8 CTBR 60+ 17(1)

13.49 Discretionary housing payments (para. 22.2) are disregarded in full as unearned income. If the claimant and any partner are under 60, they are disregarded as capital for 52 weeks from the date of payment, or longer for some large overpayments (para. 13.31). If the claimant or any partner is aged 60+, there is no disregard of the capital value of arrears.

WIDOWED MOTHER'S ALLOWANCE AND WIDOWED PARENT'S ALLOWANCE

HBR sch 4 para 14A
HBR 60+ sch 4A paras 7,8
NIHBR 60+ sch 4A paras 8, 9
TBR sch 4 para 14A
CTBR 60+ sch 4A paras 7,8

13.50 From current payments of these benefits, disregard £15 per week (subject to the rules on aggregation in para. 13.148). Arrears of these payments are counted as unearned income for the period they cover apart from the £15.00 per week disregard and there is there is no disregard of the capital value of arrears.

BEREAVEMENT PAYMENT

HBR60+ 25(1)(h)
CTBR 60+ 17(1)(h)

13.51 If the claimant or any partner is aged 60+, bereavement payment is disregarded in full as unearned income. If the claimant and any partner are under 60, it is counted in full as unearned income. There is no disregard of the capital value of arrears.

STATUTORY SICK, MATERNITY, PATERNITY AND ADOPTION PAY; ADOPTION ALLOWANCE

HBR 60+ 25(1)(h)
IHBR 60+ 25(1)(f)
HBR sch 4 para 23, sch 5 para 70
CTBR 60+ 15(1)(h)
TBR sch 4, para 24, sch 5, para 70

13.52 If the claimant or any partner is aged 60+, all these are disregarded in full as unearned income. If the claimant and any partner are under 60, only adoption allowance is disregarded as unearned income and the other items are counted in full as unearned income (and see chapter 14). If the claimant and any partner are under 60, adoption allowance is disregarded as capital. There is no disregard of the capital value of arrears of any of these items.

CARER'S ALLOWANCE

HBR 60+ sch 5ZA paras 21, 21A
CTBR 60+ sch 5ZA paras 21, 21A

13.53 Carer's allowance counts in full as unearned income. If the claimant or any partner is aged 60+, arrears are disregarded as capital for 52 weeks from the date of payment. If the claimant and any partner are under 60, there is no disregard of the capital value of arrears.

BR sch 4 para 14A
HBR 60+ 25(1)(h)
IHBR 60+ 25(1)(f)
BR sch 4 para 14A
TBR 60+ 17(1)(h)

PENSIONER'S CHRISTMAS BONUS

13.54 This is disregarded in full as unearned income.

FOSTERING, BOARDING OUT AND RESPITE CARE PAYMENTS

HBRGB sch 4 para 24, 25
NIHBR sch 4 paras 26, 27
HBR 60+ 25(1)
CTBR sch 4 paras 25, 26
CTBR 60+ 17(1)

13.55 If the claimant or any partner is aged 60+ disregard all such payments in full (as income): there are no further conditions. If the claimant and any partner are under 60, disregard these payments in full (as income) if they are received from a local authority or voluntary organisation or (in the case of respite care payments) a primary care trust; and also disregard (in the case of respite care payments), contributions required from the person cared for.

ADOPTION AND CUSTODIANSHIP ALLOWANCES

HBRGB 2(1), sch 4 para 23
NIHBR 2(1), sch 4 para 25

13.56 If the claimant or partner is aged 60+ disregard all such payments in full (as income): there are no further conditions. If the claimant and partner are under 60:

- from payments received from a local authority, disregard any amount in excess of the dependant's allowance and any disabled child premium for the child or young person concerned; and
- count any balance as unearned income;
- but if the child or young person concerned has capital valued at over £3,000 disregard the whole amount.

HBR 60+ 25(1)
CTBR 2(1),
sch 4 para 24
CTBR 60+ 17(1)

COMMUNITY CARE AND OTHER SOCIAL SERVICES PAYMENTS

13.57 If the claimant or partner is aged 60+ disregard all such payments in full (as income): there are no further conditions. If the claimant and partner are under 60, disregard in full (both as income and capital) any social services payment made for the purposes of avoiding taking children into care or to children and young persons who are leaving or have left care, and any social services community care payments.

HBRGB
sch 4 paras 26, 67,
sch 5 paras 18, 69
NIHBR sch 4
paras 28, 65,
sch 5 paras 18, 69
HBR 60+ 25(1)
CTBR sch 4
paras 37, 62,
sch 5 paras 18
CTBR 60+ 17(1)

SUPPORTING PEOPLE PAYMENTS

13.58 Supporting people payments (usually administered by social services to assist people with certain support costs in their home) are disregarded in full as unearned income.

HBR sch 4 para 75,
sch 5 para 68
HBR 60+ 25(1)
CTBR sch 4 para 74
sch 5 para 68
CTBR 60+ 17(1)

SOCIAL FUND PAYMENTS AND LOANS

13.59 Disregard payments and loans from the social fund in full (both as income and capital) – including winter fuel payments.

HBRGB sch 4 para
NIHBR sch 4 para 3
HBR sch 5 para 19
HBR 60+ 25(1)(h)
NIHBR 60+ 25(1)
CTBR sch 4 para 3
sch 5 para 19
CTBR 60+ 17(1)(h

THE MACFARLANE TRUSTS, THE FUND, THE EILEEN TRUST, THE INDEPENDENT LIVING FUNDS

13.60 The Macfarlane Trust, the Macfarlane (Special Payments) Trust, the Macfarlane (Special Payments) (No. 2) Trust, 'the Fund', and the Eileen Trust were all set up to assist certain people with HIV. The Independent Living Fund, the Independent Living (Extension) Fund, and the Independent Living (1993) Fund were all set up to enable severely disabled people to live independently. Any payment from any of these is disregarded in full (both as capital and income). Payments in kind from any of these are also disregarded. If money from any of these is passed on to a third party, it is usually also disregarded in the assessment of the third party's income and capital (and always disregarded if that third party or his or her partner is aged 60+).

HBRGB
sch 4 para 34,
sch 5 paras 23, 32
NIHBR
sch 4 para 37,
sch 5 paras 23, 32
HBR 60+ 25(1)
CTBR sch 4 para 3
sch 5 paras 23, 32
CTBR 60+ 17(1)

THE CREUTZFELDT-JACOB DISEASE TRUST

13.61 Disregard payments to sufferers of variant Creutzfeldt-Jacob disease and their families (as capital). (There are rare exceptions to this rule if the claimant and any partner are under 60: circular HB/CTB A19/2001.)

HBR sch 5 para 66
HBR 60+
sch 5ZA para 14
CTBR sch 5 para 6
CTBR 60+
sch 5ZA para 14

GOVERNMENT TRAINING SCHEMES, ETC

HBR 2(1), 40(7), sch 4 paras 11, 49, 66, 72, 73, sch 5 paras 7, 33, 43, 44, 55
NIHBR sch 4 paras 11, 52, 68 sch 5 paras 43, 53
HBR 60+ 25(1)
CTBR 2(1), 31(7), sch 4 paras 11, 49, 66, 71, 72, sch 5 paras 7, 33, 42, 43, 55
CTBR 60+ 17(1)

13.62 The following is about payments received by people on the New Deal or on other schemes run by the DWP. There are three possibilities in the assessment of HB/CTB:

- If the claimant or any partner is aged 60+, all such payments are disregarded as income: there are no further conditions; but if they form part of the claimant's capital (which is improbable) they count as capital.
- In most other cases, people on such schemes remain entitled to JSA(IB) or IS, so their income and capital are disregarded.
- In any other case, the income and capital is assessed as in the next paragraph.

13.63 The full details of the assessment depend on the nature of the training scheme concerned. More detail may be found in DWP guidance (GM paras 3.575 onwards and circular HB/CTB A6/2004). The main rules are as follows:

- Payments on the New Deal and similar schemes are ignored as income unless they are made as a substitute for JSA(IB), IS, IB or SDA, or are for basic day-to-day maintenance.
- Training grants under the New Deal 50-plus Employment Credit Scheme are disregarded as capital for 52 weeks from the date of payment.
- Access to Work payments (to enable disabled people to gain or retain employment) and payments under the Blind Homeworkers' Scheme are disregarded as both income and capital.
- Earnings received whilst undergoing Work Based Training for Young People, Work Based Training for Adults, Training for Work or Community Action, are counted as earnings in the normal way (chapter 14).
- Payments on the Employment Retention and Advancement Scheme, the Return to Work Credit Scheme, the Lone Parent Work Search Scheme, the Lone Parent In-work Scheme, and most other schemes under section2 of the Employment and Training Act 1973 or the Enterprise and New Towns (Scotland) Act 1990 are disregarded both as income and as capital.

WELFARE TO WORK BENEFICIARIES

13.64 There are several concessions in the HB and CTB schemes for welfare to work beneficiaries (see chapters 9, 10 and 12). The definition of a 'welfare to work beneficiary' is in table 13.3. Their earnings are assessed in the normal way (chapter 14).

Table 13.3: Definition of 'welfare to work beneficiary'

For all HB/CTB purposes, this means a person who: SI 1997 No. 852

- has been incapable of work for at least 28 weeks (196 days); and
- has stopped (on or after 5th October 1998) receiving a benefit or advantage which was dependent on his or her being incapable of work (the relevant benefits and advantages for HB/CTB purposes are indicated as they arise mainly in chapters 9 to 12 of this guide); and
- has – within 7 days of ceasing to be incapable of work – started:
  - remunerative work (in broad terms, 16 hours or more per week: paras. 7.29 onwards), or
  - Work Based Training for Adults (in England and Wales), or
  - Training for Work (in Scotland); and
- has notified the benefits agency of the fact that he or she has started work, and has done so within one month of the date on which he or she ceased to claim that he or she is incapable of work (or, in certain cases, has won a social security appeal relating to this).

Such a person counts as a welfare to work beneficiary for 52 weeks only. The Benefits Agency should inform authorities if someone is a welfare to work beneficiary (circular HB/CTB A41/98).

CAREER DEVELOPMENT LOANS

13.65 In Great Britain only, career development loans are paid under arrangements between the DWP and national banks (circular HB/CTB A1/97). If the claimant or any partner is aged 60+, they are disregarded as income. If the claimant and any partner are under 60, they are dealt with as follows:

HBR 34(4), sch 4 para 63
HBR 60+ 25(1)
CTBR 25(4), sch 4 para 63
CTBR 60+ 17(1)

- any amount which (over the period of the education or training to which the loan applies) relates to the claimant's or a member of the family's food, ordinary clothing or footwear (excluding school uniform and sportswear), household fuel, eligible rent (apart from any non-dependant deduction), council tax, or water charges, is counted in full as income;
- any amount relating to any other purposes (such as for course fees and course-related expenses) is disregarded in full (as both income and capital).

HEALTH BENEFITS AND PRISON VISITS PAYMENTS

HBRGB sch 4 paras 37, 44-46
NIHBR sch 4 paras 40, 47-49
HBR 60+ 25(1)
HBR sch 5 paras 39-41
CTBR sch 4 paras 39, 44, 45, sch 5 pars 38-40
CTBR 60+ 17(1)

13.66 If the claimant or any partner is aged 60+, all the following payments are disregarded in full as income, but arrears are not disregarded as capital. If the claimant and any partner are under 60, all the following are disregarded in full as unearned income and (only) the last three items are disregarded as capital for 52 weeks from the date of payment:

- hospital resettlement benefit;
- payments for travel for hospital visits;
- health service supplies or payments in lieu of free milk and vitamins;
- Home Office payments for travel for prison visits.

COUNCIL TAX REDUCTIONS

HBRGB sch 4 para 41, sch 5 para 36
NIHBR sch 4 para 44. sch 5 para 35
HBR 60+ 25(1)
CTBR 60+ 17(1)

13.67 Disregard in full (both as income and capital) council tax disability reductions and discounts (paras. 9.13-17). In other words, the fact that the claimant gets one of these does not mean that it counts as his or her income or capital.

OCCUPATIONAL AND PERSONAL PENSIONS

HBR 28(2), 33(4), sch 4 para 1, sch 5 para 30
HBR 60+ 25(1), 28(11), sch 5 para 23
CTBR 19(2), 25(4), sch 4 para 1, sch 5 para 30
CTBR 60+ 17(1), 20(11), sch 5 para 23

13.68 These count in full as unearned income, after deducting tax. However, disregard as capital any amount held in a pension scheme and of the right to receive money from it (para. 13.91).

The home, property and possessions

13.69 This section is about how things the claimant owns affect his or her entitlement to HB and main CTB, including the home, a former or future home, other property and rent received by the claimant.

HOMES AND OTHER PROPERTY

13.70 The claimant's current, former or future home can be disregarded and so can a home or other property (including non-domestic property) which the claimant has never occupied, if the conditions in the following paragraphs apply. The disregards described below can apply one after another, so long as the relevant conditions are met (as illustrated in the example).

THE CLAIMANT'S HOME

HBR sch 5 para 1
HBR 60+ 2(1), sch 5ZA para 25A
CTBR sch 5 para 1
CTBR 60+ 2(1), sch 5ZA para 25A

13.71 Disregard the capital value of the dwelling normally occupied as the claimant's home, and any land or buildings (including in Scotland croft land) which are part of it or are impracticable to sell separately. There is no time limit. This disregard is limited to one home per claim but see the other headings below.

A RELATIVE'S HOME

13.72 Disregard the capital value of the home of a partner or relative of anyone in the claimant's family, if that partner or relative is aged 60+ or incapacitated. There is no time limit. The property may be occupied by others as well as the partner or relative. Any number of properties may be disregarded under this rule. 'Relative' is defined in paragraph 10.39. 'Incapacitated' is not defined for this purpose; in particular, it is not linked to premiums or state benefits.

HBR sch 5 para 4(a)
HBR 60+ sch 5ZA para 4(a)
CTBR sch 5 para 4(a)
CTBR 60+ sch 5ZA para 4(a)

AN INTENDED HOME

13.73 Disregard the capital value of a property which the claimant intends to occupy as a home as follows:

- in all cases, for 26 weeks from the date of acquisition or such longer period as is reasonable; and/or
- if the claimant is taking steps to obtain possession (e.g. if there are squatters or tenants), for 26 weeks from the date the claimant first seeks legal advice or begins legal proceedings, or such longer period as is reasonable; and/or
- if the property requires essential repairs or alterations, for 26 weeks from the date the claimant first takes steps to render it fit for occupation or reoccupation as his or her home, or such longer period as is reasonable. This could apply for example to the normal home of a claimant in temporary accommodation

HBR sch 5 paras 2, 26, 27
HBR 60+ sch 5ZA paras 1-3
CTBR sch 5 paras 2,26, 27
CTBR 60+ sch 5ZA paras 1-3

A FORMER HOME

13.74 There is no disregard of the capital value of a claimant's former home as such. However, a former home may well fall within one of the following headings (which also apply to other property): if it does not, then it is taken into account as capital.

PROPERTY FOR SALE

13.75 Disregard the capital value of any property the claimant intends to dispose of, for 26 weeks from the date when the claimant first takes steps to dispose of it, or for such longer period as is reasonable. This can apply to a former or second home or any other property. It can apply to more than one property.

HBR sch 5 para 25
HBR 60+ sch 5ZA para 7
CTBR sch 5 para 2
CTBR 60+ sch 5ZA para 7

DIVORCED OR ESTRANGED COUPLES AND POLYGAMOUS MARRIAGES

13.76 If a claimant has actually divorced or become estranged from a former partner, disregard the whole capital value of the claimant's former home (and any land or buildings which are part of it or are impracticable to sell separately) as follows:

HBR sch 5 para 24
HBR 60+ sch 5ZA para 6
CTBR sch 5 para 2
CTBR 60+ sch 5ZA para 6

- for any period when it is occupied by the former partner if he or she is now a lone parent. This could begin straight after the divorce/estrangement, or later on, and there is no time limit in this case;
- in any other case, for 26 weeks from the date of divorce or estrangement (e.g. if the former partner is not a lone parent at the time, or the property is empty). The time limit in this case cannot be extended, but the property may fall within one of the other disregards afterwards.

Note that (unlike in the next paragraph) the claimant must have formerly lived there as his or her home for this disregard to apply. 'Estranged' is not defined in the law and so carries its ordinary English meaning that the people in question no longer regard themselves as a couple or as being in a polygamous marriage.

SEPARATED OR SPLIT COUPLES AND POLYGAMOUS MARRIAGES

HBR sch 5 para 4(b)
HBR 60+ sch 5ZA para 4(b)
CTBR sch 5 para 4(b)
CTBR 60+ sch 5ZA para 4(b)

13.77 If a claimant has not actually divorced or become estranged from a former partner, but the HB/CTB rules treat him or her as no longer being in a couple or polygamous marriage (e.g. because of the rules about absence of a partner: para. 4.11), disregard the whole capital value of any property currently occupied as a home by the former partner. There is no time limit. Note that (unlike in the previous paragraph) it is irrelevant who used to live there.

DISPUTED ASSETS WHEN A RELATIONSHIP ENDS

13.78 When a relationship ends, ownership of a property may be in dispute. This can sometimes mean the current market value of the property (paras. 13.19-20) is nil until ownership of the property is settled.

HOUSING ASSOCIATION DEPOSITS

HBR sch 5 para 10(a)
CTBR sch 5 para 10(a)

13.79 If the claimant and any partner are under 60, disregard in full as capital any amount deposited with a housing association (para. 10.17) in order to secure accommodation. There is no such disregard if the claimant or any partner is aged 60+.

MONEY FROM SELLING A HOME

HBR sch 5 para 3, 10(b)
CTBR sch 5 para 3, 10(b)

13.80 If the claimant and any partner are under 60, disregard in full as capital:

- money from the sale of the claimant's former home, including in Northern Ireland any compensation paid resulting from compulsory purchase; and
- money refunded by a housing association with which it was deposited (para. 13.79),

but only if it is intended for purchasing another home within 26 weeks, or such longer period as is reasonable. (However, interest accrued on the money is counted as capital in the normal way: para. 13.94.) If the claimant or any partner is aged 60+, a different rule applies, as follows.

Example: The capital value of a property following relationship breakdown

- A married couple jointly own the house they live in. They do not own any other property. They have one child at school. They claim CTB. The man is the claimant.

  The value of the house is disregarded as capital: it is their normal home (para. 13.71). However, they turn out not to qualify for CTB because they have too much income.

- The coupler separate (but are not estranged).The man leaves and rents a room in a shared house. He does not intend to return (and so they no longer count as a couple: para. 4.11). He claims HB and CTB for the flat.

  In the man's claim, his share of the house is disregarded: it is the home of his former partner from whom he is separated (para. 13.77).

- They divorce. The terms of the divorce are that the man retains a one-third share in the house; but that the house cannot be sold until their child is 18. The man notifies the council of this.

  In his claim, his share of the house is disregarded: it is his former home and is occupied by his former partner from whom he is divorced and who is a lone parent (para. 13.76).

- More than 26 weeks after their divorce, their child leaves school. The house is not put up for sale and the man does not seek his share of its value.

  In his claim, his interest in the house must now be taken into account (para. 13.76). As a joint owner, he is treated as possessing one-half of its value (and the other points in para. 13.20 are taken into account in valuing it).

- The house is put up for sale.

  In the man's claim, his interest in the house is now disregarded as capital for 26 weeks (or longer if reasonable: para. 13.75).

- The house is sold, and the man puts his share into a building society account and starts trying to raise a mortgage using the money. It seems likely that he will be able to buy somewhere within the next two or three months.

  In his claim, this money is disregarded: it is the proceeds of the sale of his former home and he plans to use it to buy another property within 26 weeks (para. 13.80).

MONEY FOR BUYING A HOME

HBR 60+ sch 5ZA paras 18, 20(a)
CTBR 60+ sch 5ZA para 18, 20(a)

13.81 If the claimant or any partner is aged 60+, payments (or amounts deposited in the claimant's name) for the sole purpose of buying a home are disregarded for one year from the date of receipt. Apart from lasting longer, this is wider than the rule for under 60s (para. 13.80). It includes home sale proceeds and money refunded by a housing association, but also (for example) money given or loaned by a relative for that purpose.

VALUING PROPERTY GENERALLY

13.82 The general rules about valuing capital apply to a property which has to be taken into account as capital for HB/main CTB purposes (paras. 13.19-20). In such cases, an authority can get a free valuation of property from the Valuation Office Agency (and a form which can be used for this purpose is in GM chapter C2 annex E).

VALUING PROPERTY WHICH IS RENTED OUT

HBR sch 5 para 6
HBR 60+ sch 5ZA para 5
CTBR sch 5 para 6
CTBR 60+ sch 5ZA para 5

13.83 Unless it forms part of the capital assets of a business (or in certain circumstances a former business: para. 15.7), property a claimant owns and has rented out is valued as described earlier (paras. 13.19-20). However, the fact that it is rented out will affect its market value; for example, the presence of a sitting tenant can reduce it. For information about rental income see the following.

RECEIVING RENT

13.84 Table 13.4 shows how rent received by the claimant from people living in his or her home is taken into account. See also the example. Table 13.5 shows how rent received from property other than the claimant's home is taken into account.

HBR sch 5 para 31
HBR 60+ sch 5ZA para 27
CTBR sch 5 para 31
CTBR 60+ sch 5ZA para 27

13.85 The value of the right to receive rent is disregarded as capital.

Table 13.4: Rent received from people in the claimant's home

HBRGB sch 4 para 19
NIHBR sch 4 para 21
HBR 60+ 25(1)
CTBR sch 4 para 19
CTBR 60+ 17(1)

RENT, KEEP, ETC. FROM HOUSEHOLD MEMBERS

- Disregard the whole of any rent, 'keep', etc. received from a child or young person in the family (paras. 4.12-20) or from a non-dependant (para. 4.21)

HBRGB sch 4 para 20
NIHBR sch 4 para 22
HBR 60+ sch 4A para 9
NIHBR 60+ sch 4A para 10
CTBR sch 4 para 20
CTBR 60+ sch 4A para 9

RENT FROM BOARDERS (AS DEFINED IN PARA. 4.XX)

- Disregard the first £20.00 of that rent.

- Count only half the rest as unearned income.
- If the claimant and any partner are under 60, a separate £20.00 is disregarded for each individual boarder who is charged or – even a child – regardless of whether they have separate agreements.
- If the claimant or any partner is aged 60+, only one lot of £20.00 is disregarded per HB/CTB claim, regardless of how many boarders the claimant has.

RENT FROM (SUB-)TENANTS (AS DEFINED IN PARA. 4.25)

HBRGB sch 4 para 42
NIHBR sch 4 para 45
HBR 60+ sch 4A para 10
NIHBR 60+ sch 4A para 11
CTBR sch 4 para 21
CTBR 60+ sch 4A para 10

- Disregard the first £20.00 of that rent if the claimant or any partner is aged 60+ (regardless of whether the rent includes heating).
- Disregard the first £13.80 of that rent if the claimant and any partner are under 60 and the rent includes heating.
- Disregard the first £4.00 of that rent if the claimant and any partner are under 60 and the rent does not include heating.
- Count all the rest as unearned income.
- A separate £20,00, £13.80 or £4.00 is disregarded for each (sub-) tenancy.

Example: Letting out a room

A couple in their 20s are on HB and CTB. They have a spare room and they let it out to a man for £50.00 per week inclusive of fuel for heating etc, and water charges (but not meals). He is their sub-tenant.

For the purposes of their HB/CTB, their income from this sub-tenant is £50.00 minus £13.80, which is £36.20 per week.

Later, the same couple agree with the man that if he increases what he pays to £65.00 per week, they will feed him. He is now their boarder.

For the purposes of their HB/CTB, their income from this boarder is £65.00 minus £20.00, which is £45.00, the result being divided in two, which is £22.50 per week.

Note that the rules therefore mean that a claimant is usually better off renting out a room to a boarder than to a (sub-)tenant.

Table 13.5: Rent received on property other than the claimant's home

HBR 60+ 25(1)
CTBR 60+ 17(1)

IF THE CLAIMANT OR ANY PARTNER IS AGED 60+

Rent received on property (other than the claimant's home) counts in full as unearned income in all circumstances, and there are no disregards whatever.

HBR sch 4 para 15(2)
NIHBR sch 4 para 17(2)
CTBR sch 4 para 14(2)

IF THE CLAIMANT AND ANY PARTNER ARE UNDER 60 AND THE PROPERTY'S VALUE IS DISREGARDED AS CAPITAL

This applies to rent received on one of the types of property (other than the claimant's home) whose capital value is disregarded (as described in paras. 13.71-77 and 15.7):

- Take the amount of the rental income for an appropriate period (e.g. a month, a year).
- Disregard any payment towards mortgage repayments (both interest and capital repayments) or any council tax or water charges the claimant is liable to pay during that period on the property (note that other outgoings cannot be disregarded).
- Count the balance (converted to a weekly figure) as the claimant's unearned income.

HBR 40(4), sch 4 para 17(1)
NIHBR 40(4), sch 4 para 17(1)
CTBR 31(4), sch 4 para 17(1)

IF THE CLAIMANT AND ANY PARTNER ARE UNDER 60 AND THE PROPERTY'S VALUE COUNTS AS CAPITAL

This applies to rent received on one of the types of property (other than the claimant's home) whose value is taken into account as his or her capital (even if for some reason the capital value is nil for HB/main CTB purposes):

- Take the amount of the rental income for an appropriate period (e.g. a month, a year).
- Deduct any outgoings incurred in respect of the letting (e.g. agents' fees, tax due on the income, repairs, council tax, water charges, repayments of mortgages/loans, etc.).
- The balance (if any) is capital (not income) for HB/main CTB purposes.

PAYMENTS FOR WORK ON THE HOME

13.86 The following disregard applies, for example, to money paid by a council to assist a tenant to buy a property, a home improvement grant, a loan from a bank or similar institution or from a friend or relative, or any other loan or payment. It works as follows:

HBR sch 5 paras 9, 37
HBR 60+ sch 5ZA paras 18, 20(b)
CTBR sch 5 paras 10, 36
CTBR 60+ sch 5ZA paras 18, 20(b)

- If the claimant and any partner are under 60:
  - payments solely for essential repairs or improvements to the home, and
  - grants from a local authority to purchase, alter or repair an intended home

are disregarded as capital for 26 weeks from the date of payment, or such longer period as is reasonable.

- If the claimant or any partner is aged 60+:
  - payments (or amounts deposited in the claimant's name) solely for essential repairs or improvements to the home or an intended home

are disregarded for one year from the date of receipt.

TAX REFUNDS FOR MORTGAGE INTEREST

13.87 If the claimant and any partner are under 60, tax refunds for interest on a mortgage taken out for purchasing a home, or for carrying out home repairs or improvements, are disregarded in full as capital. There is no such disregard for 60+s.

HBR sch 5 para 20
HBR 60+ 25(1)
CTBR sch 5 para 20
CTBR 60+ 17(1)

MORTGAGE AND LOAN PROTECTION POLICIES

13.88 The following applies if a claimant has taken out insurance against being unable (perhaps because of sickness) to pay his or her mortgage or some other loan (for example a car loan), and is now receiving payments under that insurance policy. In such cases, if the claimant or any partner is aged 60+, all payments received under that insurance policy are disregarded as unearned income. If the claimant and any partner are under 60 they are disregarded only insofar as they cover the cost of:

HBRGB sch 4 para 28
NIHBR sch 4 para 30
HBR 60+ 25(1)
CTBR sch 4 para 29
CTBR 60+ 17(1)

- the repayments on the mortgage or other loan; and
- any premiums due on the policy in question; and
- (only in the case of a mortgage protection policy) any premiums on another insurance policy which was taken out to insure against loss or damage to the home and which was required as a condition of the mortgage.

COMPENSATION AND INSURANCE PAYMENTS FOR THE HOME OR POSSESSIONS

HBR sch 5 para 9
HBR 60+ sch 5ZA paras 18, 19
CTBR sch 5 para 9
CTBR 60+ sch 5ZA paras 18, 19

13.89 Such payments are disregarded as capital if they are for repair or replacement following loss of, or damage to, the claimant's home or personal possessions. If the claimant and any partner are under 60, they are disregarded for 26 weeks from the date of payment, or such longer period as is reasonable. If the claimant or any partner is aged 60+, they are disregarded for one year from the date of receipt.

PERSONAL POSSESSIONS

HBR sch 5 para 11
HBR 60+ sch 5ZA para 8
CTBR sch 5 para 11
CTBR 60+ sch 5ZA para 8

13.90 Disregard in full as capital the value of the claimant's personal possessions. If the claimant and any partner are under 60, the law specifically mentions that if they were purchased for the purpose of obtaining or increasing entitlement to HB/CTB, their capital value should be taken into account. If the claimant or any partner is aged 60+, the same applies, but under the deprivation of capital rule (para. 13.132).

Savings and investments

13.91 This section is about savings, investments etc. When these are taken into account, they are valued as described in paragraphs 13.19-20. (But for national savings certificates, see para. 13.95.) The following terms are used below:

- the 'surrender value' (of an insurance policy, for instance) means what the claimant would be paid (by the insurance company, for instance) if he or she cashed it in now (rather than waiting for it to mature, for instance);
- the 'value of the right to receive income' (from an annuity, for instance) means what the claimant would be paid in return for transferring the right to receive the income to someone else.

SAVINGS AND CASH

HBR 38(1)
HBR 60+ 39(1)
CTBR 29(1)
CTBR 60+ 31(1)

13.92 These count in full as capital. For example, money in a bank or building society account (or under the mattress) is counted as capital (but see the next paragraph).

INCOME PAID REGULARLY INTO AN ACCOUNT

13.93 Regular payments of income (e.g. earnings, benefits, pensions) into a claimant's bank, building society or similar account should not be counted as capital for the period they cover (see e.g. Commissioners' decisions R(SB) 2/83 and R(IS) 3/93). For example, if earnings are paid in monthly, only what is left at the end of the month is capital. In practice, authorities often do not do this unless claimants specifically ask them to.

INTEREST

13.94 Except where other rules in this chapter state otherwise, interest or other income derived from capital (such as interest on a bank or building society account) is counted not as income but as capital. If the claimant and any partner are under 60, the law spells out that this is done from the date it is due to be credited to the claimant, and it seems logical that this would also apply to 60+s.

HBR 40(4)
HBR 60+ 25(1), sch 4A para 23
CTBR 31(4)
CTBR 60+ 17(1), sch 4A para 23

NATIONAL SAVINGS CERTIFICATES

13.95 These count as capital, but the following applies instead of the normal rules about valuing capital. From 1st July in any year to 30th June in the next year, the capital amount for HB/main CTB purposes is their value as at 1st July in the first of those years. For current issues, this means their purchase price. The DWP usually issues a circular with valuation tables each year – usually in July.

HBR 41(b)
HBR 60+ 40(b)
CTBR 32(b)
CTBR 60+ 32(b)

INVESTMENTS

13.96 These count as capital. They are valued as described in the general rules (paras. 13.19-20), with the effect that:

- shares are valued at their 'sell' price. Then disregard 10% towards the cost of their sale;
- unit trusts are valued at their 'sell' price. Normally this already allows for notional sales costs. If it does not, disregard 10% for this;
- income bonds count in full.

LIFE INSURANCE POLICIES

13.97 Disregard as capital the surrender value of a life insurance policy. But count as capital any money actually received from it (e.g. if the claimant actually cashes in all or part of it).

HBR sch 5 para 16
HBR 60+ sch 5ZA para 11
CTBR sch 5 para 1
CTBR 60+ sch 5ZA para 11

FUNERAL PLAN CONTRACTS

13.98 If the claimant or any partner is aged 60+, disregard the value of a funeral plan contract. To qualify the contract provider (which would normally be a firm or company but need not be so) must contract to provide or secure the provision of a funeral in the UK, and that must be the sole purpose of the contract. There is no such disregard if the claimant and any partner are under 60.

HBR 60+ sch 5ZA para 12
CTBR 60+ sch 5ZA para 12

ANNUITIES

HBR sch 5 para 34(2), sch 5 para 12
HBR 60+ 25(1), sch 5ZA para 24
CTBR sch 5 para 25(2), sch 5 para 12
CTBR 60+ 17(1), sch 5ZA para 24

13.99 If the claimant has an annuity, it means he or she has invested an initial lump sum with an insurance company which, in return, pays the claimant a regular income. Count this in full as unearned income. Disregard as capital the surrender value of the annuity, and also the value of the right to receive income from it (para. 13.91).

HOME INCOME PLANS

HBRGB 34(2), sch 4 para 16, sch 5 para 12
NIHBR 34(2), sch 4 para 18, sch 5 para 12
HBR 60+ 25(1), sch 4 para 11, sch 5ZA para 28
CTBR 25(2), sch 4 para 16, sch 5 para 12
CTBR 60+ 17(1), sch 4 para 11, sch 5ZA para 28

13.100 If the claimant has a home income plan, it means he or she raised a loan using his or her home as security, has invested the loan as an annuity and, in return, gets a regular income: part of this income is used to repay the loan, part may be used to repay the claimant's mortgage, and part may be left over for the claimant to use. Count the income received by the claimant as unearned income, but only after deducting (if they have not been deducted at source):

- any tax payable on that income;
- any repayments on the loan which was raised to obtain the annuity; and
- any mortgage repayments made using the income (using the figures for the repayments which apply after tax has been deducted from them).

Disregard as capital the surrender value of the annuity, and the value of the right to receive income from it (para. 13.91).

LIFE INTEREST AND LIFERENT

HBR sch 5 para 14
HBR 60+ sch 5ZA para 26
CTBR sch 5 para 14
CTBR 60+ sch 5ZA para 26

13.101 If a claimant has a life interest or (in Scotland) liferent, it means he or she has the right to enjoy an asset during his or her or someone else's lifetime, after which it will pass to someone else. The actual value to the claimant (if any) of the life interest or liferent is counted as capital; and any actual income the claimant receives from it is counted as earned or unearned income as appropriate. Disregard as capital the value of the right to receive income from it (para. 13.91).

REVERSIONARY INTEREST

HBR sch 5 para 6
HBR 60+ sch 5ZA para 5
CTBR sch 5 para 6
CTBR 60+ sch 5ZA para 5

13.102 If a claimant has a reversionary interest, it means he or he has an interest in property but will not possess it until some future event (for example, the death of a relative). Disregard in full the capital value of a reversionary interest. For HB and main CTB purposes, however, a property the claimant has rented out is not disregarded as a reversionary interest: the rules for dealing with such property are explained in table 13.5.

Trust funds and awards for personal injury, etc

13.103 This section is about awards for personal injury (and similar matters) and trust funds (whether for personal injury or not).

GENERAL RULE

13.104 The general rule is that any amount in a trust fund, and any personal injury payment, is capital and is counted in full, and that payments from trust funds are capital or income as the case may be. But there are several exceptions, described below (and see also paras. 13.60-61 in the case of trust funds relating to people with HIV and people with Creutzfeld-Jacob disease).

PERSONAL INJURY PAYMENTS ADMINISTERED BY A COURT

HBRGB sch 5 paras 46, 47
NIHBR sch 5 para 4
HBR 60+ sch 5ZA para 17
CTBR sch 5 paras 46, 47
CTBR 60+ sch 5ZA para 17

13.105 Compensation for personal injury, if paid into a court and administered by the court on the compensated person's behalf, is disregarded in full as capital without time limit. The same applies to compensation for the death of a parent, but in this case only if the compensated person is under 18.

PERSONAL INJURY PAYMENTS UNDER A COURT ORDER OR OUT-OF-COURT SETTLEMENT

HBRGB 34(5)
NIHBR 34(4)
HBR 60+ sch 4A paras 14, 1
NIHBR 60+ sch 4A paras 15, 1
CTBR 25(5)
CTBR 60+ sch 4A paras 14, 1

13.106 If the claimant or any partner is 60+, the following are disregarded as income:

- any payment made under a court order for accident, injury or disease of the claimant, partner or child;
- any periodic payment made in an out-of-court settlement for injury of the claimant or partner.

If the claimant and any partner are under 60, and a court orders that any part of a personal injury payment is to be paid periodically, then that part counts as unearned income (not capital) for HB/CTB purposes.

PERSONAL INJURY MONEY HELD IN A TRUST: CAPITAL

HBRGB sch 5 para 13
NIHBR sch 5 para
HBR 60+ sch 5ZA para 17
CTBR sch 5 para 1
CTBR 60+ sch 5ZA para 17

13.107 Any money for personal injury which is held in a trust fund is disregarded in full as capital without time limit (and if the claimant and any partner are under 60, so is the value of the right to receive income from it: para. 13.91). If the claimant or any partner is aged 60+, the law makes it clear that the particular money need not be kept track of. If, say, the award was £20,000 then £20,000 is disregarded from the person's capital for ever more.

PERSONAL INJURY MONEY HELD IN A TRUST: INCOME

HBR sch 4 para 13
HBR 60+ sch 4A para 12
NIHBR 60+ sch 4A para 13
CTBR sch 4 para 1
CTBR sch 4A para

13.108 Payments of income received from a personal injury trust are assessed as follows:

- £20.00 is disregarded from any amount intended and used for the claimant's (or a member of the family's) food, ordinary clothing or footwear (excluding school uniform and sportswear), household fuel, eligible rent (apart from any non-dependant deduction), housing costs that would be eligible for pension credit (but only if the claimant or any partner is aged 60+), council tax, or water charges (subject to the rules on aggregation: para. 13.148).
- The whole amount of any other payment is disregarded as unearned income.

PROPERTY HELD IN A TRUST

HBR 60+ sch 5ZA para 30
CTBR 60+ sch 5ZA para 30

13.109 If the claimant or any partner is aged 60+, a property held in a trust for the claimant's or partner's benefit (other than a charitable trust, or a trust for people with HIV as described in para. 13.60) is disregarded – so long as the trust makes payments or has a discretion to make payments to the claimant or partner. There is no such disregard if the claimant and any partner is under 60.

DISCRETIONARY TRUSTS: INCOME

HBR 60+ sch 4A para 12
NIHBR 60+ sch 4A para 13
BR sch 4A para 12

13.110 If the claimant or any partner is aged 60+, payments of income from any discretionary trust (one which the claimant has no absolute right to take money from) are assessed in the same way as in paragraph 13.108. There is no equivalent rule if the claimant and any partner are under 60 (but see para. 13.104).

Other items of income and capital

MAINTENANCE

HBRGB sch 4 para 47
HBR 60+ sch 5 para 20
HBR sch 4 para 50
TBR sch 4 para 46
CTBR 60+ sch 5 para 20

13.111 If there is at least one child or young person in the claimant's family, disregard £15 of any maintenance received or due to be received from:

- the claimant's former partner; or
- the claimant's partner's former partner; or
- the parent of any child or young person in the claimant's family (so long as that parent is not in the claimant's family); or
- the Secretary of State (under child support provisions) in lieu of maintenance.

13.112 The definitions of 'partner', 'child', 'young person', 'family' are in chapter 4. The £15 disregard applies whether the maintenance is payable to the claimant or to a child or young person. If two or more maintenance payments are received in any week, the maximum disregard is £15 per week.

CHARITABLE AND/OR VOLUNTARY PAYMENTS

13.113 The following rules apply if the claimant receives payments which are charitable and/or voluntary. If the claimant or any partner is aged 60+, such payments are fully disregarded as unearned income. If the claimant and any partner are under 60:

HBR 40(6), sch 5 para 32
HBRGB sch 4 paras 13, 21
NIHBR sch 4 paras 15, 23
HBR 60+ 25(1)
CTBR 31(6), sch 4 paras 13, 22, sch 5 para 32
CTBR 60+ 17(1)

- a lump sum payment counts as capital, as does a payment which is neither made nor due to be made at regular intervals;
- in the case of payments made or due to be made at regular intervals:
  - payments in kind (i.e. goods not money) from a charity are disregarded in full (para. 13.114);
  - £20.00 is disregarded from any amount intended and used for the claimant's (or a member of the family's) food, ordinary clothing or footwear (excluding school uniform and sportswear), household fuel, eligible rent (apart from any non-dependant deduction), council tax, or water charges (subject to the rules on aggregation: para. 13.148);
  - the whole amount of any other payment is disregarded as unearned income.

PAYMENTS IN KIND

13.114 Regular payments in kind (i.e. goods not money – apart from those in paras. 13.105 and 14.45) are dealt with as follows. If the claimant or any partner is aged 60+, such payments are fully disregarded as unearned income. If the claimant and any partner are under 60, they count in full as unearned income.

HBR 38(1)
HBR 60+ 25(1)
CTBR 29(1)
CTBR 60+ 17(1)

CASH IN LIEU OF CONCESSIONARY COAL

13.115 Cash in lieu of concessionary coal which is paid to a current employee of the British Coal Board counts as part of his or her earnings (chapter 14). If it is paid to an ex-miner or a miner's widow, it counts in full as unearned income, unless the claimant or any partner is aged 60+ in which case it is disregarded as unearned income.

HBR 38(1)
HBR 60+ 25(1)
CTBR 29(1)
CTBR 60+ 17(1)

SECOND WORLD WAR EX GRATIA PAYMENTS

13.116 Disregard in full as capital, without time limit, the ex gratia payments of £10,000 made by the Secretary of State in respect of imprisonment or internment of the claimant or his or her deceased partner, or the claimant's or partner's deceased spouse, by the Japanese during the Second World War. The DWP (circular HB/CTB A1/2001) has recommended that authorities need not attempt to identify the particular £10,000, but that £10,000 should simply be disregarded from the capital the claimant has.

HBRGB sch 5 para 64
NIHBR sch 5 para
HBR 60+ sch 5ZA para 13
CTBR sch 5 para 6
CTBR 60+ sch 5ZA para 13

SECOND WORLD WAR COMPENSATION PAYMENTS

HBRGB sch 5 para 67 NIHBR sch para 63 HBR 60+ sch 5ZA para 15 CTBR sch 5 para 67 CTBR 60+ sch 5ZA para 15

13.117 Disregard in full as capital, without time limit, any payment (apart from a war pension) made to compensate for the fact that, during the Second World War, the claimant or partner or either's deceased spouse:

- was a slave labourer or a forced labourer; or
- had suffered property loss or personal injury; or
- was a parent of a child who had died.

COMPENSATION FOR THE FAMILIES OF THE DISAPPEARED

IHBR sch 5 para 62

13.118 In Northern Ireland only, compensation payments to the families of the disappeared are disregarded in full for 52 weeks from the date of receipt.

GALLANTRY AWARDS

HBR sch 4 para 9 HBRGB sch 5 para 48 IHBR sch 5 para 46 HBR 60+ 25(1) CTBR sch 4 para 9, sch 5 para 48 CTBR 60+ 17(1)

13.119 Disregard in full as unearned income:

- Victoria Cross and George Cross payments;
- the lump sum payments of up to £6,000 for those who have agreed not to receive any further payments of income from those; and
- analogous awards for gallantry from this country or another country.

These amounts are disregarded as capital if the claimant and any partner are under 60. There is no such disregard for 60+s.

PARENTAL CONTRIBUTIONS TO STUDENTS

HBR sch 3 para 9 HBRGB sch 4 paras 17, 18 NIHBR sch 4 paras 19, 20 HBR 60+ sch 3A para 6, sch 4 paras 18, 19 CTBR sch 3 para 9, sch 4 paras 17, 18 CTBR 60+ sch 3A para 6, ch 4A paras 18, 19

13.120 The following rules apply to contributions made by claimants to a student son or daughter ('student' is defined in paras. 21.5-19):

- If a claimant has been assessed as being able to make a contribution to the student's grant (other than a discretionary grant) or student loan, the whole amount of the assessed contribution is disregarded in the assessment of the claimant's income.
- If a claimant contributes towards the maintenance of a student under the age of 25, who has a discretionary grant or no grant, the amount of the contribution is disregarded in the assessment of the claimant's income – but only up to a maximum weekly figure. The maximum weekly figure is £44.05 minus the amount of any discretionary grant.

So far as possible the above are disregarded from unearned income, then any balance is disregarded from earned income.

MAINTENANCE ALLOWANCES

13.121 Disregard Education Maintenance Allowances or Awards (including Assisted Places Allowances) in full as unearned income. These include (for example) bursaries for 16-to-18-year olds in non-advanced education and payments towards a child's travel to school.

HBR sch 4 para 10
HBR 60+ 25(1)
CTBR sch 4 para 10
CTBR 60+ 17(1)

13.122 If the claimant and any partner are under 60, disregard Education Maintenance Allowance bonuses in full as capital for 52 weeks from the date of payment. There is no such disregard for 60+s.

HBR sch 5 para 60
CTBR sch 5 para 60
CTBR 60+ 17(1)

ASSISTANCE WITH REPAYING STUDENT LOANS

13.123 Disregard (as unearned income) any payment made to a former student to help with repaying his or her student loan. This applies whether the payer pays it direct or via the ex-student. It includes payments by the DfES under the Teacher Repayment Loan Scheme, but also includes any other case.

HBR sch 4 para 10A
HBR 60+ 25(1)
CTBR sch 4 para 10
CTBR 60+ 17(1)

SPORTS AWARDS

13.124 If the claimant or any partner is aged 60+, these are disregarded if paid as income but counted if paid as capital. If the claimant and any partner are under 60, they are dealt with as follows:

- Any amounts awarded in respect of the claimant's or a member of the family's food (excluding vitamins, minerals or other special performance-enhancing dietary supplements), ordinary clothing or footwear (excluding school uniform and sportswear), household fuel, rent, council tax, or water charges, are counted in full as income or capital as appropriate.
- Any other amounts are disregarded in full as unearned income, and as capital for 26 weeks from the date of payment.

HBR 2(1)
HBRGB
sch 4 para 71,
sch 5 para 59
NIHBR
sch 4 para 72,
sch 5 para 57
HBR 60+ 25(1)
CTBR 2(1),
sch 4 para 70,
sch 5 para 59
CTBR 60+ 17(1)

JURORS' ALLOWANCES

13.125 If the claimant or any partner is aged 60+ these are disregarded in full. If the claimant and any partner are under 60, they are disregarded in full except in so far as they compensate for loss of earnings or loss of a social security benefit.

HBR sch 4
paras 38, 441
HBR 60+ 25(1)
CTBR sch 4 para 40
CTBR 60+ 17(1)

LOANS

13.126 A genuine loan usually increases a person's capital (until and to the extent that he or she spends it, perhaps on the thing it was lent for), though it is at least possible for a loan to be income (*Morrell v Secretary of State for Work and Pensions,* and see para 13.11) depending on the circumstances of the case, and the law requires this in the case of student loans (paras. 21.37-43) and career development loans (para. 13.65).

OUTSTANDING INSTALMENTS OF CAPITAL

13.127 There are no specific rules for outstanding instalments of capital if the claimant or partner is aged 60+, in whose case they count as capital when received.

HBR 19(2), 34(1), sch 5 para 17
CTBR 11(2), 25(1), sch 5 para 17

13.128 If the claimant and any partner are under 60 and if, at the claimant's date of claim for HB/CTB (or at the date of any subsequent reconsideration of the claim), he or she is entitled to outstanding instalments of capital (i.e. instalments due after that date), the authority must consider whether the sum of the outstanding instalments and the claimant's other capital exceeds £16,000,

- If it does, the outstanding instalments are ignored as capital but are counted as income. The law does not lay down any particular way of doing this.
- If it does not, the outstanding instalments are counted in full as capital from the date of claim (or reconsideration).

When the above rule is applied to outstanding instalments of capital to which a child or young person is entitled (para. 13.145), the only difference is that £3,000 is substituted for £16,000.

CAPITAL OUTSIDE THE UK

HBR 42, sch 5 para 22
HBR 60+ 41, sch 5ZA para 22
CTBR 33, sch 5 para 22
CTBR 60+ 33, sch 5ZA para 22

13.129 The following rules apply if a claimant possesses capital in a country outside the UK.

- If there is no prohibition in that country against bringing the money to the UK, value it at its market or surrender value in that country; then disregard 10% if selling it would incur costs; then disregard any mortgage or other incumbrance secured on it; then disregard any charge which would be incurred in converting it into sterling; and count the remainder as capital.
- If there is such a prohibition, value it at what a willing buyer in the UK would give for it; then disregard 10% if selling it would incur costs; then disregard any mortgage or other incumbrance secured on it; and count the remainder as capital.

HBRGB sch 4 paras 22, 32
NIHBR sch 4 paras 24, 34
HBR sch 5 para 15
HBR 60+ sch 4A paras 16, 17
NIHBR 60+ sch 4A paras 17, 18
CTBR sch 4 paras 23, 33, sch 5 para 15
CTBR 60+ sch 4A paras 16, 17

INCOME OUTSIDE THE UK

13.130 The following rules apply if a claimant is entitled to income payable in a country outside the UK.

- If there is no prohibition in that country against bringing the money to the UK, treat it as income in the normal way, allowing any disregard which may apply (including any earnings disregard in the case of earned income); also disregard any charge for converting it into sterling.

- If there is such a prohibition, disregard it in full; also (but only if the claimant and any partner are under 60) disregard as capital the value of the right to receive income from it (para. 13.91).

EXPENSES FOR UNPAID WORK

13.131 Expenses for unpaid work (whether for a charity, voluntary organisation, friend or neighbour) are disregarded. (For work expenses see para. 14.48.)

HBR sch 4 para 2
HBR 60+ 25(1)
CTBR sch 4 para 2
CTBR 60+ 17(1)

Notional income and capital

13.132 In the situations described below a claimant is treated, for HB/main CTB purposes, as possessing income and/or capital he or she does not in fact possess – known as 'notional' income and/or capital. The notional income or capital is assessed as if it was actual income or capital and any relevant disregards must be applied.

HBR 35(6),(7), 43(6)
HBR 60+ 42(5)
CTBR 26(6),(7), 34(6)
CTBR 60+ 34(5)

DEPRIVATION

13.133 If a claimant deliberately deprives himself or herself of capital or income in order to qualify for HB (or for more HB), he or she is treated as still having it for HB purposes. The same applies independently for CTB. Except as described in the next paragraph, it is the claimant's intention which must be taken into account (not the item he or she spent the money on).

HBR 35(1), 43(1)
HBR 60+ 36(6), 42(1)
CTBR 26(1), 34(1)
CTBR 60+ 28(6), 34(1)

13.134 If the claimant and any partner is aged 60+, there are two further rules relating to capital:

HBR 60+ 42(2)
CTBR 60+ 34(2)

- a gift to a third party is always deprivation;
- repaying or reducing a debt, or purchasing goods or services reasonable in the claimant's circumstances is never deprivation.

These rules are automatic, and apply regardless of the claimant's intention. For any other question of deprivation in the case of this age group, and for all questions of deprivation in the case of under 60s, the claimant's intention is the only determining factor.

DIMINISHING NOTIONAL CAPITAL

13.135 If a claimant is treated as having notional capital for the above reason (paras. 13.133-134), the amount of notional capital taken into account is reduced each week, broadly speaking, by the amount of any HB, CTB, JSA(IB) or IS (but not WTC or CTC), lost as a result of the claimant being treated as having notional capital. The rules for doing this are complicated, and in practice not all authorities follow them. For further details, see GM paras. C2.328-381.

HBR 43A
HBR 60+ 43
CTBR 35
CTBR 60+ 35

AVAILABLE ON APPLICATION

HBR 60+ 36(1)(a)
CTBR 60+ 28(1)(a)

13.136 If the claimant or any partner is aged 60+, the claimant is treated as having any amount of retirement pension which he or she has not claimed, but might reasonably be expected to be entitled to. No such rule applies for 60+s to any other type of income or any kind of capital.

HBR 35(2), 43(2)
CTBR 26(2), 34(2)

13.137 If the claimant and any partner are under 60, any income or capital which the claimant could have on application (in other words, simply by applying for it) is treated as possessed by him or her from the date it could be obtained. This rule does not apply to:

- working tax credit or child tax credit;
- income which could be obtained in the form of a DWP rehabilitation allowance;
- payments (of income or capital) made to a provider of a New Deal arrangement;
- income or capital which could be obtained from a discretionary trust or a trust for personal injury;
- income or capital which could be obtained from a personal pension scheme or retirement annuity contract (but see para. 13.143); or
- any kind of disregarded capital.

Also the DWP advises that this rule should not be applied in the case of income from any other social security benefit unless the authority is sure about the amount the person could receive (GM para. C3.634). This rule is, for example, commonly used in the case of unclaimed child benefit.

PAYMENTS TO OR FOR THIRD PARTIES

HBR 35(3),(8), 43(3),(3A),(7)
HBR 60+ 37
CTBR 26(3),(8), 34(3),(3A),(7)
CTBR 60+ 29

13.138 If income is paid in A's name but used by B for food, household fuel, clothing or footwear (other than school uniform and sportswear), eligible rent (apart from any non-dependant deduction), council tax or water charges, it is treated as belonging to B. If the claimant and any partner are under 60, the rule applies also to capital (but not for 60+s).

13.139 This rule must not be used in relation to occupational or personal pensions if the intended beneficiary is bankrupt or sequestered and payment is made to a trustee (or similar) for him or her and any family have no other income.

UP-RATINGS

HBR 35(4)
HBR 60+ 36(7)
CTBR 26(4)
CTBR 60+ 28(7)

13.140 If the April up-rating date for social security benefits or tax credits is different from that for HB/CTB, they are generally treated as up-rated on the same date as HB/CTB (paras. 17.34-35).

WORK PAID AT LESS THAN THE GOING RATE

13.141 This rule applies only if the claimant and any partner are under 60. If the claimant is paid less than the going rate for a job, he or she is treated as having whatever additional pay is reasonable in the circumstances. The means of the employer must be taken into account; and this rule does not apply to voluntary work, to claimants provided with a New Deal arrangement (para. 13.62) or to claimants on an 'approved work' training programme (e.g. work trials or work placements). When this rule is used, disregard notional tax and national insurance contributions and apply the earnings disregards (paras. 14.26-38).

HBR 35(5)-(5B)
CTBR 26(5)-(5B)

RELATIONSHIP TO A COMPANY

13.142 This rule applies only if the claimant and any partner are under 60. It applies to a claimant who is not the sole owner of, or a partner in, a company, but whose relationship to that company is analogous to someone who is. In such cases, the claimant's share of the capital of that company is assessed as though he or she was the sole owner or partner and any actual share of the company he or she possesses is disregarded.

HBR 43(4),(5)
CTBR 34(4),(5)

PENSION SCHEMES

13.143 If a claimant aged 60+ could get income from his or her pension scheme, but has failed to do so or chosen not to do so, then he or she is treated as having that income. Further details are given in circular HB/CTB A25/95.

HBR 35(2A)-(2C)
HBR 60+ 36(1)(b), (2)-(5)
CTBR 26(2A)-(2C)
CTBR 60+ 28(1)(b), (2)-(5)

Income and capital of children and young persons

CLAIMANT OR PARTNER AGED 60+: CAPITAL AND INCOME

13.144 If the claimant or any partner is aged 60+, the income and capital of a child or young person are always wholly disregarded.

HBR 60+ 21, 25(1
CTBR 60+ 13, 17(

CLAIMANT AND PARTNER UNDER 60: CAPITAL

13.145 This rule applies only if the claimant and partner are under 60 (para. 13.144). Except for the rule described in paragraph 13.128 (about outstanding instalments of capital), a child's or young person's capital is calculated in the same way – and with the same disregards – as for the claimant. But a child's or young person's capital is never counted as part of the claimant's capital.

HBR 19, 39
CTBR 11, 30

13.146 Instead, for any child or young person who has capital of over £3,000, the claimant is not awarded a personal allowance for him or her, nor any disabled child premium or enhanced disability premium (chapter 12). However, no matter how many children/young persons in the family have capital over £3,000, the claimant keeps his or her family premium – whether this is payable at the basic rate or the protected lone parent rate.

CLAIMANT AND PARTNER UNDER 60: INCOME

HBR 19, 36
CTBR 11, 27

13.147 This rule applies only if the claimant and partner are under 60 (para. 13.144). A child's or young person's income is calculated in the same way – and with the same disregards – as for the claimant. But the following variations apply:

- Payments of maintenance made to a child or young person are treated as if they were paid to the claimant (and dealt with as in para. 13.111).
- If a child or young person has capital over £3,000, his or her income is completely disregarded (apart from maintenance as just described).
- If a child or young person has left school and is in remunerative work (work averaging 16 hours per week or more: para. 7.29), count any unearned income and earnings he or she has. Note that the earnings disregard is £15.00 if the claimant gets a disabled child premium for the child or young person in question; otherwise it is £5.00.
- For any other child or young person, count unearned income only.
- The child's or young person's income, calculated as above, is counted as part of the claimant's income – but only up to the amount of the dependant's allowance and any disabled child premium and enhanced disability premium for the child or young person in question. Anything beyond that is disregarded.

Details of the allowances and premiums referred to above are in chapter 12.

The over-riding £20 disregard from certain income

HBRGB sch 4 para 33
HBR sch 4 para 35
HBR 60+ sch 4A para 12(3)
NIHBR 60+ sch 4A para 13(3)
CTBR sch 4 para 34
CTBR 60+ sch 4A para 12(3)

13.148 In any particular claim for HB/main CTB, the maximum weekly disregard per claim is £20 from any or all of the following:

- certain war widow's, war widower's and war disablement pensions (para. 13.38);
- widowed mother's allowance and widowed parent's allowance (para. 13.50);
- if the claimant and any partner are under 60, certain charitable and voluntary payments (para. 13.113);
- if the claimant and any partner are under 60, student loan and access fund income (chapter 21);
- if the claimant or any partner is aged 60+, certain payments from trust funds (paras. 13.108 and 13.110).

If two (or more) members of the family get any of these types of payment, the maximum weekly disregard is £20 for the whole family. In such cases, the disregard is used in whatever way is most favourable to the claimant.

13.149 Nothing in the above prevents an authority in Great Britain from running a local scheme whereby more than £10 (or all) of a war widow's, war widower's or war disablement pension is disregarded (para 22.10).

Assessing income and capital for people on savings credit

13.150 This section explains how income and capital are assessed if the claimant or any partner is on savings credit. It over-rides the rules described earlier in this chapter. If, however, the claimant qualifies for second adult rebate, the 'better buy' (para. 8.29) still applies once main CTB has been assessed as follows.

INCOME AND CAPITAL IS ASSESSED BY THE DWP

13.151 A claimant on savings credit has had his or her income and capital assessed by the DWP (i.e. the pensions service). With the exceptions mentioned below, the authority must use the DWP's assessment of income and capital in assessing the claimant's HB/CTB. HBR 60+ 23(1) CTBR 60+ 17(1)

THE DWP MUST NOTIFY THE AUTHORITY

13.152 The DWP must provide the authority with details of its assessment of income and capital within two working days of the following (or in either case as soon as reasonably practicable thereafter): HB 60+ 23(2),(3) CTB 60+ 15(2),(3)

- the date the DWP did the assessment, if the person has already claimed or is already on HB/CTB by that time; or
- the date the authority informs the DWP that the claimant or partner has claimed HB/CTB, in all other cases.

In particular, the DWP must include in the notification its 'assessed income figure' ('AIF') for the claimant.

13.153 If the DWP notifies the authority of new figures at any time, this is implemented as a change of circumstances (supersession) in the HB/CTB claim (table 17.1 and para. 17.4).

WHEN THE AUTHORITY ADJUSTS THE DWP'S ASSESSED INCOME FIGURE

13.154 Once the DWP has notified the authority of the claimant's assessed income figure, it is adjusted by the authority – but only if one (or more) of the things in table 13.6 applies. This is simply to reflect differences in assessing income for pension credit purposes as opposed to HB/CTB purposes. In making such adjustments, the authority uses (where necessary) the rules earlier in this chapter. HBR 60+ 23(4),(5 CTBR 60+ 15(4),(

Table 13.6: Claimants on savings credit: adjustments to the DWP's assessed income figure (AIF)

All the amounts mentioned in this table are weekly.

- Start with the DWP's assessed income figure
- Add the amount of savings credit payable
- Add the following (if in payment):
  - child benefit
  - child tax credit
- If the claimant receives income from the following sources, deduct the amount shown *:

• lone parent earnings	£5
• widowed mother's allowance	£5
• widowed parent's allowance	£5
• maintenance from a former partner or from a parent of a child or young person	£15
• earnings from which the child care disregard may be deducted	the whole amount of eligible child care costs (para. 14.27)
• a war widow's, war widower's or war disablement pension	any amount attributable to a local scheme (para. 22.10) apart from the first £10

- Add the income of any partner who was ignored in assessing pension credit but has to be taken account in HB/CTB (a rare circumstance indeed)
- If the authority determines that the income and capital of a non-dependant should be used instead of the income and capital of the claimant and partner (para 13.9), use this income instead of the DWP's assessment

Notes

* In each case the deduction equals the difference between what is disregarded in the assessment of pension credit and what is disregarded in

HB/CTB. The lone parent earnings disregard in pension credit is £20 and in HB/CTB is £25. The widowed mother's/parent's allowance disregard in pension credit is £10 and in HB/CTB is £15. There are no maintenance or child care disregards in pension credit, but there are in HB/CTB. The war widow's/widower's/disablement disregard in pension credit is £10 but in HB/CTB depends on the extent of any local scheme.

WHEN THE AUTHORITY ADJUSTS THE DWP'S CAPITAL FIGURE

13.155 Once the DWP has notified the authority of the claimant's capital, it is never (apart from the one exception below) adjusted. In particular, if the DWP notifies a figure above £16,000, the claimant is not entitled to HB/CTB. HB 60+ 23(6),(8) CTB 60+ 15(6),(8)

13.156 The one exception works as follows. If the DWP notified the authority that the claimant's capital was £16,000 or lower and then the claimant's capital rises above £16,000 during the course of the DWP's 'assessed income period' (the period during which the DWP does not reconsider the amount of a claimant's income or capital) then the authority must itself reassess capital using the rules earlier in this chapter. HB 60+ 23(7) CTB 60+ 15(7)

13.157 If the authority's assessment is that the claimant's capital is now over £16,000, entitlement to HB/CTB ends. If the authority's assessment is that the claimant's capital is £16,000 or lower (whether different or the same as the DWP's assessment), there is no change to the amount of the claimant's HB/CTB.

DISPUTES AND APPEALS

13.158 If a claimant disagrees with the DWP's assessed income figure (and any other income or capital figures notified by the DWP), this is something to take up using the DWP's disputes and appeals procedure. The claimant has no right to appeal to a social security tribunal via the authority about these figures. DAR sch para 6

13.159 If a claimant disagrees with an adjustment to the assessed income figure (table 13.5) or a re-assessment of capital (para. 13.157), he or she may ask the authority to reconsider (para. 17.55) and/or appeal to a tribunal via the authority (chapter 19).

Example: A war widow on savings credit

INFORMATION

A war widow aged 81 gets savings credit of £12.00 per week. She also gets a war widow's pension of £57.00 per week and retirement pension and an occupational pension, and has some capital.

The DWP notifies the authority of its assessed income figure (AIF) of £202.00 and notifies her capital as being £7,000. The authority dealing with her claim has a local scheme whereby it disregards the whole of a war widow's pension.

ASSESSMENT

The authority (table 13.5) starts with the DWP's assessed income figure (£202.00) and adds her savings credit (£12.00), giving a total of £214.00. It then disregards all but £10.00 of the war widow's pension of £57.00 (in other words, it disregards £47.00). This gives her net income for HB/CTB purposes as being £167.00 per week. It must use this figure in calculating her entitlement to HB/CTB.

The authority must accept that her capital is under £16,000 at the outset. If evidence later arises of an increase in her capital, perhaps taking it above £16,000, it then becomes the authority's duty to re-assess her capital; but no action is taken upon this re-assessment unless the amount is greater than £16,000.

14 Employed earners

14.1 This chapter describes the rules for assessing income (and capital) received by employed earners in connection with their employment.

HBR sch 3, para 10
HBR 60+ 22
CTBR sch 3 para 20
CTBR 60+ 14

14.2 The rules apply to both HB and main CTB. They do not apply where the claimant or any partner is in receipt of income support, income-based jobseeker's allowance or guarantee credit. In these cases all income and capital is disregarded. Nor does it apply to the special case where the claimant or any partner is in receipt of savings credit only (paras. 13.5 and 13.150).

HBR 2(1)
CTBR 2(1)

14.3 The term 'employed earner' means a person who is gainfully employed in Great Britain either under a contract of service, or in an office (including elective office) with emoluments (forms of gain) chargeable to income tax under Schedule E (PAYE). This definition most obviously includes an employee who works for a wage or salary but it also includes directors of limited companies, clergy, local authority councillors and sub-postpersons.

SI 2003 No. 325
Reg 2, 12
ISR 2003 No. 197
Reg 2, 12

14.4 As described in the relevant places in this chapter, there are some differences in the law depending upon whether:

- the claimant or any partner is aged 60 or over; or
- the claimant and any partner are both under 60.

HBR 60+ 25(1)
CTBR 60+ 17(1)

14.5 The rules that apply where the claimant or any partner is 60 or over are in many ways similar to those that apply where the claimant and any partner are both under 60 with one important difference. The categories of income that are relevant to calculating the HB/CTB where the claimant or any partner is 60 or over are set out in legislation. The effect of this is that if an income is not listed then it is not relevant to the HB/CTB calculation even though it is not specifically disregarded. Consequently some of the less common or more obscure types of income are ignored. Where the claimant and any partner are under 60 all income is taken into account unless specifically excluded.

14.6 The following matters are explained in this chapter:

- the assessment of earnings;
- earned income disregards generally;
- the child care disregard;
- the 16/30 hours per week disregard;

- particular kinds of earnings and expenses;
- starting work;
- absences from work and ending work.

14.7 Where the claimant and any partner are aged under 60, this chapter applies equally to the employed earnings of the claimant, a partner or a child or young person in the claimant's family. Where the claimant or any partner is aged 60-plus, this chapter only applies to the employed earnings of the claimant and any partner. In such cases the employed earnings of a child or young person in the claimant's family are totally disregarded. References to 'a claimant' should be read accordingly.

HBR 19(1)
HBR 60+ 19(4)
CTBR 11(1)
CTBR 60+ 19(4)

14.8 This chapter does not apply to the employed earnings of a non-dependant or a second adult: the law does not lay down any particular way of assessing employed earnings in such cases – although it must be gross income (less necessarily incurred expenses: para. 14.49) not net.

The assessment of earnings

14.9 The key steps for assessing employed earnings for HB/main CTB purposes are:

- identifying earned income;
- establishing the gross earnings;
- deducting tax and national insurance contributions;
- deducting half of any approved pension contribution;
- converting the result, if necessary, to a weekly figure;
- deducting a fixed 'earned income disregard' and, if appropriate, amounts for child care costs and for certain people working 16/30 hours or more per week.

14.10 In certain circumstances, notional (rather than actual) earnings are used (para. 13.141) but this does not apply where the claimant or any partner is aged 60 or over (DWP *Pension Credit Handbook,* part 1, para. 162).

ESTABLISHING GROSS EARNINGS

14.11 The authority must first identify an appropriate assessment period that can be used as the basis for calculating or estimating the gross earned income. The aim is to identify the period that provides the most accurate basis on which to estimate average weekly earnings.

HBR 2(1), 22(1)(b
HBR 60+ 2(1), 28(2)
CTBR 2(1), 14(1)(
CTBR 60+ 2(1), 20(2)

14.12 Where the claimant and any partner are under age 60 and earnings have not fluctuated, the earnings are averaged over the five weeks immediately preceding the date of claim if the claimant is paid weekly; or the two months immedi-

HBR 22(1)(a),(b)
CTBR 14(1)(a),(b)

ately preceding the date of claim if the claimant is paid monthly. But if averaging the earnings over some other period would produce a more accurate estimate of what will be the claimant's earnings, they should be averaged over that period. (See also para. 13.141 in the case of work paid at less than the going rate.)

HBR 22(2)(a) CTBR 14(2)(a)

14.13 If the claimant has not been employed for long enough to assess earnings on the above basis, but has received some earnings that are likely to represent average weekly earnings, then the authority should use those earnings to estimate average weekly earnings.

HBR 22(2)(b) CTBR 14(2)(b)

14.14 In any other circumstance, the authority should ask the claimant to provide an estimate from their employer of likely weekly earnings over an appropriate period. Most authorities have standard certificate of estimated earnings forms that can be used for this purpose.

HBR 22(3) CTBR 14(3)

14.15 Where the amount of a claimant's earnings changes during an award, the authority should estimate average weekly earnings by reference to the likely earnings from the employment over an appropriate period not exceeding 52 weeks.

HBR 60+ 28(1),(2) CTBR 60+ 20(1),(2)

14.16 Where the claimant or any partner are aged 60 or over, and they work the same hours each week, and their income does not fluctuate, the rules with regard to establishing earnings are less prescriptive. Where the period for which a payment of earnings is made is a week or less, the weekly amount will be the amount of the payment and there are rules for the conversion of non-weekly to weekly amounts (paras. 7.40 and 7.43). Where, however, the claimant's regular pattern of work means that they do not work the same hours every week, or where the claimant's earnings fluctuate and have changed more then once, the authority should average the claimant's weekly earnings as described in the following paragraphs.

HBR 60+ 28(2)(a)(i) CTBR 60+ 20(2)(a)(i)

14.17 Where the claimant does not work the same hours every week and there is a recognised cycle of work, the authority should work out the average weekly earnings over the period of the complete cycle (including any periods where the claimant does no work, but not including any other absences).

HBR 60+ 28(2)(a)(ii) CTBR 60+ 20(2)(a)(ii)

14.18 Where the claimant does not work the same hours every week but there is no recognizable cycle of work or where the claimant's earnings fluctuate and have changed more than once, the authority should work out the claimant's average earnings on the basis of:

- the last two payments before the date of claim or supersession if those payments are one month or more apart; or
- the last four payments if the last two payments are less then one month apart; or
- some other number of payments if this means a more accurate average weekly amount can be calculated.

Calculation of net earnings

14.19 Net earnings are gross earnings less:

- income tax;
- Class 1 National Insurance contributions;
- half of any sum paid by the employee towards an occupational or personal pension scheme.

HBR 29
HBR 60+ 31
CTBR 20
CTBR 60+ 23

GROSS EARNINGS

14.20 Gross earnings means the amount of earnings after the deduction of expenses wholly and exclusively and necessarily incurred in the performance of the employment (R(IS) 16/93) (para. 14.49) but before any authorised deductions by the employer for tax, etc.

DEDUCTING INCOME TAX AND NATIONAL INSURANCE CONTRIBUTIONS

14.21 If the claimant's actual gross earnings were used as described above, any income tax or Class 1 National Insurance contributions actually paid (or made from them) must be deducted from those earnings.

HBR 29(3),(4)
HBR 60+ 31(2),(5
CTBR 20(3),(4)
CTBR 60+ 23(2),(5

14.22 If the claimant's gross earnings were estimated, notional amounts for the income tax payable in the year in which the claim was made (using only the lower and basic rate of tax as appropriate and less only the personal allowance for a person aged under 65, whatever the claimant's actual circumstances) and Class 1 National Insurance contributions must be deducted from those estimated earnings on a pro-rata basis.

HBR 29(4)(a)(b)
HBR 60+ 31(5)(a)(b)
CTBR 20(4)(a)(b)
CTBR 60+ 23(5)(a)(b)

14.23 Where, in Northern Ireland, the claimant works in the Republic, the amounts deducted are those which the NIHE estimates would have been deducted if they worked in Northern Ireland.

NIHBR 29(5)
NIHBR 60+ 31(6)

DEDUCTING HALF OF PENSION CONTRIBUTIONS

14.24 Where the claimant's actual or estimated gross earnings are used, half of any contributions they make or which would be payable on the estimated earnings to an occupational or personal pension scheme, must be deducted from the gross earnings figure.

HBR 29(3)(b), (3A), (3B)
HBR 60+ 31(2)(b),(3),(4),(5
CTBR 20(3)(b), (3A), (3B)
CTBR 60+ 23(2)(b),(3),(4),(5

CONVERSION TO A WEEKLY FIGURE

14.25 If a claimant's earnings are paid other than weekly, they must be converted to a weekly figure as described in paragraph 7.43.

Earned income disregards generally

HBR 29(2), sch 3
HBR 60+ 31(1)
CTBR 20(2), sch 3
CTBR 60+ 23(1)

14.26 An earned income disregard must be deducted from each claimant's earnings. The amount depends on the type of case: the figures are given in table 14.1 (which also applies to self-employed earners). As shown in that table, only one of the amounts shown there is deducted from the combined earnings of a couple or polygamous marriage. (In certain cases, there are further disregards: paras. 13.120, 14.27 and 14.36.)

Table 14.1: Weekly earned income disregards

£25 – LONE PARENTS

The weekly disregard is for any one who counts as a lone parent for HB/CTB purposes.

£20 – CERTAIN PEOPLE WHO ARE DISABLED OR LONG-TERM SICK

This weekly disregard (per single claimant or per couple) applies in all the following cases:

- where the claimant and any partner are under 60 and the claimant's applicable amount includes a disability premium (para. 12.12) or severe disability premium (para. 12.23)
- where the claimant or any partner are 60+ and in receipt of:
  - long-term incapacity benefit
  - severe disablement allowance
  - attendance allowance
  - disability living allowance
  - a mobility supplement;
  - the disability or severe disability element or working tax credit

  or are

  - registered blind
  - treated as incapable of work (para. 12.15) for a continuous period of:
    - 196 days if terminally ill; or
    - 364 days in any other case.

Note: If the claimant or any partner to whom a £20 disregard applies becomes 60 and either had an award of HB/CTB within 8 weeks of becoming 60 then they re-qualify for the £20 disregard provided that:

- they qualified for the £20 disregard under the previous award; and
- continued in employment after that award ended, and
- there is no break of more than 8 weeks in HB/CTB entitlement or employment.

£20 – CERTAIN CARERS AND CERTAIN PEOPLE IN SPECIAL OCCUPATIONS

Except where the preceding disregards of £25 or £20 apply, this weekly disregard (per single claimant or per couple) applies in the following cases:

- single claimants and couples who are awarded a carer premium.
- single claimants and couples employed in the special occupations listed in paragraph 14.43.

OTHER SINGLE CLAIMANTS AND COUPLES

In any case not mentioned above, the weekly disregard is:

- £10 per couple;
- £5 per single claimant.

CHILDREN AND YOUNG PERSONS (WHERE THE CLAIMANT AND ANY PARTNER ARE UNDER 60)

The weekly disregard per child or young person is:

- £15 if he or she qualifies for a disabled child premium;
- £5 in any other case.

Notes

Other earned income disregards are described in paragraph 14.27 and 14.36.

HBR 60+ 27(1), (11), (14)
HBRGB 21(1A), (7), (8)
NIHBR 21(1A), (7)(a),(b)
CTBR 13(1A), 13A(7),(8)

The child care disregard

14.27 In addition to the disregards in table 14.1, up to £135.00 (for one child) or £200 (for two or more children) per week per HB/main CTB claim is disregarded for child care costs in the circumstances described below (A2/2004(Revised)).

WHO CAN QUALIFY?

HBR 21A(1),(4),(5)
HBR 60+ 27(1), (8), (9)
CTBR 13A(1),(4),(5)
CTBR 60+ 19(1),(8),(9)

14.28 The following groups qualify for the child care disregard in the circumstances described:

- lone parents in remunerative work;
- couples if both are in remunerative work;
- couples if one of them (claimant or partner) is in remunerative work and the other one incapacitated (para. 14.30).

REMUNERATIVE WORK

HBR 60+ 27(11),(14)
HBRGB 21A(7),(8)
NIHBR 21A(7)(a),(b)
CTBR 13A(7),(8)
CTBR 60+ 19(1),(14)

14.29 'Remunerative work' means the same as it does in paragraphs 7.29 onwards, except that for the following purposes a person on maternity leave, paternity leave or adoption leave from remunerative work still counts as being in remunerative work. (However, they cannot get the child care disregard in respect of the child they are on that leave for.)

INCAPACITATED

HBR 21A (4)
HBR 60+ 27 (8)
CTBR 13A(4)
CTBR 60+ 19(8)

14.30 The other member of the couple is 'incapacitated' where:

- they are aged 80 or over;
- the claimant's applicable amount includes a disability premium on account of the other member's incapacity;
- they are aged less than 80 and apart from the age criteria would satisfy the conditions for the disability premium (para. 12.12) or would satisfy one of those conditions but have not been treated as incapable of work because the DWP has decided that their incapacity has arisen from their own misconduct; failure to take up medical treatment (under section 171E of the Social Security Contributions and Benefits Act 1992 or in Northern Ireland section 167E of the Social Security Contributions and Benefits (Northern Ireland)Act 1992);
- the claimant's applicable amount would include a disability premium (para. 12.12) on account of the other member's disability but they have been disqualified by the DWP;
- the claimant has been treated as incapable of work (para. 12.15) for a continuous period of at least 196 days (breaks in continuity of 56 days should be ignored in calculating the 196 days);

- In Great Britain a payment equivalent to the following is payable under Northern Ireland law in respect of the other member's incapacity or in Northern Ireland the equivalent benefits under the law in Great Britain:
  - short-term higher rate or long-term incapacity benefit;
  - attendance allowance (AA);
  - severe disablement allowance (SDA);
  - disability living allowance (DLA);
  - industrial injuries constant attendance allowance;
  - an increase of a war pension or disablement pension analogous to AA, DLA or an increase in disablement pension;
- where any of the pensions or allowances, except short-term higher rate or long-term incapacity benefit, have ceased because of hospitalisation;
- claimant has an invalid carriage or other vehicle provided under the relevant legislation.

IN WHAT CIRCUMSTANCES DO THEY QUALIFY?

14.31 The above groups qualify for the disregard if the claimant or partner pays one or more of the following to care for at least one child in their family (so long as that child satisfies the age condition – see below):

HBR 21A(2ZB), (2ZC)
HBR 60+ 27(4), (5
CTBR 13A(2ZB), (2ZC)
CTBR 60+ 19(4),(5

- a registered child-minder, nursery or play scheme; or
- a child-minding scheme for which registration is not required (e.g. run by a school, local authority or, in Northern Ireland, Crown property); or
- child care approved for tax credit purposes; or
- any other out-of-school-hours scheme provided by a school on school premises or by a local authority (in Northern Ireland an education and library board or HSS trust) – but, in this case only, the child must be aged 12 or more.

The disregard does not, however, apply to payments in respect of compulsory education, nor to payments made by a claimant to his or her partner (or *vice versa*) if the child is the responsibility of at least one of them (para. 4.16).

THE AGE CONDITION

14.32 A child satisfies the age condition until the first Monday in September after their 15th birthday or, in the case of a child who meets the conditions for a disabled child premium (para.12.19), the first Monday in September after their 16th birthday.

HBR 21A(2ZA)
HBR 60+ 27(3)
CTBR 13A(2ZA)
CTBR 60+ 19(3)

AMOUNTS, ETC

HBR 21(1)(c), (1ZA), (1A) HBR 60+ 26(1)(c), (2), (3) CTBR 13(1)(c), (1ZA), (1A) CTBR 60+ 18(1)(c),(2),(3)

14.33 The amount of the disregard equals what the claimant or partner pays, up to a maximum of:

- £135.00 per week per HB/main CTB claim for claimants with one child who meets the above criteria (paras. 14.31-32); or
- £200.00 per week per HB/main CTB claim for claimants with two or more children who meet those criteria.

14.34 The disregard is made as far as possible from the earnings (from employment or self-employment) of a claimant and/or partner who satisfies the conditions in paragraph 14.28. Any balance, if the earnings are insufficient, is disregarded from any working tax credit or child tax credit the claimant or partner receives (para. 13.44). Apart from that, it cannot be disregarded from unearned income.

14.35 The amount the claimant or partner pays is averaged over whichever period, up to a year, gives the most accurate estimate of the charges, taking account of information provided by the person providing the care.

The 16/30 hours per week disregard

HBR sch 3 para 16 HBR 60+ sch 3A para 9 CTBR sch 3 para 16 CTBR 60+ sch 3A para 9

14.36 In addition to the earned income disregards mentioned above, a disregard of £12.32 per week is made if at least one of the following conditions is met (but see para. 14.38 for the exception to this rule):

- the claimant, or any partner receives the working tax credit 30 hours element; or
- the claimant or any partner is aged at least 25 and that person is engaged in remunerative work for on average at least 30 hours per week; or
- the claimant is in a couple who have at least one dependent child or young person and at least one member of the couple is engaged in remunerative work for on average at least 16 hours per week; or
- the claimant is a lone parent who is engaged in remunerative work for on average at least 16 hours per week; or
- the claimant's applicable amount includes a disability premium because of their disability and the claimant is engaged in remunerative work for on average at least 16 hours per week;
- the claimant's applicable amount includes a disability premium because of their partner's disability and the partner is engaged in remunerative work for on average at least 16 hours per week;

- the claimant or any partner receives the 50-plus element of working tax credit (DWP HB/CTB A3/2004, para 15, advises that this is shown on the tax credit award notice or can be confirmed by the Inland Revenue);
- the claimant or any partner would qualify for the 50-plus element of working tax credit if they were to make an application (regulation 18 of the Working Tax Credit (Entitlement and Maximum Rate) Regulations 2002 sets out the entitlement conditions for the 50-plus element and DWP A3/2004 Appendix A provides the procedures to help identify this group);
- the claimant is aged at least 60, meets the conditions for the disabled/ long-term sick earned income disregard (table 14.1) and does paid work averaging at least 16 hours per week;
- The claimant or partner is aged at least 60, one of them does paid work averaging at least 16 hours per week and that person's circumstances meet the condition for the disabled/long-term sick earned income disregard (table 14.1).

14.37 For the above purposes, the question of whether anyone works 16 hours or more per week on average is decided as in paragraphs 7.29 onwards; and the question of whether anyone works 30 hours or more per week on average is decided in the same way (apart from the different number of hours).

14.38 The above £12.32 earned income disregard is not made if it (along with the other earned income disregard(s) which apply in any particular case) would result in a negative earned income figure. In such a case, a similar disregard is instead made from working tax credit (para. 13.44).

Particular kinds of earnings and expenses

BONUSES, TIPS AND COMMISSION

14.39 All forms of bonuses, tips and commission derived from the employment are included in the assessment of gross earnings. HBR 28(1) HBR 60+ 30(1) CTBR 19(1) 60+CTBR 22(1)

ARREARS OF EARNINGS

14.40 Where the claimant or any partner is aged under 60, any arrears of pay count as earnings for the period they cover if they relate to periods on or after 6th March 1995 (para. 13.25). They count as capital if they relate to periods before then. HBR 68(7) CTBR 59(9)

TAX REFUNDS

14.41 Where the claimant and any partner are aged under 60, tax refunds on earnings count as capital (not earnings) including in Northern Ireland any analogous payments from the Irish Republic. HBR 40(2) CTBR 31(2)

EARNINGS PAID IN A LUMP SUM

HBR 34(3)
CTBR 25(3)

14.42 Where the claimant and any partner are aged under 60 and have earnings that are paid in a lump sum (or in any other form which could in broad terms be characterised as capital), they are nonetheless counted as earnings. They are averaged over the period they cover.

SPECIAL OCCUPATIONS ANNUAL BOUNTY

HBR 40(1)
CTBR 31(1)

14.43 Where the claimant and any partner are aged under 60 and receives a bounty paid by the special occupations this counts as capital (not earnings) if it is paid annually or at longer intervals. For these purposes the 'special occupations' means part-time fire-fighters, auxiliary coast guards, part-time life-boat workers, and members of the Territorial Army or similar reserve forces.

NON-CASH VOUCHERS

HBR 28(1)(k)
HBR 60+ 30(1)(g)
CTBR 19(1)(k)
CTBR 60+ 22(1)(g)

14.44 If an employee receives non-cash vouchers that are taken into account for the purposes of calculating National Insurance contributions, their value is counted as employed earnings. The value of such vouchers should appear on pay slips (circular HB/CTB A17/99).

PAYMENTS IN KIND

HBR 28(2)(a)
HBR 60+ 30(2)(a)
CTBR 19(2)(a)
CTBR 60+ 22(2)(a)

14.45 With the exception of certain non-cash vouchers (para. 14.44) and where the claimant and any partner are under 60 concessionary coal (para. 13.81), payments in kind (i.e. payments of goods rather than money) are completely disregarded in the assessment of earnings. The DWP advises (GM paras. C3.99-101) that credits received via Local Exchange Trading Schemes ('LETS') do not count as payments in kind, but should be given a cash value as earnings.

COUNCILLORS' ALLOWANCES

14.46 Councillors' allowances, apart from expenses payments, count as employed earnings. (For general advice on these, see GM paras. C3.83-95.)

COMPANY DIRECTORS

14.47 In the case of a claimant who is a director of a company registered with Companies House:

- the income paid by the company to the director is assessed as earned income under the usual rules;
- his or her interest (or share of it) in the company is assessed as capital.

WORK EXPENSES

14.48 The treatment of work expenses met by an employer is as follows: HBR 28(1)(f),(2)(b) sch 4 para 3 HBR 60+ 30(1)(f), (2)(b) CTBR 19(1)(f),(2)(b) sch 4 para 3 CTBR 60+ 22(1)(f), (2)(b)

- if they are for travel to work, or for the cost of caring for a child or other dependant, these must be added in as part of the employee's earnings;
- if they are for other items necessary for performance of the job, these are disregarded in full.

14.49 Work expenses met by an employee and not reimbursed by the employer may not be disregarded against the employee's earnings (but see paragraph 14.27 as regards child care expenses); but where they are wholly and exclusively and necessarily incurred in the performance of the employment (e.g. travel costs between work places as opposed to travel to work costs) they should be deducted from the earnings figure to arrive at the gross earnings figure that is used as the starting point for the calculation of net earnings (R(IS) 16/93 followed in CIS 507/94).

EXPENSES IN UNPAID WORK

14.50 Expenses received by a person doing unpaid work are disregarded in full if they are paid by a charitable organisation or non-profit-making voluntary organisation. HBR sch 4 para 2 HBR 60+ 25(1) CTBR sch 4 para 2 CTB 60+ 17(1)

Starting work

14.51 Although in HB and main CTB there are no specific rules about the period to which earned income should be attributed, the general principle is that, when a claimant starts work, earnings should be taken into account from the beginning of the job – not (if different) the first pay day. (However, for Access to Work and similar schemes, see para. 13.63; for 'extended payments', see para. 17.81; and for the general rules about when changes of circumstances are taken into account, see chapter 17.)

ADVANCES OR LOANS FROM AN EMPLOYER

14.52 Advances and loans from an employer do not count as earnings. They count as capital if (and for as long as) the person has the money. HBR 40(5) CTBR 31(5)

Absences from work and ending work

14.53 The general rules are described below but note that where the claimant or any partner is aged 60 or over any earnings (other than royalties, etc) derived from employment which ended before the first day the claimant becomes entitled to HB/CTB, are disregarded. More details are in tables 14.2 and 14.3. These rules may appear complicated. This is because (for example) during a holiday a person may get sick pay, or while on sick leave a person may get holiday pay. (For the HBR 28 HBR +60 30, sch 3A para 8 CTBR 19 CTBR +60 22, sch 3A para 8 general rules about when changes of circumstances are taken into account, see chapter 17.)

HOLIDAY PAY

HBR 28(1)(d), 40(3)
HBR 60+ 30(1)(d), sch 3A para 8
CTBR 19(1)(d), 31(3)
CTBR 60+ 22(1)(d), sch 3A para 8

14.54 Holiday pay counts as earnings (but see tables 14.2 and 14.3). Where the claimant or any partner is aged 60 or over, any holiday pay from employment which ended before the first day of HB/CTB entitlement is disregarded. Where the claimant and any partner are aged under 60, any holiday pay payable more than four weeks after the following event counts as capital:

- the beginning of an absence or break from work (table 14.2), or
- ending work (table 14.3).

HBR 2(1), 28(1)(i), 29(3)
HBR 60+ 30(1)(h)-(j)
CTBR 2(1), 19(1)(i), 20(3)
CTBR 60+ 22(1)(h)-(j)

SICK PAY, MATERNITY PAY, PATERNITY PAY AND ADOPTION PAY

14.55 Statutory sick, maternity, paternity and adoption pay and employer's sick, maternity, paternity and adoption pay, and corresponding Northern Ireland payments, count as earnings (but see tables 14.2 and 14.3).

RETAINERS

HBR 28(1)(e)
HBR 60+ 30(1)(e)
CTBR 19(1)(e)
CTBR 60+ 22(1)(e)

14.56 Retainers are payments made for a period when no actual work is done, for example to employees of school meals services during the school holidays. These count as earnings (but see tables 14.2 and 14.3).

STRIKE PAY

HBR 60+ 25(1)
60+ CTB 17(1)

14.57 Strike pay does not count as earned income (since it is not paid by an employer). If the claimant and any partner are under 60, it counts as unearned income (but see tables 14.2 and 14.3). If the claimant or any partner are aged 60-plus, it is disregarded because it is not defined as income for HB/CTB purposes.

REDUNDANCY PAYMENTS

HBR 28(1)(b),(g)
HBR 60+ 30(1)(b)
CTBR 19(1)(b),(g)
CTBR 60+ 22(1)(b)

14.58 Redundancy payments (including those paid periodically rather than in a lump sum) do not count as earnings. Redundancy payments count as capital if (and for as long as) the person actually has the money (but see table 14.3 for the treatment of other payments which may be made on redundancy – such as payments in lieu of notice and compensation payments).

Table 14.2: Absences from work

PERIODS WHILST SOMEONE RECEIVES A RETAINER

- Reassess earnings if they change (for example, if the person is paid less during the summer holidays).

HOLIDAYS, ABSENCES WITHOUT GOOD CAUSE, AND STRIKES

- Reassess earnings if they change (for example, if the person is paid less during holidays, or nothing during a strike). (See also the general rule about holiday pay: para. 14.54.)

SICK LEAVE, MATERNITY LEAVE, PATERNITY LEAVE, ADOPTION LEAVE, LAY OFF, SUSPENSION AND OTHER ABSENCES WITH GOOD CAUSE

The following rules apply so long as the employment has not terminated.

- If the absence for any of these reasons began before the person's 'date of claim' (para. 5.52). Count only the following as earnings (and only if they are received during the absence):
  - holiday pay – but only if it is an absence from remunerative work (paras. 7.29 onwards). (See also the general rule about holiday pay: para. 14.54.)
  - retainers;
  - statutory or employer's sick, maternity, paternity or adoption pay;
- If the absence for any of these reasons begins on or after the person's 'date of claim' (para. 5.52). Reassess earnings if they change (for example if the person receives a lower rate of pay for any of these reasons). (See also the general rule about holiday pay: para. 14.54.)

Table 14.3: Ending work

'Remunerative work' is described in paragraphs 7.29 onwards.

ENDING REMUNERATIVE WORK

Where the claimant or any partner is aged 60 or over any earnings (other than royalties) derived from employment which ended before the first day the claimant becomes entitled to HB/CTB are disregarded.

Where the claimant and any partner are aged under 60:

- If the termination of employment occurred before the person's 'date of claim' (para. 5.54) for any reason other than retirement. During the period following termination disregard all earnings except:
    - payments in lieu of remuneration (but periodic redundancy payments count as capital: para. 14.58);
    - payments in lieu of notice or compensating for loss of income;
    - holiday pay (see also the general rule about holiday pay: para. 14.54);
    - retainers;
    - compensation awards made by industrial tribunals for unfair dismissal. Other compensation payments count as capital (not earnings).
    - a sum payable in respect of: arrears of pay following an order for reinstatement or re-engagement under the Employment Rights Act 1996, or following an order under that Act or the Trade Union and Labour Relations (Consolidation) Act 1992 for the continuation of a contract of employment, or by way of remuneration following a protective award under the Trade Union and Labour Relations (Consolidation) Act 1992.
- If the termination occurs on or after the person's 'date of claim' (para 5.52). Reassess to take changes and ending of earnings into account. There are no special rules.

ENDING WORK WHICH IS NOT REMUNERATIVE WORK (PART-TIME WORK)

- If the termination occurred before the person's 'date of claim' (para. 5.52) disregard all earnings apart from retainers.
- If the termination occurs on or after the person's 'date of claim' (para. 5.52). Reassess to take changes and ending of earnings into account. There are no special rules.

15 The self-employed

15.1 This chapter describes the rules for assessing income (and capital) received by the self-employed. In particular it describes the following necessary steps for assessing income from self-employment:

- deciding who is self-employed;
- deciding what assessment period to use;
- assessing the total income during that period;
- assessing allowable expenses during that period;
- calculating pre-tax profit (chargeable income) for that period;
- allowing for tax and national insurance;
- allowing for half of any pension contributions;
- calculating net profit.

HBR sch 3 para 10
HBR 60+ 22
CTBR sch 3 para 20
CTBR 60+ 14

15.2 The rules apply to both HB and main CTB. They do not apply where the claimant or any partner is in receipt of income support, income-based jobseeker's allowance or the guarantee credit. In these cases all income and capital is disregarded. Nor do they apply where the claimant or any partner is in receipt of savings credit only (para. 3.150).

SI 2003 No 325
Reg 2, 12

15.3 As described in the relevant places in this chapter, there are some differences in the law depending upon whether:

- the claimant or any partner is aged 60 or over; or
- the claimant and any partner are both under 60.

HBR 19(1)
HBR 60+ 19(4)
CTBR 11
CTBR 60+ 11(4)

15.4 Where the claimant and any partner are aged under 60 this chapter applies equally to the self-employed income of the claimant, a partner or a child or young person in the claimant's family. Where the claimant or any partner is aged 60 or over this chapter only applies to the self-employed income of the claimant and any partner. In such cases the self-employed income of a child or young person in the claimant's family are totally disregarded. References to 'a claimant' should be read accordingly. This chapter does not apply to the self-employed income of a non-dependant or second adult: the law does not lay down any particular way of assessing income from self-employment in such cases (although it must be gross income, not net). The special rules for self-employed people on the New Deal are given at the end of this chapter (paras. 15.41-43).

Who is self-employed?

15.5 A 'self-employed earner' means someone who is gainfully employed in Great Britain (or in Northern Ireland gainfully employed in NI or the Republic) except anyone employed under a contract of service (i.e. an employee) or employed in an office (e.g. a company director). A person may be a sole trader or in a business partnership (para. 15.28), and therefore be a self-employed earner. But someone who has set up a company, and is a director of it, counts as an employed earner (para. 14.47). The DWP advises that the claimant's word should generally be accepted as to whether he or she is self-employed unless there are grounds for uncertainty (GM para. C3.37).

CBA 2(1)(b)
HBR 2(1)
CTBR 2(1)

15.6 The following are not self-employed income: fostering payments, 'respite care payments' (para. 13.55); or receipt of a Sports Council award (para. 13.124). Additionally, where the claimant or any partner is aged 60-plus, the regulations explicitly exclude from self-employed income payments from boarders in the claimant's home. Such payments should also be excluded from self-employed income where the claimant and any partner are under 60 and with both categories of claimant payments from a sub-tenant should additionally be excluded. Separate rules apply to income from these sources (table 13.4). If, however, board and lodging accommodation is provided somewhere other than the claimant's home the payments should be taken into account as earnings from self-employment. Where the claimant receives rent on a property other than the home this also should be excluded from self-employed income, unless the renting of property constitutes gainful self-employment, as again separate rules apply to the income derived from a property (para. 13.69).

HBR 30(2)
HBR 60+ 33(2)
CTBR 21(2)
CTBR 60+ 25(2)

Capital

15.7 Assets of a business wholly or partly owned by a claimant are disregarded in the assessment of capital if he or she:

- is self-employed; or
- has ceased to be self-employed – the assets are disregarded for as long as reasonably needed to dispose of them; or
- is not self-employed because of sickness or disability, but intends to be afterwards – the assets are disregarded for 26 weeks from the date of any claim; or for such longer period as is reasonable to enable them to return to self-employment.

HBR sch 5 para 7
HBR 60+ sch 5ZA, para 9, 10
CTBR sch 5 para 7
CTBR 60+ sch 5ZA para 9, 10

15.8 It is sometimes necessary to decide whether capital is personal or part of the business. The DWP advises (presumably following R(SB) 4/85) that the test depends on whether the capital is (part of) 'a fund employed and risked in the business' (HB/CTB(93)16). For example, an amount in a self-employed claimant's personal bank account would not be disregarded as a business asset if it is neither employed nor risked in the business.

The assessment period

HBR 21(1), 23
HBR 60+ 32
CTBR 13(1), 15
CTBR 60+ 24

15.9 The income and expenses of a self-employed person are estimated by reference to an 'assessment period'. This is whatever period is appropriate to enable an accurate estimation of average weekly earnings. Where the claimant and any partner are aged under 60 the period must not be longer than one year. Surprisingly, where the claimant or any partner is aged 60 or over it must be for a one year period unless the circumstances are as set out in paras. 15.12-14. The year does not need to be the year immediately before the claim or the date the claim is looked at. The general principle is that income and expenses in the past (in the assessment period) are used to calculate HB and CTB in the future.

PEOPLE WHO HAVE BEEN SELF-EMPLOYED FOR MORE THAN A YEAR

15.10 For people who have been self-employed for some time the DWP advises that the assessment period should normally be that of the last year's trading accounts, but that a shorter or different period may be used if appropriate (GM para. C3.300).

15.11 If claimants have not kept accounts, or the accounts don't cover an appropriate assessment period, it will be necessary for the claimant to provide the authority with information on business-related income and expenditure during the assessment period. Most authorities have a standard form for the collection of this information. The authority may also request supporting evidence such as invoices and receipts, particularly if the information provided by the claimant is improbable or inconsistent. In rare cases, drawings from a business (what they have paid themselves) may provide some evidence. Drawings must not be used, however, where there is evidence of actual business income.

PEOPLE SETTING UP IN BUSINESS

HBR 23(1)
HBR 60+ 32(1)(b)
CTBR 15(1)
60 CTBR 24(1)(b)

15.12 No self-employed earnings should be taken into account until the first earnings are actually received. The receipt of such earnings is a change of circumstance that the claimant has a duty to notify the authority about. We would offer the following approach to the assessment of self-employed earnings in these circumstances. The authority first needs to determine an assessment period from the date the claimant became self-employed to the date of receipt of the first earnings (or a shorter period up to the date of the first earnings if it would give a more accurate earnings figure) and calculate net earnings from self-employment. The assessment period should then be extended (say) every three months until:

- where the claimant and any partner are aged under 60 – an appropriate period of no more than a year is reached; or
- where the claimant or any partner is aged 60 or over – a period of one year is reached.

At each point that the assessment period is extended and net earnings from self-employment recalculated the authority should supersede the previous award.

BUSINESS TRADING FOR LESS THAN A YEAR

15.13 Where the claimant has been engaged in the current self-employment for less than a year, the assessment period should be a period that allows the authority to calculate the earnings with the greatest accuracy.

HBR 23(1)
HBR 60+ 32(1)(b)
CTBR 15(1)
CTBR 60+ 24(1)(b

IF THE NATURE OF A BUSINESS CHANGES

15.14 If the nature of a claimant's business changes in such a way as to affect the normal pattern of business, e.g. the loss of a major customer or changing from full-time to part-time self-employment, the authority should again identify an assessment period that allows it to calculate the earnings with the greatest accuracy, e.g. starting with the date the change occurred and ending on the date for which the most recent figures regarding earnings and expenditure are available.

HBR 23(1)
HBR 60+ 32(1)(b)
CTBR 15(1)
CTBR 60+ 24(1)(b

CAN THE FIGURES BE ALTERED LATER?

15.15 Once the various figures have been assessed as described above, they can be altered later if they were based on a mistake of fact or law or there was an official error, or if there has subsequently been a relevant change of circumstances (e.g. as in para. 15.14). It is incorrect in any other case to revise the figures.

A NOTE ON ACCOUNTING METHODS

15.16 Self-employed people commonly account for their income and expenditure using one of the following methods:

- a 'cash' basis – counting income as being received on the day they receive the money and counting expenses as being incurred on the day they pay the money out; or
- an 'on paper' basis – counting income as being received on the day they issue their bill or invoice for it and counting expenses as being incurred on the day they receive a bill or invoice for them; or
- the basis required (roughly speaking) for income tax purposes – counting income as being received on the day they issue their bill or invoice

or the day they receive the money, whichever happens first and counting expenses as being incurred on the day they receive a bill or invoice or the day they pay the money out, whichever happens first.

15.17 In relation to the rules that operate where the claimant and any partner are under age 60, there is a body of opinion that HB and CTB entitlement should reflect the claimant's cash flow – the first method above. On the other hand, there is evidence that the HB and CTB regulations were drafted on the assumption that income and expenditure should be dealt with under the second or third method above. For example, the rules about debts referred to in items (k) and (l) of table 15.1 would not be needed if income and expenditure were dealt with on a purely cash flow basis. The rules that operate where the claimant or any partner is aged 60-plus are drafted on the assumption that income and expenditure is to be dealt with on a cash flow basis – note the absence of the previously mentioned items in table 15.1 for these claimants. Consequently, where accounts 'on a paper basis' have been submitted for such claimants the information they contain needs to be converted to a cash flow basis, i.e. to reflect gross receipts actually received – not money owed to the business and expenses actually paid – not unpaid bills.

Assessing total earnings

HBR 30(1), 31(1),(3) HBR 60+ 33(1) CTBR 21(1), 22(1),(3) CTBR 60+ 25(1)

15.18 The total earnings of the employment means all the income/receipts of the business during the assessment period. There are two general points to bear in mind.

- Only payments of income are taken into account. A payment of capital into a business (e.g. an investment in the business by, say, a relative) is not a payment of income. It is disregarded under the general rule about disregarded capital (para. 15.7).
- Only income 'derived from' the employment is taken into account. Income from some other source (e.g. as described in para. 15.19) falls under whatever rules apply to that kind of income (chapter 13).

GRANTS, LOANS AND THE ACCESS TO WORK SCHEME

15.19 The following additional points apply:

- Typically, but not always, grants are not 'derived from' self-employment. If not, they should be regarded as a separate source of income or capital – typically voluntary or charitable (para. 13.113).
- Genuine loans are not income (para. 13.126). Money from a loan forms part of the claimant's capital. If it is a loan to the business it is therefore disregarded (para. 15.7).

- Disabled people setting up in self-employment can get payments under the government's Access to Work scheme: these are disregarded as income (para. 13.63).

SINGLE REGENERATION BUDGET (BUSINESS START-UP ALLOWANCES)

HBR 30(1)
HBR 60+ 33(1)
CTBR 21(1)
CTBR 60+ 25(1)

15.20 The Single Regeneration Budget (SRB) has replaced various employment related national schemes and programmes including the Business Start up Allowance (GM para. C3.340-42). Any regular payments to the business from the SRB received by the claimant during the assessment period (except for capital payments) must be counted as part of the total income of the employment. They must not be counted as a separate source of income. But they are not included as income if payments ceased before the date of claim for HB or CTB.

Assessing allowable expenses

HBRGB 31(3)(a), (7
HBR 60+ 34(2)(a)
CTBR 22(3), (7)
CTBR 60+ 26(2)(a
NIHBR 31(3), (7)

15.21 Having worked out the total income in the assessment period, the next step is to allow for the expenses incurred in running the business during the assessment period. The two general principles are:

- expenses are allowed for so long as they are 'wholly and exclusively incurred' for the purpose of the business; but
- the authority cannot allow for an expense if it is not satisfied, given the nature and the amount, that it has been 'reasonably incurred'.

15.22 The law contains rules about special kinds of expenses. These are summarised in table 15.1.

WORKING FROM HOME

15.23 A rent-paying claimant who works from home may regard part of their rent as a business expense. Whether it is an allowable expense depends on the circumstances of the case. It is clear that if part of the home is exclusively used for the business (e.g. an annexe), then the rent on this is an allowable expense but is also disregarded in the assessment of the claimant's eligible rent (paras. 10.5 and 10.108). In all cases, however, an allowance should be made for a reasonable proportion of heating the home and of similar overheads.

DRAWINGS TAKEN BY THE CLAIMANT FROM THE BUSINESS

15.24 Claimants may take 'drawings' from their business as a kind of wages or salary for themselves. These must not be allowed as a business expense.

Table 15.1 SPECIAL TYPES OF EXPENSES

		Allowable?
(a)	Interest payments on any business loan	Yes
(b)	Sums (other than interest payments) employed or intended to be employed in setting up or expanding the business	No
(c)	Income spent on repairing an existing business asset (except to the extent that any sum is payable under an insurance policy for this)	Yes
(d)	Capital repayments on loans for repairing an existing business asset (except to the extent that any sum is payable under an insurance policy for this)	Yes
(e)	Capital repayments on loans for replacing business equipment or machinery	Yes
(f)	Capital repayments on any other business loans	No
(g)	Any other capital expenditure	No
(h)	Depreciation of any capital asset	No
(i)	Losses incurred before the beginning of the assessment period	No
(j)	Excess of VAT paid over VAT received in the assessment period	Yes
(k)	Proven bad debts	Yes/NA*
(l)	Other debts	No/NA*
(m)	Expenses incurred in the recovery of any debt	Yes
(n)	Business entertainment	No
(o)	Any sum for a domestic or private purpose	No

* Not applicable where the claimant or any partner is aged 60 or over (para. 15.17)

Example: Expenses

A self-employed technical writer's accounts include the following expenditure. Before the purchase of her computer and laser printer, she used to do all her writing by hand. The references (a), (b), etc, are to table 15.1.

A cash payment to buy her computer.	Not allowable (g).
Repayments on the loan she took out to buy her laser printer.	The capital element of the repayments is not allowable (f). The interest element is allowable (a).
Repayments on a smaller loan covering half the cost of repairing her laser printer, which was not insured.	Capital and interest elements are both allowable (d), (a).
A cash payment covering the other half of the cost of the laser printer repair.	Allowable (c)
Repayments on a general purpose business loan to help with her cash-flow.	The interest element of the repayments is allowable (a). The capital element is not (f).
A figure for depreciation in the value of the computer and laser printer.	Not allowable (h).

Example: A self-employed childminder

A claimant earns £120 per week from working as a self-employed childminder. She is a lone parent with no other form of earned income. She does not make pension contributions. She does not use a childminder for her own children. Her income from childminding is assessed as follows:

- From the gross amount, two-thirds (£80) is disregarded. The remaining amount is — £40.00
- £40 per week is too low for a deduction to be made for notional tax and national insurance (tables 15.2, 15.3).
- She qualifies for an earned income disregard. For a lone parent (table 14.1) this is — £25.00
- So her assessed weekly earned income for HB/main CTB purposes is — £15.00

EMPLOYING A HUSBAND, WIFE OR UNMARRIED PARTNER

15.25 If the claimant pays their husband, wife or unmarried partner to work for the business, this is allowable as a business expense. It will then count as the partner's earnings. The rules are different if the couple are in a business partnership (para. 15.28).

SELF-EMPLOYED CHILDMINDERS

HBR 31(9)
HBR 60+ 34(8)
CTBR 22(9)
CTBR 60+ 26(8)

15.26 For claimants who are self-employed childminders, instead of working out what their actual expenses are, two-thirds of their total earnings are disregarded in lieu of expenses. No actual expenses can be allowed for.

Pre-tax profit

HBR 31(1)(a), (3)
R 60+ 34(1)(a),(3)
CTBR 22(1)(a), (3)
R 60+ 26(1)(a),(3)

15.27 The next step is to work out the claimant's 'pre-tax profit' (referred to in the regulations as 'chargeable income'):

Total income (paras. 15.18-20)

MINUS

- allowable expenses (paras. 15.21-26)

= pre-tax profit.

BUSINESS PARTNERSHIPS

HBR 31(1)(b),(4)
HBR 60+ 34(1)(b)
CTBR 22(1)(b),(4)
TBR 60+ 26(1)(b)

15.28 If the claimant is self-employed in a partnership, the pre-tax profit (as defined above) should be assessed for the partnership and then split between the business partners. This split should reflect how the business partners actually split their income. This split is required even if the business partners are a couple because it will ensure the correct calculation of notional tax and national insurance (para. 15.34). The rules are different if one partner in a couple employs the other (para. 15.25).

15.29 The rules regarding the business partner's share of the net profit also apply to 'share fishermen' where the claimant and any husband, wife or unmarried partner are under age 60 but not where either is aged 60 or over. In such cases they should be assessed under the self-employed earner provisions described above (DWP, HB/CTB *Pension Credit Handbook* – part 2, para. 520).

NIL INCOME FROM SELF-EMPLOYMENT

15.30 If the claimant's allowable expenses exceed his or her total income, then pre-tax profit is nil. So his or her income from the self-employment is nil.

MORE THAN ONE EMPLOYMENT

15.31 If a self-employed claimant is engaged in any other employment or self-employment, the losses from one cannot be set against the income from the other. HBR 31(10) HBR 60+ 34(9) CTBR 22(10) CTBR 60+ 26(9)

IF THE PRE-TAX PROFIT APPEARS UNREPRESENTATIVE

15.32 If the pre-tax profit appears unlikely to represent the claimant's income, the authority should consider whether selecting a different assessment period would produce a more accurate estimate (para. 15.9). HBR 23(1) HBR 60+ 32(1)(b) CTBR 13(1) CTBR 60+ 24(1)(b)

Notional income tax and notional NICs

15.33 Allowances are made for income tax and national insurance contributions ('NICs'). However, the authority must work these out itself, based on the claimant's pre-tax profit. The figures calculated by the authority are known as 'notional income tax' and 'notional NICs'. They usually differ from the actual income tax and NICs paid by the claimant. One reason for the difference is that an amount for depreciation and certain expenses which are allowed by the Inland Revenue cannot be allowed for HB/CTB purposes. In Northern Ireland, if the claimant is employed in the Republic the authority will deduct what it considers would have been deducted had they worked in Northern Ireland. HBR 32 60 + HBR 35 NIHBR 31(12) CTBR 23 60 + CTBR 27

Table 15.2: Calculating notional income tax (2004-05 tax year)

(a) Start with the annual pre-tax profit figure.

(b Subtract £4,745*.

(c) If there is a remainder:
multiply the first £2,020 (or all, if it is under £2,020) by 10%;
multiply the rest (if any) by 22%, and add to the result of the above.**

(d) The result is the amount of notional tax.

Notes

* £4,745 is the personal allowance.

** The 40% tax rate is not used in assessing notional income tax, nor are any allowances taken into account other than as above. (The regulations have in fact referred to apparently out-of-date tax law for some years. The above appears to be the intention of the law and the best interpretation available.)

THE CALCULATIONS

HBR 26, 32 **15.34** The calculations are given in tables 15.2 and 15.3. An example is given
HBR 60+ 35 CTBR 23 near the end of this chapter. The tables apply to annual amounts of pre-tax profit.
CTBR 60+ 27 If a claimant's assessment period was a different length (e.g. three months), convert pre-tax profit into an annual figure before doing the calculations (para. 7.43). In the case of a couple, work through the calculations separately for each one who has self-employed income.

Table 15.3: Calculating notional NI contributions (2004-05 tax year)

CLASS 2 NICS

If the annual pre-tax profit figure is £4,215* or more, then the amount of notional class 2 NICs is £106.60.**

CLASS 4 NICS

(a) Start with the annual pre-tax profit figure (unless this is greater than £31,720***, in which case start with £31,720).

(b) Subtract £4,745.***

(c) If there is a remainder, multiply it by 8%. The result is the amount of notional class 4 NICs.

Notes

The person may have class 2 notional NICs alone, or may have both class 2 and class 4 notional NICs.

* £4,215 is the lower threshold for class 2 NICs. If the person's pre-tax profit is lower, then the notional class 2 NICs figure is nil (regardless of whether he or she has in fact applied to the Inland Revenue for exemption).

** £106.60 is 52 times £2.05 (the weekly rate of class 2 NICs), there being 52 Sundays in the 2004-05 tax year.

*** £4,745 is the lower threshold, and £31,720 the upper threshold, for class 4 NICs. The 1% class 4 NIC rate for income above £31,720 is not used in assessing notional NICs. (The regulations have not been amended to keep them up-to-date with NIC rules, but this appears to be their intention.)

15.35 Tables 15.2 and 15.3 give the figures for the tax year from 6th April 2004 to 5th April 2005. Authorities must use the figures applying at the date of claim for HB/CTB (para. 5.52). However, they may disregard for up to 30 benefit weeks any change in tax and NICs caused by a change in the law (typically the Budget). So 2003-04's tax and national insurance figures may continue to be used if the date of claim occurs on or before Sunday 7th November 2004.

HBR 26
HBR 60+ 29
CTBR 18
CTBR 60+ 21

Pension contributions

15.36 An allowance is made for half of any pension contributions payable by self-employed claimants towards:

HBRGB 31(11),(12
60+HBR 34(10),(11)
NIHBR 31(11),(11A
CTBR 22(11),(12)
CTBR 60+ 26(10),(12)

- a self-employed personal pension scheme if they are payable on a periodical basis (e.g. monthly). No allowance is made for the lump sum payments some self-employed people make (often for tax purposes); or
- an annuity for a retirement pension for the claimant or a dependant (including husbands, wives and unmarried partners) – if the scheme is approved by the Inland Revenue as eligible for tax relief. People can no longer enter such schemes, but those who entered them in the past may still be in them.

15.37 The allowance applies only while the claimant is making such payments. So if a claimant starts or ceases making such payments while he or she is on HB or CTB (or the amount of the payments changes), this is taken into account as a change of circumstances and HB and/or CTB must be reassessed.

15.38 To find the annual equivalent of pension contributions:

- for contributions payable calendar monthly, multiply the monthly contribution by 12;
- in any other case, divide the contribution by the number of days it covers (e.g. in the case of a weekly contribution, divide by 7) and multiply by 365.

Example: Pension contributions

When a claimant claims HB and CTB, he is paying pension contributions of £50 per month. The annual equivalent is 12 x £50 = £600. Half of this (£300) is allowable in calculating his annual net profit.

After making three monthly payments, he reduces his payments to £40 per month. The annual equivalent is 12 x £40 = £480. Half of this (£240) is allowable in calculating his annual net profit. His claim must be reassessed taking his new annual net profit into account from the Monday after the day on which the first payment of £40 was due.

Net profit

HBR 31(1)-(3)
HBR 60+ 34(1)-(3)
CTBR 22(1)-(3)
CTBR 60+ 26(1)-(3)

15.39 The final step is to work out the claimant's net profit. It is always advisable to work this out initially on an annual basis.

Pre-tax profit (paras. 15.27-32)

MINUS

- notional income tax and notional NI contributions (paras. 15.33-35)
- half of pension contributions (paras. 15.36-38)

= net profit.

CONVERSION TO A WEEKLY FIGURE

15.40 The result must be converted to a weekly figure. Divide the annual figure by 365 and then multiply the result by 7. This weekly figure is the one used in calculating entitlement to HB and main CTB (subject to the earned income disregards: paras. 14.26-38).

Example: Notional tax and NI contributions and net profit: 2004-05

A married woman's annual pre-tax profit is £9,000. She contributes £480 per year to a personal pension scheme. Her husband has no source of earned income.

NOTIONAL INCOME TAX (TABLE 15.2)

(a)	Start with the annual pre-tax profit figure. This is	£9,000.
(b)	Subtract the personal allowance of £4,745. This leaves	£4,255.
(c)	Of this,	
	multiply the first £2,020 by 10%	
	10% of £2,020 is:	£202.00
	multiply the rest (£4,255 – £2,020 = £2,235) by 22%	
	22% of £2,235 is	£491.70
	Adding these together gives:	£693.70
(d)	So her notional tax is:	£693.70

NOTIONAL CLASS 2 NICS (TABLE 15.3)

The annual pre-tax profit figure (£9,000) is greater than £4, 215, so the amount of her notional class 2 NICs is £106.60.

NOTIONAL CLASS 4 NICS (TABLE 15.3)

(a) Start with the annual pre-tax profit figure (which is not greater than £31,720). This is £9,000.

(b) Subtract £4,745.

(c) Multiply the remainder (which is £4,255) by 8%.

This is £340.40 – which is the amount of her notional class 4 NICs.

NET PROFIT

Annual pre-tax profit	£9,000.00
minus notional income tax	£693.70
minus notional class 2 NICs	£106.60
minus notional class 4 NICs	£340.40
minus half of annual contributions to pension scheme	£240.00
Equals annual net profit:	£7,619.30
On a weekly basis this is (£7,619.30 ÷ 365 x 7 =)	£146.12
She qualifies for an earned income disregard of	£10.00
So her weekly net profit (after the disregard) is	£136.12

People on the self-employed employment option of the New Deal

15.41 The following rules apply to people on the 'self-employed employment option' of the New Deal, and to people assisted with pursuing self-employment on an Employment Zone programme or on the 'intensive activity period' of the New Deal (para. 13.41 and table 13.2). Most such people should be entitled to income support or income-based jobseeker's allowance: in their case, all their income and capital is disregarded for HB and main CTB purposes (paras. 7.7, 13.2). The following rules apply in the uncommon cases in which such people are not on either of those benefits: in their case, their income and capital is assessed, for HB and main CTB purposes, in a special way (which differs from the rules in the other parts of this chapter).

BACKGROUND

15.42 A person on the self-employed employment option gets assistance from the Jobcentre with his or her 'commercial activity'. The Jobcentre keeps a 'special account' for that commercial activity, the main features of which are as follows:

- any income he or she makes on the commercial activity is payable into the special account;
- payments may be taken from the special account to meet business expenses or the repayment of business loans relating to the commercial activity;
- the amounts in the special account are treated as capital for IS and JSA(IB) purposes;
- when he or she reaches the end of the self-employed route, the balance in the special account is assessed for IS and JSA(IB) purposes in a special way as income for the future.

ASSESSMENT FOR HB/MAIN CTB PURPOSES

HBRGB 40(7)
sch 4 paras 64,66
5 paras 7, 53, 55
HBR 60+
HBR 40(7), sch 4
paras 66, 67
h 5 paras 7,51, 53
CTBR 31(7)
sch 4 paras 64,66
5 paras 7, 53, 55

15.43 Where the claimant and any partner are aged under 60, the following rules apply in the assessment of HB and main CTB for people on the self-employed employment option (for references to 'commercial activity' and 'special account', see above):

- the gross receipts of the commercial activity are treated as capital for HB and main CTB purposes – but only to the extent that they are payable into the special account;
- payments the person takes from the special account are disregarded as unearned income for HB and main CTB purposes – but only if they are to meet expenses wholly and necessarily incurred in the commercial activity; or are used or intended to be used to maintain repayments on a loan taken out to establish or carry on the commercial activity;
- any capital acquired by the person for the purposes of establishing or carrying on the commercial activity (from whatever source) is disregarded for HB and main CTB purposes for 52 weeks from the date on which it was acquired;
- any business assets acquired by the person for establishing or carrying on the commercial activity (from whatever source) are disregarded as capital for HB and main CTB purposes for as long as the person remains on the self-employed route and then for as long as is reasonable in the circumstances to allow for their disposal (or, if they remain self-employed, see para. 15.7).

In broad terms, the effect of these rules is that, so long as the self-employment is run through the Jobcentre's 'special account', the monies have no impact on the claimant's JSA(IB), HB or CTB.

16 Decisions, notification and payment

16.1 This chapter describes the process of decision-making, notification and payment. It covers the following:

- how quickly should the claim be dealt with and benefit paid?
- who must be notified of the authority's decision;
- information that must be provided to the claimant and others;
- how, and when, HB/CTB should be paid;
- when a payment on account should be made in a rent allowance case;
- how often a rent allowance should be paid;
- when a landlord is paid direct (except for pathfinder authorities: see paras. 22.53-62);
- when a payment of HB/CTB is suspended; and
- who else may receive payment of a rent allowance/CTB.

Dealing with claims and changes

HOW QUICKLY SHOULD THE CLAIM BE DEALT WITH AND BENEFIT PAID?

16.2 Once the authority has received a claim and all the information and evidence it reasonably requires from the claimant it must:

HBR 76(3) CTBR 66(3)
- reach a decision on the claim within 14 days or as soon as reasonably practicable after that;

HBR 77(1)(a) CTBR 67(1)(a)
- notify persons affected (para. 16.7) as soon as the claim is decided; and

HBR 88(3)
- in the case of HB, make payment within 14 days of the receipt of the claim or as soon as possible after that.

In all rent allowance cases if the authority is unable to meet the 14 day decision-making timetable it must normally make a payment on account (para. 16.16).

EXCEPTIONS TO THE REQUIREMENT TO DECIDE

16.3 The authority does not have to meet the above time limits however where a claim: HBR 76(2) CTBR 66(2)

- is not made in the proper time and manner (para. 5.30); or
- is not supported by reasonably required information or evidence from the claimant (para. 5.33); or
- has been withdrawn (para. 5.51).

TIME PERIOD IN WHICH OTHER DECISIONS SHOULD BE MADE

16.4 From time to time authorities have to make other decisions on a claim, e.g. to supersede an original decision following a change of circumstance. Notification of such decisions must be made within 14 days or as soon as possible after that. Notification is not required, however, where a change in CTB entitlement relates solely to a reduction in the council tax where government 'tax-capping' or a delayed award of transitional relief, disability reduction or discount leads to an overpayment of CTB. HBR 77(1)(b) CTBR 67(1)(b)

REMEDIES FOR DELAYS

16.5 Authorities are expected to meet the time limits in the majority of cases. Delays are normally only justifiable, for example, in periods of peak pressure such as the annual up-rating or while handling a high level of enquiries following a take-up campaign. Many authorities fail to meet the time limit and it may be necessary for outside agencies and individuals to place pressure upon such authorities via campaigns and legal and other remedies to ensure that they meet this obligation in the future. Such remedies include:

- complaints to the local government ombudsman;
- action in the High Court or Court of Session in Scotland for judicial review to require authorities to make a determination; and
- action in the County Court or Sheriff Court to require authorities to make a payment if they have agreed that the claimant is entitled.

16.6 *R v Liverpool CC ex parte Johnson No. 1* considered a sample of the many applications made for judicial review of the authority's failure to meet its statutory duties. The judge said that 'in their discretionary decisions as to allocation of resources, authorities must, in making their arrangements for carrying the housing benefit regulations into effect, have specific regard to the time limits'. In response to the authority's assertion that it should not be singled out because the Audit Commission had found that many authorities were in breach of the regulations, the judge said 'if the legal rights of disadvantaged people to expeditious determination of their claims for benefit are being denied across the country, the need for the court's intervention is all the greater'.

Who should be notified and how?

PERSONS AFFECTED

HBR 77, 2(1)
CTBR 67, 2(1)
DAR 3

16.7 The authority is required to notify all persons affected by a decision. A 'person affected' means any of the following where their rights, duties or obligations are affected by a decision:

- the claimant;
- where a claimant, or would-be claimant, is unable to act on his or her own behalf:
  - a receiver appointed by the Court of Protection;
  - an attorney with a general power or a power to claim or as the case may be receive benefit appointed under the Powers of Attorney Act 1971 or the Enduring Powers of Attorney Act 1985;
  - a person appointed by the Council to act on behalf of someone who is unable to act on his or her own behalf;
  - a person appointed by the Secretary of State (in practice a manager at the DWP office) to act on behalf of someone who is unable to act on his or her own behalf;
- the landlord – but only in relation to a decision (not) to make direct payments (where the payment is made to an agent acting for the landlord the agent is the person affected); or
- anyone – including the landlord – from whom the Council has decided that an overpayment is recoverable.

16.8 There may be more than one person affected by any decision made by the authority. For example, where the authority decided to recover an overpayment from the claimant's landlord, both the landlord and the claimant are 'persons affected' and both should be notified of the relevant decisions. The 'person affected' label is not confined to natural persons; it also applies to legal entities such as housing associations and letting companies.

INFORMATION TO BE PROVIDED

HBR 77, sch 6
CTBR 67, sch 6

16.9 The authority must send a written notification to a person affected by a decision. Table 16.1 illustrates the minimum amount of information that an authority must make available automatically following its decisions on a claim. In practice, it is a regrettable fact that many notification letters contain insufficient information and/or are very hard to understand. It is also regrettable that many authorities do not keep copies of their own notification letters, thereby placing their own staff in the impossible position of being unable to explain to claimants what they have said to them.

16.10 Notifications are also required, for instance, where rent allowances are paid direct to the landlord (para. 16.29); where, in the case of HB or main CTB the income of a non-dependant is treated as the claimant's (para. 13.9); and in any case where a recoverable overpayment exists.

HBR 77, sch 6 paras 11-14
CTBR 67, sch 6 paras 11, 16

16.11 All notifications must include statements explaining the right of the person affected to:

HBR sch 6 part 1
CTBR sch 6 part 1

- obtain a written statement of the authority's reasons for the decision; and
- make an application for a revision (para. 17.55) and, where appropriate, to appeal against that decision (i.e. where it is an appealable decision – paras. 19.16-18).

Table 16.1: Information to be notified following decisions on a claim

(HB and CTB notifications should be separate)

A. WHERE THE CLAIMANT IS ENTITLED TO HB/MAIN CTB

*Claimant on income support (IS)/income-based JSA(IB) or guarantee credit **

- Weekly eligible rent/weekly amount of council tax.
- HB – amount and explanation of fuel deductions from eligible rent where they have been estimated using the standard figures in table 10.6, together with the fact that the amount may be varied if the claimant supplies reasonable evidence.
- Amount and category of any non-dependant deductions.
- Normal weekly amount of benefit.
- Rent allowances – date of payment and period for which payment is made.
- First day of entitlement.
- End of benefit period.

- The claimant's duty to notify the authority of changes of circumstance and examples of the kinds of change that should be reported.
- CTB – details of any 'rounding' of figures.

Where a claimant on state pension credit is not entitled to the guarantee credit (i.e. savings credit only) the following additional information must be provided:*

- The applicable amount and the basis of calculation.
- The amount of the savings credit and any child tax credit, child benefit or child special allowance taken into account.
- The amount of the person's income and capital as notified to the authority by the DWP and taken into account for the purposes of the HB/CTB assessment.
- Any modification of the claimant's income or capital.
- The amount of the claimant's capital where applicable.

Claimant not on state pension credit or JSA(IB)

- The information given where the claimant is on IS/or guarantee credit* or JSA(IB).
- The applicable amount and how it is worked out.
- Weekly earnings.
- Weekly unearned income.

B. WHERE THE CLAIMANT IS NOT ENTITLED TO HB/MAIN CTB BECAUSE OF INCOME OR THE MINIMUM HB PAYMENT RULE

*IS, JSA(IB) or state pension credit**

- Weekly eligible rent/weekly amount of council tax.
- HB – amount and explanation of fuel deductions from eligible rent where they have been estimated using the standard figures in table 10.6, together with the fact that the amount may be varied if the claimant supplies reasonable evidence.
- Amount and category of non-dependant deductions.
- HB – normal weekly amount of benefit and the fact that it is not payable because it is below the minimum.

*Claimants not on IS, JSA(IB) or state pension credit**

- The information given where the claimant is on IS, state pension credit or JSA(IB).
- The applicable amount and how it is worked out.
- Weekly earnings.
- Weekly unearned income.

C. WHERE THE CTB CLAIMANT IS BETTER OFF ON SECOND ADULT REBATE

- The fact that the claimant is better off on second adult rebate and the amount.
- The lesser amount of main CTB.

D. WHERE THE CTB CLAIMANT IS ENTITLED TO SECOND ADULT REBATE

- Normal weekly amount of council tax rounded to nearest penny.
- Normal weekly amount of second adult rebate rounded to nearest penny.
- Rates of second adult rebate and related gross income levels.
- First day of entitlement.
- End of benefit period.
- Gross income of any second adult or the fact that the second adult is on IS/state pension credit or JSA(IB).
- The claimant's duty to notify the authority of changes of circumstance and examples of the kinds of change that should be reported.
- Details of any 'rounding' of figures.

E. ITEMS TO BE NOTIFIED WHERE SECOND ADULT REBATE IS NOT PAYABLE

Where gross income of second adult(s) too high

- Normal weekly amount of council tax rounded to nearest penny.
- Rates of second adult rebate and related gross income levels.
- Gross income of any second adult or the fact that the second adult is on IS, state pension credit or JSA(IB).

Where claimant better off on main CTB

- The fact that the claimant is better off on main CTB.
- The lesser amount of second adult rebate.

F. CLAIMANT NOT ENTITLED FOR SOME OTHER REASON

- The reason why the claimant is not entitled.

G. ITEMS TO BE NOTIFIED IN ALL CASES

- The right, time and manner in which to request a written explanation of a decision.
- The right, time and manner in which to apply for a revision (para. 17.55) and, where appropriate, to appeal against the decision (i.e. where it is an appealable decision – paras. 19.16-18).
- Any other appropriate matters.

* The state pension credit will be made up of two elements: the guarantee credit (which replaces income support) and the savings credit, a new benefit paid to over-65s with a private income.

Time and manner of payment

PAYMENT OF HB

HBR 88(1)
DAR sch para 1

16.12 Authorities may decide on the time and manner in which to make payments of HB on the basis of the circumstances of the individual case. They are expected to have regard to the reasonable needs and convenience of the person they are paying, as well as the time and frequency with which the liability to make payments arises. Decisions on payment method/frequency are not appealable but a person affected can request the authority to revise its decision at any time.

16.13 The requirement that the authority must have regard to the reasonable needs and convenience of the person receiving payment means that they should not make unreasonable demands, such as collection from a place not easily accessible, or insistence upon crossed cheques or credit transfer arrangements when the payee does not have a bank account (GM para. A6.120).

16.14 In the case of rent rebates, payment is in the form of a rebate applied to the rent account.

16.15 Where the claimant is a private tenant, he or she is normally paid direct, though in certain circumstances a rent allowance may be paid to the landlord (paras. 16.29-40). HBR 88(1), 92(1)

PAYMENTS ON ACCOUNT (INTERIM PAYMENTS)

16.16 A payment on account, (sometimes known as an interim payment), must be paid within 14 days if the following circumstances are met: HBR 91(1)

- the authority is unable to make a decision on the amount of benefit payable within 14 days of receipt of the claim; and
- that inability has not arisen out of the claimant's failure to provide necessary information or evidence (which the authority has requested from the claimant in writing) without good cause.

The authority must pay an amount it considers reasonable on the basis of whatever information is available to it about the individual claimant's circumstances, such as sources of income, and any relevant determination made by a rent officer (para. 23.45).

16.17 Payments on account are not discretionary and must be paid if the circumstances set out in paragraph 16.16 apply. In the case of *R v Haringey LBC ex parte Ayub,* the judge confirmed that a rent allowance claimant 'who has done all that he should is to be paid something within 14 days of a claim being made'. The judge also confirmed that no separate claim or request need be made in respect of a payment on account. The DWP (GM A6.137) considers it important for authorities to note that the duty to make a payment on account rests entirely with the authority. 'It is not the claimant's responsibility to ask for a payment on account and [authorities] must not wait for them to ask.' It should also be emphasised that the rule applies to all rent allowance claims including those from housing association tenants.

16.18 Many authorities fail to make payments on account or only make such payments when the claimant's tenancy is at risk. Such authorities are acting illegally. The DSS (HB/CTB(93)37) expresses its 'concern about continuing reports of delays by some authorities in processing rent allowance claims, and their failure to make payments on account where appropriate'. The authority's decisions relating to payments on account, (except subsequent adjustments to take account of an under or overpayment) are not appealable but may be the trigger for an application for judicial review or a complaint to the local government ombudsman. A high proportion of complaints to the local government ombudsman concern failure to make payments on account. The ombudsman is likely to find maladministration with injustice and make a recommendation that compensation be paid in such cases. DAR sch para 1(b)

16.19 Good cause for the claimant failing to provide necessary information and evidence would include, for example, a landlord's unwillingness to provide evidence of rent payments. The DWP (GM A6.140) points out that a claimant cannot be held responsible for delays in receiving confirmation of IS entitlement from the local DWP office. The DSS also reminded authorities (HB/CTB(93)37) that a claimant cannot be held responsible for a failure to supply evidence and information which he or she has not been asked specifically to provide. The claimant must also be given a reasonable time to provide any information which has been asked for before he or she can be judged to have failed to have done so. For example, if the authority does not write to the claimant asking for verification of, say, his or her earnings until the 13th day after the date on which the claim was made and the verification is supplied a few days later, the authority cannot then reasonably argue that it was impractical to decide the claim within 14 days because of the claimant's failure to provide the necessary information. The DSS advises that, in such a case, the claimant would clearly have good cause for failing to provide the information within the 14-day period. The authority is obliged to make initial payment on account on the 14th day following receipt of the claim based on the information originally available to it. This is the case even when the post-1996 payment rules (para. 16.21) apply.

HBR 91(2),(3) **16.20** If the authority finds, when it makes its formal decision on the claim, that HB entitlement is different from the amount it has paid on account, further rent allowance payments will be adjusted to allow for under- or overpayments. The authority's decisions regarding adjustments to payment on account of rent allowance to take account of an under or overpayment are appealable to an independent appeal tribunal.

DAR sch para 1(b) The letter advising of a payment on account must include a statement informing the claimant that if the payment is in excess of actual entitlement it will be recoverable from the person to whom the payment is made.

FREQUENCY OF RENT ALLOWANCE PAYMENTS

HBR 90(1),(2),(2A) **16.21** Following any 'payment on account', or first payment, the authority may choose to pay a rent allowance at intervals of two or four weeks or one calendar month or, with the consent of the person entitled to payment, at intervals greater than one month. Since the 7th October 1996, except where the claimant is entitled to transitional protection (para. 16.23), the authority must make payments to claimants at the end of the period to which they relate as follows:

- where payment is being made direct to the landlord every four weeks (or, at the authority's discretion, monthly where there is a monthly rent liability); or

- in any other case every two weeks or other period in accordance with paragraph 16.24.

16.22 Where the authority is paying benefit direct to a landlord for more than one claimant the first payment to a new claimant may be made at a shorter interval than four weeks if it is 'in the interest of efficient administration'. In practice this allows the authority to align any new claimants of a landlord who they already pay direct into the same payment cycle as their other claimants. HBR 90(2B)

FREQUENCY OF RENT ALLOWANCE CASES FOR CERTAIN PRE-1996 CASES

16.23 The rules in paragraphs 16.21-22 do not apply to claimants who: SI 1996 No. 965 reg 11 NISR 1996 No. 181 reg 11

- were in receipt of HB before 7th October 1996; and
- have been on HB continuously since without any breaks; and
- have not moved home since that date.

Any break in the claim is ignored if the claimant dies provided their surviving partner makes a within four weeks of the death But no other reason). In these cases authorities have a duty, as far as possible, to make payments two weeks before the end of the period covered in accordance with the same rules about frequency of payment as described in paragraph 16.24. So a fortnightly rent liability should be paid in advance, while four-weekly or monthly liabilities should be met midway through the period. However, where the tenancy allows for rent is paid in arrears the authority has the discretion to make payments at the end of the period.

16.24 Where payment is being made to the claimant they can require the authority to make payments every two weeks if their weekly HB is greater than £2. Where the amount of weekly benefit is £2 or less then the authority may pay HB according to the following rules: HBR 88(2),90(3),(5

- if they are a student once a term (para 21.34);
- where the amount of weekly HB is less than £1 per week, every six months;
- in any other case the authority may choose to pay either at intervals of two weeks, four weeks, one month or, where the claimant has given their consent, any other interval greater than a month.

In all these cases the authority retains discretion to pay the claimant weekly where the circumstances in paragraph 16.25 apply.

AUTHORITY'S DISCRETION TO PAY WEEKLY

HBR 90(4) **16.25** Except where HB is paid direct to a landlord, authorities have discretion to pay HB weekly if it considers that:

- paying HB over a longer period would lead to an overpayment; or
- the claimant pays rent weekly and it is in his or her interest (or that of the family) to receive weekly payments.

The former instance covers cases where there is only a short period of entitlement to HB, or where a change of circumstance is anticipated in the near future. The latter instance may be helpful in cases where claimants have difficulty in budgeting over a longer period.

PAYMENT OF CTB

CTBR 77 **16.26** Normally authorities pay CTB by means of a rebate (credit) to the individual's council tax account and thus reduce the liability for the tax. Where the rebate is greater than the tax liability the authority may reduce the liability for the tax in subsequent years. However, where the tax has been paid for the financial year, and the claimant requires it, or the claimant is jointly and severally liable for the tax and the authority considers it appropriate, the balance of any CTB must be paid direct to the claimant. Also where a person has met the tax liability in full and the tax account has been closed, e.g. because he or she has left the area or is no longer liable, the authority must pay the outstanding amount of CTB direct to the claimant. In all cases where the payment is direct to the claimant rather than to the claimant's council tax account, payment should normally be made within 14 days or as soon as reasonably practicable after that.

PAYMENT OF RATE REBATES IN NORTHERN IRELAND

NIHBR 89 **16.27** In Northern Ireland the rate rebate can be paid with the claimant's rent allowance provided they are not billed directly by the rates collection agency (i.e. they pay their rates as part of their rent).

To whom should the payment be made?

AA 134(1A),(1B), 138(1) NIAA 126(1) HBR 92 CTBR 78 **16.28** HB for council and NIHE tenants and CTB (in Northern Ireland HB for rates (para.11.40)) is normally paid by way of a rebate to their rent/council tax/rates account. In all other cases the normal requirement is that the benefit is paid to the claimant. However, in particular circumstances:

- a rent allowance can be paid to the claimant's landlord, or someone else to whom rent is payable, e.g. a lettings agent, or a nominee (note that these rules are different in the Pathfinder areas (paras. 22.53-62)); and

- a rent allowance or CTB is paid to an appointee or, in the case of a claimant who has died, a personal representative or next of kin aged 16 or over.

When an amount of rent allowance is paid to a landlord or lettings agent this discharges the claimant's liability to pay that amount of rent, unless the authority recovers any overpayment from that landlord or lettings agent (para. 18.58).

FIRST PAYMENT OF A RENT ALLOWANCE MADE PAYABLE TO A LANDLORD OR LETTINGS AGENT BUT SENT TO THE CLAIMANT

16.29 The authority has the discretion to make the first payment of a new or renewed rent allowance claim by sending the claimant a cheque or other instrument of payment payable to the landlord for part or all of the amount due. The DWP advises that this 'is to avoid the possibility of a claimant misusing a first payment covering several weeks' entitlement' (GM A6.142). The authority is, however, only able to make the first cheque, etc, payable to the landlord where: HBR 94(1A)

- the authority is of the opinion that the claimant has not already paid the landlord for the period in respect of which any payment is to be made; and
- it is in the interests of the efficient administration of housing benefit.

The DWP has advised authorities (GM A6.145) to consider using this power where:

- the amount due is £100 or more; or
- it has reason to think that the claimant might default; or
- there is a rent debt but the case is not appropriate for longer term direct payment arrangements.

MANDATORY DIRECT PAYMENTS

16.30 Except where paragraph 16.31 applies, the authority must make direct payments of a rent allowance to a landlord where: HBR 93(1)

- an amount of income support, state pension credit or either kind of JSA payable to the claimant, or partner, is being paid direct to the landlord to meet arrears; or
- the claimant has rent arrears equivalent to eight weeks or more, except where the authority considers it to be in the overriding interest of the claimant not to make direct payments.

16.31 The exception to the above rules requiring direct payment is where the authority is not satisfied that the landlord is a 'fit and proper person' to receive direct payments. The DWP advises (GM A6.164) that a landlord should be assumed to be a 'fit and proper person' in the absence of evidence to the contrary. The test HBR 93(3), 94(1B) enables the authority to refuse direct payments in cases where the landlord is involved in fraudulent acts related to HB. The DWP suggests (GM A6.166) that the authority might also consider whether the landlord has habitually failed to:

- report changes in tenants' circumstances which he or she might reasonably be expected to know might affect entitlement; or
- repay an overpayment which the authority has decided is recoverable – despite the fact that a proper notification was issued and that the rights of review had been exercised or made available.

16.32 In deciding whether the landlord is 'fit and proper', the authority should not base its judgment on:

- the landlord's undesirable activity in non-HB matters; or
- the fact that the landlord makes use of the right to request a revision or appeal before repaying any recoverable overpayment; or
- the fact that the landlord has made complaints of maladministration to the local government ombudsman.

HBR 94(1) **16.33** Where the authority is satisfied that the landlord is not a 'fit and proper person' but it appears to be in the overriding interest of the claimant to pay the landlord direct – then direct payments may still be considered under the discretionary direct payment rules (para. 16.38).

16.34 In the case of *R v Haringey LBC ex parte Ayub* the judge found that the duty to pay a landlord direct once the claimant is eight weeks or more in rent arrears only arises if the landlord or someone else informs the authority that there are eight weeks or more arrears. It is not up to the authority to find this out for itself. If the tenant disputes that there are eight weeks' arrears the authority must consider the available evidence and come to a finding of fact on the balance of probability. Either party (the claimant or landlord) can appeal about the authority's decision.

HBR 96(3),(5) **16.35** If the claimant dies but the authority has already decided to make payment direct to the landlord, any amount of benefit outstanding at the time of the claimant's death must be paid to the landlord if a written application has been made for it (see also para. 16.45).

16.36 Where deductions are being made from income support/JSA to meet rent arrears, direct payments of HB to the landlord should continue until such time as the DWP ceases to make the relevant deductions. DWP local offices should advise authorities of appropriate cases (GM A6.154).

16.37 Where the authority is making direct payments because the claimant is eight or more weeks in rent arrears, the direct payment should cease once the arrears fall below the eight-week level, unless one of the circumstances in paras. 16.34 or 16.35 applies.

DISCRETIONARY DIRECT PAYMENTS

16.38 Except in the Pathfinder authority areas (table 22.1), where different rules apply (paras. 22.53-62), an authority may implement direct payment arrangements where: HBR 94(1)

- the claimant requests, or consents to, such an arrangement; or
- the authority considers it to be in the interest of the claimant and family; or
- benefit is owing to a claimant who has left a dwelling with rent arrears.

In the last circumstance direct payment is limited to an amount equivalent to the rent owing.

16.39 As with mandatory direct payments, the authority may decide not to make direct payments where the landlord is not a 'fit and proper person' to receive such payments. However, where it appears to be in the overriding interest of the claimant for the landlord to be paid direct, and there are no practicable alternatives, the authority may make direct payments. This would apply, for example, where the risk to the claimant of not paying the landlord outweighs any risk associated with direct payment. HBR 94(1B)

16.40 Authorities might use their power to pay direct in the interest of the claimant and family where, for example, the claimant has a history of rent arrears at a previous address or where social or medical problems (such as mental illness or drug addiction) indicate that help with budgeting is needed.

INFORMATION TO BE PROVIDED TO CLAIMANTS AND LANDLORDS OR LETTINGS AGENTS

16.41 When a decision has been made that HB is to be paid direct to the landlord both the claimant and landlord should be notified of that fact within 14 days (para. 16.2). The notification must include the date from which the arrangement will commence and their right to obtain a written statement of reasons and make written representations. The notification must also inform both the landlord and claimant that where: HBR 77, sch 6 part IV

- an overpayment is recoverable from the landlord (para. 18.26); and
- the overpayment is recovered from direct payments made on behalf of a tenant to whom the overpayment does not relate (para. 18.47),

that tenant's rent must be treated as paid to the value of the amount recovered.

16.42 The landlord must also be informed of his or her duty to report any change of circumstances which might affect the claimant's amount of, or right to, HB and the kind of change which should be notified.

Other people who may receive a rent allowance or CTB

APPOINTEE

HBR 92(2) CTBR 78(2) **16.43** Where an appointee acts on behalf of a claimant who is incapable of managing his or her own affairs (para. 5.6) then payment may be made to that person. In most cases, however, CTB will be paid by rebating the claimant's tax liability. The authority should also consider whether the claimant should be exempt from the council tax on grounds of severe mental impairment (para. 9.11).

NOMINEE

HBR 92(3) **16.44** In the case of HB, if the claimant requests in writing that the authority makes payment to another person (who must be 18 or more), the authority may make payments to that person. The DWP incorrectly refers to this person as an agent and advises that the claimant must be unable to collect the money himself or herself (GM para. A6.148). This is not the case, however, as the relevant regulation specifically identifies that the claimant may be able to act on their own behalf.

A DEAD CLAIMANT'S PERSONAL REPRESENTATIVE OR NEXT OF KIN

HBR 96(1)-(3) CTBR 81(1)-(3) **16.45** Following a claimant's death, the authority must, if a written application is received within 12 months (or such longer period as the authority may allow), pay a rent allowance – or any CTB above the dead claimant's residual council tax liability – to his or her personal representative or, if there is none, the next of kin. The next of kin take priority in the following order: spouse, issue (children, grandchildren), other relatives (parents, brothers, sisters or their children); and must be aged 16 or over.

17 Changes to entitlement

17.1 This chapter explains how a claimant's entitlement to HB or CTB can change or end – perhaps because of a change in the claimant's (or other) circumstances, or perhaps because the claimant has asked the authority to reconsider its decision. It covers:

- how a decision can be changed;
- general rules about 'revisions' and 'supersessions';
- the duty to notify a change of circumstances;
- when changes of circumstances take effect from;
- how mistakes and errors are corrected;
- asking the authority to reconsider a decision and how the authority deals with this; and
- the rules about 'extended payments' and 'continuing payments'.

The rules have changed this year, mainly because 'benefit periods' have been abolished (paras. 5.74-75).

How a decision can be changed

CPSA sch 7 paras 2, 11

17.2 Once an authority has decided a claim (para. 16.2), its decision cannot be changed unless:

- the authority changes the decision by 'revising' it – usually because it was wrongly decided in the first place; or
- the authority changes the decision by 'superseding' it – usually because there has been a change of circumstances; or
- the authority corrects an accidental error in the decision; or
- an appeal tribunal, Commissioner, tribunal of Commissioners, or court alters the decision on appeal.

The first three are described in this chapter; appeals are described in chapter 19.

TERMINOLOGY

17.3 The terms 'revise', 'revision, 'revised decision', 'supersede', 'supersession' and 'superseding decision' were introduced on 2nd July 2001, and they are explained in the next few paragraphs. Table 17.1 summarises which applies in which circumstances, and gives the date from which it applies. Accidental errors are explained in paragraph 17.45.

Table 17.1: Revisions and supersessions: main points

SITUATION	REVISION OR SUPERSESSION? AND DATE IT TAKES EFFECT
CHANGES OF CIRCUMSTANCES	
A change which the claimant had a duty to notify and which he or she notified to the authority more than one month after it occurred (this time limit can be extended) and the claimant qualifies for more HB/CTB	**Supersession:** From the Monday following the day when the authority receives the notification (or for some rent increases, earlier)
Any other change of circumstances	**Supersession:** From the Monday following the day the change occurs (or for some rent increases, earlier)
OFFICIAL ERROR	
An official error arising at any time (whether resulting in an overpayment or an underpayment)	**Revision:** From the date the decision took effect or should have (or supersession: para. 17.46)
OVERPAYMENTS (OTHER THAN AS ABOVE)	
A mistake of fact meaning the claimant was overpaid	**Revision:** From the date the decision took effect or should have (or supersession: para. 17.49)
REQUESTS BY PERSON AFFECTED	
A person affected requests the authority to reconsider its decision within one month (which can be extended)	**Revision:** From the date the decision took effect or should have
A person affected requests this benefit outside the above time limits	**Supersession:** From the Monday of the week in which the authority received the request
A person affected appeals within the time limits for appeal and the authority chooses to revise instead	**Revision:** From the date the decision took effect or should have

RENT OFFICER RE-DETERMINATIONS

A rent officer re-determination is in the claimant's favour	**Revision:** From the date the decision took effect or should have
A rent officer re-determination is against the claimant's favour	**Supersession:** From the Monday following the rent officer re-determination

OTHER MISTAKES OF FACT OR LAW

Other mistake of fact arising within one month of the decision	**Revision:** From the date the decision took effect or should have
Any other mistake of fact or law	**Supersession:** From the Monday of the benefit week in which the authority was notified of it or became aware of it

Examples: Revisions and supersessions when there is a change or dispute

A CHANGE RESULTING IN A SUPERSESSION

A claimant writes to tell the authority that her wages went down some months into her HB/CTB benefit period. Her letter gets to the authority within one month of the change, and she provides acceptable evidence.

The authority should make a superseding decision, so that the increase in her HB/CTB is awarded from the Monday following the date her wages went down.

A LATE-NOTIFIED CHANGE RESULTING IN A SUPERSESSION

The same as the above story, except that the claimant took six months to inform the authority (and has no reason for her delay).

The authority should make a superseding decision, so that the increase in her HB/CTB is awarded from the Monday following the date it received the information from her.

A DISPUTE RESULTING IN A REVISION

A claimant has been awarded HB/CTB on the basis that the maximum non-dependant deduction is to apply in respect of her son (because he works full-time but she has been unable to provide evidence of his income). Within one month of notification of the decision on her claim, she writes in with acceptable evidence of his true (low) income.

The authority should revise its decision, so that the lower non-dependant deduction applies from the beginning of her claim.

A DISPUTE RESULTING IN A SUPERSESSION

The same as the last story, except that the claimant took eight months to provide the evidence (and has no reason for her delay).

The authority should make a superseding decision, so that the lower non-dependant deduction applies from the Monday of the week it received the evidence from her.

'REVISION', 'SUPERSESSION' AND 'RECONSIDERATION'

17.4 'Revision' and 'supersession' are the legal terms for what is more commonly called in day-to-day work a 'reconsideration'. Generally speaking the distinction between them is as follows:

- **Revision:** A revision is typically required when a decision was wrong from the outset. When a decision is revised, the revision goes back to the beginning (to the date of the decision in question).
- **Supersession:** A supersession is typically required when there has been a change of circumstances. When a decision is superseded, the supersession does not go right back: there will always be a 'before' and an 'after'.

17.5 Depending on the circumstances (described in the next sections of this chapter), the authority may have to revise or supersede a decision:

- because a claimant or other person affected requests this (para. 17.55) – in which case he or she does not have to get the terminology right; or
- because the authority has the power to do so without such a request; or
- because the regulations require it.

In each case there are rules about what factors are relevant to a revision or supersession and how to obtain the information and evidence needed (paras. 17.65-66).

17.6 If more than one event occurs in a case (such as a two successive changes in circumstances), each is dealt with in turn. However, if a single event apparently requires both a revision and a supersession, it is dealt with as a revision. For example, a claimant may request a reconsideration so late that it can only be dealt with as a supersession (para. 17.60), but the authority realises it has made an official error (para. 17.46) which has to be treated as a revision: the revision 'wins'. DAR 7(4)

CPSA sch 7 paras 1(2), 3(1), 4(1)-(2),(4) DAR 7(1)

17.7 Once a decision has been revised or superseded, the result is a decision itself, which can in turn be revised or superseded in the same way as an original decision can be. This applies also to a decision imposed by an appeal tribunal, a Commissioner, or a tribunal of Commissioners.

Duty to notify a change of circumstances

HBR 75(1),(4) CTBR 65(1),(5)

17.8 The claimant has a duty to notify the authority's 'designated office' (para. 5.25), in writing, of any 'relevant' change of circumstances. What counts as a 'relevant' change is in the next paragraph. The duty to notify begins on the date the claim is made and continues for as long as the person is in receipt of HB or CTB (except in relation to 'extended payments' and 'continuing payments': paras. 17.81 and 17.94). If HB/CTB is payable to someone other than the claimant (e.g. a landlord or an appointee), that person is also required to notify relevant changes.

HBR 75(1) CTBR 65(1)

17.9 For these purposes a 'relevant' change is one which the claimant (or other person) could reasonably be expected to know might affect:

- entitlement to HB/CTB; or
- amount of HB/CTB; or
- method of payment (e.g. whether to pay HB to the landlord rather than the claimant or *vice versa*).

17.10 Whether a claimant (or other person) could reasonably be expected to know a change might affect HB or CTB, is of importance if failure to notify a change results in an overpayment and the question of recovering the overpayment arises (chapter 18), or results in an underpayment and the question of whether it should be awarded arises (para. 17.37).

17.11 Apart from the specific rules mentioned in the next paragraph, the following are a selection of things the claimant should inform the authority of:

- changes of address;
- changes in rent (unless the claimant is a council or NIHE tenant);
- changes in rates if they are not collected by the RCA (Northern Ireland only);
- changes in the status of non-dependants/second adults;
- changes in family circumstances affecting the applicable amount;
- changes in capital and/or income;
- changes relating to payment of HB direct to a landlord.

17.12 The law lists certain things which the claimant must inform the authority of (table 17.2) and certain other things which the claimant need not inform the authority of (table 17.3).

Table 17.2: Changes the claimant must notify *

CLAIMANT AND ANY PARTNER UNDER 60

- The end of his or her (or any partner's) entitlement to JSA(IB) or IS
- Changes where a child or young person ceases to be a member of the family: for example, when child benefit stops or he or she leaves the household

CLAIMANT OR ANY PARTNER AGED 60+

- Changes in the details of their letting (HB rent allowances only)
- Changes affecting the residence or income of any non-dependant
- Absences exceeding or likely to exceed 13 weeks

ADDITIONAL MATTERS FOR CLAIMANTS ON SAVINGS CREDIT

- Changes affecting any child living with the claimant (other than age) which might affect the amount of HB/CTB
- Changes to child tax credit or child benefit
- Changes to capital which take it (or may take it) above £16,000
- Changes to a non-dependant if the non-dependant's income and capital was treated as being the claimant's (para. 13.9)
- Changes to a partner who was ignored in assessing savings credit but is taken into account for HB/CTB (para. 13.104 and table 13.5)

ADDITIONAL MATTERS FOR CLAIMANTS ON SECOND ADULT REBATE **

- Changes in the number of adults in their home
- Changes in the total gross incomes of the adults in their home
- The date any adult in their home ceases to receive JSA(IB) or IS

Notes

* This is a list of the items specifically mentioned in the law. The claimant's duty is wider (para. 17.9).

** In the first two cases, the duty arises only if the change might reasonably be expected to alter the claimant's entitlement to second adult rebate. In the third case, the duty arises whenever such a change occurs – regardless of whether it could affect entitlement. The word 'adult' is not defined for these purposes, but may be presumed to mean anyone aged 18 or more.

HBR 75(2)(e),(3)
HBR 60+ 75(1),(5)-(7)
CTBR 65(2)(e),(3),(4)
CTBR 60+ 65(1),(6)-(8)

Table 17.3 Changes the claimant need not notify *

HBR 75(2)
HBR 60+ 75
CTBR 65(2)
CTBR 60+ 65

- Beginnings or ends of awards of pension credit (either kind) or changes in the amount
- Changes which affect JSA(IB) or IS but do not affect HB/CTB
- Changes in rent (HB rent rebates only)
- Changes in council tax
- Changes in rates paid direct to the RCA (Northern Ireland only)
- Changes in the age of any member of the family or non-dependant
- Changes in the HB or CTB regulations

Notes

* In the first case, it is the DWP's duty (and no-one else's) to notify the authority of the change. In the second, the change has no impact on HB. In the third, fourth and fifth, the authority has made the changes, and so should not need to be informed of them. In the last two cases, the authority shoul implement the change automatically.

Changes of circumstances which are notified on time or do not require notification

17.13 This section describes how authorities should deal with changes of circumstances which:

- are notified to the authority on time ('on time' means within a month of the occurrence of the change – or longer in special circumstances: para. 17.40); or
- do not require to be notified to the authority (table 17.3).

In each case, in broad terms the general principle is that the change is taken into effect from a date at or very near to the occurrence of the change. Late-notified changes are dealt with in the next section (para. 17.36 onwards).

17.14 The authority may alter a decision if there has been a change of circumstances or one is anticipated. The effect of this may be to:

- alter the claimant's entitlement to HB/CTB; or
- end the award of HB/CTB.

17.15 This is normally a supersession (in the second case a supersession at nil) but in limited circumstances it can be a revision (paras. 17.46 and 17.49). The following paragraphs explain which option is available to the authority in each circumstance.

NOTIFYING THE OUTCOME

17.16 The claimant and any other person affected must be notified in writing of the alteration in entitlement (or of the end of the award), within 14 days or as soon as reasonably practicable, including the following matters: HBR 77(1)(b), sch 6 part I CTBR 67(1)(b), sch 6 part I

- a statement of what the authority has altered;
- the person's right to request a written statement, to request a reconsideration, and to appeal to an appeal tribunal, and how and when to do these things.

THE DATE THE CHANGE ACTUALLY OCCURS

17.17 The date a change actually occurs is an important concept: it affects the date on which the change is implemented in HB/CTB (which may be before, on, or after the date of claim, depending on the other circumstances of the case, as described later in this chapter).

17.18 Determining the date a change actually occurs can be straightforward (e.g. in the case of a claimant's birthday) or difficult (e.g. in the case of acquiring a partner). In four cases there are specific rules:

- If entitlement to any social security benefit ends, the date the change actually occurs is defined as being the day after the last day of entitlement to that benefit. HBR 68(1) CTBR 59(1)
- If there is a change in tax, national insurance or the maximum rate of working tax credit or child tax credit, and this is caused by a change in the law (e.g. the Budget), it may be disregarded (i.e. treated as not occurring) until up to 30 benefit weeks later. This applies to the income of a claimant, partner, non-dependant or second adult. HBR 26 CTBR 18
- If the claimant or partner is aged 65+, changes in non-dependant deductions are delayed for 26 weeks (paras. 7.37-38); HBR 60+ 68(9)-(12) CTBR 60+ 59(10)-(13)
- There are special rules about arrears of income (para. 13.25).

Example: A claimant's birthday

A claimant receiving HB and CTB (but not income support or JSA(IB)) reaches the age of 60 on Wednesday 7th July. The effect is that her HB and CTB increase.

She has no duty to notify the authority of this. The authority should alter her entitlement to HB and CTB.

The new amounts of HB and CTB are awarded from the Monday following the change, i.e. Monday 12th July.

This is a supersession.

IMPLEMENTING CHANGES: THE GENERAL RULE

17.19 The following general rule applies for all changes other than those mentioned in the remainder of this chapter. Typical examples are changes in income, capital, age or household composition.

HBR 68(1)
CTBR 59(1)
DAR 7(2)(a)(i), 8(2)

17.20 So long as the result of a change is that entitlement to HB/CTB continues, the authority alters the claimant's entitlement to HB/CTB. The new amount of HB/CTB is awarded from the Monday after the date the change occurs, even if the change occurs on a Monday. This is a supersession. (If the result of the change is that entitlement ends, see paragraph 17.21.)

CHANGES ENDING AN AWARD OF HB/CTB

HBR 68(1)
CTBR 59(1)
DAR 8(2)

17.21 If the result of a change of circumstances is that the claimant's HB/CTB reduces to nil (for example, a claimant dies or becomes a millionaire through the lottery), the authority must inevitably end the award of HB/CTB. In such cases:

- the last week of HB/CTB entitlement is the benefit week (para. 5.53) in which the claimant's circumstances change; and
- in the last week, the claimant is entitled to a full week's HB/CTB (i.e. calculated as if the change had not occurred).

This is a supersession. For an exception and a special case, see paragraphs 17.23 and 17.25 respectively.

WHEN JSA(IB), IS, IB OR SDA CEASE AFTER 26 WEEKS OR MORE

17.22 The following rule applies to people who have been on income-based jobseeker's allowance (JSA(IB)), income support (IS), incapacity benefit (IB) or severe disablement allowance (SDA) for 26 weeks or more, and who have found a job or similar. The full details are in table 17.4. The DWP is thought to be considering changing this rule during 2004-05: details were not available at the time of writing.

Table 17.4: Ending an award of HB/CTB when someone has been on certain benefits for 26 weeks or more

CLAIMANTS WHO HAVE BEEN ON JSA(IB) AND/OR IS

HBR 65A, 65B
CTBR 56A, 56B

AN AWARD OF HB/CTB MUST END IF:

- the claimant or any partner starts employment or self-employment, or (except in the case of a lone parent*) increases his or her hours or earnings; and
- this is expected to last for at least 5 weeks; and
- the claimant or partner has been entitled to JSA or IS continuously for at least 26 weeks (or any combination of those two benefits in that period**); and
- entitlement to JSA(IB) or IS ceases as a result***

CLAIMANTS WHO HAVE BEEN ON IB AND/OR SDA

AN AWARD OF HB/CTB MUST END IF:

- the claimant or any partner starts employment or self-employment, or (except in the case of a lone parent*) increases his or her hours or earnings; and
- this is expected to last for at least 5 weeks; and
- the claimant is not on pension credit and nor is any partner; and
- the claimant or partner has been entitled to IB or SDA continuously for at least 26 weeks (or any combination of those two benefits in that period**); and
- entitlement to IB or SDA ceases as a result.

Notes

* These exceptions for lone parents relate to the 'lone parent run-on' (para. 17.88) and cease to apply from 25th October 2004.

** A combination of JSA/IS over the 26 weeks is sufficient, or a combination of IB/SDA is sufficient. No other combination (such as IS/IB) is sufficient.

*** Over the 26 weeks no distinction is made between JSA(IB) and JSA(Cont), but the claimant must be on JSA(IB) (not JSA(Cont)) for at least one day before starting the job, etc.

HBR 65A(1), 65B(1) CTBR 56A(1), 56B(1)

17.23 In such cases, the award of HB/CTB ends. It does so at the end of the benefit week which contains the last day of entitlement to JSA(IB), IS, IB or SDA. (This is a different rule from the one in paragraph 17.25. Although the two rules sound similar, they have different effects – as illustrated in the examples, 'When JSA(IB) ends'.) This is a supersession (at nil). If the claimant wishes to be awarded HB/CTB thereafter, he or she must re-claim (para. 17.89).

17.24 In such cases, subject to further conditions, the claimant qualifies for a four-week 'extended payment' or a two-week 'lone parent run-on', as explained in paragraphs 17.81 onwards. But the award of HB/CTB must end even if the claimant does not meet those further conditions (for example does not notify the fact that he or she has begun work, etc) and even if the claimant has no entitlement to an extended payment or lone parent run-on (for example now lives in accommodation where he or she is not eligible for HB/CTB)

WHEN JSA(IB), IS, IB OR SDA CEASE FOR OTHER REASONS

HBR 68(1) CTBR 59(1)

17.25 If JSA(IB), IS, IB or SDA cease in any circumstances other than as above (para. 17.22), the general rule applies (para. 17.19). In other words:

- if the claimant continues to qualify for at least some HB/CTB, this is awarded from the Monday following the first day of non-entitlement to JSA(IB), IS, IB or SDA;
- if the claimant no longer qualifies for any HB/CTB, the former amount continues until the end of the benefit week containing the first day of non-entitlement to JSA(IB), IS, IB or SDA.

17.26 This applies if, for example, the claimant gets a job but has not been on JSA/IS/IB/SDA for 26 weeks, or simply does not sign on, etc. When JSA(IB) or IS cease because the claimant or partner starts getting pension credit, the claimant may qualify for a four-week 'continuing payment' (paras. 17.94 onwards). In other circumstances, until the authority obtains the details of the claimant's new circumstances, it is likely to suspend HB/CTB (para. 17.67).

CHANGES RELATING TO PENSION CREDIT

17.27 If a change in either guarantee credit or savings credit, whether due to a change in the claimant's circumstances or due to an official error (as defined in para. 17.46), affects the claimant's entitlement to HB/CTB, this takes effect from the date shown in table 17.5. These are supersessions.

Examples: When JSA(IB) ends

A woman on HB/CTB gets a job which starts on Monday 1st November 2004. She has been on JSA(IB) for more than 26 weeks and meets the relevant conditions in table 17.4. Her last day of entitlement to JSA(IB) is Sunday 31st October.

Her award of HB/CTB ends. It ends at the end of the benefit week containing her last day of entitlement to JSA(IB), i.e. on Sunday 31st October. (The claimant will then get a four weeks extended payment, and can also reclaim HB/CTB)

A man on HB/CTB gets a job which starts on Monday 1st November 2004. He has been on JSA(IB) for less than 26 weeks and so does not meet the conditions in table 17.4. His last day of entitlement to JSA(IB) is Sunday 31st October. He informs the authority promptly of these matters and provides all the information and evidence reasonably required.

His award of HB/CTB continues. The new amount of HB/CTB (based on his new income) takes effect from the Monday following the first day of non-entitlement to JSA(IB), Monday 8th November.

These are both supersessions.

Table 17.5: When pension credit starts, changes or ends

HB 68B(1)-(8)
HBR 60+ 36(8)
CTB 59B(1)-(8)
CTBR 60+ 28(8)
DAR 8(2),(3)

WHAT THE CHANGE IS	WHEN IT TAKES EFFECT IN HB/CTB *
Pension credit starts, increasing entitlement to HB/CTB	The Monday following the first day of entitlement to pension credit
Pension credit starts, reducing entitlement to HB/CTB	The Monday following the date the authority receives notification from the DWP about the change (or, if later, the Monday following the date of the pension credit change)
Pension credit changes or ends, increasing entitlement to HB/CTB	The Monday of the benefit week in which pension credit changes
Pension credit changes or ends, reducing entitlement to HB/CTB:	
◆ if this is due to a delay by the claimant in notifying a change in circumstances to the DWP	The Monday of the benefit week in which pension credit changes

◆ in any other case	The Monday following the date the authority received notification from the DWP about the change (or, if later, the Monday following the pension credit change)
But if the claimant is on savings credit, and the 'assessed income figure' (para. 13.152) changes during 1st to 15th April in any year	The new 'assessed income figure' applies in HB/CTB from the date the HB/CTB up-rating applies (para. 17.34).

Note

* If any of the above would take effect during a claimant's 'continuing payment' period (para. 17.94), the change is instead deferred until afterwards.

RETROSPECTIVE CHANGES TO SOCIAL SECURITY BENEFITS

DARGB 4(7B),(7C), 7(2)(i), 8(14)
NIDAR 4(6B), (6C), 7(2)(h), 8(11)

17.28 Changes relating to social security benefits (other than those described above) fall within the general rule (paras. 17.19-20). However, for mainly technical reasons it is made clear in the law that:

- ◆ if a social security benefit, or an increase in a social security benefit, is awarded back to a date before the start of an HB/CTB award, that award is revised as necessary;
- ◆ if a social security benefit, or an increase in a social security benefit, is awarded back to a date after the start of an HB/CTB award, that award is superseded as necessary;
- ◆ if an award of HB/CTB ended due to the end of an award of a social security benefit, but that social security benefit is reinstated, then the decision to end HB/CTB is revised as necessary (to reinstate the award of HB/CTB if appropriate).

MOVES AND CHANGES IN RENT OR COUNCIL TAX LIABILITY

17.29 The rules about moves and changes in liability are the same, and are explained in table 17.6. In each case these are supersessions (at nil if there is no further entitlement). The next two paragraphs explain when the changes are taken into account.

R 68(2), 69(4),(5)
CTBR 59(2)

17.30 If entitlement to HB/CTB continues after the move or change in liability, this is done from the benefit week in which the date of change occurs (but see paras. 17.42-43 for changes in eligible rent caused by a rent officer re-determination or NIHE rent decision):

- if rent is expressed on a weekly basis (or in multiples of weeks), a whole week's new HB entitlement is awarded in that benefit week;
- if rent is expressed on a non-weekly basis (e.g. daily or calendar-monthly), HB entitlement for that benefit week is assessed on a daily basis for both the old and new entitlements;
- CTB entitlement for that benefit week is assessed on a daily basis for both the old and new entitlements.

17.31 If entitlement to HB/CTB following the move or change in liability is nil, the change takes effect as follows: HBR 68(2), 69(4),(5),(13),(14) CTBR 59(2)

- if rent is expressed on a weekly basis (or in multiples of weeks), no HB is awarded in the last benefit week; unless the claimant is liable for rent up to and including the Sunday, in which case a whole week's HB is awarded for that benefit week;
- if rent is expressed on a non-weekly basis (e.g. daily or calendar-monthly), a whole week's HB is always awarded for that benefit week (this rule is new this year);
- CTB entitlement in the last benefit week is calculated on a daily basis.

17.32 In the case of CTB, the law mentions that the above rules (paras. 17.29-30) apply when a change in liability is due to a change in entitlement to a council tax discount or disability reduction or council tax capping, or the claimant acquiring a partner, or the claimant's partner dying, or the claimant and partner separating. They also apply in all other cases of changes in council tax liability. CTBR 59(2),(3),(5),(6)

Table 17.6: Moves and changes in liability

HBR 68(2), 69(4),(5),(13),(14) CTBR 59(2)

THE CHANGE	HOW THE CHANGE IS DEALT WITH
The claimant moves outside the authority's area (and there is no agency arrangement: para. 1.25)	The authority ends the award of HB/CTB
The claimant moves within the authority's area to an address where he or she is ineligible for HB/CTB	The authority ends the award of HB/CTB

The claimant moves within the authority's area to an address where he or she is eligible for HB/CTB	The award of HB/CTB continues based on the new eligible rent/ eligible council tax *
The amount of the claimant's eligible rent/council tax changes	The award of HB/CTB continues based on the new eligible rent/ council tax *

Notes

* In practice the authority may need to suspend the award of HB/CTB in order to find out the new rent and council tax details (para. 17.67).

Examples: Moves and changes in liability

A man on HB pays his rent weekly on Saturdays. It increases on Saturday 10th July 2004. In his case, the effect is that his HB increases.

The award of HB continues. The new amount of HB (based on his new eligible rent) takes effect from the benefit week in which the change occurs, i.e. from Monday 5th July.

A woman on HB gets a transfer from one housing association tenancy to another. Her rent (at both addresses) is due on Mondays and she moves on Monday 12th July.

The award of HB continues. The new amount of HB (based on her new eligible rent) takes effect from the benefit week in which the change occurs, i.e. from Monday 12th July.

These are both supersessions.

LOCAL GOVERNMENT REORGANISATION

SI 1995 No. 531
SI 1996 No. 548
SI 1996 No. 549

17.33 Following local government reorganisation (in Great Britain only) a newly-constituted authority may, within six months of reorganisation (or, in Scotland, twelve months), end an award of HB/CTB being made to any claimant whose claim was formerly administered by a different authority. A determination to do this is not appealable. (The law is slightly out-of-date but its intentions appear clear.)

CHANGES IN THE REGULATIONS

17.34 When regulations relevant to HB/CTB are amended, the authority alters the claimant's entitlement to HB/CTB from the date on which the amendment takes effect. This is a supersession. In HB only, there are two exceptions:

HBR 68(3),(13),(14
HBR 60+ 68B(7A)
CTBR 59(4)
CTBR 60+ 59B(7A
DAR 8(10)

- if the claimant's entitlement reduces to nil, and the regulations are amended from a day other than a Monday, in the week of the change the claimant qualifies for a full week's HB;
- if the claimant's rent is due weekly or in multiples of weeks, the annual HB/CTB up-rating (which for everyone else takes effect on 1st April) takes effect from the first Monday in April (5th April in 2004).

WHEN THERE IS MORE THAN ONE CHANGE

17.35 If two or more changes occur in relation to the same claim, they are dealt with in turn, following the above rules. The exceptions to this are as follows:

HBR 68(1A), (4), (
CTBR 59(1A), (6)

- In HB only, when one of the changes is the annual April HB/CTB up-rating and it is required (as described in the previous paragraph) to take effect from the first Monday in April, and the other change also occurs in the benefit week commencing with that Monday, then both changes take effect from that Monday.
- In any other HB/CTB case, the following rules apply when changes which actually occur in the same benefit week would have an effect (under the earlier rules in this chapter) in different benefit weeks.
  - For HB if one of the changes is in the amount of rent liability, the other changes in entitlement instead apply when that applies.
  - For HB in any other case, work out the various days on which the changes have an effect (under the earlier rules): all the changes instead apply from the earliest of these.
  - For CTB in all cases, work out the various days on which the changes have an effect (under the earlier rules): all the changes instead apply from the earliest of these.

Changes of circumstances which are notified late

LATE NOTIFICATION OF CHANGES WHICH REDUCE ENTITLEMENT

17.36 If a claimant delays (no matter how long) notifying the authority of a change which would have the effect of reducing his or her entitlement to HB or CTB, the authority must nonetheless implement the change according to the rules in the previous section. This is a supersession. It creates an overpayment (which may or may not be recoverable: chapter 18). The authority's duty to notify the outcome is the same as in paragraph 17.16. An example appears below.

Example: Late notified change reducing entitlement

A claimant's wages went up four months ago, but the claimant did not inform the authority until today.

The change is implemented from the Monday following the day the wages went up – thus creating an overpayment (which will very likely be recoverable).

This is a supersession.

LATE NOTIFICATION OF CHANGES WHICH INCREASE ENTITLEMENT

17.37 The rules in the previous section do not, however, apply if the claimant delays notifying the authority of a change which would have the effect of increasing his or her entitlement to HB or CTB (or would otherwise be 'advantageous' to the claimant) – and which he or she had a duty to notify (para. 17.9 and table 17.2). A claimant counts as having delayed notifying a change if his or her written notification is received by the authority more than one month after the change occurred (though this time limit can be extended: para. 17.40).

17.38 In such cases the change is instead deemed to have occurred on the date the authority received the written notification – and then the change is taken into account using the rules in the previous section but based on that date. In other words, the claimant loses money (as in the first example below). This is a supersession. The authority's duty to notify the outcome is the same as in paragraph 17.16.

17.39 The following points are worth noting in connection with this rule.

- The rule applies only to changes which the claimant has a duty to notify, and therefore does not apply to the changes mentioned in paragraph 17.8 (and see also para. 17.10 for what a claimant could be expected to know he or she had to notify).
- A claimant cannot be held to have a duty to notify something which he or she cannot know. For example, a claimant waiting for the outcome of an appeal about entitlement to (say) disability living allowance cannot have a duty to notify a successful outcome until it turns out to be successful. He or she has a month to notify the authority (which can be extended) from being informed of the outcome of the appeal, and (assuming this is done) does not lose his or her arrears of HB/CTB.

- The effect of the rule can be mitigated by the rule about underlying entitlement (para. 18.17) as illustrated in the second example below.
- The claimant can take longer to provide the notification if the circumstances in the next paragraph apply.

Examples: Late notified changes increasing entitlement

GENERAL EXAMPLE

A claimant's wages went down four months ago, but the claimant did not inform the authority until today. The authority asks why she delayed, but she has no special circumstances.

The change is implemented from the Monday following the day the claimant's written notification of the change was received by the authority. The claimant does not get her arrears. (However, if the claimant has 'special circumstances', she may get her arrears: para. 17.40). This is a supersession.

EXAMPLE INVOLVING UNDERLYING ENTITLEMENT

A claimant on HB/CTB (but not on JSA(IB) or income support) had a baby in May 2004 and did not inform the authority of this until September 2004 (when she made a renewal claim). Nor did she inform the authority of her award of child benefit till then. She has no special circumstances for failing to notify these things.

The increase in her HB/CTB due to the addition to her family cannot (because of her delay in notifying it) be awarded for the period from May to September: for that period it is 'underlying entitlement'. However, it must be used to reduce the HB/CTB overpayment that has arisen due to the award of child benefit (para. 18.17). Typically the underlying entitlement in a case like this would be greater than the overpayment. So no overpayment would be recoverable (but also no increase would be awarded for the period).

EXTENDING THE TIME LIMIT FOR NOTIFYING A CHANGE THAT INCREASES ENTITLEMENT

17.40 In the case of a change of circumstances which increases entitlement, the one month time limit for notifying it is extended (and the claimant does not lose money) if:

- the notification is received by the authority within 13 months of the date on which the change occurred; and
- the claimant, when writing to notify the change, also notifies the authority of the reasons for his or her failure to notify the change earlier; and

- the authority is satisfied that the change of circumstances is relevant; and
- the authority is satisfied that there are or were 'special circumstances' as a result of which it was not practicable to notify the change within the one month time limit. The longer the delay (beyond the normal one month), the more compelling those special circumstances need to be; and
- the authority is satisfied that it is reasonable to grant the claimant's request. In determining this, the authority may not take account of ignorance of the law (not even ignorance of the time limits) nor of the fact that a Commissioner or tribunal of Commissioners or court has taken a different view of the law from that previously understood and applied.

17.41 If the authority refuses the claimant's request, the claimant has no right to ask it again to accept late notification of the same change. However, the authority must implement the change from some date (the late date: para. 17.38) – which is a supersession. That supersession (and the date it is to apply from) is a decision itself (para. 17.7), and so the claimant has the right to ask the authority to reconsider (para. 17.55) or to appeal (chapter 19)

Implementing rent officer re-determinations

17.42 The following rules apply (in England, Wales and Scotland only) if the claimant or an authority appeals to the rent officer and he or she issues a re-determination, or if the authority applies for a correction in a rent officer determination or re-determination and he or she issues a substitute determination or substitute re-determination (paras. 6.41-50). In such cases, the new rent officer figures apply as follows.

- If the effect of the new figures would be to increase the amount of the claimant's eligible rent, the authority alters its original decision from the date it took effect (or should have). So the claimant gets his or her arrears. This is a revision.
- If the effect of the new figures would be to reduce the amount of the claimant's eligible rent, the authority alters its original decision from the Monday following the rent officer's re-determination, substitute determination or substitute re-determination. So the claimant (if the authority acts promptly) does not suffer from an overpayment. This is a supersession.

In either case, the authority's duty to notify the outcome is the same as in paragraph 17.16.

17.43 The above rules do not apply in Northern Ireland, since decisions about restricting the eligible rent are made by the NIHE and unlike in Great Britain there is no special procedure for appealing (paras. 6.40 and 6.51). The equivalent situation is where the claimant asks the NIHE to reconsider its decision. Except where as a result of the request the NIHE decides to restrict the rent still further, where the request is made within the one month time limit (paras. 17.55 and 17.59) any increase in benefit will be payable from the date of the original decision (para. 17.58). This is a revision. Where the request is made outside one month and it results in an increase in benefit the new decision will take effect from the date of the request (paras 17.51-52). This is a supersession. If the request is made within the one month time limit but the new decision is that the rent should be restricted still further, then normal NIHE practice, except perhaps in the case of misrepresentation or fraud, is to treat the request as a change of circumstances (i.e. a change in the housing market conditions) from the date of the request (paras. 17.51-52) and not to restrict benefit from the date of the original decision. This is a supersession.

Mistakes and errors

17.44 This section is about what an authority can or must do when there has been a 'mistake of fact' or a 'mistake of law' in a decision – or an 'accidental error' or other 'official error' in it. These four terms are distinguishable as follows:

- A 'mistake of fact' means that the decision was based (at least partly) on an incorrect fact (without at this stage saying that it was necessarily anybody's fault).
- A 'mistake of law' means that the decision was based (at least partly) on an incorrect understanding of the law.
- An 'accidental error' is something on the lines of a slip of the pen – a failure by the authority to put into action (or to record) its true intentions.
- An 'official error' is defined independently (para. 17.46) but might be one or a combination of the above.

The example contrasts the first two.

Example: 'Mistake of fact' and 'mistake of law'

In deciding a claim for HB/CTB, an authority determined that a man and a woman were not a couple.

This would be a mistake of fact if the authority made its decision not knowing that they were actually married (e.g. because the claimant had lied or the authority misread the application form).

It would be a mistake of law if the authority wrongly believed that two unmarried people could never be a couple.

CORRECTING ACCIDENTAL ERRORS

17.45 The authority may correct an accidental error in any decision (including a revised or superseding decision), or the record of any decision, at any time. The correction is deemed to be part of the decision or record, and the authority must give written notice of the correction as soon as practicable to the claimant and any other person affected.

CORRECTING OTHER OFFICIAL ERRORS

17.46 The authority may revise (or supersede: CH/216/2003) a decision at any time if the decision arose from an 'official error'. An 'official error' means an error by an authority, a contractor to an authority, or an officer of the DWP or the Commissioners of Inland Revenue acting as such. However, something does not count as an 'official error' if it was caused wholly or partly by any person or body other than the above, nor if it is an error of law which is shown to have been an error only by a subsequent decision of a Commissioner or tribunal of Commissioners.

17.47 The effect may be that there has been an underpayment of HB/CTB (in which case the arrears must be awarded – no matter how far back they go) or an overpayment (which may or may not be recoverable: chapter 18).

BECOMING AWARE THAT AN APPEAL DECISION APPLIES TO A CASE

17.48 The authority may revise a decision at any time to take account of an appeal decision in the same case (by an appeal tribunal, Commissioner, tribunal of Commissioners or court) which the authority was not aware of at the time it made the decision.

MISTAKES OF FACT RESULTING IN AN OVERPAYMENT

17.49 The authority may revise (or supersede: CH/216/2003) a decision at any time if the decision was made in ignorance of, or was based on a mistake as to, some material fact – and the decision was, as a result, more favourable than it would otherwise have been. This creates an overpayment (which may or may not be recoverable: chapter 18).

MISTAKES OF FACT DISCOVERED WITHIN ONE MONTH

17.50 The authority may revise a decision if, within one month of the date of notifying it, the authority has information sufficient to show that it was made in ignorance of, or was based on a mistake as to, some material fact. This is something the authority may do without a request from anyone else. This one month time limit cannot be extended (though the person affected could write asking the authority to reconsider and ask for this to be considered late because of special circumstances: para 17.59).

OTHER MISTAKES OF FACT – SUPERSESSION RATHER THAN REVISION

17.51 If none of the previous rules in this section apply, the authority may supersede a decision at any time if the decision was made in ignorance of, or was based on a mistake as to, some material fact. This could arise only in the case of increases to entitlement (because decreases are all covered by the earlier rules). This is something the authority may do because the claimant or other person affected has asked it to, or without anyone asking it to. An example follows.

Example: Mistake of fact resulting in a supersession

A claimant with a non-dependant in remunerative work was unable to provide the authority with details of the non-dependant's income. So the authority applied the highest level of non-dependant deduction in assessing her HB and CTB (para. 7.27). Now, four months later, the claimant provides evidence which is acceptable to the authority. It means a lower deduction applies.

Because this is outside the time limit for a revision (para. 17.57), the authority alters the amount of the claimant's HB/CTB from the Monday of the benefit week in which it received the evidence. The claimant does not get her arrears.

Note that the outcome would be different if the claimant wrote giving her reasons for the delay and the authority accepts these amount to special circumstances (para. 17.59). She would then get her arrears.

17.52 The supersession in such a case takes effect from the Monday at the beginning of the benefit week in which:

- the request was received from the claimant or other person affected (if a request was indeed made); or
- the authority first had information to show that the original decision was made in ignorance or mistake of fact (in any other case).

OTHER ERRORS OF LAW

17.53 A final rare rule applies if a decision was based on an error of law but was not due to 'official error' (para. 17.46). (This could arise if the Commissioners or courts interpret the law in an unexpected way.) The authority may supersede the decision at any time. This is something the authority may do because the claimant or other person affected has asked it to, or without anyone asking it to. In such a case, the supersession takes effect from the date on which it is made (or, if earlier, from the date the person's request was received).

NOTIFYING THE OUTCOME

17.54 Whenever the authority alters a decision under the above rules (except in the case of correcting accidental errors, for which a different rule applies: para. 17.45), it must write notifying the claimant and any other person affected, of the same matters as in paragraph 17.16.

Asking the authority to reconsider a decision

GENERAL RULES

17.55 This section is about requests to the authority to reconsider its decision. Such requests must be in writing and may be made either by the claimant or by any other 'person affected' (para. 16.7). This could be done either instead of or before making an appeal to the appeal tribunal (chapter 18). Although the law refers to requests for a 'revision' or 'supersession', the person does not have to remember to use either term in his or her request, and it does not matter if he or she uses those terms wrongly. The authority should treat any letter raising queries about entitlement as a request to reconsider its decision (unless the claimant is simply asking for a written statement of reasons: para. 19.20).

TIME LIMIT FOR REQUESTS

17.56 If the request for a reconsideration is received:

- within the time limit, the authority must consider revising its decision (para. 17.58)
- outside the time limit, the authority must consider superseding its decision (para. 17.60).

17.57 A request is within the time limit if it is received by the authority within one calendar month of the date the decision was notified. In calculating this time limit:

- any time is ignored from the date the authority received a request for a statement of reasons (para. 19.20) to the date the authority provided the statement (both dates inclusive); and
- any time is ignored before the date on which the authority gave notice of the correction of an accidental error (para. 17.45); and
- the time limit may be extended by the authority as described below (para. 17.59).

REQUESTS RECEIVED WITHIN THE TIME LIMIT

17.58 If the request for reconsideration is received within the time limit, and the authority alters entitlement to HB/CTB, this takes effect from the date of the original decision – unless the authority determines that the original decision took effect from a wrong date, in which case it takes effect from the correct date. This is a revision. Whether or not the authority alters entitlement, the outcome must be notified (para. 17.61).

EXTENDING THE TIME LIMIT FOR REQUESTS

17.59 The one-month time limit is extended if:

- the request is received in writing by the authority within 13 months of the date on which the decision was notified; and
- the request says that the person is asking for it to be accepted late, and gives the reasons for his or her failure to request a reconsideration earlier; and
- the person gives sufficient details to identify the disputed decision; and
- the request for revision 'has merit'; and
- the authority is satisfied that there are or were 'special circumstances' as a result of which it was not practicable to request a reconsideration within the one month time limit. The longer the delay (beyond the normal one month), the more compelling those special circumstances need to be; and
- the authority is satisfied that it is reasonable to grant the claimant's request. In determining this, the authority may not take account of ignorance of the law (not even ignorance of the time limits) nor of the fact that a Commissioner or tribunal of Commissioners or court has taken a different view of the law from that previously understood and applied.

REQUESTS RECEIVED OUTSIDE THE TIME LIMIT

17.60 If the request for reconsideration is received outside the one month time limit, and the authority refuses to extend this limit, the person affected has no right to ask it to accept a further late request to reconsider the same matter. However, the authority should nonetheless reconsider its decision and should consider making a superseding decision instead: the details are in paragraph 17.51.

Example: Late request for the authority to reconsider its decision

In May 2004, the authority notified a claimant of its decision on his claim. Amongst other things, the decision depended upon an assessment of the claimant's self-employed income.

In September 2004, the claimant asks the authority to reconsider its decision, as he forgot to tell them about part of his expenditure. He has no special circumstances for his delay. However, the authority accepts that (if it had known) it would have allowed that additional expenditure (and he would therefore have qualified for more HB/CTB).

The change is implemented from the Monday following the day the claimant's written notification of the change is received by the authority. The claimant does not get his arrears. This is a supersession. (However, if the claimant has 'special circumstances', he may get his arrears: para. 17.59).

NOTIFYING THE OUTCOME

17.61 In all the circumstances described in this section, the authority must notify the claimant of the outcome of his or her request for reconsideration, including the following matters

- whether it has changed its decision;
- if it has not changed its decision, the reasons why it has refused the claimant's request;
- if it has changed its decision, the same matters as in paragraph 17.16.

Revisions prompted by an appeal

17.62 The authority may revise a decision if an appeal to an appeal tribunal is made against it within the relevant time limits, and the appeal has not yet been determined. This takes effect from the date of the original decision – unless the authority determines that the original decision took effect from a wrong date, in which case it takes effect from the correct date. Generally speaking, if the authority does revise a decision in these circumstances, the appeal lapses. More information is in paragraph 19.33.

Information and evidence

WHAT MATTERS ARE TAKEN INTO ACCOUNT

17.63 When considering revising or superseding any decision, the authority need not consider any matter which was not raised in the request (if a request was made) or did not cause it to act on its own initiative. An authority may ask experts for help when considering any decision it has made (in order to decide whether it should be revised or superseded). The authority may 'stay' (i.e. not make) a revision or supersession when an appeal is pending against a Commissioner or tribunal of Commissioners or court in another similar case – or, in certain circumstances, make that revision or supersession by following special rules: further details are in paragraph 19.85.

17.64 In considering revising a decision, the authority must ignore any change of circumstances which has occurred since the decision was made and must ignore any future change of circumstances which may be about to occur. (In relation to these, the authority must consider supersession instead.) This rule ensures that decisions relating to different events do not become muddled up.

REQUESTS FOR INFORMATION AND EVIDENCE

17.65 When a revision or supersession is being considered as a result of a request from a claimant or other person affected, and the authority requires further evidence or information in order to consider all the issues raised, the authority has a duty to request this in writing from the person affected. Then:

- if the information or evidence is provided within one calendar month of the date of the authority's request – or within such longer period as the authority may allow – the authority must consider the revision or supersession taking it into account;
- if the information or evidence is not provided within the above time limit, the authority must consider the revision or supersession on the basis of the original request from the claimant or other person affected.

In the second case, if doubt arises about entitlement to HB/CTB, the authority may suspend HB/CTB (paras. 17.67 onwards).

17.66 When a revision or supersession is being considered without a request, but because the authority has the power to do so, it has the same rights to require information, evidence, documents and certificates as in the case of a claim (para. 5.33). If the claimant fails to provide these, the authority may suspend HB/CTB (paras. 17.67 onwards).

Suspending, restoring and terminating HB/CTB

17.67 The authority may suspend HB/CTB in the circumstances set out in the following paragraphs. To suspend simply means stopping making payments for the time being, in order to seek information and evidence or for other reasons. Eventually, entitlement to HB/CTB will either be restored (as described at all the relevant places below) or terminated (para. 17.79). The claimant has a right of appeal to a social security tribunal (para. 19.16) about a decision terminating HB/CTB, or restoring HB/CTB at a different level (which is a supersession) but not about a decision suspending HB/CTB.

SI 2001 No. 1605
NISR 2000 No. 215
DAR Part III

DOUBT REGARDING ENTITLEMENT

DAR 11(1),(2),12 **17.68** The authority may suspend, in whole or in part, any payment of HB/CTB where there is doubt as to whether the conditions for entitlement are or were fulfilled. The authority may also suspend, in whole or in part, any HB/CTB payment where it is considering whether a decision about an award should be revised or superseded. Obviously where a revised or superseded decision would result in an increase in entitlement, there is no need for the authority to consider suspension.

17.69 Payments should be made in both cases once the authority is satisfied that the suspended benefit is properly payable and no outstanding issues remain to be resolved. This should be done so far as practicable within 14 days of the decision to make or restore the payment.

SUSPENSION WHERE AN APPEAL IS PENDING

DAR 11(1),(2)(b) **17.70** The authority may suspend, in whole or in part, any payment of HB/CTB where an appeal is pending against a decision of an appeal tribunal, a Commissioner or a court.

17.71 An appeal is pending where an appeal against the decision has been made, but not determined, or an application for leave to appeal against the decision has been made, but not yet determined.

DAR 12(2) **17.72** Payments should be made when the appeal is no longer pending and the suspended benefit remains payable following the decision of the appeal. This should be done so far as practicable within 14 days of the decision to make or restore payment.

SUSPENSION WHERE AN APPEAL IS PENDING AGAINST A DECISION IN A DIFFERENT CASE

DAR 11(2)(b) **17.73** The authority may suspend, in whole or in part, any payment of HB/CTB where an appeal is pending against a decision given by a Commissioner or a court in a different case, and it appears to the authority that if the appeal were to be determined in a particular way an issue would arise as to whether the award of HB/CTB in the case under consideration ought to be revised or superseded.

DAR 12(1)(b),(2) **17.74** Payments should be made when the appeal is no longer pending and the benefit suspended remains payable following the determination of the appeal. This should be done so far as practicable within 14 days of the decision to make or restore payment.

POSSIBLE OVERPAYMENTS

17.75 The authority may suspend, in whole or in part any payment of HB/CTB when an issue arises as to whether an amount of HB/CTB is recoverable. Again once resolved payment of any outstanding amount should be made. Again, so far as practicable, this should be done within 14 days of the decision to make or restore payment. DAR 12(2)(c)

SUSPENSION FOR FAILURE TO FURNISH INFORMATION ETC

17.76 The authority may suspend in whole or in part any payment of HB/CTB that relates to someone who fails to comply with the requirements to provide information or evidence needed by the authority in deciding whether a decision should be revised or superseded. DAR 13(1),(2)

17.77 The authority must notify the person concerned of this power. The person concerned must:

DAR 13(3),(4),(5)

- furnish the information or evidence required within:
  - one month beginning with the date on which the notification was sent to them; or
  - such longer period as the authority considers necessary to enable them to comply with the requirement; or
- satisfy the authority within the relevant period that:
  - the information or evidence required does not exist; or
  - it is not possible for them to obtain the required information or evidence.

17.78 Where a person satisfies the requirements the authority must, so far as practicable, make, or restore, payment within 14 days of making the decision to make or restore payment.

TERMINATING HB/CTB

17.79 When someone's HB/CTB has been suspended and he or she fails to comply with the information requirements (para. 17.77), HB/CTB entitlement is terminated (in other words, simply ends). Except when only part of the HB/CTB in question was suspended, this is done from the date on which the payments were suspended, or from whatever earlier date HB/CTB entitlement ended. DAR 14

17.80 The exception is that if only part of the HB/CTB was suspended, then entitlement continues for one month longer before the HB/CTB is terminated.

Example: Suspending, restoring and terminating HB/CTB

SUSPENSION IN FULL

The authority obtains information that a man on HB/CTB and currently being paid income support is in fact working full-time.

The authority suspends his award immediately, and writes to him allowing him one month to respond.

If he responds and provides the necessary information and evidence within the month, the authority restores his HB/CTB from the appropriate date (and makes any supersession needed to take account of his new income), probably thereby creating an overpayment from that date until the date HB/CTB were suspended.

If the claimant refuses to respond, or responds insufficiently, the authority terminates the award of HB/CTB. In this case, the authority needs to establish when the termination should occur.

SUSPENSION IN PART

A woman on HB/CTB (but not on JSA(IB), IS or pension credit) is currently awarded a carer premium. The authority considers this entitlement may have ceased.

The authority suspends only the part of HB/CTB attributable to the carer premium, and writes to the woman allowing her one month to respond.

If she responds and provides the necessary information and evidence within the month, showing that she is still entitled to carer premium, the authority simply restores the award so it runs continuously.

If she refuses to respond, or responds insufficiently, the authority notifies her that it intends to terminate HB/CTB in a further month's time, and continues to award the (lower) amount.

The law does not spell the next step out, but it is clear that if within that month she does provide the necessary information and evidence, then it would be appropriate for the authority to allow the award to continue. (Alternatively she could simply re-apply within that month and provide the necessary information and evidence with that application.)

Extended payments

17.81 The following rules are designed to help long-term unemployed people who are returning to work, by giving them an 'extended payment' of two or four weeks extra HB/CTB. HBR 62A, sch 5A CTBR 53A, sch 5A

ENTITLEMENT TO EXTENDED PAYMENTS

17.82 A claimant is entitled to an extended payment ('EP') if:

- the claimant's award of HB/CTB ends in the circumstances described in paragraph 17.23 and table 17.4 (in broad terms, because he or she has been on JSA(IB)/IS/IB/SDA for 26 weeks or more and this has ceased because of a new job, etc); and
- the claimant or partner remains liable (or treated as liable) for rent or liable for council tax (at the same or a new address).

CLAIMS, ETC

17.83 There is no requirement for a written claim. Instead, a person who fulfils the conditions is treated as having claimed an EP so long as he or she notifies the authority or the DWP of the matters in table 17.4. This must be done within four weeks of the day the new job, new hours or new rate of pay, began. Although it could be done in person or by telephone, it is wise for claimants to follow this up with written confirmation. This notification is not, however, required at all in 'lone parent run-on cases' (described later), in which cases the DWP should notify the authority automatically of entitlement to EPs.

17.84 The authority has a duty to determine EP claims and notify the outcome – even if a claimant does not qualify for an EP – and even if the only reason is that the DWP has said that the claimant does not satisfy the '26-week condition' (table 17.4). Unlike the other conditions (in that table and para. 17.82), it is for the Secretary of State (via the DWP) to 'certify' whether or not the claimant fulfils this condition – and this is binding on the authority. If the claimant disagrees with this particular matter he or she may negotiate with the DWP, but the only formal method of appeal would be to seek judicial review.

17.85 As regards whether the claimant satisfies the other conditions (in para. 17.82) the DWP's advice is that authorities should normally accept what the claimant has said – though, of course, an authority may well not accept it if a claimant said, in late December, that his new job impersonating Father Christmas would last five weeks.

PERIODS AND AMOUNTS OF EXTENDED PAYMENTS

17.86 Except in lone parent run-on cases (described below), an EP is awarded for the four weeks following the Sunday on which the authority ends the HB/CTB benefit period as a result of the claimant ceasing to be entitled to IS/JSA(IB) or (if relevant) moving (para 17.23). An EP is treated as though it was ordinary HB/CTB for other purposes (such as whether the claimant falls within the New Scheme or Old Scheme for eligible rent purposes: chapter 10). Also it may be replaced, later, by a new ongoing HB/CTB benefit period as described in paragraph 17.89.

17.87 In each of those four weeks, the amount of HB/CTB EP equals the amount awarded in the last benefit week of the (recently ended) award of HB/CTB – ignoring any part-week of entitlement and ignoring any rent-free period in that week. The one exception is that no HB EP is awarded in a rent-free week. (For example, if the normal four-week EP period contains one rent-free week, the claimant will get only three weeks' worth of EPs.) Otherwise all changes of circumstances are ignored.

'LONE PARENT RUN-ON' CASES

17.88 In broad terms, 'lone parent run-on' is available for certain lone parents who have been on income support and who start work after being out of work for 26 weeks or more (table 17.4). It means they get two weeks' extra income support after they start the job. During these two weeks they continue to qualify for HB/CTB in the ordinary way. Their entitlement to an EP is for only two weeks (rather than the usual four). (The idea behind this is that they get the 'other' two weeks during their lone parent run-on.) The rules about the amount of the EP are the same as in other cases. The EP is awarded for the two weeks following the Sunday on which the authority ends the HB/CTB benefit period as a result of the claimant ceasing to be entitled to IS/JSA(IB) (para 17.23).

Lone parent run-on is abolished from 25th October 2004, from which date lone parents qualify for extended payments in the same way as anyone else.

FURTHER AWARDS OF HB/CTB FOLLOWING EXTENDED PAYMENTS

17.89 Claimants may remain entitled to HB/CTB despite their (or their partner's) new job or increase in hours or earnings. A further claim (by the claimant or partner) for ongoing HB/CTB runs consecutively as follows:

- If the claimant is entitled to less ongoing HB/CTB than the amount of the EP (or exactly the same amount), the new amount is awarded from the benefit week immediately following the end of the EP period.
- If the claimant is entitled to more ongoing HB/CTB than the amount of the EP, the balance is awarded for the EP period, and the whole amount is awarded thereafter. (This could arise, for example, if a non-dependant left the household and the increase in entitlement due to this was greater than the decrease in entitlement due to the new income of the claimant or partner.)

Table 17.7: Extended payments for movers

HB: A MOVE FROM RENT ALLOWANCE TO RENT ALLOWANCE

The amount of HB at the new address is exactly equal to the amount of HB at the old address (including any rate rebate in NI*).

If the move is to a new authority area, the old authority makes this payment.

HB: A MOVE FROM RENT ALLOWANCE TO RENT REBATE

The amount of HB at the new address is calculated using:

- the eligible rent (and rates*) at the new address, but
- the non-dependant deduction(s) (if any) at the old address.

If the move is to a new authority area, the new authority makes this payment.

HB: A MOVE FROM RENT REBATE TO RENT REBATE

The amount of HB at the new address is calculated using:

- the eligible rent (and rates*) at the new address, but
- the non-dependant deduction(s) (if any) at the old address.

If the move is to a new authority area, the new authority makes this payment.

HB: A MOVE FROM RENT REBATE TO RENT ALLOWANCE

The amount of HB at the new address is exactly equal to the amount of HB at the old address (including any rate rebate in NI*).

If the move is to a new authority area, the new authority makes this payment.

CTB: ALL CASES

The amount of CTB at the new address is calculated using:

- the eligible council tax liability at the new address, but
- the non-dependant deduction(s) (if any) at the old address.

If the move is to a new authority area, the new authority makes this payment.

RATE REBATE ONLY PAYABLE

The amount of HB at the new address is calculated using

- the eligible rates at the new address, but
- the non-dependant deduction(s) (if any) at the old address.

* In Northern Ireland, where a rent rebate is paid together with HB in respect of rent, follow the appropriate rent rebate or allowance category. Where a rate rebate only is payable, including cases where the claimant is a tenant but does not qualify for any HB in respect of their rent, follow the table as for 'Rate Rebate only'.

MISCELLANEOUS MATTERS

17.90 The following are the main further matters relating to EPs.

- A separate determination should be made (and notified) about whether to pay HB to a landlord during an EP period.
- A separate determination should be made (and notified) about whether to recover recoverable overpayments of HB by deduction from an EP for HB.
- The question of whether an EP has been overpaid depends on who has to notify and/or determine what. For example, if a claimant said that his new job would last at least five weeks and then the employer (unforeseeably) closed down, the extended payment was correctly paid: there has been no overpayment.

EXTENDED PAYMENTS FOR MOVERS

17.91 Except in 'lone parent run on' cases (para. 17.88), claimants who are entitled to an EP are entitled to it even if they move home during the week before, or the week in which, they or a partner take up employment or self-employment – but not in cases of increasing hours or earnings.

17.92 The amount of the EP for HB at the new address (during the EP period) depends on whether the claimant's entitlements at the old and new addresses are to a rent allowance or a rent rebate, as shown in table 17.7, which also shows the amount of the EP for CTB at the new address.

17.93 In any case when the claimant moves to a new authority area, the law allows authorities to exchange information relevant to extended payments. The DWP advises that the old authority should keep all the documentation and write to the new authority confirming the details.

Continuing payments

17.94 The following rules are designed to 'tide someone over' when he or she transfers from JSA(IB) or IS to pension credit. The person has no need to claim a continuing payment: it is awarded automatically. HBR 60+ 62B CTBR 60+ 53B

ENTITLEMENT TO CONTINUING PAYMENTS

17.95 Someone on HB/CTB and either JSA(IB) or IS is entitled to a continuing payment if:

- he or she reaches 60 (or 65 if he has stayed on JSA(IB) beyond age 60); and
- the DWP certifies to the authority that the claimant has claimed or is treated as having claimed pension credit, and IS or JSA(IB) has therefore stopped.

17.96 Someone on HB/CTB and either JSA(IB) or IS is also entitled to a continuing payment if:

- he or she has a partner and the partner claims pension credit; and
- the DWP certifies this to the authority.

PERIODS AND AMOUNTS OF CONTINUING PAYMENTS

17.97 In such cases the person (so long as he or she otherwise remains entitled to HB/CTB) gets four weeks of HB/CTB, starting on the day after his or her last day of entitlement to IS/JSA(IB), calculated as follows:

- he or she is treated as having no income or capital;
- his or her eligible rent and/or council tax are treated as being the same as they were immediately beforehand – except in the case of an increase (in either) in which case the increased amount is used;
- but non-dependant deductions are done according to the actual circumstances of the case.

17.98 If the four weeks in question would not run out on a Sunday, the continuing payment is lengthened by up to six days to ensure that it does end on a Sunday.

17.99 The idea behind continuing payments is that the award of HB/CTB can then continue seamlessly. The amount awarded during the continuing payment period is not an overpayment (unless, say, the claimant lied about his or her age, perhaps).

Example: Continuing payments

A man is on HB/CTB and JSA/(IB) when he reaches 65. He reaches 65 on Tuesday 13th April 2004. The DWP tells the authority that he has been treated as having claimed pension credit.

His continuing payment of HB/CTB is awarded from Tuesday 13th April 2004 to Sunday 16th May 2004 – a total of four weeks six days.

By then the authority knows the claimant qualifies for guarantee credit from his birthday.

He is awarded HB/CTB based on this from Monday 17th May 2004.

18 Overpayments

18.1 This chapter explains:

- what an overpayment is;
- why the cause of an overpayment is important;
- when an overpayment is recoverable;
- how the amount of the overpayment is worked out;
- when, from whom, how, and at what rate an overpayment should be recovered;
- whether recovered overpaid benefit results in rent arrears;
- the information that should be provided to the claimant and any other person affected;
- how far recovery of an overpayment may be pursued; and
- when an administrative penalty may be added to a fraudulent overpayment.

AA 75(1), 76(1)
NIAA 73(1)
HBR 98
CTBR 83

18.2 Where more HB is paid than someone is entitled to, this is referred to as an 'overpayment'. The term includes not only overpayments made by way of instruments of payment such as cheques but also any overpayment by way of a rebate to a rent account and in Northern Ireland a rebate of rates paid into a rates account. Where more CTB is allowed (by way of a rebate to a council tax account or otherwise) than a claimant is entitled to, this is referred to as 'excess benefit'. As most of the rules relating to 'overpayments' and 'excess benefit' are the same, the term overpayment is used in this chapter to refer to both.

18.3 The overpayment and recovery of benefit has created major difficulties for claimants, landlords and authorities. Claimants and landlords have had their rights denied and unnecessary debts created. Many authorities have failed to follow the correct decision-making process, notify claimants, keep adequate records, or account for overpayments properly. As a consequence they have made inaccurate subsidy claims and created rent and council tax arrears for themselves and debts for landlords.

What is an overpayment?

18.4 Overpayments are established through revision of benefit entitlement. They are amounts of benefit which have been paid but to which there is no entitlement under the regulations. They include any overpayment of: HBR 98 CTBR 83

- a rent allowance paid on account;
- CTB due to a backdated award of a council tax discount (para. 9.16), or council tax disability reduction (para. 9.13) or council tax transitional relief (para. 9.19).

Example: An overpayment

The claimant receives HB and CTB from 9th April 2003. On 14th May 2003 her adult son comes to live with her. The claimant has a duty to inform the authority of this change of circumstances but does not do so until 6th August 2003. The authority determines that a non-dependant deduction should have been made for the son from the benefit week commencing Monday 19th May 2003 (the date from which the change of circumstances should have taken effect). The claimant has received benefit up to and including the benefit week commencing 11th August 2003. An overpayment of benefit has occurred for 19 weeks.

18.5 Having identified that an overpayment has occurred the authority must:

- establish the cause of each overpayment;
- decide whether or not the overpayment is recoverable;
- identify the period and calculate the amount of the overpayment;
- consider whether or not recovery should be sought;
- decide from whom the recovery should be sought;

and, within 14 days (para. 18.63), notify the claimant and other persons affected, for example the landlord where recovery is sought from them, accordingly.

18.6 In the case of HB overpayments of rebates to an authority's rent account or overpaid CTB allowed to its council tax accounts, the regulations must not be circumvented by the automatic creation of debits applied retrospectively with the resulting creation of arrears for the claimant. The authority must perform the duties imposed by the regulations and make each decision required.

Establishing the cause of the overpayment

18.7 The authority must establish the cause of an overpayment in order to:

- decide whether or not it is recoverable;
- correctly notify the claimant, the person the authority is seeking to recover from (if not the claimant), and any other person affected;
- claim the correct amount of subsidy;
- in some cases, determine the method of recovery.

18.8 An overpayment might arise due to:

- local authority error, e.g. the authority fails to act on notification of a change of circumstances provided by the claimant;
- Job Centre Plus or Pensions Service error, e.g. the Job Centre Plus office makes a mistaken award of income support or income-based JSA;
- claimant error or claimant fraud, e.g. the claimant fails to inform the authority of a change in circumstance which he or she has a duty to report, such as the end of entitlement to income support or income-based JSA; or
- other reasons, e.g. the claimant obtains a retrospective award of a council tax discount and this reduces the council tax liability for that period.

Technical and advance overpayments are amounts of CTB or rent and rate rebates (but not rent allowances) that are paid in advance by way of a rebate to an account.

18.9 Consecutive overpayments may result from different causes. For example, the claimant may fail to notify the authority that their earnings have increased. The authority may then delay acting on that information once it is informed, in which case that part of the overpayment would be classified as authority error (DWP, HB/CTB *Overpayments Guide,* paragraph 2.41). In such a case the cause and amount of each overpayment must be separately identified.

Recoverable overpayments

R 91(3), 99(1),(2)
HBRGB 99(4)
NIHBR 99(4),(4A)
TBR 84(1),(2),(3)

18.10 An overpayment of a rent allowance payment on account may, where there is ongoing benefit once entitlement has been decided, be recovered whatever the cause of the overpayment. An overpayment of CTB may be due to a retrospective reduction in the claimant's council tax as a result of a delayed award of a discount or disability reduction. Such overpayments are recoverable in all cases. All other amounts that have been overpaid are recoverable, except where they are due to official error. Even an official error overpayment is recoverable if:

- the claimant, someone acting on their behalf, or the person to whom the payment was made, could reasonably have been expected to realise that an overpayment was taking place at the time of payment or upon receipt of any notification relating to the payment; or

- it is an amount of rent rebate or CTB that has been overpaid in respect of a period following the date on which the revision took place that identified the overpayment;
- in Northern Ireland, it is an overpayment of rate rebates which has arisen as a result of reduction in the regional rate.

18.11 An official error is a mistake, whether in the form of an act or omission made by the authority, an external contractor acting for the authority, or an officer of the DWP; or the Commissioners of the Inland Revenue, or a person providing services to either Department or to the Commissioners. The definition of an official error does not include circumstances where the claimant, or someone acting on the claimant's behalf, or the person to whom payment has been made, caused or materially contributed to that error. In *R v Cambridge CC ex parte Sier* it was argued that the DWP office failure to notify the authority that IS had ceased meant that there was a non-recoverable 'official error' overpayment. The Court held that, while it was an official error, it was the claimant's failure to inform the authority of a change in his circumstances that caused the overpayment. Such overpayments are categorised as claimant or third party error and are recoverable. An official error occurs, for example, where there is a mistaken award of IS by the DWP or where the authority puts the wrong information into its computer or delays acting upon information it has received. However, DWP guidance advises that the rule that claimants are expected to report changes to the authority does not apply in Pension Credit cases because 'the authority relies on the Pensions Service to report any change of circumstance to them'. In these cases, it advises that any changes are only taken into account when the authority receives details from the Pensions Service (DWP HB/CTB *Overpayments Guide,* para. 2.41). HBR 99(3) CTBR 84(3)

18.12 Where the claimant, a person acting on his or her behalf, or the person to whom the payment has been made, could reasonably have been expected to realise that it was an overpayment at the time of payment, or of any notice relating to that payment, an official error overpayment is recoverable. In *R v Liverpool CC ex parte Griffiths* it was held that this rule requires the reasonable expectation, not that a payment might be an overpayment, but that it was an overpayment. A decision regarding recoverability requires examination of all the relevant facts. If, for example, the claimant has learning difficulties it may be that he or she could not reasonably have been expected to realise that it was an overpayment. DWP guidance also points out that a person may not be expected to realise they were being overpaid if they were 'wrongly advised by an official source' (DWP HB/CTB *Overpayments Guide,* para. 2.100). HBR 99(2) CTBR 84(2)

18.13 If the claimant, etc, did not have the information necessary to know that benefit was being overpaid at the time of payment or notification relating to the payment, then an official error overpayment is not recoverable. The DSS (HB/CCB(90)23) advises that when in rent rebate cases credits are made to the landlord's rent accounts before the claimant receives a written notification of the award, the claimant cannot know if they are being overpaid unless or until they receive written notification of the rebate. This will also be the case, for example, where HB is paid direct to a landlord (unless the landlord could reasonably have been expected to realise it was an overpayment) or CTB is paid into a council tax account. The claimant and/or any other person affected may apply for a revision of the authority's decision that an overpayment is recoverable or appeal the decision.

18.14 The rules regarding HB/CTB overpayments differ from those applicable to the other social security benefits. With the latter, the power to recover rests on the adjudicating authority being satisfied that a material misrepresentation or non-disclosure has been proved.

Working out the amount of a recoverable overpayment

UNDERLYING ENTITLEMENT

HBR 104 CTBR 90 **18.15** When calculating the amount of a recoverable overpayment, any amount 'which should have been determined to be payable' must be deducted. This means whatever would have been awarded if the authority had known the true facts of the case throughout, all changes of circumstances had been notified on time, and any necessary claims had been made. Money kept by a claimant (i.e. not recovered from him or her) under this rule is often called 'underlying entitlement' to distinguish it from an actual award of HB/CTB. Underlying entitlement must be deducted (if there is any) in all situations in which an overpayment occurs *(Adan v London Borough of Hounslow and Another)*.

Example: Underlying entitlement in a straightforward case

A claimant has been doing undeclared work whilst signing on, and JSA is cancelled back to the time he began this.

Because of underlying entitlement, the recoverable overpayment of HB/CTB is only the difference between what he or she was awarded and what he or she would have been awarded if the true facts had been known throughout. This might be all of the HB/CTB he was paid in this period (if he was well-paid in the job) or none of it (if he was paid less than he was getting on JSA) or any amount in between.

18.16 When the authority deals with a recoverable overpayment for a particular period, there are three stages at which underlying entitlement is considered:

- Any underlying entitlement for that period which has already been identified as belonging to that period must be used to reduce the overpayment. This arises if the claimant had been late notifying a change of circumstances and had thus not been awarded arrears of entitlement for all or part of that period (para. 17.36).
- The authority should invite the claimant (or other overpaid person) to provide information which may establish underlying entitlement. This is part of the process of determining the amount of the overpayment. In day-to-day work, the authority may use the rules about suspension, restoration and termination (paras. 17.67-80) whilst considering possible underlying entitlement.
- Once the authority has decided and notified the amount of the overpayment, the claimant (or other overpaid person) may ask the authority to reconsider (para. 17.55) or appeal to a tribunal (chapter 21), and in doing so may include information which would establish underlying entitlement.

8.17 Also, the following calculation rules apply when considering underlying entitlement (and are illustrated in the examples):

- only underlying entitlement falling (in whole or part) within the period of the overpayment is used to reduce the overpayment;
- although underlying entitlement (within that period) is used to reduce an overpayment – maybe even to nil, it can never be used to actually pay money out.

18.18 It is for each authority to decide what level of evidence it will require in order to determine underlying entitlement. Since it is the authority that is asserting that there is an overpayment, it is not appropriate to require a claimant to prove underlying entitlement beyond reasonable doubt. In particular, the Verification Framework does not apply to the assessment of underlying entitlement. It appears that 'balance of probabilities' is the correct test (chapter 1).

Examples: Underlying entitlement: calculation rules

UNDERLYING ENTITLEMENT PERIOD FALLS WHOLLY WITHIN OVERPAYMENT PERIOD

Information: In a particular case, there is a recoverable overpayment of £15 per week for weeks 1 to 20 inclusive (20 x £15 = £300), and only in weeks 6 to 15 inclusive is there underlying entitlement of £20 per week (10 x £20 = £200).

Assessment: The whole of the underlying entitlement (£200) is used to reduce the overpayment (£300). So the recoverable overpayment is £100.

UNDERLYING ENTITLEMENT PERIOD FALLS PARTLY WITHIN OVERPAYMENT PERIOD

Information: In a particular case, there is a recoverable overpayment of £5 per week for weeks 1 to 20 inclusive (20 x £5 = £100), and underlying entitlement (because the claimant did not notify a beneficial change on time) in weeks 11 to 30 inclusive of £15 per week.

Assessment: Only the underlying entitlement in weeks 11 to 20 inclusive (10 x £15 = £150) is used to reduce the overpayment (£100). It is enough to reduce the recoverable overpayment to nil. The remainder of the underlying entitlement cannot be awarded. (It lurks instead.)

ONE CHANGE WITH TWO EFFECTS

Information: Six months ago, a claimant (not on JSA(IB), IS or pension credit) had a baby and started to receive child benefit but did not report these things to the authority, simply because she did not get round to it.

Assessment: The recoverable overpayment (caused by the her income from child benefit) is smaller than the underlying entitlement (caused by the increase in her applicable amount to take account of the baby). The recoverable overpayment is therefore nil (but the remainder of the underlying entitlement cannot be awarded).

ANOTHER CHANGE WITH TWO EFFECTS

Information: Three months ago, the claimant's daughter moved in with him as his non-dependant, but he did not report this to the authority because he hoped he would get away with it. He rents from a private landlord.

Assessment: The recoverable overpayment (caused by the presence of the non-dependant) is in this case bigger than the underlying entitlement (caused by the increase in his eligible rent because he now requires a room for his daughter). The recoverable overpayment is only the net amount (i.e. the difference between the two figures).

WHERE THE CLAIMANT HAS CONTINUED TO PAY RENT OR COUNCIL TAX TO THE AUTHORITY

18.19 During the period of the overpayment the claimant may have paid money into a local authority rent or council tax/rates account above their erroneous liability. If this is the case such payments may be deducted for the purpose of working out the amount of the recoverable overpayment. HBR 104(3) CTBR 90(3)

DIMINISHING CAPITAL RULE

18.20 Where the overpayment arose as: HBR 103(1) CTBR 89(1)

- a result of a misrepresentation or failure to disclose relevant information relating to the claimant's capital, or that of a child or young person; or
- an error relating to capital (other than a non-recoverable official error, paras. 18.10-11); and in either case
- the overpayment is in respect of more than 13 weeks;

the authority must treat the amount of the capital as having been reduced by the amount overpaid during the first and each subsequent period of 13 benefit weeks for the purpose of working out the overpayment.

18.21 The reasoning behind this rule is that if the capital had been taken into account, so that the benefit was reduced or not awarded, the claimant's capital would in all probability have been reduced to meet his or her housing costs, council tax liability, or day-to-day living expenses.

18.22 This notional reduction of capital does not count for any other purpose, e.g. calculating entitlement. This rule is entirely separate from, and should not be confused with, the notional capital rule (para. 13.132). HBR 103(2) CTBR 89(2)

Example: Diminishing capital rule

The claimant has been in receipt of a £5.73 rent allowance each week since 25th May 1998. She visits the authority's housing benefit office on 15th October 1998, to query the amount of benefit she is receiving.

During the course of her interview it emerges that she had accidentally forgotten to include on her original application form £250 which she has retained throughout the period in a building society account. When this amount is added to her previously declared and still existing capital of £15,783 it brings the amount that counts for HB purposes to £16,033. With capital above the maximum limit there has been no entitlement to benefit from the start of the claim.

The overpayment arose due to the claimant's failure to disclose a material fact relating to capital and is recoverable. The overpayment has taken place over 21 benefit weeks so the diminishing capital rule applies. There is only one complete 13-week period.

The amount of HB overpaid by the end of 13 benefit weeks is:

£5.73 x 13 =	£74.49

With the application of the diminishing capital rule for the rest of the period of payment – and for the sole purpose of calculating the overpayment – the claimant's capital is assumed to be £15,958.51, i.e.

Claimant's capital	£16,033.00
MINUS amount of overpaid HB during 13-week period	£74.49
Claimant's assumed capital for purpose of calculating overpaid HB =	£15,958.51

The original calculation of HB had taken into account the declared capital of £15,783. The tariff income from the actual and 'diminished' capital amount is the same. Therefore, under the diminishing capital rule, no overpayment has occurred between the 14th and last week in which the benefit has been paid. The total amount of recoverable overpayment is £74.49.

The claimant still actually has capital of £16.033. She is not entitled to HB until such time as the amount of her capital falls below £16,000.01 (as would be the case if, for example, she repaid the overpayment).

When should a recoverable overpayment be recovered?

18.23 A recoverable overpayment may be recovered at the authority's discretion. The law says that such overpayments are recoverable and not that they must be recovered. The DWP advises authorities to note that the question of whether an overpayment is recoverable is quite separate from the question of whether to recover it. Due regard should be given to the circumstances relating to individual cases when deciding if recovery is appropriate (GM A7.166).

AR 16, sch para 3

18.24 The authority is not obliged to make recoveries. The exercise of the discretionary power contained within the legislation is governed by a number of legal principles that are long established. Each and every individual case must be decided on its merits. This means that the authority must be satisfied that it is reasonable to make a recovery in the individual case. A person affected can ask the authority to revise its decision to recover a recoverable overpayment but there are no appeal rights against a decision as to the exercise of discretion to recover an overpayment. An authority which acted unreasonably or irrationally would be susceptible to judicial review. However, a decision will not be unreasonable merely because it is not the most reasonable course of action but only if it is so unreasonable that no reasonable authority could have reached that conclusion.

From whom may recovery be sought?

18.25 A recoverable HB/CTB overpayment may be recovered from: AA 75(3) NIAA 73(3) HBR 101(1),(2)(a)-

- the claimant in every case;
- the person to whom it was paid (e.g. landlord, landlord's agent) in every case, except the circumstances described in paragraphs 18.28-30;
- any person who misrepresented or failed to disclose a material fact which resulted in the overpayment being made (e.g. an appointee) in every case (para. 18.31-34); and
- the partner of the claimant but only in the limited circumstances described in paras. 18.35-37 below.

LIABILITY OF LANDLORDS AND AGENTS

18.26 Note that the rules above do not give an authority the power to recover from landlords *per se,* but only if the landlord was either the person who actually received the payment or was the person who misrepresented or failed to disclose a fact which caused the overpayment. This means that if, for example, an overpayment arose during a period in which the claimant was living in accommodation provided by their former landlord, and the error is subsequently discovered after the claimant has moved to accommodation provided by a new landlord, then that overpayment cannot be recovered from their new landlord even if the new landlord is currently receiving direct payments on their behalf. It could, however, be recovered from the claimant (para. 18.27). Where the landlord employs a managing agent and benefit is paid to the agent, any overpayment it will not be recoverable from the landlord, unless they caused it by their misrepresentation or failure to disclose.

18.27 Where an overpayment is made in respect of a period during which the claimant was living with a previous landlord, and the authority subsequently decides to recover it, the recovery can be made by reducing any ongoing direct payments made to their current landlord (para. 18.39).

WHEN OVERPAYMENTS CANNOT BE RECOVERED FROM LANDLORDS

18.28 Overpaid benefit cannot be recovered from a landlord/agent if:

- it was never paid to them in the first place (para. 18.26); or
- it was paid to them but it is unreasonable to recover from them (para. 18.30); or

- it was paid to them and the conditions in para. 18.29 apply (landlord reports a suspected fraud).

HBR 101(1)(a)-(d) **18.29** From 1st October 2001, an authority cannot recover HB overpayments from the landlord who received the benefit direct where:

- the landlord has notified the authority or the DWP in writing that they suspect there has been an overpayment;
- it appears to the authority that:
  - there are grounds for instituting proceedings against any person for an offence under section 111A or 112(1) of the Administration Act (dishonest or false representations for obtaining benefit)(in Northern Ireland s.105A or 106 of the NIAA);
  - there has been a deliberate failure to report a relevant change of circumstances and the overpayment occurred as a result of that deliberate failure;
- the authority is satisfied that the landlord has not:
  - colluded with the claimant so as to cause the overpayment
  - acted, or neglected to act, in such a way so as to contribute to the period, or the amount, of the overpayment.

18.30 The Court of Appeal, in *Warwick DC v Freeman,* confirmed that a recoverable overpayment may be recovered from a landlord where the overpayment was paid directly to the landlord, even where the landlord did not contribute to, or have any knowledge of, the overpayment. In a later case, *Secretary of State for Work and Pensions v Chiltern District Council and Warden Housing Association,* the Court of Appeal confirmed that if recovery is made from a landlord then that landlord will be a 'person affected' and will have the right to challenge the authority's decision to recover from them. However, a subsequent decision by a tribunal of Commissioners, CH 5216 2001, held that these types of challenge are limited to challenging the factual basis on which the decision was made (e.g. the amount of the overpayment) and the legality of the decision to recover from the landlord. The legality of the decision to recover is restricted to those grounds available under judicial review, that is: whether the authority has exceeded its powers in recovering from them. This does not include a challenge as to the particular merits of a decision to recover from the landlord provided it is within the margin of discretion allowed by the courts (which is wide). The courts will not consider whether the decision of the authority is the most reasonable course of action but will only consider a decision to be unlawful if it was so unreasonable that no reasonable authority could have reached that conclusion. However, a decision to recover from a landlord will always be unlawful if the facts are such that the conditions under which an authority may recover from a landlord are not satisfied (para. 18.28).

LIABILITY OF A PERSON WHO MISREPRESENTS OR FAILS TO DISCLOSE

18.31 Where an overpayment of HB (but not CTB) has arisen due to a misrepresentation or failure to disclose a relevant fact by: HBR 101(2)(a)

- the claimant; or
- someone on their behalf, such as an appointee or agent; or
- the person to whom a payment may be made, such as a landlord or the claimant's partner

then it may also be recovered from that person. This does not apply in the case of overpaid CTB.

18.32 A misrepresentation is a statement that is untrue or misleading. A misrepresentation could be a written or verbal statement.

18.33 A failure to disclose occurs where a person has a duty to disclose information (paras. 17.8-12), they do not disclose it and there was some 'failure' on that person's part because there was a reasonable expectation that they should disclose it having regard to all the circumstances. A person may not be expected to disclose if they were given clear advice to the contrary by an official of the authority or the DWP (Commissioners decision R(SB) 3/89).

18.34 A person will be liable for recovery even if the misrepresentation or failure to disclose was innocent. Neither does the misrepresentation or failure to disclose have to be the sole cause of the overpayment; the fact that it was a contributing factor will be sufficient to make that person liable to recovery (Commissioners decision CSB 64/1986).

LIABILITY OF THE CLAIMANT'S PARTNER

18.35 An overpayment of HB or CTB can only be recovered from the claimant's partner in certain limited circumstances (assuming they have not misrepresented or failed to disclose) and even if these conditions are met the method of recovery is limited to deductions of any ongoing HB or CTB that is being paid to them. Further, recovery can only occur if the claimant and partner are members of the same household (para. 4.11) both at the date of the overpayment and the date it is recovered. HBR 101(2)(b),(4

18.36 This rule may appear unduly restrictive. However, it affirms the principle that overpayments should not normally be recovered from a partner. However, if this option was not available, a couple could avoid recovery from any ongoing HB by simply swapping who claims.

18.37 Since recovery is dependent on a couple continuing to live as partners at the time the overpayment is recovered, if the claimant dies then any overpayment cannot normally be recovered from their surviving partner, but instead will have to be recovered from the claimant's estate (GM A7.491 and A7.495). However, the DWP advises authorities that in the case of rent allowance payments, if the overpaid allowance is issued before the authority is notified of the tenant's death but is cashed after the tenant's death then the cause of the overpayment would be 'payment irregularity' and recovery could be made from the person who cashed it (GM A7.492). This can justified on the grounds that it is a failure to disclose (paras. 18.31 and 18.33)

Method of recovery

AA 75(4),(5), 76(2)(b),(3)
NIAA 73(4),(5)
HBR 102, 105
CTBR 87, 91
SI 1997 No. 2435
NISR 1997 No.454

18.38 Authorities may recover a recoverable overpayment by any lawful method but an overpayment of HB cannot be recovered from a payment of CTB or *vice versa*. The following are the main methods adopted by authorities:

(a) in the case of HB only, by deduction from any on-going benefit payable to them (subject to maximum amounts, paras. 18.60-62) in every case;

(b) from arrears of HB or CTB which becomes payable while there is an outstanding overpayment in every case;

(c) by deduction from certain social security benefits payable to the claimant in certain circumstances;

(d) in the case of HB only, where the overpaid benefit was paid direct to the landlord on behalf of one of their tenants, from any benefits including HB to which the landlord themselves may be personally entitled (e.g. if the landlord was entitled to HB in their own right because of a low income);

(e) in the case of HB only, where the overpaid benefit was paid direct to the landlord on behalf of one of their tenants, from any ongoing HB payable to that landlord in respect of their other tenants (e.g. by deduction from a bulk payment schedule);

(f) by setting up a sundry debtors' account and billing for the overpayment;

(g) in the case of CTB, by adding the overpaid CTB on to the claimant's council tax account as an amount of council tax owing, or in the case of HB paid by way of rent rebate by adding a charge to the claimant's rent account – but if this is the case the debt will not normally constitute rent arrears and will simply be a separate debt owed to the landlord (paras. 18.57-58).

The particular method used will be a determining factor as to whether the recovery creates rent arrears in respect of the tenant to whom the overpayment relates (paras. 18.57-58).

RECOVERY BY DEDUCTIONS FROM ON-GOING HB, INCLUDING HB PAID DIRECT TO A LANDLORD

18.39 Where the authority is recovering an overpayment by deduction from the claimant's on-going benefit (including any offsetting against any underpayment) paid direct to a landlord or, in the case of a council tenant, in the form of a reduction to the rebate to the rent account, the position is no different than if the reduced HB was paid to the claimant. With the sole exception of rent allowance claims, to which paragraph 18.41 applies, the reduced HB payments represent part payment of the rent and so the claimant must make up the subsequent shortfall in HB to avoid rent arrears accruing (GM A7.293, example 1). This method represents recovery from the claimant, not the landlord, and consequently the landlord is not a 'person affected' and does not have any right to apply for a revision of the decision or appeal it (Commissioners decision CSHB 615 2003).

AA 75(5)(b)
NIAA 73(5)(b)

18.40 Note that in the case of council/NIHE tenants paid by rent rebate a distinction should be made between a reduction in an on-going rebate (i.e. an increase in the rent payable each period as it arises) and a charge added to the rent account representing the overpayment. Such a charge will not normally constitute rent arrears as it is an addition to the rent that has already been paid (paras. 18-57-58) (albeit by overpaid HB). Charges of this kind will be easily identifiable, since the total charge for the rental period in which it is made will be more than the gross un-rebated rent. In the case of CTB, any overpayment can be added to the council tax account and be charged as additional council tax.

18.41 Where a rent allowance claim is paid direct to the landlord and the cause of the overpayment is landlord fraud (para. 18.77) which has resulted in a conviction or the landlord agreeing to pay a penalty as an alternative to prosecution (18.81), then any arrears of rent which result from the reduced housing benefit cannot be pursued by the landlord. If this rule is applied, then both the landlord and the tenant must be notified (paras. 18.64 and 18.66) and the landlord would be able to appeal. In practice however, this rule is hardly ever used. The DWP advises (GM A7.320-321) that where this rule is applied the legislation imposes no penalty on landlords who attempt to recover or evict a tenant due to the non-closure of their rent liability, but that the courts have been advised that landlords would be in breach of the relevant legislation if they attempted this action.

AA 75(5)(b)
NIAA 73(5)(b)
SI 1997 No. 2435
NISR 1997 No.45

RECOVERY FROM ARREARS OF BENEFIT OWED

18.42 An existing overpayment can be recovered at some future date by offsetting it against any underpaid benefit. Any underpaid benefit in excess of the overpayment will constitute a payment towards any rent owed for the period to which it relates. If the tenant fails to make up any shortfall for that period then it will result in rent arrears. If the underpayment is not sufficient to meet the full

HBR 102(1)
CTBR 87(1)

debt, the question of whether the remaining debt creates rent arrears will depend on the method employed to recover it (para. 18.38).

RECOVERY FROM OTHER SOCIAL SECURITY BENEFITS

HBR 105
CTBR 91

18.43 In the case of IIB where methods (a), (b) or (d) in paragraph 18.38 are not possible because the person from whom the recovery is being sought is not entitled to HB, or in the case of CTB methods (a), (b) or (g) are not possible, the authority may request the DWP to recover any overpayment from any person identified in paragraph 18.31 by deductions from certain social security benefits payable to them.

18.44 Recovery can be made from most social security benefits including: income support, jobseeker's allowance, pension credit, retirement pension, invalid care allowance, widow's benefits, maternity allowance, disability living allowance, attendance allowance and industrial injuries benefits; or from any equivalent social insurance benefit of these paid to the recipient by an European Union member state. Recovery is not permitted from guardian's allowance, child benefit, war pensions, statutory sick/maternity pay or child/working tax credits. Some commentators have expressed doubts as to whether recovery can be made from incapacity benefit as the legislation only permits recovery from benefits specified (pension credit, IS and JSA) or benefits payable under the Social Security Act 1975 (which incapacity benefit is not).

18.45 The DWP will recover overpayments from social security benefits where it is:

- requested by the authority to do so; and
- satisfied that the overpayment arose as a result of a misrepresentation or failure to disclose a material fact by, or on behalf of, the claimant, or by some other person to whom a payment of HB/CTB has been made; and
- that person is receiving sufficient amounts of one or more benefits to enable deductions to be made.

RECOVERY FROM THE LANDLORD BY DEDUCTIONS FROM THE LANDLORD'S PERSONAL BENEFIT

AA 75(5)(a)
NIAA 73(5)(a)
SI 1997 No. 2435
SR 1997 No. 454

18.46 In a rent allowance case the authority may, in appropriate circumstances, decide to recover the overpayment from the landlord by deduction from any benefit to which the landlord is personally entitled (e.g. the landlord's income is low enough to qualify for HB in their own right). Where the overpayment arose from the landlord's misrepresentation or failure to disclose but the landlord does not qualify for HB in their own right, recovery can be made from the landlord's other social security benefits as described in paragraphs 18.43-45. In either case, the landlord will normally wish to recover their loss by recharging the tenant (paras. 18.56-58). In practice, recovery from a landlord's personal benefits is rare.

RECOVERY FROM THE HB OF TENANT(S) UNRELATED TO THE OVERPAYMENT (DEBIT OF BULK PAYMENT SCHEDULE)

18.47 Where the overpaid benefit was paid to the landlord and the landlord receives on-going direct payments of rent allowance in respect of other ('innocent') tenants to whom the overpayment does not relate, the authority may recover the overpayment by deducting from the direct payments of other tenants to whom the overpayment does not relate. This method is often employed by authorities to recover from landlords who have substantial numbers of tenants on HB who are all paid in the same payment cycle by a single payment (e.g. cheque) accompanied by a bulk payment schedule. Recovery is made by deducting the overpayment from the gross HB owed in respect of all its tenants.

AA 75(5)(c),(6)
NIAA 73(5)(c),(6)
SI 1997 No. 2435
NISR 1997 No. 454

18.48 Any amount recovered by this method from 'innocent' tenants will be deemed to have been paid as rent by them to the value of the recovered sum. In these circumstances, the landlord is a 'person affected' and should be notified (para. 18.64-65) but the 'innocent' tenant/claimant from whose benefit the deductions are being made is not. Consequently such tenants/claimants should not receive an overpayment notification and do not have the right to appeal or request a decision. The authority should, however, have notified all claimants and landlords at the time direct payments commenced that:

- it had the power to make deductions from the amount paid to the landlord in order to recover an overpayment of benefit relating to another tenant; and
- that in such a case the claimant's rent liability will have been discharged to the full value of their HB entitlement.

HBR sch 6
para 11(c)

18.49 Where this method has been employed, the landlord will wish to recover their loss from the tenant to whom the overpayment relates. Whether this consequent recovery constitutes rent arrears will be determined by the rules in paragraphs 18.57-58.

RECOVERY BY SETTING UP A SUNDRY DEBTORS ACCOUNT

18.50 An authority may implement a recovery by simply sending a demand for payment to any person liable to recovery. Recovery can be enforced by registering the debt in the courts as described by paragraphs 18.73-76 below.

HBR 102(1)
CTBR 87(2)(a)

18.51 A bill sent directly to the tenant paid by rent allowance does not constitute rent arrears. A bill sent to a local authority/NIHE tenant paid by rent rebate from their landlord may create rent arrears if their tenancy agreement so stipulates (paras. 18.56-58).

RECOVERY BY CHARGING THE CLAIMANT'S RENT/COUNCIL TAX ACCOUNT

HBR 102(1)
CTBR 87(2)(b)

18.52 Authorities are able to recover any overpaid CTB by simply adding the debt to the council tax and issuing a new bill. They will then be able to enforce this debt by the usual council tax enforcement procedures.

18.53 This method is not available for tenants paid HB by rent allowance, although where the recovery has been made from their landlord the landlord will probably wish to recover their loss from the tenant. For the circumstances in which the landlord may pass this charge on as rent arrears, see paras. 18.56-58.

18.54 Except in the circumstances described in paragraphs 18.57-58, authorities who recover overpaid rent rebates by debiting the rent account of the claimant cannot claim that the debt constitutes rent arrears. Instead, the debt created is separate housing benefit debt which cannot be enforced by possession proceedings as it is not an amount of rent lawfully due (para. 18.57) and the claimant would have a defence against any such action.

18.55 Authorities may, however, use their rent accounting systems to collect contributions towards overpayment debts and some tenants may prefer this as being the most convenient way to pay. The DWP advises that authorities should be able to distinguish 'recovered' overpaid HB from arrears of rent. Authorities should also make it clear to claimants that the payments being sought represent overpaid HB (GM A7.363) and should be able to distinguish payments the claimant makes to cover the overpayment and payments of rent. Where the tenant is not on full HB or has existing rent arrears, authorities would be well advised to issue the tenant with a separate HB overpayment account so that when the tenant makes a payment there can be no doubt against which debt the payment is to be attributed, otherwise over time the true position is likely to become increasingly difficult to unravel. Common law rules stipulate that where a person owes more than one debt they may elect to attribute any payments they make towards each debt in the proportions they choose (GM A7.365-67). If they do not so specify, then normally the payment will be attributed to the earliest debt first.

METHODS BY WHICH THE LANDLORD MAY RECOVER THE REPAID OVERPAYMENT FROM THE CLAIMANT

18.56 The landlord may seek to recover the sum repaid to the authority from the claimant to whom the overpayment relates. Landlords are perfectly entitled to recover their losses under general legal principles; however, where they do so the question often arises as to whether this constitutes rent arrears.

CIRCUMSTANCES IN WHICH A LANDLORD RECHARGE CREATES RENT ARREARS

18.57 The general rule is that once rent has been paid, even though it was paid by benefit to which the claimant was not entitled, any liability for it has been extinguished for all time *(R v Haringey LBC ex p Ayub)*. The fact that the authority can recover it is a consequence of a power they have been given by legislation and does not alter this position. Therefore, if the landlord recharges the tenant for the past period to which the overpaid benefit relates, any charge that they make cannot be 'rent' because in effect the tenant would be charged twice for the same period. However, this general rule has been modified by legislation and may also be modified by contractual agreement (para. 18.58).

18.58 The general rule against the creation of retrospective rent arrears is modified in the following circumstances;

- where the tenancy agreement expressly stipulates that overpaid HB recovered from the landlord can be recharged as 'additional rent' – this applies equally to claimants paid by rent rebate as well as rent allowance; or
- where the claimant is a non local authority tenant (i.e. paid by rent allowance, not rent rebate) and the overpayment relates to a period after 6th April 1997, the landlord is able to treat the sum it has repaid to the authority as rent arrears. HBRGB 93(2) NIHBR 93(1A)

In both cases the landlord has the ultimate sanction of eviction to secure payment. However, these exceptions can never be applied to 'innocent' tenants to whom the overpayment does not relate (paras. 18.47-49). AA 75(6) NIAA 73(6)

18.59 Where the claimant to whom the overpayment relates is no longer the landlord's tenant, the landlord may invoice the former tenant and then pursue the debt through normal civil debt recovery procedures.

Rate of recovery

18.60 The current rules which prescribe the maximum permitted rate of recovery where deductions are to be made from a claimant's on-going housing benefit, came into effect from 2nd October 2000. The amounts are tied to a formula based on a single person's personal allowance, and so change annually. There are two maximum permitted rates of deduction depending on whether or not the overpayment has arisen as a result of fraud.

18.61 Where the claimant has been found guilty of fraud; or admitted fraud after caution; or agreed to pay a penalty (para. 18.81) the maximum permitted weekly deduction is £11.20 plus 50% of any of the earned income disregards shown HBR 102(2)-(5)

in table 14.1 or any disregarded regular charitable or voluntary payments (para. 13.113) or war disablement pension or war widow's pension (para. 13.38) if they apply to the claim. In any other case the maximum permitted weekly deduction is £8.40 plus 50% of the income disregards previously identified if they apply to the claim. In both cases the amounts are subject to an overall maximum deduction which does not reduce the balance of benefit payable to less than 50p. The council should deduct less than the maximum permitted amount in any case where, after considering all of the claimant's circumstances, this is justified in order to avoid undue hardship.

18.62 In deciding the rate of recovery from organisations, the authority has the power to effect large recoveries in a single lump sum (para. 18.47) but it will often not be appropriate to do so. The authority should act reasonably in deciding a rate of recovery. In particular, as a matter of good practice, the authority should discuss the rate of recovery with the organisation concerned to ensure the rate of recovery does not undermine that organisation's financial stability or essential activities.

Information to be provided to claimants, landlords, etc

HBR 77(1)(b)
CTBR 67(1)(b)

18.63 When the authority decides that a recoverable HB/CTB overpayment has occurred, and exercises its discretion to recover it, a letter should be sent to the person from whom recovery is sought and any other person affected by the decision. So, for example, if the authority decides to recover from the landlord, it must send letters to both the claimant and the landlord. This should happen within 14 days of the decision being made or as soon as reasonably practicable thereafter.

R sch 6 para 14(1)
TBR sch 6 para 16

18.64 Overpayment letters to claimants, landlords and other persons affected must state:

- the fact that there is a recoverable overpayment;
- the reason why there is a recoverable overpayment;
- the amount of the recoverable overpayment;
- how the amount was calculated;
- the benefit weeks to which the recoverable overpayment relates;
- where recovery of HB is to be made by deduction from future HB, the amount of that deduction;
- in the case of overpaid CTB, the method of recovery to be adopted;

- the person's right to request a written statement setting out the authority's reasons for its decision on any matter set out in the letter and the manner and time in which to do so; and
- the person's right to apply for a revision of the decisions or appeal them and the manner and time in which to do so; and
- any other appropriate matter, e.g. the opportunity to make representations with regard to hardship.

18.65 Where the authority is seeking to recover an overpayment from another claimant's direct payments to the landlord (para. 18.47), the decision notice to that landlord must also identify both: HBR sch 6 para 14(2)

- the original claimant on whose behalf the recoverable amount was paid to that landlord; and
- the other claimant from whose benefit recovery is going to be made.

18.66 Where the authority has decided to recover an overpayment from a rent allowance paid direct to the landlord by the method described in paragraph 18.41 (as a result of landlord fraud) the authority must also notify both the landlord and the tenant that: SI 1997 No. 2435 NISR 1997 No. 45

- the overpayment which it has recovered, or decided to recover, is one for which the landlord has been convicted of fraud or has agreed to pay a penalty; and
- any tenant from whose benefit the recovery is made must be deemed to have paid his or her rent to the value of the amount recovered.

18.67 The DWP advises (GM para. A7.231) that overpayment notifications should include an invitation to the person in question to either make a full repayment or negotiate some other arrangement within 28 days. A more appropriate period in fact is the one month normally allowed for a request for revision/appeal to be made.

DEFECTIVE NOTIFICATION

18.68 Failure by authorities to notify persons affected clearly and correctly of decisions about overpayments has caused problems for claimants, landlords and authorities. Experience has shown that overpayment notification letters, particularly those to landlords, are often defective in a number of ways. A significant number, for example, fail to give an adequate and intelligible reason why there is a recoverable overpayment or advise landlords of their appeal rights. In *R v Thanet DC ex parte Warren Court Hotels Ltd,* for example, it was held that the phrase 'change of circumstances' was not itself a statement of the reason why there was a recoverable overpayment, since it covered a multitude of possible reasons. The failure to provide the required information constitutes maladministration. Additionally, authorities that have deficient notifications should be aware that they are undermining the legal basis of their debt recovery action *(Warwick DC v Freeman)*. There is no legally recoverable debt until such time as the authority makes the appropriate determinations and issues the required notification.

18.69 A more recent Court of Appeal decision *(Haringey LBC v Awaritefe, CA)* while agreeing with the approach taken in Warwick and Freeman, ruled that where the failure to provide a valid notification was only trivial, and no substantial harm was caused as a result, the authority was still entitled to pursue recovery of the overpaid amount.

18.70 *Jones v Waveney DC* concerned a case where the authority failed to follow the statutory procedures provided and had recovered an alleged overpayment from the landlord by making deductions from benefit due to him on other properties. The court, applying Warwick and Freeman, held that the landlord was entitled to bring a county court action to recover from the authority the amount that the authority had recovered illegally. This point may be contrasted with the decision in *Norwich CC v Stringer, CA,* where the court held that the landlord could not seek restitution of the sums paid to the council on the basis that if the landlord had not repaid the money the council would have been unable to recover it.

The pursuit of recovery

18.71 The DWP advises (GM para. A7.192) that 'it is for authorities to decide how far to pursue recovery…' In the past, many authorities have failed to pursue recovery actively if legal proceedings were required. Where an authority has decided an overpayment is recoverable, exercised its discretion and decided to recover, the DWP expects it to make a serious attempt at recovery. The GM (para. A7.192) advises that at least two letters requesting payment should be issued, that an interview will often be appropriate and that a home visit might be cost-effective. As a matter of good practice, authorities should include in their recovery work procedures that ensure that the claimant is receiving all the HB/CTB and other benefits to which they may be entitled, with the aim of reducing the overpayment and increasing resources to meet the debt.

18.72 The authority may take civil proceedings for debt in an appropriate court but the simplified debt recovery procedure described in the following paragraph is a more appropriate procedure.

SIMPLIFIED DEBT RECOVERY PROCEDURE

AA 75(7), 76(6) NIAA 73(7) **18.73** The authority has the power to recover HB overpayments by execution in the County Court in England and Wales as if under a court order; and in Scotland as if it were an extract registered decree arbitral.

18.74 In England and Wales, this procedure allows an HB overpayment determination to be registered directly as an order of the court without the need to bring a separate action. This procedure remains intact under the Civil Procedure Rules 1998, introduced in April 1999. The authority applies to the court on a standard county court form (N 322A), attaching a copy of the overpayment decision notice and accompanied by the relevant fee. The DWP advises (GM A7.462) that the overpayment notification can only be used as proof of debt where it complies fully with the requirements for such notifications under schedule 6 of the benefit regulations (para. 18.64-66). An officer of the court then makes an order and a copy is sent to the authority and the debtor. Once an order has been made, the normal methods of enforcement are available to the authority, i.e. attachment of earnings, a garnishee order allowing the authority to obtain money owed to the debtor by a third party, a warrant of execution against goods executed by the county court bailiff, or a charging order, normally against land.

18.75 There is no provision for any appeal against an order made by the 'proper officer' of the court. Consequently, where the claimant or landlord disputes the determination that there is a recoverable overpayment or from whom it should be recovered, this is a matter which can only be taken up by applying for a revision of, or appealing, the relevant decision(s) (chapter 19). However where, for example, overpayment notification is defective or appeal rights ignored by the authority an application for the setting aside of the order can be made to the court.

18.76 In Scotland, the HB determination is immediately enforceable as if it were an extract registered decree arbitral. There is no requirement to register the overpayment determination with the Sheriff Court. The usual methods of enforcement are available, i.e. arrestment of earnings; poinding and warrant sale; arrestment of moveable property and inhibition of heritable property.

Overpayments and fraud

18.77 The subject of HB/CTB fraud and the authority's response goes beyond the remit of this Guide. The interested general reader is referred to the Audit Commission's *Countering housing benefit fraud: a management handbook* (1997) while officers working for an authority should also refer to the DWP *Local authority fraud investigators manual* and the DWP Fraud Circulars. Overpayments are, however, often related to charges of fraud. The effective recovery of overpayments is one tool in the authority's anti-fraud strategy and as anti-fraud work increases, in the short term at least, the number and amount of overpayments that are identified by the authority increases.

The administrative penalty

AA 115A NIAA 109A **18.78** Since 1997 (para. 18.82) authorities have had the power to levy an administrative penalty (a fine) as an alternative to bringing a prosecution for fraud. The power to levy a penalty is closely related to the administration of overpayments. The penalty is equivalent to 30 per cent of the recoverable overpayment due from the person concerned and is recoverable by the same methods available to the authority as when seeking recovery of the overpayment.

WHEN WILL A PENALTY APPLY?

18.79 The authority has the discretion to levy the penalty as an alternative to bringing a prosecution for fraud. Prosecutions for HB/CTB offences are in fact rare. In 2002-02 there were approximately 1,700 successful prosecutions for HB fraud in the UK (*Hansard,* Commons Written Answers, 24/07/2002, 389c1556W). Where the overpayment is substantial or there are other aggravating factors (such as being in a position of trust) the person suspected will not normally be offered the alternative of a penalty.

18.80 The question of a penalty cannot arise until the authority has decided that an overpayment is recoverable under the regulations and the person from whom recovery is sought has been properly notified. The authority then has the discretion to invite a person to pay a penalty where it is satisfied that:

- the overpayment was caused by an 'act or omission' on the part of that person; and
- there are grounds for bringing a prosecution against that person for fraud relating to that overpayment under the Social Security Administration Act or any other enactment.

18.81 Where the conditions for a penalty apply, it can only be levied with the agreement of the person concerned. However, if that person refuses to agree to pay a penalty they could be liable to fraud proceedings instead.

CALCULATION OF THE PENALTY

18.82 The penalty is equivalent to 30 per cent of the recoverable overpayment due from the person concerned. Where an ongoing overpayment started before the penalty provision came into force, a penalty can only be calculated on the amount of recoverable overpayment that accrued on or after 18th December 1997. (See also section 25(7) of the Social Security Administration (Fraud) Act 1997; in Northern Ireland article 1(4) of the Social Security Administration (Fraud) Order 1997 (SI 1997 No 1182) and NISR 1997 No. 508.)

AGREEING TO PAY A PENALTY

18.83 It is up to the authority to decide how any agreement to pay a penalty will be made. However, where the authority considers that a penalty may be appropriate in any particular case it must give a written penalty notice to the person liable for prosecution.

18.84 This notice advises them:

- that they may be invited to agree to pay a penalty; and
- that if they make the agreement to do this in the manner specified by the authority (e.g. by signing a standard written undertaking) no fraud proceedings will be brought against them for the overpayment in question.

18.85 The penalty notice must, by law, contain the following points of information about the penalty system:

- the manner specified by the authority by which the person may agree to pay a penalty;
- that the penalty only applies to an overpayment which is recoverable under section 75 or 76 of the Social Security Administration Act 1992 (in Northern Ireland s73 of the Social Security Administration (Northern Ireland) Act 1992);
- that the penalty only applies where it appears to the authority that the overpayment was caused by an act or omission by the person and that there are grounds for commencing criminal proceedings for an offence relating to the overpayment;
- the penalty is 30 per cent of the overpayment, is payable in addition to repayment of the overpayment and is recoverable by the same methods as those by which the overpayment is recoverable;
- a person who agrees to pay a penalty may withdraw the agreement within 28 days (including the date of the agreement) by notifying the authority in the manner specified by the authority (i.e. in writing or by using a notice provided by the authority for this specific purpose, etc);
- where the person withdraws their agreement, any amount of the penalty which has already been recovered will be repaid and the person will no longer be immune from proceedings for an offence;
- where it is decided on revision or appeal (or in accordance with regulations) that the overpayment is not recoverable or due, any amount of the penalty which has already been recovered will be repaid;
- where the amount of the overpayment is revised on revision or appeal, except as covered by a new agreement to pay the revised penalty, any amount of the penalty which has already been recovered will be repaid

and the person will no longer be immune from proceedings for an offence; and

- the payment of a penalty does not give the person immunity from prosecution in relation to any other overpayment or any offence not relating to an overpayment.

19 Appeals

19.1 New arrangements for changing and appealing HB and CTB decisions were introduced from 2nd July 2001. These arrangements are similar and in many instances identical to the arrangements that apply to other social security benefits. Chapter 17 describes the related decision-making arrangements. This chapter describes what can be done if a claimant (or in certain cases other people such as a landlord or a landlord's agent) disagrees with the authority's decision or simply does not understand it. The system contains a right of appeal from the authority's decisions to an independent, legally qualified appeal tribunal. This tribunal replaces the former HB/CTB review board. See paragraphs 21.80-81 of the 2001-02 edition of the Guide for a description of the transitional rules and saving rules that made provision for the transfer of outstanding cases in the former system of review/further review on the 1st July 2001.

The legislative framework

19.2 In Great Britain section 68 and Schedule 7 of the Child Support, Pensions and Social Security Act, 2000 (abbreviated to CSPSSA) provides for:

- a right of appeal from the authority's HB/CTB decisions to an appeal tribunal administered by the Appeals Service agency;
- a right of appeal from a decision of the tribunal, on a point of law, to a Social Security Commissioner.

The equivalent legislation in Northern Ireland is section 59 and schedule 7 of the Child Support Pensions and Social Security Act (Northern Ireland) 2000 (abbreviated to NICSPSSA).

19.3 The Housing Benefit and Council Tax Benefit (Decisions and Appeals) Regulations 2001 (SI 2001 1002, in Northern Ireland SR 2001 No. 213 abbreviated to DAR, NIDAR) set out in detail the procedures to be followed in the making of an appeal. The regulations cross-refer to the Social Security and Child Support (Decisions and Appeals) Regulations 1999 (SI 1999 No. 991, in Northern Ireland SR 1999 No. 162) (abbreviated to DAR99, DAR99GB, NIDAR99) where they relate to the powers and procedures of appeal tribunals. The Housing Benefit and Council Tax Benefit (Decisions and Appeals)(Transitional and Savings) Regulations 2001 (SI 2001 No. 1264, in Northern Ireland SR 2001 No. 214) deal with the treatment of any business outstanding on the 2nd July 2001. Social Security Commissioners (Procedure) Regulations 1999 (SI 1999/1495, in

Northern Ireland SR 2001 No. 225) have been amended by the Social Security Commissioners (Procedure) (Amendment) Regulations 2001 (SI 2001 No. 1095) to extend them to cover HB/CTB appeals.

Overview of the appeal service

APPEAL TRIBUNALS AND THE APPEALS SERVICE

19.4 The appeal tribunal that decides HB/CTB appeals is part of an independent tribunal body responsible for hearing appeals on decisions on social security, child support, vaccine damage, tax credit and compensation recovery. Appeal tribunals are one arm of the Appeal Service (TAS). The other arm consists of the executive agency responsible for the administration of appeals. The Appeal Service web site can be found at *www.appeals-service.gov.uk*

THE DISPUTES PROCESS

19.5 While not a term contained in the legislation, the matters described in this chapter are often referred to as part of a 'disputes process'. In the first instance a person affected (para. 19.14) may seek to have a disputed decision changed via one of two routes:

- by requesting the authority to look at it again (i.e. apply for a revision); or
- by making an appeal against it.

19.6 In both cases, applications must be made in writing and sent to the authority, normally within one calendar month of the date the authority notified the relevant decision. If the first route is taken, once the person affected has the result of their application for revision they normally have one calendar month from the date that was sent out in which to appeal. If the second route is taken, the authority will normally take the opportunity provided by receipt of an appeal to reconsider the disputed decision.

19.7 There are three ways in which the authority may change a disputed decision. It can be:

- revised (see chapter 17);
- superseded – where it cannot be revised (see chapter 17);
- changed on appeal.

19.8 As mentioned above, when an appeal is received, the authority may consider whether the decision can be revised. If it can be revised to the advantage of the person affected, the authority should revise the decision and the appeal lapses. This applies even though the person affected may not receive all that has been asked for in the appeal. The person affected then has a fresh decision with a fresh dispute period, and fresh rights to apply for a revision or appeal.

19.9 From the perspective of the person affected, the appeal should automatically proceed to an independent appeal tribunal if:

- the decision is not revised by the authority; or
- the decision is revised, but not in favour of the person affected; or
- the decision is superseded by the authority.

Performance standards

19.10 There are no statutory performance standards relating to how quickly:

- an authority should refer an appeal to the Appeal Service; or
- a tribunal should hear a case once it has been lodged with the Appeal Service.

19.11 The Local Government Ombudsmen have described how a 'pattern of delays by some councils in the referral of housing benefit appeals to the Appeal Service is a particular concern…'

(Foreword to *Advice and guidance on arrangements for forwarding housing benefit appeals to the Appeals Service,* 2004, The Commission for Local Administration in England – *www.lgo.org.uk/pdf/sp-2-web.pdf).*

19.12 The DWP's suggested Service Level Agreement between authorities and the Appeal Service (DWP A20/2003 Appendix B: para. A65) indicates that the authority should aim to complete the submission and issue it to all parties within four calendar weeks. Where the appeal is particularly complex or more information is required, it is accepted that this timescale may be exceeded. The suggested service level agreement also indicates that the authority should inform the Appeal Service of all cases which have been outstanding for more than three months where a submission has not been issued and explain the reasons for the delay and confirm when the submission will be provided. The Local Government Ombudsmen's report identified above advises authorities how they might go about meeting the four-week target and also illustrates the remedies available to complainants, including recommendations regarding compensation.

19.13 The Secretary of State sets the Appeals Service a number of targets in relation to the administration of appeals. In 2003-04 the target for the time between the Appeal Service receiving the completed enquiry form (TAS 1) from the person affected (paras. 19.34-35) and the date of the tribunal hearing was no more than 13 weeks. For HB appeals the average time between receipt at the Appeal Service and the first hearing is eight weeks. The average time between being lodged at an authority and the first hearing is 30.2 weeks (*Hansard,* Written Answers, 26/2/02).

Who may appeal

19.14 The people who have a right to appeal an HB/CTB decision are referred to as 'persons affected'. Someone is a 'person affected' by a decision where their rights, duties or obligations are affected by it. Additionally, to be a 'person affected' they must be: DAR 3

- a claimant;
- in the case of a person who is unable for the time being to act:
  - a receiver appointed by the Court of Protection with power to claim, or as the case may be, receive benefit on his behalf;
  - in Scotland, a tutor, curator or other guardian acting or appointed in terms of law administering that person's estate; or
  - an attorney with a general power or a power to receive benefit appointed by the person liable to make those payments under the Powers of Attorney Act 1971 or the Enduring Powers of Attorney Act 1985;
- a person appointed by the authority to act for the claimant;
- the landlord, or agent where a decision has been made by the authority under regulation 93 (circumstances in which payment is to be made to a landlord) or 94 (circumstances in which payment may be made to a landlord) of the Housing Benefit Regulations (where payment of benefit is to the landlord's agent – the agent is the person affected); or
- a person from whom the authority decides that an HB/CTB 'overpayment' is recoverable (para. 18.25).

19.15 An appeal made by someone who is not a 'person affected' is not 'duly made' and should be identified as such by the auth ority. It will be turned down by the tribunal member because it fails to satisfy the legal requirement. The tribunal member should inform the appellant and the authority of the determination. DAR 20(7)(b)

Decisions that may be appealed

19.16 A person affected has a right of appeal (via the authority) to an independent appeal tribunal against any relevant decision (whether as originally made or as revised or superseded) the authority makes on a claim for, or on an award of, HB/CTB; and certain other prescribed decisions. Table 19.1 sets out other decisions that cannot be appealed. CPSA sch 7, para 6(1)(a),(b)

Table 19.1: Decisions which cannot be appealed

CPSA sch 7 para 6 DAR 16(1) and sch

- Any decision made by the authority as to the application or operation of a local scheme (i.e. disregard of war disablement and war widows' pensions);
- Any decision made by the authority that adopts a decision of a rent officer (i.e. the authority's decision regarding the maximum rent where the authority is bound by the figures produced by the rent officer);
- Any decision as to the amount of benefit to which a person is entitled in a case in which the amount is determined by the rate of benefit provided for by law;
- A decision made by virtue of, or as a consequence of any of the provisions in Part X of the main HB Regulations or Part VIII of the main CTB Regulations (claims) except a decision regarding:
    - the date of claim (including backdating);
- A decision made under any of the provisions in Part XII (Payments) except a decision regarding:
    - adjustments to payment on account of rent allowance to take account of an under or overpayment;
    - the circumstances in which payment is to be made to a landlord;
    - the circumstances in which payment may be made to a landlord;
- A decision made by virtue of, or as a consequence of any of the provisions in Part XIII (overpayments) of the main HB Regulations or Part XI (excess benefit) of the main CTB Regulations except a decision regarding:
    - recoverable overpayments;
    - person from whom recovery may be sought;
    - diminution of capital;
    - sums to be deducted in calculating recoverable overpayments;
- A decision as to the exercise of discretion to recover an 'overpayment' (para. 18.25);
- A decision involving issues that arise on appeal to the Commissioners or the courts in other cases;
- A decision relating to the suspension of benefit or payment following a suspension;
- The assessed income figure (AIF) provided by the Pension Service that the authority must use (subject to prescribed modifications) where the claimant or any partner is in receipt of the pension savings credit only.

The treatment of non-appealable decisions

19.17 If an appeal is made against one of the decisions set out in table 19.1 it should be identified as 'out of jurisdiction' by the authority and struck out by the appeal tribunal clerk or member. For example, as table 19.1 indicates, there is no right of appeal via the authority to the tribunal against the assessed income figure (AIF) the authority must use in the calculation of HB/CTB in a savings credit only case. If the authority receives an appeal that is clearly about the AIF, the claimant should be advised that the correct thing to do is to lodge an appeal with the Pension Service. The claimant should also be advised that the appeal lodged with the authority will be processed, but as there is no right of appeal via the authority against the AIF, it will be treated as 'out of jurisdiction' and the Appeals Service will be asked to strike it out (DWP, *Pension Credit Handbook,* para. 1103). The claimant does, however, have a right of appeal via the authority to the tribunal against any modification the authority may or may not make of the Pension Service's AIF.

19.18 In appropriate cases, certain of the non-appealable decisions set out in table 19.1 can be revised or superseded on request. For example, the claimant or landlord could request the authority to revise its discretionary decision to recover a recoverable overpayment in a case of hardship. Were the authority to act irrationally, unreasonably or in bad faith in relation to many of these non-appealable decisions it would be susceptible to judicial review or a complaint of maladministration.

Notification of appealable decisions to persons affected

19.19 The authority has an obligation to notify its appealable decisions (para. 19.16) to all persons affected. The notification should set out

- the decision against which the right of appeal lies;
- the right to request the authority to provide them with a written statement of the reasons for that decision – in a case where the notice does not include a statement of reasons;
- the right of appeal against that decision.

OBTAINING A WRITTEN STATEMENT EXPLAINING THE DECISION

19.20 If no written statement is included in the notification of the decision, a person affected may request one at any time. The authority must then, 'so far as practicable', provide one within 14 days. DAR 10(2)

Making an appeal

DAR 18(1), 19(2),(4), 20(1),(4)

19.21 Authorities are expected as a matter of good practice to make available forms on which an appeal may be made. An appeal may also be accepted in a letter. To be properly made an appeal should meet the conditions set out in table 19.2 and should normally be made within one month of the date of notification of the decision against which it is made. Out of time appeals may be made in particular circumstances but must be made at the latest within 13 calendar months of the date of notification of the decision. Such out of time applications should describe the particular circumstances that caused the delay. Where an appeal form is not used, the person seeking the appeal is advised to head their letter 'Appeal' and use the phrase 'I wish to appeal against…' in the body of the letter. In this way the authority should not mistake it for an application for revision (para. 19.5).

Table 19.2: Necessary attributes of a valid appeal

DAR 20(1)

The appeal must:

- be in writing on a form approved for the purpose by the authority or in such other form (e.g. letter) as the authority may accept; and
- be signed by the person who has a right of appeal; and
- be delivered, by whatever means (e.g. post, fax, e-mail) to the authority; and
- contain details of the grounds on which it is made (it is not enough, for example, for the claimant to say that they are unhappy with the decision – they must state why they think the decision is wrong); and
- contain sufficient particulars of the decision to enable that decision to be identified.

DAR 20(7)(b)

19.22 An appeal made by someone who is not a 'person affected' is not 'duly made' and should be identified as such by the authority. It will be turned down by a legally qualified tribunal member because it fails to satisfy the legal requirement. The tribunal member should inform the appellant and the authority of their determination.

WITHDRAWING AN APPEAL

19.23 An appeal may be withdrawn by an appellant in writing at any time before it is decided. If the authority has not sent the appeal to the Appeal Service any request to withdraw can be accepted by the authority. If the authority has referred the appeal to the Appeal Service any request from the appellant to withdraw the appeal must be sent to the Appeal Service. DAR 20(9)

WHAT HAPPENS IF THE APPELLANT DIES DURING THE APPEAL PROCESS?

19.24 If the appellant dies during the appeal process the authority may appoint anyone it thinks fit to proceed with the appeal in the place of the deceased. DAR 21(1)

Out of time appeals

19.25 An appeal must normally be made to the authority within one month of the date of notification of the decision against which it is made or in particular circumstances 13 months. The decision is notified when it is posted or handed to the person affected. The authority should ensure that it has an accurate record of when notifications are actually posted or handed to persons affected. An appeal is treated as made on the day that it is received by the authority. DAR 18(1) DAR 2(a)

19.26 An application for an extension of the time limit within a further 12 months should be successful where:

- the authority, or if not the authority the tribunal member, is satisfied that it is in the 'interests of justice' for the application to be granted; or
- a tribunal member is satisfied that if the application is granted there are reasonable prospects that the appeal will be successful.

19.27 Under the first bullet point the authority may admit an appeal without involving the Appeals Service. The DWP (A28-2002, para. 31) advises that the authority should make sure that the Appeal Service knows that it has admitted the late appeal by including the following paragraph in its appeal submission: 'The appeal was made on [date] but the reason(s) for the late application has been accepted by the relevant authority under regulation 32 of the SS&CS (D&A) Regs. Accordingly, the issue does not need to be considered by the tribunal.'

If the authority does not admit the late appeal the question must be referred to the Appeal Service for consideration. The authority should advise the Appeal Service why it does not support the 'out of time' appeal. As soon as practicable, a copy of the decision on the out of time appeal made by the tribunal member must be sent or given to principal parties to the proceedings.

NECESSARY CONDITIONS FOR AN OUT OF TIME APPEAL TO BE ACCEPTED BY THE TRIBUNAL MEMBER

19.28 An application cannot be granted unless the tribunal member is satisfied that:

- there are reasonable prospects that the appeal will be successful; or
- it is in the interests of justice for the application to be granted.

Note that it is sufficient if the application satisfies one of the two tests.

The 'interests of justice'

DAR 19(6)(a),(7) **19.29** With regard to the interests of justice, the regulations prescribe that it is not in the interests of justice to grant an application unless the authority or tribunal member is satisfied that one of the following circumstances exists and is relevant to the application:

- the applicant or a spouse or dependant of the applicant has died or suffered serious illness; or
- the applicant is not resident in the United Kingdom; or
- normal postal services were disrupted; or
- some other special circumstances exist which are wholly exceptional and relevant to the application.

Additionally, it must be as a result of those special circumstances that it was not practicable for the application to be made within the time limit.

GUIDING PRINCIPLE

DAR 19(8) **19.30** In determining whether it is in the interests of justice to grant the application, the authority or tribunal member must have regard to the principle that the later the application for the extension of time the more compelling the special circumstances for lateness must be.

FACTORS THAT CANNOT BE TAKEN INTO ACCOUNT

DAR 19(9)(a)-(b) **19.31** In determining whether it is in the interests of justice to grant an application, the authority or tribunal member cannot take account of the following factors:

- that the applicant was unaware of or misunderstood the law or the time limits; or
- that a Commissioner or a court has taken a different view of the law from that previously understood and applied.

The authority's action on receipt of an appeal

19.32 On receipt of an appeal the authority should:

- consider revising the decision appealed against (para. 19.6);
- classify the appeal (i.e. not duly made, out of time and/or involves a third party) if not revised to the advantage of the person affected;
- send the appropriate forms (the pre-hearing enquiry form (TAS1) to the appellant and the notification of appeal (AT37) to the Appeal Service) and its submission to:
  - the appellant; and
  - the Appeal Service.

19.33 The authority must send all appeals to the Appeals Service unless the appeal lapses following revision or is withdrawn by the appellant. The authority should indicate on the notification of appeal form (AT37) sent to the Appeal Service if it knows that eviction proceedings have begun. Such cases can be heard urgently by tribunals.

The pre-hearing enquiry form (TAS1)

19.34 The pre-hearing enquiry form the authority sends to the person affected includes questions as to whether that person:

- wants to withdraw their appeal;
- wants an oral hearing (at which they and/or their representative can be present) or paper hearing (which does not require their attendance);
- agrees to having less than 14 days notice where they have opted for an oral hearing;
- has an outstanding appeal against another benefit decision; and/or
- needs an interpreter or signer.

NORMALLY 14 DAYS TO RETURN ENQUIRY FORM TO THE APPEAL SERVICE

19.35 The person affected should normally return the pre-hearing enquiry form (TAS1) to the appropriate regional office of the Appeal Service within 14 days of the date it was sent out by the authority. If it is not returned within 14 days the Appeal Service will assume that the person affected does not wish to continue with the appeal and the appeal will be struck out. The tribunal clerk may give a longer period for reply, for example where the appellant is in hospital or some other reason exists which would prevent the appellant from replying on time. If the form cannot be returned within 14 days the regional office of the Appeal Service DAR99 39(2)-(3)

should be advised. If the authority is aware of any reason that might prevent the appellant from replying on time, this must be clearly marked on the notification of appeal (AT37) it sends to the Appeal Service.

The appeal hearing

MEMBERSHIP OF TRIBUNAL

DAR 22(1)-(2) **19.36** All tribunal members are independent of the authority. In the case of an appeal concerning HB/CTB the tribunal normally consists of just one person who will be legally qualified. In rare instances where financial questions are raised, e.g. regarding a difficult question relating to a self-employed claimant's accounts, there may also be a financially qualified tribunal member. An additional member may also be present to provide that member with experience or to assist with the monitoring of standards.

VENUES

19.37 The hearing normally takes place at a tribunal venue near to the appellant. The Appeal Service has a network of around 140 tribunal venues that it uses to hear cases across England, Wales and Scotland. The Appeal Service (Northern Ireland) currently holds appeal hearings at 19 venues in towns and cities throughout the province.

The oral hearing

NOTICE

DAR99 49(2) **19.38** At least 14 days before the hearing (beginning with the day on which the notice is given and ending on the day before the hearing of the appeal is to take place) notice of the time and place of any oral hearing must be given to every party to the proceedings. If such notice has not been given to someone who should have been given it, the hearing may proceed only with the consent of that person.

POSTPONEMENT

DAR99 51(1) **19.39** A tribunal member or the clerk may at any time before the beginning of the hearing postpone the hearing. Where a person affected wishes to request a postponement of the hearing they should do so in writing to the clerk stating the reasons for the request. If it is too late to request a postponement, an adjournment may be requested at the hearing. The clerk or tribunal member may grant or refuse the request as they think fit.

PUBLIC OR PRIVATE HEARINGS

19.40 The initial presumption is that a hearing will be in public. A (part) private DAR99 49(6) hearing may be held, however:

- in the interests of national security, morals, public order or children;
- for the protection of the private or family life of one of the parties; or
- in special circumstances, because publicity would prejudice the interests of justice.

19.41 Certain persons such as trainee panel members or trainee clerks are enti- DAR99 49(9) tled to be present at an oral hearing (whether or not it is otherwise in private) but are not able to take part in the proceedings.

DECIDING TO PROCEED IN THE ABSENCE OF ANY OF THE PARTIES

19.42 If a party to the proceedings to whom notice has been given fails to appear DAR99 49(4) at the hearing the Chair may, having regard to all the circumstances including any explanation offered for the absence:

- proceed with the hearing notwithstanding the absence; or
- give such directions with a view to the determination of the appeal as they think proper.

19.43 If a party to the proceedings has waived the right to be given 14 days DAR99 49(5) notice of the hearing, the Chair may proceed with the hearing notwithstanding the absence.

THE PARTIES' RIGHTS AT THE HEARING

19.44 While the procedure for an oral hearing is determined by the Chair, the DAR99 49(1),(7) parties to the proceeding have certain rights which the Chair must respect. Any party to the proceedings is entitled to:

- be present; and
- be heard at an oral hearing.

Parties entitled to be present do not have to be physically present, but can attend by a live television link, e.g. a video conference facility, but only where the Chair gives permission and the appellant consents. DWP advises (A17-2002, para. 31) that the facility for a live television link will only be used in TAS Liverpool as a pilot scheme.

19.45 A person who has the right to be heard at a hearing: DAR99 49(8)

- may be accompanied; and
- may be represented by another person whether they have professional qualifications or not.

DAR99 49(8) **19.46** For the purposes of the proceedings at the hearing, any representative has all the rights and powers to which the person represented is entitled.

DAR99 49(11) **19.47** Any person entitled to be heard at an oral hearing may:

- address the tribunal;
- give evidence;
- call witnesses; and
- put questions directly to any other person called as a witness.

Order of the hearing

AR99 38(2), 49(1) **19.48** The procedure for an oral hearing is determined by the Chair. The Chair may at any stage of the proceedings, either of their own motion or on a written application made to the clerk by any party to the proceedings:

- give such directions as they consider necessary or desirable for the just, effective and efficient conduct of the proceedings; and
- direct any party to the proceedings to provide such particulars or to produce such documents as may be reasonably required.

19.49 The way in which the tribunal actually hears the appeal varies according to the issue that the tribunal has to decide. Each Chair has their own way of conducting a hearing. Nevertheless the appellant should expect to have those present in the room introduced and their function explained at the start. The Chair should also explain the procedure they wish to follow and seek the agreement of the parties to going ahead in that way. The Chair may wish the appellant to start by explaining why they think the decision is wrong. If there is a Presenting Officer for the authority in attendance, they will be asked to explain the basis of the authority's decision. At some point the Chair is likely to ask questions of the parties. Usually the appellant is offered the opportunity of having the final word before the tribunal goes on to consider its decision.

ADJOURNMENT

DAR99 51(4) **19.50** An oral hearing may be adjourned by the Chair at any time on the application of any party to the proceedings or of their own motion. This might be, for example, to allow new evidence to be looked at. Where a hearing has been adjourned and it is not practicable, or would cause undue delay, for it to be resumed before a tribunal with the same tribunal member(s) there must be a complete rehearing (DWP A17/2002, para. 33).

WITHDRAWING AN APPEAL

AR99 40(1)(a),(2) **19.51** An appeal may be withdrawn by the appellant at the oral hearing. If this happens the clerk must send a notice in writing to any party to the proceedings who is not present when the appeal or referral is withdrawn, informing them that the appeal has been withdrawn.

The tribunal's decision

19.52 The tribunal reaches a decision once it has considered all the evidence from an oral or paper hearing. If the appellant attends an oral hearing they may be given the decision on the day but it will be confirmed in writing as soon as practicable by the Chair. The Appeal Service aims to issue a copy of the tribunal's decision to the authority, appellant and appellant's representative, where one exists, within two days of the tribunal hearing (DWP A20-2003, Appendix B, Annex B, para. A59).

THE WRITTEN DECISION NOTICE

19.53 Every decision of an appeal tribunal must be recorded in summary by the Chair. The decision notice must be in the written form approved by the President of Appeal Tribunals. The Chair must sign it. Where there was a legally qualified member and a financially qualified member the decision notice should state if the decision is unanimous or not. DAR99 53(1),(2),(

COMMUNICATION OF THE DECISION

19.54 As soon as practicable after an appeal has been decided, a copy of the decision notice must be sent or given to every party to the proceedings. They must also be informed of: DAR99 53(3)

- the right to apply for a statement of reasons; and
- the conditions governing appeals to a Commissioner.

19.55 The decision notice is the legal document that enables the authority to correct and pay benefit in line with the tribunal's decision.

WHAT IS A 'STATEMENT OF REASONS'?

19.56 A statement of reasons sets out the findings of fact and the reasons for the decision. If an appeal to the Social Security Commissioners is being considered, a statement of reasons must be asked for.

TIME LIMIT FOR APPLICATION FOR STATEMENT OF REASONS

19.57 A party to the proceedings may apply to the tribunal member for a statement of the reasons for the tribunal's decision. A statement of reasons can be asked for at the tribunal. Otherwise the application must normally be made within one month of the date the decision notice was given or sent. If this is not asked for in time the chance of appealing may be lost. DAR99 53(4)

AR99GB 54(1),(13) NIDAR99 54(1),(12A) **19.58** Late applications for the statement of reasons can only be accepted if the application is made in writing to the Clerk within three months of the date the decision note was sent. In calculating this three month period no account is to be taken of time that elapses before the day on which notice was given of:

- a correction of a decision or the record of a decision; or
- a decision to refuse to set aside.

Where a correction is made, or where set-aside is refused, the three month period will be counted from the day notice of the correction or refusal is given.

DAR99 54(2)-(5) **19.59** The application must explain why the application is late, including details of any relevant special circumstances. A legally qualified panel member will consider the application and decide the matter. Similar considerations apply to those that apply to late appeals.

REQUIREMENT TO SUPPLY WRITTEN STATEMENT OF REASONS

DAR99 54(11) **19.60** Following receipt of an accepted application for a written statement of reasons the tribunal member must:

- record a statement of the reasons; and
- send or give a copy of that statement to every party to the proceedings as soon as practicable.

The Appeal Service aims to issue a full statement of reasons within four weeks of a request being received (DWP A20-2003, Appendix B, Annex B, para. A61).

RECORD OF TRIBUNAL PROCEEDINGS

DAR99 55(1)-(2) **19.61** A record of the proceedings at an oral hearing, which is sufficient to indicate the evidence taken, must be made by the tribunal member. This record must be preserved by the Appeal Service for six months from the date of the decision. Any party to the proceedings may within that six month period apply in writing for a copy of that record. The copy must be supplied.

Implementing the tribunal's decision

19.62 The authority should action the tribunal's decision as soon as practicable. The DWP indicatea that the authority should seek to complete the necessary actions within four calendar weeks (A20-2003, Appendix B, Annex B, para. A70).

What actions can be taken if a tribunal's decision is wrong?

19.63 Once a tribunal has made and communicated its decision it may be:

- altered if the authority supersedes the decision;
- corrected, where there is an accidental error;
- set aside on certain limited grounds;
- appealed to the Social Security Commissioners.

WHEN MAY THE AUTHORITY SUPERSEDE THE TRIBUNAL'S DECISION?

19.64 A decision of a tribunal may be superseded, either on application or on the authority's own initiative, where: DARGB 7(2)(a),(2) NIDAR 7(2)(b),(c)

- the decision was made in ignorance of a material fact; or
- the decision was based on a mistake as to a material fact; or
- there has been a relevant change of circumstances since the decision had effect.

WHEN MAY A TRIBUNAL'S DECISION BE CORRECTED?

19.65 The clerk, or a tribunal member, may at any time correct accidental errors such as a mistake in a date or an amount in any decision, or the record of any such decision. A correction made to, or to the record of, a decision is deemed part of the decision or record of that decision. Any of the parties to the appeal can ask for a correction to be made. A written notice of the correction must be given as soon as practicable to every party to the proceedings. There is no right of appeal against a correction or a refusal to make a correction. DAR99 56(1)-(2)

SETTING ASIDE DECISIONS ON CERTAIN GROUNDS

19.66 If a tribunal decision is 'set aside' this means that the decision is cancelled and a new tribunal must be arranged. Any party to the proceedings may apply for a decision of an appeal tribunal to be set aside by a legally qualified tribunal member. The member may set the decision aside where it appears just on the ground that: DAR99 57(1)

- a document relating to the proceedings was not sent to, or was not received at an appropriate time by, any of the parties to the proceedings or their representatives or was not received at an appropriate time by the person who made the decision;
- any party to the proceedings or their representative was not present at the hearing.

DAR99 57(2) **19.67** In determining whether it is just to set aside a decision on the ground that someone was not present, the tribunal member must consider whether the party making the application gave notice that they wished to have an oral hearing. If that party did not give such notice, the decision cannot be set aside unless the tribunal member is satisfied that the interests of justice obviously support acceptance of the set aside application.

DAR99 57(3) **19.68** An application for a set aside must:

- be made within one month of the date on which:
  - a copy of the decision notice is sent or given to the parties; or
  - the statement of the reasons for the decision is given or sent in,

  whichever is the later;
- be in writing; and
- signed by a party to the proceedings or, where the party has provided written authority to a representative to act on their behalf, that representative;
- contain particulars of the grounds on which it is made; and
- be sent to the clerk to the appeal tribunal.

EXTENSION OF THE TIME LIMITS IN WHICH TO APPLY FOR A SET ASIDE

DAR99 57(6) **19.69** Late applications for set aside may be accepted up to one year after the end of the one month time limit.

DAR99 57(7) **19.70** An application for an extension of time must include details of any relevant special circumstances. It must be determined by a legally qualified panel member.

WHEN MAY A TRIBUNAL'S DECISION BE CORRECTED?

DAR99 57(8) **19.71** An application for an extension of time cannot be granted unless the panel member is satisfied that:

- if the application is granted there are reasonable prospects that the application to set aside will be successful; and
- it is in the interests of justice for the application for an extension of time to be granted.

DAR99 57(9)(b),(10) **19.72** It is not in the interests of justice to grant an application for an extension of time unless the panel member is satisfied that:

- the applicant or a spouse or dependant of the applicant has died or suffered serious illness;
- the applicant is not resident in the United Kingdom; or

- normal postal services were disrupted; or
- some other special circumstances exist which are wholly exceptional and relevant to that application,

and as a result of those special circumstances, it was not practicable for the application to set aside to be made within the one month time limit.

19.73 In determining whether it is in the interests of justice to grant an application for an extension of time, the panel member must have regard to the principle that the greater the amount of time that has elapsed between the expiry of the time within which the application to set aside is to be made and the making of the application for an extension of time, the more compelling should be the special circumstances on which the application for an extension is based. DAR99 57(11)

19.74 Where an application to set aside a decision is entertained every party to the proceedings must be sent a copy of the application. They must also be afforded a reasonable opportunity of making representations on it before the application is determined. DAR99 57(4)

COMMUNICATION OF THE DECISION ON THE APPLICATION TO SET ASIDE

19.75 Every party to the proceedings must receive a written notice of the decision on an application to set aside as soon as practicable. The notice must contain a statement giving the reasons for the decision. DAR99 57(5)

19.76 There is no right of appeal against the outcome of a set aside request. If the request is refused, however, the time limit for appealing to the Commissioner does not start until the notification of the set aside decision has been issued. DAR99 57A(2)

19.77 An application under this regulation for an extension of time which has been refused may not be renewed. DAR99 57(12)

Appeals to Social Security Commissioners

19.78 The Social Security Commissioners are appointed to decide appeals on questions of law from appeal tribunals. The Commissioners' role is to give interpretations of the law which are binding on all decision makers and appeal tribunals. The Commissioners are barristers, solicitors or advocates of not less than ten years' standing who are specialists in social security law. Commissioners have a legal status comparable to that of a High Court judge in their specialised area. Any appeals from their decisions are to the Court of Appeal or the Inner House of the Court of Session, and from there to the House of Lords. Cases involving European Union law are referred by the Commissioners direct to the European Court of Justice.

19.79 DSS Circular A25/2001, supplemented by DWP Circular A5/2002, provides detailed guidance on appeals to Commissioners. Most appeals are determined on paper without a hearing. Parties make their submissions in writing. However, parties may ask for an oral hearing. Hearings take place at the Commissioners' offices in London (Harp House, 83-86 Farringdon Street, London EC4A 4DH – correspondence should be sent to 5th Floor, Newspaper House, 8/16 Great New Street, London EC4A 3NN) and Edinburgh (23 Melville Street, Edinburgh EH3 7PW). In Northern Ireland the address for the Commissioners is Headline Building, 10-14 Victoria Street, Belfast, BTI 3GG. Hearings may take place at other locations in particular circumstances.

WHEN CAN AN APPEAL BE MADE TO THE COMMISSIONERS?

CPSA sch 7 paras (1), (2), (7)(c), (8)
DAR99 58(1)(3)
CPR 9, 10, 12, 13

19.80 An appeal can only be made to the Social Security Commissioners where the following points are satisfied:

- the ground for seeking an appeal is that the appeal tribunal made an error on a point of law (para. 19.82) in arriving at its decision; and
- the appeal is being made by someone entitled to make it (para. 19.83); and
- the appellant has applied to the tribunal – preferably on form OSSC1 (or OSSC2 for authorities) for leave to appeal to the Commissioner; and
- the application for leave to appeal is made within one month of the date the tribunal's statement of reasons was sent; or a late application made within 13 months of that date is accepted by the Chair; and
- the tribunal Chair accepts the application for leave to appeal; or
- where a tribunal chair has rejected an application for leave an application has been made directly to a Commissioner (again on Form OSSC1/ OSSC2) normally within one month (though out of time applications may be considered if there are special reasons) of the tribunal Chair's rejection of the application for leave being sent and the Commissioner considers that there are special reasons to accept the application for leave; and
- the appellant has submitted the appeal, together with all the necessary accompanying documents, to the Commissioner within one month (or longer if there are special reasons) of the date the tribunal's decision granting leave was sent.

Where the Commissioner granted leave to appeal the appellant will not normally have to a make a separate appeal. Detailed advice on appealing to the Commissioners in Great Britain and Forms OSSC1/OSSC2 can be found on the Social Security and Child Support Commissioners' web site: *www.osscsc.gov.uk*

The equivalent advice and forms in use in Northern Ireland can be found on the Northern Ireland Court Service web site:

www.courtsni.gov.uk/en-GB/Services/Tribunals/OfficeOfSSC/HowTo/

What is an error in a point of law?

19.81 An appeal to a Commissioner can only be made on an error in a point of law. CPSA sch 7 para 8(1)

19.82 An error in a point of law is where, for example (R(IS) 11/99), the appeal tribunal:

- failed to apply the correct law;
- wrongly interpreted the relevant Acts or Regulations;
- followed a procedure that breached the rules of natural justice;
- took irrelevant matters into account, or did not consider relevant matters, or did both of these things;
- did not give adequate reasons in the full statement of its decision;
- gave a decision which was not supported by the evidence;
- decided the facts in such a way that no person properly instructed as to the relevant law, and acting judicially, could have come to the decision made by the tribunal.

Who can apply for leave to appeal?

19.83 Where the disputed decision relates to housing benefit, the following can apply for leave to appeal to the Commissioners:

- the claimant;
- any other 'person affected' by the decision (para. 19.14) such as a landlord who has been found liable to repay an amount of overpaid housing benefit (paras. 18.25, 18.41 and 18.46-47);
- the authority against whose decision the appeal to the appeal tribunal was brought;
- the Secretary of State (the Department for Social Development in Northern Ireland).

Appeals against a Commissioner's decision

CPR 33 **19.84** There is a right to appeal against a Commissioner's decision to the Court of Appeal or the Court of Session in Scotland. An appeal can only be made on a point of law. Leave to appeal must be obtained from the Commissioner or, if the Commissioner refuses, from the relevant Court. The time limit for applying for leave to appeal to the Commissioner is three months. The time limit may be extended by the Commissioner. If leave to appeal is refused the application may be renewed in the relevant Court within six weeks. If the Commissioner grants leave the appeal must be made to the relevant Court within six weeks.

Errors of law: restrictions on entitlement

CPSA sch 7 para 18 **19.85** The rules about this apply when:

- the result of an appeal to a Commissioner or court (i.e. the High Court, Court of Appeal, Court of Session, House of Lords or Court of Justice of the European Community) is that the authority's decision was erroneous in point of law (including cases where all or part of a Regulation or Order has been held to be invalid); and
- after the date of the determination of that appeal, that authority or another authority has to make a decision in accordance with it; and
- the authority's decision would be about:
  - a claim (regardless of whether the claim was made before or after the appeal determination), or
  - a revision (and if this is as a result of an application to do so, regardless of whether the application was made before or after the appeal determination), or
  - a supersession following an application for one (regardless of whether the application was made before or after the appeal determination).

In such cases, in respect of the period before the appeal determination, the authority must make the decision as though it had not been found to be wrong in law. This does not, however, apply where the decision would have been made before the appeal determination apart from the fact that it was stayed as described above.

20 Immigration status, rights of residence and habitual residence

20.1 Certain claimants are not entitled to HB or CTB if they are:

- 'subject to immigration control' (paras. 20.6-14); or
- considered not habitually resident in the United Kingdom, the Channel Islands, the Isle of Man or the Republic of Ireland (paras. 20.32-49); or
- from 1st May 2004, a person who does not have the right to reside in the United Kingdom, the Channel Islands, the Isle of Man or the Republic of Ireland (paras. 20.15-24).

20.2 The rules about who is excluded from HB/CTB are complex and have been subject to various amendments. Transitional provisions also apply. Certain persons who would be excluded under the current rules nevertheless remain entitled because of the date they first claimed HB/CTB.

The relevant legislation

20.3 Section 115 (which applies to Great Britain and Northern Ireland) of the Immigration and Asylum Act 1999 which came into force on 3rd April 2000 excludes persons subject to immigration control from HB/CTB entitlement (and most other forms of assistance).

20.4 Exceptions to this general exclusion, and transitional provisions, are prescribed in the Social Security (Immigration and Asylum) Consequential Amendment Regulations (SI 2000 No. 636, in Northern Ireland SR 2000 No. 71).

20.5 HB regulation 7A and the equivalent CTB regulation 4A additionally exclude from HB/CTB entitlement certain persons who are not habitually resident in the United Kingdom, the Channel Islands, the Isle of Man or the Republic of Ireland (sometimes referred to as the Common Travel Area). From 1st May 2004 this rule is extended so that a person who does not have the 'right to reside' in the Common Travel Area cannot be considered as habitually resident. This change in the rules effectively creates a new condition in addition to the existing immigration status and habitual residence tests. These new rules are set out in the Social Security (Habitual Residence) Amendment Regulations 2004 (SI 2004 No. 1232) or, in Northern Ireland, the Social Security (Habitual Residence) Amendment (Northern Ireland) Regulations 2004 (SR 2004 No. 197) and are described in paragraphs 20.15-24 below.

Persons 'subject to immigration control'

20.6 Section 115(9) of the Immigration and Asylum Act 1999 defines 'a person subject to immigration control' as someone who is not an EEA national (para. 20.11) and who:

- requires leave (permission) to enter or remain in the United Kingdom but does not have it (i.e. an illegal entrant or someone who has overstayed his or her leave);
- has leave to enter or remain in the United Kingdom which is subject to a condition that he or she does not have recourse to public funds (such as a visitor or student);
- has leave to enter or remain in the United Kingdom given as a result of a maintenance undertaking (i.e. a resident has formally agreed to sponsor him or her);
- has had leave extended to allow an appeal against a decision on the grounds that he or she is an asylum seeker;
- has leave to enter or remain in the United Kingdom only as a result of a pending appeal against:
  - a decision to vary, or to refuse to vary, any limited leave to enter or remain in the United Kingdom; or
  - a requirement to leave the United Kingdom because he or she is an asylum seeker.

PERSONS 'SUBJECT TO IMMIGRATION CONTROL' WHO REMAIN ENTITLED

20.7 Claimants who fall into any of the categories identified in the following paragraphs are exempt from the general exclusion from HB/CTB contained in the Immigration and Asylum Act 1999. SI 2000 No. 636 NISR 2000 No. 71

CLAIMANTS WITH LIMITED LEAVE – FUNDS DISRUPTED

20.8 Claimants with limited leave to remain in the UK (and thus normally ineligible for HB/CTB), but whose funds from abroad have stopped temporarily, are entitled to HB/CTB for up to 42 days in any one period of leave where they are temporarily without funds from abroad and there is a reasonable expectation that the funds will resume with three months.

SPONSORED IMMIGRANTS – SPONSOR(S) DIE

20.9 A person given leave to enter or remain in the UK on the condition that one or more sponsors have given a formal, written undertaking under the 1971

Immigration Act to be responsible for maintaining and accommodating them during their stay, but where all such sponsors have subsequently died.

SPONSORED IMMIGRANTS – RESIDENT FOR FIVE YEARS OR MORE

20.10 People admitted to the UK as sponsored immigrants who have been resident in the UK for five years or more.

EUROPEAN UNION AND EUROPEAN ECONOMIC AREA NATIONALS

20.11 The EEA consists of the member states of the European Union plus a small number of other European states. Prior to 1st May 2004 the EEA comprised 16 states: Austria, Belgium, Denmark, Finland, France, Germany, Greece, Iceland, Ireland, Italy, Liechtenstein, Luxembourg, Netherlands, Norway, Portugal, Spain, and Sweden. On 1st May 2004 the following ten countries – known as the accession states – became members of the European Union: Cyprus, Czech Republic, Estonia, Hungary, Latvia, Lithuania, Malta, Poland, Slovakia and Slovenia. However, from the same date all claimants will be required to show that they have the right to reside in the Common Travel Area (paras. 20.1, 20.5 and 20.15) to be entitled to benefit. The effect of these new rules will be to exclude many, but not all, nationals from the accession states as well as certain people who are nationals of other states (including the 16 EEA states prior to 1st May 2004).

ECSMA/CESC AND SWISS NATIONALS

20.12 A person who is a national of a state which has ratified the European Convention on Social and Medical Assistance (ECSMA) or a state which has ratified the Council of Europe Social Charter (CESC) and who is lawfully present in the United Kingdom.

20.13 In addition to EEA states the only countries that had ratified either the ECSMA or CESC as at March 2003 were Croatia and Turkey. Turkish Cypriots are not considered to be nationals of either Turkey or Cyprus.

20.14 Switzerland is not a member of the EEA or ECSMA/CESC. However, from 1st June 2002 the European Union-Swiss agreement gives Swiss nationals the same rights to HB/CTB (and other benefits) as nationals of other European Union member states.

The right of residence test

SI 2004 No. 1232
SR 2004 No. 197

20.15 The right of residence test applies from 1st May 2004. The new test was proposed following concern that the expansion of the European Union might result in an influx of nationals from Eastern Europe intending to exploit the UK benefit system. However, the new test applies to all claims, not just those from the new EU states.

20.16 Strictly speaking the test works by treating those who fail it as not being habitually resident (para. 20.32) in the common travel area (para. 20.5) and so disqualifies them from benefit. The overall effect is the same as adding an additional test on top of the existing immigration status and habitual residence tests. Its intention is to complement the habitual residence test by guarding against the possibility that a person who has no intention of working could otherwise acquire rights to benefit simply by living in the UK for a reasonably lengthy period.

PERSONS WITH A RIGHT OF RESIDENCE

20.17 In order to qualify for benefit the claimant will have to show that they have a right of residence in the UK, the Channel Islands, Isle of Man or the Republic of Ireland (sometimes collectively known as the Common Travel Area). A person will have right of residence in the Common Travel Area and so pass this test if they are:

- a British Citizen or Citizen of the Irish Republic;
- exempt from the habitual residence test (para. 20.33)
- an EEA worker (paras. 20.34-38) from one of the 16 EEA states prior to 1st May 2004 (para. 20.11);
- a work seeker from one of the 16 EEA member states prior to 1st May 2004 for a period up to six months (or longer if genuinely seeking work);
- certain persons who are economically inactive from one of the 16 EEA member states prior 1st May 2004 whose claim for benefit is not considered to be an unreasonable burden on the state (para. 20.24);
- a foreign national who has been granted limited leave to remain but whose funds are temporarily disrupted (para. 20.8);
- a foreign national granted leave as a result of a sponsorship agreement who has lived in the UK for at least five years or a lesser period if their sponsor has died (paras. 20.9-10);
- a national of an EEA state, including those states which joined the EEA on 1st May 2004, who is self employed;
- a national of Malta, Cyprus or Switzerland to whom any of the above applies (including conditions which apply to nationals of the original 16 EEA member states);
- a national of one of the A8 states (para.20.20) who has acquired a right to reside in the UK as a result of working for a continuous period of 12 months (para. 20.22);

- a national of a state which has ratified the ECSMA or CESC treaties (paras. 20.12-13) provided they were granted leave to enter the UK which has not subsequently expired;
- a claimant who has transitional protection (para. 20.18-19).

TRANSITIONAL PROTECTION FROM THE RIGHT OF RESIDENCE TEST

20.18 The main effect of these rules is expected to be on those nationals from the original 16 EEA member states (i.e. the EEA prior to 1st May 2004) who did not enter the UK as workers, for example, students, people incapable of work or pensioners. The DWP's intention is that existing claimants who would otherwise be affected by this change will be transitionally protected.

SI 2004 No. 1232 Reg 6 NISR 2004 No. 197

20.19 A claimant will be transitionally protected from the rights of residence test if they were entitled to HB/CTB on 30th April 2004 (including a claim back-dated to that date). Protection will continue until such time as their claim ends for some other reason. Protection will also continue provided the claimant remains entitled to either HB, CTB, IS, JSA(IB) or the guarantee credit for a continuous period which includes 30th April 2004. Therefore, while the claim for HB or CTB may be broken protection can continue and will apply to a later claim provided the claimant remained entitled to least one of these benefits for a continuous period from 30th April 2004. Likewise, continued entitlement to HB or CTB (or both) will preserve protection for IS, JSA or the guarantee credit to be used at some later date.

NATIONALS OF THE NEW EUROPEAN UNION (ACCESSION) STATES

20.20 The Accession Treaty to the European Union allows for the rights of nationals from accession states (para. 20.11) to live and work in another member state to be restricted for a transitional period of up to five years. This restriction does not apply to the self-employed nor to nationals of Malta and Cyprus, who will gain full rights to live and work in the UK from 1st May 2004. The result is that, with the exception of those accession nationals who eventually acquire 'EEA worker' status (para. 20.21) and the self employed, nationals of the remaining eight accession states (known as the A8) will not have the right to reside in the UK and so will be excluded from benefit.

HBR 7A(4)(e) CTBR 4A(4)(e)

20.21 Accession nationals from the A8 states who want to work in the UK will be required to register with the Home Office. The requirement to register will cease when they have been working in the UK continuously for 12 months without interruption. Accession nationals from the A8 states who are not registered will not have the right to reside in the UK. The requirement to register does not apply to self-employed persons, but would apply if they ceased to be self employed.

20.22 Following 12 months continuous employment in the UK, A8 nationals will have the same rights as other EEA nationals from the original 16 EEA member states, such as those enjoyed by persons with EEA worker status (para. 20.34). This also applies to those who have been legally working in the UK for a continuous period of 12 months prior to 1st May 2004.

20.23 A8 nationals who are not in work (e.g. students, pensioners, others incapable of work through sickness or disability) or who are looking for work will not have the right to reside in the UK unless it is considered that they will not be an unreasonable burden on the UK benefits system (that is social assistance, rather than contributory benefits). If they are considered to be an unreasonable burden they will not have the right to reside in the UK and so will be excluded from benefit.

ECONOMICALLY INACTIVE EEA NATIONALS CONSIDERED AN UNREASONABLE BURDEN

20.24 Whether a person is considered an unreasonable burden on the UK benefits system is a question to be determined after 'taking into consideration the personal circumstances of the applicant and, where appropriate, their dependants'. DWP Guidance on deciding this question published as part of its memorandum on the new rules to the Social Security Advisory Committee stated that 'EEA nationals who have no prospect of finding work or becoming self sufficient may be considered an unreasonable burden [but] it would be open to those [not in work] to demonstrate that their private funds would resume before long would not be an unreasonable burden [...]. If EEA nationals claim benefits after having been in the UK for some time, the fact they have been self sufficient will be a factor in the decision [...] as well as the length of time they are likely to be claiming [...]'.

Asylum seekers, refugees and persons granted leave outside the immigration rules

EXCLUSION OF ASYLUM SEEKERS

20.25 An asylum seeker is someone normally subject to immigration control who seeks to enter or remain in the UK by applying for asylum as a refugee, or who otherwise indicates a fear of being required to return to his or her country of origin. Except for transitionally protected claims (para. 20.26) from 3rd April 2000 asylum seekers are excluded from HB/CTB and other social security benefits. Their only rights to support are through the Home Office asylum support scheme managed by the National Asylum Support Service (NASS). From January 2003 NASS support can be denied to any person who does not apply for asylum immediately on entering the UK, effectively leaving these persons destitute.

TRANSITIONALLY PROTECTED ASYLUM SEEKERS

SI 2000 No. 636 Reg 12
SI 1996 No. 30 Reg 12
NISR 2000 No. 71 Reg 11
NISR 1996 No. 11 Reg 11

20.26 The following asylum seekers are entitled to HB/CTB:

- a claimant who was entitled to benefit on 4th February 1996 and who has not yet received an adverse decision on their asylum claim. A break in benefit does not bring protection to an end: *Yildiz v Secretary of State for Social Security;* or
- a claimant who applied for asylum before 3rd April 2000 who made their application either before entering the UK or at immigration control when first entering the UK; or
- a claimant who applied for asylum before 3 April 2000 after arriving in the UK following declaration by the Home Secretary that their country of origin was in a state of 'significant upheaval'. This only applies to persons from the former Zaire from 16th May 1997 and from Sierra Leone from 1st July 1997.

20.27 In the last two cases, a break in the claim will not affect entitlement to benefit – but it may mean that benefit is not payable in respect of a partner. Protection continues until the first negative decision on their asylum application. Note that this protection does not apply to those who illegally entered the UK but who were subsequently granted 'temporary admission'. All benefit for these cases ended on 3rd April 2000.

PERSONS GRANTED ASYLUM – REFUGEES

HBR 7A(4)(e), 7B, sch A1
CTBR 4A(4)(e), 4D, sch A1

20.28 Asylum seekers who have their applications for asylum accepted (i.e. are granted refugee status) become entitled to benefit in the normal way from the date their refugee status is confirmed. They also become entitled to benefit for the whole of their exclusion period immediately prior to their refugee status being confirmed. A claim for this retrospective period is not subject to the normal rules for backdating (para 5.76), instead a strict time limit of four weeks applies from the date their refugee status is decided by the Home Office. Time starts to run from the date of the decision, not from the date the refugee receives the confirmation letter (which may be some time later). The time limit cannot be extended. Since many asylum applications can take years to be decided, the claimant could be due substantial arrears – a prompt claim is essential.

PERSONS GRANTED HUMANITARIAN PROTECTION OR DISCRETIONARY LEAVE FOLLOWING REFUSAL OF ASYLUM

HBR 7A(4)(e)
CTBR 4A(4)(e)

20.29 From 1st April 2003, Exceptional Leave to Remain for asylum seekers refused refugee status was replaced by two new forms of leave. As with exceptional leave, both are granted outside the immigration rules at the discretion of the Home Secretary. These two forms of leave are known as Humanitarian Protection and Discretionary Leave: details can be found in circular A11/2003. Exceptional leave still remains, but is now only granted to those who do not apply for asylum (para 20.39-40).

20.30 A person refused asylum may be granted humanitarian protection or discretionary leave at the discretion of the Home Secretary. Humanitarian protection is granted to those who would be at risk of their life or degrading treatment if they returned to their country of origin. Discretionary leave is granted to those who do not fit the criteria for humanitarian protection and is only granted in exceptional circumstances. Persons granted humanitarian protection or discretionary leave are entitled to benefit in the normal way from the date their status is confirmed. However, unlike refugees they are not entitled to benefit retrospectively.

OTHER PERSONS REFUSED ASYLUM

20.31 If an application for asylum is refused and the applicant is not granted humanitarian protection or discretionary leave then there will be no entitlement to HB/CTB, regardless of the personal circumstances of the claimant.

The habitual residence test

20.32 If the claimant is not exempt from the 'habitual residence' the authority should decide that they are a 'person from abroad' and not entitled to HB/CTB where it considers that they are not habitually resident in the United Kingdom, the Channel Islands, the Isle of Man or the Republic of Ireland (formerly referred to as the Common Travel Area). The rule applies to all claimants who are not exempt from the test irrespective of nationality.

HBR 7A(4)(e)
CTBR 4A(4)(e)

EXEMPT CLAIMANTS

20.33 The following claimants are exempt from the habitual residence test:

HBR 7A(4)(e), (5)(d)-(f)
CTBR 4A(4)(e), (5)(d)-(f)

- recipients of income support, state pension credit or income-based jobseeker's allowance;
- EEA nationals who are 'workers' for the purposes of Council Regulation (EEC) No. 1612/68 or (EEC) No. 1251/70;
- EEA nationals who have a right to reside in the UK under Council Directive No. 68/360/EEC or No. 73/148/EEC (e.g. the self-employed);
- refugees;
- claimants given exceptional leave to enter or remain the UK;
- former asylum seekers granted Humanitarian Protection or Discretionary Leave by the Home Secretary;
- claimants who left the territory of Montserrat after 1st November 1995 because of the effect on that territory of volcanic eruption;

- claimants not subject to immigration control who have been deported, expelled or otherwise removed by compulsion of law from another country to the United Kingdom.

In addition, DWP guidance states that 'persons that have lived in the Common Travel Area (para. 20.32) for at least two years will not normally be subject to the test on the basis that they are very likely to satisfy it' (GM C7.42-43).

EEA WORKER

20.34 The EEA states are identified in paragraph 20.11. The definition of an EEA worker has become ambiguous due to a growing body of case law. To be classed as an 'EEA worker' a person must be currently, or in certain circumstances (see below) have been, engaged in remunerative work in the UK which is both:

- 'effective and genuine'; and
- not 'on such a small scale as to be purely marginal and ancillary'.

20.35 European case law has established that no-one should be denied EEA worker status simply because they are working part-time or because they are low paid and need to supplement their income with social security benefits. The DSS suggests that a number of factors should be considered before the authority decides whether any work done by the claimant is 'effective and genuine'. These include:

- the period of employment;
- the number of hours worked;
- the level of earnings; and
- whether the work is regular or erratic.

These factors are meant to be considered as a whole. The presence or absence of any one factor is not, by itself, conclusive.

20.36 The definition of an EEA worker does not include a UK citizen who is working in the UK. Such individuals do not need to exercise rights under European law in order to be able to work in their home state. However British citizens can obtain the status of EEA worker by living and working in another EEA country and then returning to the UK.

20.37 A former worker who retains EEA worker status is one who has worked in the UK in the past and who is:

- actively seeking to rejoin the workforce; or unemployed and undergoing retraining; or
- voluntarily unemployed in order to take up vocational training linked to a previous job; or

- retired after working in the UK for at least 12 months before pensionable age (60 for a woman, 65 for a man) and who has either resided continuously in the UK for more than three years or whose spouse is (or was at the time of marriage) a British national; or
- incapable of work through illness or injury sustained while working in the UK and who either:
  - is entitled to UK invalidity or disablement benefit, or
  - previously resided in the UK for two years or more, or
  - has a spouse who is (or was at the time of marriage) a British national; or
- seeking reinstatement or re-employment with the same employer after being temporarily laid off.

20.38 Self-employed people have a right to reside in the UK under specific EEC directives and are therefore also exempt.

PERSONS WITH EXCEPTIONAL LEAVE TO ENTER OR REMAIN

20.39 Exceptional leave to enter or remain in the UK is a form of leave given by the Home Secretary outside the normal immigration rules. It is granted to people when it is considered that they should be allowed to enter or remain in the United Kingdom on humanitarian grounds.

20.40 Prior to 1st April 2003 this form of leave was mostly given to asylum seekers who had not been recognised as refugees. Exceptional leave is no longer granted to applicants who have made a claim for asylum (para. 20.29). However, exceptional leave can continue to be granted to other types of applicant at the discretion of the Home Secretary.

The meaning of 'habitual residence'

20.41 The term 'habitual residence' is not defined in the regulations. The DWP (GM C7.58) described the term as 'intended to convey a degree of permanence in the claimant's residence in the Common Travel Area'. The term 'habitual residence' arises in European legislation, in particular EEC Regulation 1408/71 dealing with social security for migrant workers and in family law.

'HABITUAL RESIDENCE' IN EUROPEAN SOCIAL SECURITY LAW

20.42 In *Angenjeux v. Hakenberg* the court ruled that 'the place where one habitually resides must be understood in the case of a business representative [...] as the place in which he has established the permanent centre of his interests and to which he returns in the intervals between his tours'. In *Di Paolo v. Office National de l'Emploi* the court ruled that where a person habitually resides also corresponds with where the habitual centre of his interests is situated. The court also ruled that account should be taken of the length and continuity of residence before the person concerned moved, the length and purpose of his absence, the nature of the occupation found in the other member state and the intention of the person concerned as it appears from all the circumstances.

20.43 The judgment in the Di Paolo case emphasised that whenever a worker has stable employment in a member state there is a presumption that he resides there, even if he has left his family in another state.

20.44 The authority must establish the relevant facts on which it can make a decision as to whether or not someone is 'habitually resident'. Drawing on the relevant European case law, the DWP suggests (GM C7.63) that the authority, in deciding this question, should consider the following factors:

- length and continuity of residence;
- future intentions;
- employment prospects;
- reasons for coming to the UK; and
- centre of interest.

'HABITUAL RESIDENCE' IN FAMILY LAW

20.45 The prime authority on the ordinary and natural meaning of 'habitual residence' is the speech of Lord Brandon in *Re J (A Minor) (Abduction)*. This was a case on the Convention on the Civil Aspects of International Child Abduction. Lord Brandon emphasised that 'there is a significant difference between a person ceasing to be habitually resident in country A, and his subsequently becoming habitually resident in country B. A person may cease to be habitually resident in country A in a single day if he or she leaves it with a settled intention not to return to it but to take up long-term residence in country B instead. Such a person cannot however, become habitually resident in country B in a single day. An appreciable period of time and a settled intention will be necessary to enable him or her to become so.'

PERSUASIVE COMMISSIONER'S DECISIONS

20.46 There are a number of Commissioner's decisions relating to the test of habitual residence within the income support scheme that must be considered persuasive for HB/CTB purposes. These decisions have adopted the key criteria of 'an appreciable period of time' and a 'settled intention'. The following key points arose from CIS 1067/1995:

- residence implies a more settled state than mere physical presence, thereby excluding short stay visitors;

- to be a resident the claimant must be seen to be making a home here;
- the home need not be his or her only home, nor need it be intended to be a permanent one, but it must be a genuine home for the time being;
- the length, continuity and general nature of a claimant's actual residence are more important than his or her intentions as to the future;
- a person may abandon habitual residence in a single day but this does not mean that he or she becomes a habitual resident of another country to which he or she intends to move;
- an appreciable period of time, as well as a settled intention, is necessary to enable the claimant to become habitually resident; and
- what counts as an 'appreciable period of time' must depend on the facts in each case; it must, however, be the kind of period which demonstrates a settled and stable pattern of living as a resident.

20.47 Commissioner's Decision CIS/2326/1995 agreed with the main points of CIS 1067/1995. It emphasised, however, that no particular periods should be mentioned as amounting to an appreciable period of time except in relation to actual cases that arise for decision. The Commissioner considered that the question in each individual case must be whether, in all the circumstances, including the settledness of the person's intentions as to residence, the residence has continued for a sufficient period for it to be said to be habitual.

RECENT UK COURT DECISIONS

20.48 The House of Lords upheld the Commissioner decision in CIS 2326/1995. It found that an appreciable period of time of actual residence is needed to establish habitual residence for people coming to the UK for the first time *(Nessa v. Chief Adjudication Officer)* whereas the European Court of Justice in *Swaddling v. Chief Adjudication Officer* has ruled that a UK claimant who had returned to Britain after living and working in France for several years could not have his right to benefit made subject to any period of actual residence here after his return by the 'habitual residence' test.

20.49 The DWP accepts that people returning to the UK from an EU member state and re-establishing their ties here should be treated as habitually resident immediately upon their return (GM C7.53). Authorities should do the same. Indeed the DWP has gone further than the principle established in the European Court case. The DWP advises authorities (GM C7.54) to extend the effect of the judgment to people of any nationality returning from any country overseas and re-establishing their ties in the UK, Republic of Ireland, Channel Islands or Isle of Man. In other words, they should be treated as habitually resident immediately on return.

21 Students

21.1 The general rules in this guide apply to students, but with a number of variations. This chapter explains all these variations. It covers:

- the terminology used in student cases;
- which students can get HB and CTB;
- how HB and CTB are assessed for students; and
- the rules for assessing students' income and rent.

21.2 The student figures given in this chapter apply for the 2003-04 academic year. These and other relevant figures for the 2003-04 academic year are summarised in DWP circular HB/CTB A20/2002. Figures for the 2004-05 academic year were not available in time for this edition of the guide.

21.3 As described in this chapter, the student rules vary between HB and CTB, and also between main CTB and second adult rebate. Also, the rules have changed frequently in the past few years – and, despite welcome simplification this year, remain unnecessarily complex.

Who counts as a 'student'?

21.4 For the HB/CTB student rules to apply, the person in question must be a 'student'. The definition is given below. Other important terms are defined after that. Paragraph 21.22 compares these with the definitions used in council tax law – which are different.

DEFINITION OF 'STUDENT'

HBR 2(1), 46, 47, 52
CTBR 2(1), 38, 39

21.5 For HB and CTB purposes, a student is defined as any person 'who is attending or undertaking a course of study at an educational establishment… [or a New Deal qualifying course]'. This includes:

- study at any level (from school onwards) whether full-time or part-time;
- students with or without loans or grants;
- both state-funded and private establishments; and
- both term-times and vacations.

Some special cases are mentioned below.

21.6 Once a course has started, a person carries on counting as a student until his or her course finishes or he or she abandons it or is dismissed from it. So someone does count as a student during the Christmas and Easter vacations and any summer vacation(s) occurring within the course, even if he or she takes up full-time work then. But someone does not count as a student during the summer vacation after the end of a course or between two different courses.

STUDENTS WITH PARTNERS

21.7 In the case of a couple, the HB and CTB rules vary depending on whether one or both are students and which partner makes the claim. Details are given as each rule is described (and see table 21.2).

HBR 47, 52
CTBR 39

INTERCALATED PERIODS

21.8 Although the general rule is that a person must be 'attending or undertaking' the course to count as a 'student', a person continues to count as a 'student' during 'intercalated periods': *O'Connor v Chief Adjudication Officer.* An intercalated period is one during which a student temporarily suspends attendance, for example because of sickness or for personal reasons, but still remains registered with his or her educational establishment.

SANDWICH COURSES

21.9 People on sandwich courses do count as students – both when they are studying and during their periods of work experience.

HBR 46(1)
CTBR 38(1)

HEALTH CARE STUDENTS

21.10 The following count as students if (as is almost always the case) they fit the definition given above (para. 21.5):

- students undertaking nursing and midwifery diploma courses;
- NHS-funded students undertaking degree programmes.

QUALIFYING COURSES UNDER THE NEW DEAL

21.11 Studying on a 'qualifying course' is one of the options under the New Deal (paras. 13.62-63) for certain people. Such people count as students. All the student rules apply to them, apart from following variations:

- they carry on counting as a student until either the last day of their course or the date of their last examination, whichever comes later (and the points in para. 21.6 do not apply);
- discretionary payments made to them under the New Deal (table 13.2) are disregarded:
  - as income: the one exception is that no discretionary payment for travel is disregarded if the normal student disregard for travel applies to them (tables 21.3 and 21.4);

HBR 35(3),(3A), 43(3),(3A), 46
HBRGB sch 4 para [illegible]
sch 5 para 56
NIHBR sch 4 para 6[illegible]
sch 5 para 54
CTBR 26(3),(3A), 34(3),(3A), 38
sch 4 para 67, sch [illegible]
para 56

- as capital in all cases – but only for 52 weeks from the date of payment;
- as notional income and as notional capital in all cases.

21.12 However, most people on a 'qualifying course' continue to receive income-based jobseeker's allowance: in their case, all their income and capital is disregarded for HB and main CTB purposes (and they are eligible for HB and CTB: table 21.1).

TRAINING SCHEMES

HBR 46(1) CTBR 38(1) **21.13** People on the New Deal (except as described above) do not count as students; nor do people on other government training schemes. The question of whether anyone else on a training scheme counts as a student is decided by reference to the definition of 'student' quoted above: they usually do not count as a student.

'Full-time' *versus* 'part-time' students

21.14 Some of the HB and CTB rules apply to both full-time and part-time students; some apply only to full-time students. Details are given as each rule is described.

GENERAL CASES

HBR 46(1) CTBR 38(1) **21.15** There is no general-purpose definition of 'full-time' (or 'part-time'). Some special cases do have definitions (as in the next few paragraphs). In any other case, the law goes no further and authorities usually rely on factors such as how the educational establishment and local education authority treat the course. The DWP observes (GM para. C5.06) that full-time 'covers [full-time] university degree courses in England and Wales [and full-time] privately run courses', but does not offer further guidance.

FURTHER EDUCATION COURSES

HBR 46(1) CTBR 38(1) **21.16** A student studying at a further education college counts as a full-time student if (and only if) his or her course involves:

- ◆ in England, more than 16 hours per week of 'guided learning', as set out in the 'learning agreement' obtainable from his or her college;
- ◆ in Wales, more than 16 hours per week of 'guided learning', as set out in a college document;
- ◆ in Scotland:
  - more than 16 hours of classroom-based or workshop-based 'guided learning', or

- more than 21 hours per week of a combination of that and additional hours using structured learning packages,

as set out (in either case) in a college document.

SANDWICH COURSES

21.17 All students on sandwich courses count as full-time. HBR 46(1) CTBR 38(1)

MODULAR COURSES

21.18 A modular course is one which contains two or more modules, a specified number of which have to be completed in order to complete the course. They often permit full-time, part-time or mixed attendance. In such cases, the DWP advises (GM chapter C5 annex A para. C5.19) that a student counts as full-time only during the parts of the course for which he or she is registered as full-time (so a student in fact changing from full-time in, say, her second year to part-time in her third would count for HB/CTB purposes as part-time in her third year). HBR 46(2),(4) CTBR 38(2),(4)

RETAKES ON MODULAR COURSES

21.19 The following applies only to the parts of modular courses that count as full-time for HB/CTB purposes. If someone fails a module or an exam in such a case, he or she continues to count as full-time for any period in which he or she continues to attend or undertake the course for the purposes of retaking the exam or module (including any vacations within that period other than vacations after the end of the course). HBR 46(3) CTBR 38(3)

Other definitions

HIGHER EDUCATION

21.20 Whether a student is in higher education or not, is one of the main descriptions used in HB and CTB to distinguish different levels of education. Higher education is defined as meaning: HBR 46, 48A CTBR 38, 40

- first degree, postgraduate and higher degree courses;
- courses for the further training of teachers and youth and community workers;
- courses for the Diploma of Higher Education, the BTEC/SVEC Higher National Diploma (HND) or Higher National Certificate (HNC), the Diploma in Management Studies, or the Certificate in Education;
- any other courses at a level higher than GCE A level or BTEC/SVEC Ordinary National Diploma (OND) or Ordinary National Certificate (ONC), whether or not leading to a qualification.

PERIOD OF STUDY AND SUMMER VACATION

HBR 46(1) CTBR 38(1)

21.21 Some of the rules refer to a student's period of study:

- the period of study for any course requiring more than 45 weeks study in a year (e.g. for many postgraduate courses) runs from the first day of the academic year to the day before the first day of the next academic year. The course is treated as not having a summer vacation;
- for courses of less than one year, the period of study is the whole of the course;
- in all other cases, the period of study runs from the first day of the academic year to the last day before the summer vacation (or in the final year of a course of more than one year, to the last day of the course). This usually means three terms plus the Christmas and Easter vacations;
- subject to the above points, for students on sandwich courses, periods of work experience are included in the period of study.

HB AND CTB DEFINITIONS *VERSUS* COUNCIL TAX DEFINITIONS

21.22 For council tax purposes, four groups of people – including certain foreign language assistants and student nurses – are defined in the law as being 'students' (categories 5 to 8 in appendix 6). These council tax definitions are relevant for considering whether a dwelling is completely exempt from council tax (para. 9.11) and whether a council taxpayer can get a discount (para. 9.16). The council tax definitions rather than the HB and CTB definitions are also used for certain purposes to do with second adult rebate (paras. 8.6, 8.17-18). But for all the HB and CTB rules described in this chapter, the council tax definitions are irrelevant: only the definitions given earlier are relevant.

21.23 There is some overlap between the council tax definitions and the HB and CTB definitions. For example, a person who counts as a 'student' in council tax law (apart from a foreign language assistant) is usually a 'student' in HB and CTB law. However, this does not guarantee that he or she will count as a 'full-time student' (category 10 in appendix 6). (For example, there are small but growing numbers of further education students who count as full-time for council tax purposes but not for HB/CTB purposes – usually because of the nature of their studies.) Matters such as these depend on the individual circumstances of the case.

Which students can get HB and CTB?

21.24 To be eligible for HB a student must satisfy all of the following rules. To be eligible for main CTB a student need satisfy only the first rule. None of the rules affects eligibility for second adult rebate. The three rules are dealt with in turn below:

- the primary rule – which prevents full-time students from getting HB or main CTB (but not second adult rebate) unless they fall within certain groups;
- the rule preventing full-time and part-time students from getting HB on halls of residence, etc, but which is irrelevant in CTB;
- the rule preventing full-time students from getting HB (but not main CTB or second adult rebate) on their term-time accommodation if they are absent during their summer vacation.

THE PRIMARY RULE: SUMMARY

21.25 This primary rule prevents full-time students from getting HB or main CTB unless they fall within certain groups. This rule does not apply to second adult rebate. The rule works as follows:

HBR 6(1)(e), 48A
CTBR 40
Regs 9(a) and 18(a
of SI 2003 No 325

- Students aged 60 or more (or who have a partner who is) are always eligible for HB and main CTB.
- Students who are single claimants are eligible for HB and main CTB only if they are in one (or more) of the groups in table 21.1.
- Students who are lone parents are in all cases eligible for HB and main CTB.
- Couples are eligible for HB and main CTB in all cases unless both are students and neither of them is in any of the groups in table 21.1. (Information about which partner should claim is given below.)

THE PRIMARY RULE: WHICH PARTNER IN A COUPLE SHOULD CLAIM?

21.26 Table 21.2 explains which partner in a couple is eligible to claim HB and main CTB on behalf of both. In all cases where a claim may be made, it takes into account the income, capital and applicable amount relating to them both. Authorities who receive claims from the 'wrong partner' (i.e. in the cases in the second and fifth rows of the table) should return the application form with an explanation and a suggestion that the other partner should be the claimant.

HBR 6(1)(e), 48A
CTBR 40

Table 21.1: HB and main CTB eligible groups: the primary rule

(a) All students who are currently receiving income support or income-based jobseeker's allowance (but student eligibility for IS and JSA(IB) is also restricted).

(b) All part-time students.

(c) Students under 19 not in higher education.

(d) Students aged 60 or more or whose partners are.

(e) Students (couples or lone parents) who are responsible for a child or young person.

(f) Students who are responsible for a foster child.

(g) Students who qualify for a disability premium (para.12.19).

(h) Students who are disqualified from incapacity benefit.

(i) Students who have been incapable of work for 28 weeks or more.*

(j) Students whose grant assessment (if made by an English, Welsh, Scottish or Northern Ireland grant-awarding body) includes a disabled student's allowance for deafness – even if they get a grant for fees only.

(k) Students who were absent, with the consent of their educational establishment, due to illness or because of providing care for another person, and who have now ceased to be ill or providing care, and who are now not eligible for a grant or loan – but in this case only from the date of ceasing to be ill or providing care until the day before resuming the course (or, if earlier, the day their establishment agrees they can resume it) – and only up to a maximum of one year.

Note

* 'Incapable of work' means what it does for incapacity benefit purposes (para. 12.17). The student is not eligible during the first 28 weeks of incapacity for work – referred to here as a 'waiting period'.

In calculating the 'waiting period', periods of incapacity for work are added together if they are separated by gaps of eight weeks or less.

Once the waiting period is completed, the student is eligible. After a gap (i.e. a period in which the student is capable of work or is disqualified from incapacity benefit) of eight weeks or less, the student does not have to start a new waiting period: he or she becomes eligible again straightaway. But after a gap of more than eight weeks, the student is not eligible until he or she has completed a fresh waiting period.

Table 21.2: Summary: student couples: HB and main CTB

Partner A	Partner B	Who can claim HB and main CTB?	HB on two homes?
◆ Student in the eligible groups	Student in the eligible groups	Either	Yes on both, if reasonable, and if maintaining two is unavoidable
◆ Student in the eligible groups	Student not in the eligible groups	Partner A only	Only on the home occupied by partner A
◆ Student in the eligible groups	Non-student	Either	Yes on both, if reasonable, and if maintaining two is unavoidable
◆ Student not in the eligible groups	Student not in the eligible groups	Neither	Not on either
◆ Student not in the eligible groups	Non-student	Partner B only	Only on the home occupied by partner B
◆ Non-student	Non-student	Either	Student rules do not apply

The 'eligible groups' referred to in this table are those listed in table 21.1

THE PRIMARY RULE: STUDENTS WHO MAINTAIN TWO HOMES

21.27 Some students have to maintain two homes, one near their educational establishment and one elsewhere. There are special rules for students in these circumstances which apply for HB purposes only: HBR 5(3),(5)(b)

- students without partners (i.e. single claimants and lone parents) can, if they are in one of the eligible groups in table 21.1, get HB on only one home (paras. 3.26);

- for couples, the rules are given in table 21.2 and paragraph 3.28.

There are other rules about HB on two homes (para. 3.6) which apply in addition to these. For CTB there are no special rules for students maintaining two homes.

HALLS OF RESIDENCE, ETC

HBR 46, 50 **21.28** In addition to the previous rules, students (whether full-time or part-time, and including couples whether one or both are students) are not eligible for HB on halls of residence or any other accommodation where the rent is payable to the educational establishment they attend. This rule only applies in the period of study (para. 21.21), so such students are eligible for HB during their summer vacation (if they have one).

21.29 This rule applies to any accommodation which the establishment owns, leases under a lease granted for more than 21 years, or rents from another educational establishment or an education authority. It does not apply (i.e. the students are eligible for HB) if the establishment itself rents accommodation on a temporary basis from a council, housing association or private landlord and then sublets it to its students – unless it has arranged this in order to take advantage of the HB scheme.

21.30 There is no equivalent rule in CTB. This is because halls of residence are exempt from council tax (para. 9.11).

ABSENCE DURING THE SUMMER VACATION

HBR 48 **21.31** Finally, full-time students are not eligible for HB on their term-time accommodation if they are absent from it during the summer vacation. The rule does not apply unless the student is absent for at least one Sunday/Monday midnight. Once the rule applies, it continues to apply (but only during the summer vacation) until the end of the benefit week in which the student returns to the accommodation. (This is because of the ordinary rules about start of entitlement to HB: chapter 5.) This rule never applies to part-time students, and for couples it applies only if both are full-time students.

21.32 Furthermore the rule applies only if the student's main purpose in occupying the accommodation during his or her period of study is to facilitate attendance on the course. Authorities should take into account any other relevant factor in reaching a decision. For example, if the student lived in the accommodation before starting the course, or moved to the area to be near relatives, or is a council or housing association tenant, it is unlikely that the main purpose of occupying the home is to attend the course.

21.33 There is no equivalent rule in CTB. There may therefore be rare cases in which a student is eligible only for CTB during a period of absence from his or her term-time accommodation.

TERMLY PAYMENT OF HB

21.34 The authority may pay a student's HB once a term. However, if the student is entitled to more than £2.00 HB per week, he or she can insist on being paid under the normal rules about frequency of payment (paras. 16.21-25). This rule applies to full-time and part-time students, and to couples where either or both are students. In practice it is never used. HBR 90(5)

Assessing HB and main CTB for students

STUDENTS OR PARTNERS AGED 60+

21.35 In the case of a student who is aged 60 or more, or a student whose partner is aged 60 or more, all student income (grants, loans, hardship funds, etc) is disregarded in the assessment of HB and main CTB. (Such students are always eligible for HB and main CTB: para. 21.25.) HBR 60+ 25(1) CTBR 160+ 15(1)

OTHER STUDENTS

21.36 For any other student who is eligible (paras. 21.24-33) there are special rules about the assessment of student loans as income and about how grant and other student income is assessed for HB and main CTB purposes. This chapter describes these.

Student loan income

WHO CAN GET A STUDENT LOAN?

21.37 With the exceptions mentioned in the following paragraph, all full-time UK students in higher education are eligible to apply for a student loan. Parents, spouses and students themselves may, depending on the circumstances, be assessed as having to make a contribution to a student loan.

21.38 Students undertaking nursing and midwifery diploma courses (para. 21.10) are never eligible for a student loan; and the following are not normally eligible for a student loan:

- part-time students;
- postgraduates (except that students studying for a Postgraduate Certificate of Education (PGCE) are eligible for a student loan);
- students aged 50 or more.

The situation is complex in these three cases, and it is advisable for an authority to enquire of the student himself or herself as to whether he or she can get a student loan, and to seek supporting documentation as appropriate.

AMOUNTS

21.39 In the 2003-04 academic year, for students living away from home, the maximum student loan is shown in table 21.3. The figures for NHS-funded students are lower (and may be found in DWP circular HB/CTB A34/2003).

ASSESSMENT

HBR 57A CTBR 47 **21.40** In calculating HB and main CTB, all students who are eligible to apply for a student loan are treated as receiving one at the maximum level applicable to them (as shown in table 21.3) if they 'could acquire [a student loan] in respect of that year by taking reasonable steps to do so'. This is done regardless of whether they actually apply for a student loan and/or actually receive one. In the case of a couple this means taking up to two student loans into account as appropriate.

HBR 46, 53, 57A CTBR 38, 43, 47 **21.41** The student loan is then assessed for HB and main CTB purposes as shown in table 21.3 (and an example also follows). Table 21.3 covers all the main types of student course. Further variations are given in paragraphs 21.54 onwards, covering students who fall within the 'old rules', courses that start other than in autumn and students who leave part way through their course.

HBR 58(1), 58A CTBR 48, 48A **21.42** If a student loan is assessed on the assumption that the student, or his or her partner, will make a contribution, the amount of that contribution is disregarded from the student's or partner's other income. (There may also be circumstances in which a parent who makes a contribution can have that amount disregarded in the assessment of his or her own HB and main CTB: para. 13.120.)

REPAYING A STUDENT LOAN

R sch 4 para. 10A CTBR sch 4 para. 10A **21.43** If someone else repays a former student's student loan, that payment (whether made to the student or direct to the Student Loans Company) is disregarded as that student's income. This includes DfES payments under the 'Teacher Repayment Loan Scheme' – and any other such payments. However, when a student himself or herself repays a student loan this is not disregarded from his or her other income for HB/CTB purposes.

Student grant income

HBR 53(1) CTBR 42(1) **21.44** The rules for assessing grant income apply to any kind of educational grant, award, scholarship, studentship, exhibition, allowance or bursary, whether paid by an education authority or anyone else. In the 2003-04 academic year, the main grant figures for education authority grants may be found in DWP circular HB/CTB A34/2003.

ASSESSMENT

21.45 Grant income is assessed for HB and main CTB purposes as shown in table 21.4.

HBR 46,53,57,57A
CTBR 38,42,46,47

21.46 If a student's grant is assessed on the assumption that the student, or his or her partner, will make a contribution, the amount of that contribution is disregarded from the student's or partner's other income. (Similarly, a parent who makes a contribution has that amount disregarded in the assessment of his or her own HB and main CTB: para. 13.120.)

HBR 58(1), 58A
CTBR 48, 48A

Other income

ACCESS FUND PAYMENTS OR HARDSHIP FUND PAYMENTS

21.47 'Access fund payments' (also known as 'hardship fund payments') are administered by educational establishments, who may make payments to:

HBR 46(1)
CTBR 38(1)

- students who fall within the student loan scheme (para. 21.37);
- postgraduates (of all kinds); and
- students aged 19 or more in further education.

The rules about access fund payments apply identically to payments from the Welsh Assembly's financial contingency funds.

21.48 Access fund payments are treated as follows:

HBR 57B, 59(2),(
HBRGB sch 4 para
NIHBR sch 4 para
CTBR 47A, 49(2),
sch 4 para 34

- if they meet costs which are not met through a grant, but would be disregarded if they were met through a grant (as in table 21.4), they are disregarded in full;
- any other regular payments towards certain necessities (defined below) are:
  - disregarded in full as income if they are made before the student's course begins and are made in anticipation of the person becoming a student;
  - disregarded in full as income if they are made on or after 1st September (or the first day of the course if later) to tide a student over till receipt of his or her student loan;
  - in any other case, treated as income (averaged over the period they cover), then £20 per week is disregarded (subject to the over-riding £20.00 limit on certain disregards (para. 13.148).
- regular payments towards any other amount are completely disregarded;
- single lump sum payments are treated as capital; but if they are for certain necessities (defined below), the capital is disregarded for 52 weeks from the date of payment.

Table 21.3: Student loans: 2003-04 academic year

AMOUNTS	Final year	Other years	Per extra week
Courses in London:	£4,275	£4,930	£92
Courses outside London:	£3,470	£4,000	£71

Note: Figures are for English, Welsh and Scottish students living away from home in the 2003-04 academic year. In each case, they are the maximum amount a student could obtain. The figures do not apply to NHS-funded courses or to nursing and midwifery diploma students. Figures are taken from DWP circular HB/CTB A34/2003.

TREATMENT FOR HB/MAIN CTB PURPOSES

(a) Take the whole amount into account as income (even though it is in fact a loan). Include any amount from extra weeks. Treat any parental or spouse's (or student's own) assumed contribution to it as being received (even if not actually paid).

(b) Disregard £605 in all cases. This is a standard amount including £270 towards travel and £335 towards books and equipment.

(c) Average the resulting amount over the period described below.

(d) Then disregard £10 from the weekly figure (in the case of a couple, disregard £10 from each one's weekly figure), subject to the over-riding £20.00 limit on certain disregards (para. 13.109).

PERIOD OVER WHICH THE LOAN IS AVERAGED

General rule

Average over the period from the first Monday in September to the last Sunday in June. (In 2003-04 this is 43 weeks: 1.9.03 to 27.6.04. In 2004-05 it will also be 43 weeks: 6.9.04 to 26.6.05.)

Exceptions

First years only: If the course begins after the first Monday in September, still average over the period described above, but then ignore it as income for the week(s) before the course begins.

Final years and one-year courses only: Average over the period from the first Monday in September to the last Sunday in the course.

All years (but likely to apply only in Scotland): If any year of the course starts before the first Monday in September, average over the period from the first Monday in the course to the last Sunday in June (or, in final year and one-year courses, the last Sunday in the course).

Further exceptions and special cases are given in paras. 21.54 onwards.

Example: A student loan

In the 2003-04 academic year, a student in his second year of a degree course in Wales could get a student loan of £4,000. (He is not in receipt of a grant of any kind.) His wife is not a student and has claimed HB and CTB for them both. His student loan is assessed as follows in the assessment of his wife's HB/CTB claim.

Whether or not he applies for or receives it, he is treated as receiving it and it is assessed as follows (see also table 21.3):

(a) Treat the whole £4,000 as income (even though it is in fact a loan).

(b) Disregard £605 for books and equipment and travel, leaving £3,395.

(c) Average this over the 43 weeks from 1.9.03 to 27.6.04, which is £78.95 per week.

(d) Disregard £10, which gives £68.95 per week.

So this student has student loan income of £68.95 per week from 1.9.03 to 27.6.04. This is the case even if his second year did not start until a date in October 2003. (But if he had been a first year, the £68.95 per week would have been ignored as income until the first Monday in his first year.)

Table 21.4: Student grants: 2003-04 academic year

TREATMENT FOR HB/MAIN CTB PURPOSES

(a) Treat any parental or spouse's (or student's own) assumed contribution to it as being received (even if not actually paid).

(b) No standard disregard is made for travel or for books and equipment – unless the student neither receives nor is treated as receiving a student loan, in which case disregard £605. (But see also step (c).)

(c) Disregard any amount included in the grant for:

- all additions because the student has a disability;
- all additions for books and equipment and/or travel (in addition to the standard £605 if appropriate);
- child care additions;
- the allowance for lone parents with formal childcare costs;
- the DES parents learning allowance;
- the National Assembly for Wales' learning grant;
- tuition or examination fees;
- expenses for term-time residential study;
- two homes grant;
- additions for anyone outside the UK so long as the student's applicable amount does not include an amount for that person.

(d) Average the resulting amount over the period described below.

PERIOD OVER WHICH THE GRANT IS AVERAGED

Awards for (adult or child) dependant(s) from an education authority or government department

Average over the same period as the student loan (table 21.3: the general rule and exceptions all apply).

Grants for day-to-day maintenance and any other amount (other than the disregarded amounts)

If it is attributable to the student's period of study (para. 21.21): Average over the period from the first Monday to the last Sunday in that period of study omitting, for sandwich students, any benefit weeks falling wholly or partly within the period of work experience.

If it is attributable to any other period: Average over the period from the first Monday to the last Sunday in that period.

Exceptions

Nursing and midwifery diploma students: They get a bursary towards their maintenance (and cannot get a student loan). Their bursary (after any appropriate disregards) is averaged over the full calendar year (52/53 weeks).

NHS-funded students on degree courses: They get a bursary towards their maintenance (and can get a student loan at a lower rate than other students). Their bursary (after any appropriate disregards) is averaged over the full calendar year (52/53 weeks) – and their loan is dealt with as in table 21.3.

Students to whom the old rules apply: See paragraph 21.54.

21.49 The 'certain necessities' mentioned above are food, ordinary clothing and footwear, household fuel, eligible rent (apart from any amount attributable to non-dependant deductions), council tax or water charges – of the claimant or any member of the family.

PRIVATE LOANS

21.50 Regularly paid loans may conceivably be income (para. 13.11) in which case the authority would have to consider whether or not they were charitable or voluntary payments (paras. 13.113-114).

COVENANT INCOME

HBR 46, 54-56 CTBR 38, 43-45 **21.51** In the past, many parents paid their student son or daughter income through a covenant (a legally enforceable promise to pay money). The tax advantages of creating a covenant ended on 15th March 1988, and so such covenants probably do not exist. There remain, however, special rules for assessing any covenant paid to a full-time student by his or her parent. The details are in GM paragraphs C5.311-330.

OTHER INCOME

21.52 If a full-time or part-time student receives earned or unearned income other than (or as well as) grant or covenant income or a student loan, the ordinary earned and unearned income disregards apply to it (chapters 13-15).

THE EXTRA STUDENT INCOME DISREGARD

HBR 57 CTBR 46 **21.53** In addition to the above points, there is a further disregard for student expenditure, which works as follows. If the student has loan or grant income, certain amounts are disregard from it, as shown in tables 21.3 and 21.4. If the student necessarily spends more on those items than the amounts indicated in the tables, the excess is disregarded from his or her other income (as illustrated in the example). This important disregard is often overlooked: students are advised to check that it has been applied properly.

Example: The extra student income disregard

A student receives a student loan. In the assessment of the loan for HB/CTB purposes, £335 is disregarded towards books and equipment and £270 towards travel. She is not in receipt of any grant for travel, but can satisfy the authority that her actual travel costs for the year will be £700 (£430 more). She uses money from a part-time job to pay for this.

The additional £430 per year for travel is disregarded in assessing her income from her part-time job (as well as any other earned income disregards which may apply: paras. 14.11-19). There is no particular rule for which weeks to allow this in. Since her loan income has to be averaged over 43 weeks, it may be fair to average this £430 over those 43 weeks.

Special cases

VARIATIONS FOR STUDENTS WHO FALL WITHIN THE 'OLD RULES'

21.54 A student falls within the 'old rules' if he or she:

- started his or her course of study before 1st September 1998 (1st August 1998 in Scotland); or
- started his or her course of study before 1st September 1999 (1st August 1999 in Scotland) but only if he or she had the formal agreement (usually this means written agreement) of the educational establishment concerned to defer starting a course from the previous year.

So, during this 2003-04 academic year, this means a seventh (or later) year student; or a sixth year who deferred starting his or her course for a year.

21.55 Most undergraduate students who fall within the old rules can get a student loan (but at a rate lower than the figures given in table 21.3) plus some government grant towards their maintenance (plus additions for specific needs such as for a disability or for dependants).

21.56 With two variations, all the student rules in this chapter apply to students who fall within the old rules. The two variations are to do with how grants are assessed (table 21.4) and are as follows: HBR 53(3A), 60 CTBR 42(4A), 50

- awards or additions for (adult or child) dependants are averaged over the full calendar year (52/53 weeks); and
- once grant income has been assessed, any change in the standard maintenance grant occurring during the summer vacation is ignored until the end of the summer vacation. The standard maintenance grant is up-rated with effect from 1st September each year. So for a student whose autumn term begins on a date in October, the change is ignored until then.

COURSES THAT START OTHER THAN IN AUTUMN

21.57 The following rules cater for courses that do not start in the autumn. They use the concepts 'academic year' (as defined in para. 21.61) and 'quarter' (as defined in para. 21.60) in ways that do not always match day-to-day expectations. HBR 46(1), 57A(CTBR 38(1), 47(

21.58 For students whose 'academic year' (para. 21.61) begins on 1st September, their loan is averaged over the benefit weeks falling wholly within the ten months from 1st September to 30th June, both dates inclusive (as described in table 21.3).

21.59 But for students whose 'academic year' (para. 21.61) begins on 1st January, 1st April or 1st July, their loan is averaged over the benefit weeks falling wholly within:

- the whole academic year beginning on that date;
- but excluding the whole of the 'quarter' (para. 21.60) in which, 'in the opinion of the Secretary of State', the longest of any vacation is taken.

DEFINITION OF 'QUARTER'

HBR 57A(2)(aa)
CTBR 47(2)(aa)

21.60 For the purposes of the above rules, the following (despite the fact that they are of different lengths in two cases) are the four 'quarters':

- 1st January to 31st March (3 months);
- 1st April to 30th June (3 months);
- 1st July to 31st August (2 months);
- 1st September to 31st December (4 months).

DEFINITION OF 'ACADEMIC YEAR'

HBR 46(1)
CTBR 38(1)

21.61 For the purposes of the above rules, 'academic year' means the twelve months beginning on:

- 1st January if the course begins in the winter;
- 1st April if the course begins in the spring;
- 1st July if the course begins in the summer – but see below for an exception;
- 1st September if the course begins in the autumn.

But if a student is required to begin attending a course during August or September and continue attending through the autumn, his or her academic year is the one beginning on 1st September.

21.62 The seasons are not in turn defined in the law, but the following is believed to be correct (indeed the last three lines in para. 21.61 would not work in law if the following were wrong):

- winter starts on the winter solstice in late December;
- spring starts on the spring equinox in late March;
- summer starts on the summer solstice in late June;
- autumn starts on the autumn equinox in late September.

LOAN INCOME AND DEPENDANT INCOME OF STUDENTS LEAVING PART WAY THROUGH A COURSE

21.63 A student who leaves part way through his or her course is treated for HB and main CTB purposes as having income from a student loan or dependant grant – but only if a payment of a student loan and/or a dependant grant has actually been paid to the student in the 'academic year' (defined as in para. 21.61) in question. In such cases there are four steps: HBR 33(3A)-(3C) CTBR 24(4A)-(4C)

(a) Take the total amount of student loan and/or grant for dependants which he or she would have received if he or she had remained till the end of the academic term in which he or she left. Then deduct the standard amount for travel and books and equipment (£592). In the law (and guidance), the result is 'A'.

(b) Calculate how much student loan income and/or dependant grant has been taken into account already in that academic year (up to – and including – the benefit week in which he or she left) under the normal rules (table 21.3) but pretending that there was no £10 disregard. In the law (and guidance), the result is 'B x C' (B being the number of weeks and C the weekly amount in those weeks).

(c) Subtract B x C from A. Average the result over the benefit weeks from (and including) the benefit week following that in which the student abandoned or was dismissed from the course up to (and including) the final benefit week in the last 'quarter' (as defined in para. 21.60) for which the student loan and/or dependant grant was paid to that student. In the law (and guidance) the number of weeks in this period is 'D'; and the amount taken into account as income in each of those weeks is the formula:

$$\frac{A - (B \times C)}{D}$$

(d) This counts as the ex-student's income only from (and including) the benefit week following that in which the student abandoned or was dismissed from the course up to (and including) the final benefit week in the last 'quarter' (para. 21.60) for which a student loan or a grant for dependants was paid to the student.

Example: Student income assessment: 2003-04 academic year

INFORMATION

Student claimant	Single woman, student aged 20, lives alone. She is eligible for HB because of her disability (table 21.1)
Course	2003-04, outside London, first year of course, full-time, undergraduate.
Period of study	Tuesday 7.10.03 to Thursday 18.6.04 inclusive.
Student loan	She receives £4,000 (the maximum amount available in her case).
Grant	She gets a disabled student's grant only.
Other income	Net earnings (after all appropriate disregards) of £50 per week at all material times; no capital.

INCOME FROM LOAN

She qualifies for a student loan, and is treated as receiving one at the maximum level available – which in her case is £4,000. (In fact she actually receives this amount.)

Disregard £605 for books and equipment and travel, leaving £3,395.

Average this (£3,395) over the 43 weeks from 1.9.03 to 27.6.04, giving £78.95 per week.

Disregard £10.00, giving £68.95 per week.

INCOME FROM GRANT

Her disabled student's grant is disregarded completely.

HB: ASSESSED INCOME* AND ELIGIBLE RENT

Monday 1.9.03 to Sunday 12.10.03: She is not yet a student and the income from her loan is ignored. So her assessed income is £50.00 per week (from the job alone).

Monday 13.10.03 to Sunday 27.6.04: Her assessed income is £118.95 per week which is £68.95 from the loan and £50 from earnings and her eligible rent is £60.00 per week

Monday 28.6.04 to Sunday 5.9.04: This is outside the period over which her loan is averaged. So her assessed income is £50.00 (from the job alone) and her eligible rent is £60 per week.

Monday 6.9.04 to Sunday 26.6.05: Figures not yet available, but this is the 42-week period over which her loan is averaged.

* Not applicable in CTB because her home is exempt.

22 Discretionary housing payments, local schemes, pilots and pathfinders

22.1 This chapter sets out the various local variations to the HB and CTB schemes permitted by the law, including government pilot schemes that from time to time are introduced to test future reforms. Although the sections on 'pathfinders' describe what is in effect an entirely separate housing benefit scheme within the areas in which they operate, they may be of interest to the general reader, professional adviser or benefit administrator as they are likely to form the basis on which the HB scheme will operate in the future. This chapter covers:

- discretionary housing payments;
- 'local schemes', that is authorities' powers in Great Britain to operate schemes in their areas which disregard the whole of any war pension as income;
- government powers to vary the HB and CTB schemes locally;
- the HB 'pathfinders' operating in nine local authority areas in Great Britain in which the eligible rent is based on standard flat rate allowance – known as the local housing allowance.

Discretionary housing payments

SI 2001 No. 1167
SI 2001 No. 2340
SR 2001 No. 216
NISR 2001 No. 80

22.2 The Child Support, Pensions and Social Security Act 2000 (and the Child Support, Pensions and Social Security (Northern Ireland) Act 2000) introduced a scheme of discretionary housing payments with effect from 2nd July 2001.

22.3 These payments are an independent scheme administered by authorities which also administer HB/CTB. However, they are not a form of HB or CTB, and so the HB/CTB appeals procedures (chapter 19) do not apply.

22.4 Discretionary housing payments (DHPs) are available to claimants who:

- in Great Britain are entitled to HB or CTB, or in Northern Ireland are entitled to HB in respect of their rent which has been restricted under the New Scheme rules (paras. 10.33 onwards); and
- in Great Britain and Northern Ireland, 'appear to [the] authority to require some further financial assistance... in order to meet housing costs'.

22.5 Discretionary housing payments cannot be awarded towards any of the following:

- ineligible service or support charges (chapter 10);
- in Great Britain any rent liability if the claimant is entitled to CTB only;
- in Great Britain any council tax liability if the claimant is entitled to HB only or to second adult rebate only;
- in Northern Ireland any liability to meet rates;
- increases to cover rent arrears which are not eligible for HB (para. 11.30);
- reductions in any benefit as a result of Jobseeker's sanctions, Child Support sanctions or sanctions following certain benefit related offences (para. 7.48);
- HB/CTB that is suspended (paras. 16.43-54).

22.6 Furthermore the total weekly amount of the award, taken together with the claimant's award of HB or CTB, must not exceed:

- the claimant's eligible rent calculated as though he or she were a council tenant (paras. 10.21-24);
- the claimant's liability for council tax.

22.7 So, for example, DHPs could be used for such things as the following:

- to make up the shortfall in eligible rent in a 'New Scheme' case caused by the rent officer's/ NIHE figures being used;
- in Great Britain only to make up the shortfall in eligible rent in an 'Old Scheme' case where the authority considers there is no other way of doing this;
- to make up for the effect of the 65 per cent and 20 per cent tapers used in the calculation of benefit;
- to make up for the effect of non-dependant deductions.

22.8 Unlike the pre-July 2001 exceptional hardship and exceptional circumstances payments, there is no requirement in the law for the claimant's family circumstances to be 'exceptional' – nor does there to have to be 'hardship'. The payments are, however, entirely discretionary and authorities vary in their willingness to award them. While it may well be worth enquiring about and/or claiming a DHP, no claimant should rely on his or her authority actually awarding him or her payment in the above (or any other) circumstances.

22.9 The DWP partially subsidises DHPs and its predecessor the DSS issued guidance to authorities in a circular letter (not part of the normal HB/CTB series), 'Discretionary Housing Payments', 16.3.01, which can be viewed on-line at *www.dwp.gov.uk/housingbenefit/manuals/dhpguide/pdf*

Local schemes

AA 138(8)-(10), 139(6)-(8) HBR 33(2A) CTBR 24(2A) SI 1996 No. 677 SI 1996 No. 678

22.10 The HB and CTB schemes as described in this guide are those which authorities are required by law to operate. However, authorities in England, Wales and Scotland (not Northern Ireland) may grant extra benefit under a 'local scheme' – that is, an improved version of the scheme. The only improvement authorities are permitted, however, is to disregard war disablement pensions, war widows' pensions and war widowers' pensions, in whole or part, over and above the fixed disregard required by law (usually £10: para. 13.28). The vast majority, but not all, authorities have decided to do this and in 2003 only 16 authorities in England were not taking advantage of the higher disregard (Ivan Caplin MP, Minister for Veterans, 15/07/2003). The decision to run a local scheme is made by a resolution of the authority. A separate resolution is required for HB and CTB. The question of whether or not an authority should run a local scheme is not open to the appeal procedure.

SI 1995 No. 2792

22.11 For technical reasons, part of the cost of a local scheme is subject to a 'permitted total' of 0.7 per cent of the authority's HB/CTB expenditure. This should have no effect on an authority's power to operate a local scheme (circular HB/CTB A31/95).

Miscellaneous government powers to vary HB and CTB schemes locally

CBA 175(6) NICBA 171(6)

22.12 Unlike other welfare benefits the Government possesses wide powers to vary both the HB and CTB regulations to make different rules for different areas. This power has been exercised to set the rules for local housing allowance pathfinders.

22.13 Powers exist in the Jobseekers Act 1995 (s29) to run pilot schemes. These powers allow the government to vary the rules for HB, CTB, IS and JSA within a particular area or to a particular class of claimant provided it will test whether the change will improve work incentives. However, these schemes have a maximum life of one year and do not permit variation of the maximum eligible rent or council tax. There are no such schemes currently in place.

22.14 From time to time specific legislation is passed to facilitate a new policy initiative which cannot be accommodated by existing powers. For example, s79 of the Welfare Reform and Pensions Act 1999 allowed payments to be made to HB claimants who trade down if their home was larger than they require. A small scheme was piloted but wound up after it proved ineffective.

Local housing allowance pathfinders

22.15 In November 2002 the government published its proposals for major reform of the housing benefit scheme in its paper *Building choice and responsibility: a radical agenda for housing benefit* (DWP 2002). The intention was to test these reforms, initially to tenants of private landlords only (para. 22.22), in a number of local authority areas. These areas were to be known as 'pathfinders'. The reform package consisted of three main elements:

- instead of HB being calculated on the actual rent subject to a cap (i.e. the eligible rent) as at present, the eligible rent will be based on a flat rate allowance determined by the rent officer. A set of allowances will be fixed for each category of dwelling (within a defined geographic area). Each category of dwelling will be appropriate to a particular household size and the rates for each category of dwelling will be the eligible rent for all claims within that area. This rate will be payable even if the claimant's actual rent is lower;
- instead of the practice at present where the majority of payments of HB are made direct to the landlord, payment of HB in the pathfinder areas will, except in exceptional circumstances, normally be paid to the claimant;
- claims are no longer referred to the rent officer for individual assessment. Instead the rent officer will publish a set of allowances for each category of dwelling size of household within a defined 'broad rental market area'. There may be more than one broad rental market area in or partly in each authority area.

22.16 In authorities where these reforms are to be piloted, transitional protection will apply so that no claimant will receive less HB than they were entitled to immediately before the change in the rules. If the new allowance is more generous then they will benefit from the increase as soon as their claim is revised.

LEGISLATIVE AUTHORITY AND REFERENCES

22.17 The power to make changes to the HB regulations for pathfinder schemes are a pre-existing feature of the Benefit Acts (para. 22.12) as are the powers to change the rent officer rules (s122 of the Housing Act 1996). Under these powers the rules for the pathfinder authorities and rent officers in pathfinder areas are made by the Housing Benefit (General) (Local Housing Allowance) Amendment Regulations 2003 (SI 2003 No.2399) and the Rent Officers (Housing Benefit Functions) (Local Housing Allowance) Amendment Order 2003 (SI 2003 No. 2398). For the most part these regulations work by incorporating changes within the main regulations for non-pathfinder authorities. Therefore throughout the remainder of this chapter the majority of the marginal references are expressed as such. Occasionally references are made to the amendment regulations themselves. These relate to purely transitional provisions which have not been incorporated within main regulations (e.g. para. 22.50).

LOCAL HOUSING ALLOWANCE AND MAXIMUM RENT STANDARD LOCAL RATE

22.18 Strictly speaking, the term 'local housing allowance' (LHA) is a determination made by the rent officer in a pathfinder area instead of the determinations made in non-pathfinder authorities (paras. 6.16-6.34), whereas the 'maximum rent (standard local rate)' is the equivalent in the pathfinder area to the 'maximum rent' (paras 10.33-35). In a non-pathfinder authority the maximum rent is the lowest of the various rent officer determinations, whereas in a pathfinder authority the 'maximum rent (standard local rate)' will simply be the same as the appropriate (published) local housing allowance for the area in which the claimant's home is situated. Therefore in a pathfinder area the local housing allowance will be, subject to any transitional protection that may apply, identical to the figure used by the authority to calculate the eligible rent. In the remainder of this chapter the term local housing allowance (LHA) is used interchangeably to refer to both the LHA and the maximum (standard local rate).

22.19 The appropriate local housing allowance determination will depend on the area in which the claimant's home is situated and the number of occupiers in their household (para. 6.25). The area will be a 'broad rental market area' determined by the rent officer (paras. 22.20 and 22.48).

22.20 The broad rental market will replace 'locality, vicinity and neighbourhood' (paras. 6.18-21 and 22.48) and unlike those concepts, which are centred on the claimant's dwelling, will be demarcated by a boundary line which can be drawn on a map (but which may change over time as markets change). In most other respects, it works in a similar way to the local reference rent (paras. 6.28-30) and is the mid-point of the range of rents for the whole of the broad rental market area for dwellings with that number of rooms, excluding any exceptionally high or low rents. For further details about the assumptions on which each determination is made, see paragraph 22.48.

EXTENT OF THE PATHFINDERS

HBR 11A(1)(a),(b), sch 8

22.21 There are nine local authorities in Great Britain participating as pathfinder authorities. Where the authority takes part, the HB regulations are modified for those types of tenancy which come within the scope of the scheme (para. 22.22). Each pathfinder scheme is expected to run for two years. There are two basic types of pathfinder scheme, 'phased' or 'big bang' (these are not terms used in the regulations but are the accepted jargon in the pathfinder areas). In 'big bang' authorities the whole of the qualifying caseload is converted to the new scheme on the date the pathfinder starts. In 'phased' authorities all new claims go straight to the local housing allowance but existing claims are converted as and when the claim comes up for renewal. Table 22.1 sets out the nine pathfinder authorities, their start date and whether they are phased or big bang.

Table 22.1: Pathfinder authorities and start dates

Authority	Start date	Pathfinder type
Blackpool	17 November 2003	Phased
Brighton and Hove	2 February 2004	Big Bang
Conwy	9 February 2004	Phased
Coventry	12 January 2004	Phased
Edinburgh	9 February 2004	Big Bang
Leeds	9 February 2004	Phased
Lewisham	1 December 2003	Phased
North East Lincolnshire	9 February 2004	Big Bang
Teignbridge	12 January 2004	Phased

22.22 The pathfinder scheme only applies to certain types of letting within a pathfinder authority area, broadly lettings by private sector landlords. Within a pathfinder authority, the scheme will apply to any letting which is not listed in the following exceptions: HBR 11A(2),(6), 12A(1)(a),(b)

- the tenant is a council tenant paid by rent rebate (paras. 10.21-22);
- the 'rent' payable includes a mooring or site charge for a houseboat, caravan or mobile home;
- the landlord is a registered social landlord (para. 10.18) or a housing action trust;
- the claimant occupies 'exempt accommodation' (para. 10.14);
- the tenancy is let on a pre-1989 agreement (para. 10.67);
- the claim relates to rent payable in a hostel (para. 6.10), bail hostel or probation hostel (para. 10.72);

- the rent officer has determined that a substantial part of the rent is attributable to board and attendance (paras. 22.49-52).

22.23 If any of these exceptions apply then the claim will be treated in the same way as if it was not in a pathfinder authority (chapter 10 and paras. 16.48-42). A special procedure applies if a substantial part of the rent is attributable to board and attendance (paras. 22.49-52).

Eligible rent in pathfinder authorities

LOCAL HOUSING ALLOWANCE CASES

HBR 10(3A), 11A(3),(8)

22.24 Except where the claimant is entitled to the protected rate because it is higher (paras. 22.26-34), the eligible rent in the pathfinder area will be the same as the rate for the appropriate local housing allowance (para. 22.41). In these cases the eligible rent is technically known as the maximum rent (standard local rate).

22.25 Unlike non-pathfinder claims the maximum rent (standard local rate) cannot be reduced to take account of the fact that:

- the actual rent the claimant pays to the landlord is lower (paras. 10.5, 10.21, 10.33, 10.51);
- the claimant is a joint tenant (10.6);
- part of the property is used for business purposes (10.108);
- the rent includes an amount for ineligible services such as fuel or water (para. 10.75 onwards) because the rent officer is bound to exclude these in their determination of the local housing allowance (para. 22.48);
- the authority considers the rent officer's determination to be unreasonable and decides to restrict the rent still further (paras 10.48-49).

TRANSITIONALLY PROTECTED CASES

22.26 There are three types of protected claims these are:

- Existing claimants who were in receipt of housing benefit at the start of the pathfinder. These types of claim, except where they qualify for one of the other types of protection (para. 22.29), can be protected for an unlimited period; however their protection will take the form of their eligible rent being frozen;
- Claimants who have had a death in their household can be protected for up to 12 months;
- Claimants who were previously paying their own rent who have not claimed HB in the previous year can be protected for the first 13 weeks of their claim.

PROTECTION FOR EXISTING CLAIMANTS

22.27 Existing claimants will be protected if: HBR 10(3B),(3C)

- they have been continuously in receipt of housing benefit since the start of the pathfinder (table 22.1); and
- their eligible rent which applied immediately prior to the first revision of their claim following the start of the pathfinder is higher than the maximum rent (standard local rate) (para. 22.24) which applies in their case.

In such circumstances their eligible rent is frozen until their local housing allowance is equal to or higher than their protected rate. Except where protection is lost or the circumstances in para. 22.29 apply, the eligible rent continues at this frozen rate indefinitely. All protection is lost as soon as the claimant moves home or loses entitlement to HB altogether. There are no linking rules which ignore short breaks in entitlement or because the claimant takes part in a welfare to work scheme.

22.28 The frozen rate includes any eligible rent calculated as an 'Old Scheme' case (paras. 10.51-10.66) because the claimant has been on HB since January 1996, but not as a result of the claimant living in 'exempt accommodation' (para. 10.14) as these cases are not subject to the local housing allowance (para. 22.17).

22.29 There are two exceptions to the frozen rate being applied indefinitely: HBR 10(3C)(b),(c), (3I),(b),(c)

- where an existing claimant first claimed HB following the death of a household member, their eligible rent will be based on their actual rent for the first 12 months of their claim (para. 22.30); or
- they are an existing claimant whose eligible rent is based on their actual rent during the first 13 weeks of their claim (para. 22.33).

In both cases, their eligible rent continues for the remainder of their 12 month or 13 week protection period as appropriate. At the end of this period their eligible rent reverts to what it would have been without any protection except where a relevant change of circumstance has occurred (para. 22.39) which has triggered a higher maximum rent (standard) local rate than the one that applied at the beginning of the protection period.

PROTECTION FOR HOUSEHOLDS FOLLOWING A DEATH

22.30 Except where the claimant's maximum rent (standard local rate) is equal to or higher than the claimant's actual rent, then the eligible rent will be protected following the death of a household member. The circumstances when these rules apply are identical to those in paras. 10.41-44. The protected rate will be their actual rent, subject only to a reduction if the property is partly used for business (para. 10.108) or if the authority applies a restriction using its general powers (para. 10.48). HBR 10(3D),(3I)(d

22.31 The protected rate will continue for 12 months from the date of the death or until such time as the authority determines a local housing allowance which is greater than the protected rate. The authority can only determine a new local housing allowance if it is notified of a further relevant change of circumstances.

HBR 11A(1)(b)(iv) **22.32** A relevant change of circumstances only occurs if the circumstances in paragraph 22.39 apply or there is a further death of a household member (other than the claimant) but one which does not affect the category of dwelling (para. 22.42 and table 22.2) which applies in their case.

PROTECTION FOR HOUSEHOLDS DURING THE FIRST 13 WEEKS OF THEIR CLAIM

HBR (3F),(3G), (3I)(e),(3J) **22.33** Except where local housing allowance would be higher, where the authority is satisfied that the claimant could previously afford to pay their rent, then their eligible rent is worked out in the same way as a council tenant's (para. 10.21). These rules mirror the protection in non-pathfinder authorities (paras. 10.38-40). Note that this protection only applies in the 'phased' pathfinders (para. 22.21 and table 22.1) to claims made after the pathfinder start date; this is because in the 'big bang' pathfinders all claims will be covered by the rules in paragraph 22.29.

22.34 Protection continues until the earliest of either

- the end of the 13 week protection period; or
- until a relevant change of circumstance occurs (para. 22.39) which results in a maximum rent (standard local rate) being applied which is equal to or higher than the protected rate.

At the end of the 13 week period the eligible rent will be the relevant local housing allowance that would have applied had they have not been protected, except where there has been a relevant change of circumstance during the 13 week protection period in which case the eligible rent will be equivalent to the maximum rent (standard local rate) (i.e. local housing allowance) which would have otherwise applied on the date the change occurred.

TRANSFER OF CASES IN PATHFINDER AREAS

HBR 11A(1)(a) **22.35** In big bang pathfinders (para. 22.21 and table 22.1) the entire caseload is transferred to the local housing allowance or the protected rate if higher on the pathfinder start date.

HBR 11A(1) (b)(i)-(iii),(c) SI 2003 No. 2399 Reg 14 **22.36** In phased pathfinders (para. 22.29 and table 22.1) cases are transferred to the local housing allowance or the protected rate as appropriate from the pathfinder start date on the earliest of the following dates which occurs:

- when a new or renewal claim is made;
- there has been a relevant change of circumstances which would have led to referral to the rent officer in a non-pathfinder authority (table 6.3);

- where the claimant or their partner is aged at least 60 and not in receipt of IS or JSA(IB), the date on which their claim would next be referred to the rent officer if they were not in a pathfinder area (para. 6.8) (i.e. 52 weeks after the previous referral).

22.37 In both the big bang and phased pathfinders, on transfer the eligible rent will either be equivalent to the appropriate local housing allowance that applies in their case (paras. 22.42 and table 22.2) or the 'frozen' protected rate (paras. 22.26-34) if that is higher.

LENGTH OF AWARD FOLLOWING TRANSFER TO LHA AND SUBSEQUENT AWARDS

22.38 Where the claimant's eligible rent has been based on the local housing allowance instead of the protected rate, it will continue until the claimant has a relevant change of circumstances (para. 22.39) or until a year after it was set, at which point the award will come to an end. HBR 8A

RELEVANT CHANGE OF CIRCUMSTANCES FOLLOWING LHA AWARD

22.39 Once an award based the local housing allowance has been made it will remain in force for one year unless a relevant change of circumstance has occurred. A relevant change of circumstance only occurs if: HBR 11A(1)(b)(iv)

- there has been a change in the category of dwelling which applies in determining the local housing allowance (para. 22.42);
- there has been a rent increase under a term of the tenancy which was part of the tenancy agreement when the claim was made.

22.40 The revised award or new award will be based on the appropriate local housing allowance for the claimant's household which was in force during the month in which the decision on the claim is made. It is therefore possible that the award is revised following the notification of a rent increase but that the eligible rent falls because the local housing allowance rates for that month are lower than the rates that applied when the original claim was made.

Rate of local housing allowance

22.41 In all cases the eligible rent will be equivalent to the appropriate local housing allowance set by the rent officer for the month in which the award is made. Technically this is known as the maximum rent (standard local rate) – but this is misleading because it is also the minimum eligible rent. The appropriate local housing allowance will be determined by the 'broad rental market area' in which the property is situated (paras. 22.20 and 22.48) and the appropriate category of dwelling (by number of rooms) which applies to the claimant's household (para. 22.42 and table 22.2).

Table 22.2: Appropriate category of dwelling and rate of LHA for each household type within a broad rental market area

Household type	Category of Dwelling/ Rate of LHA
(a) single claimant (para. 4.4) aged under 25 except where: ◆ a non-dependant lives with them; ◆ they are paid the severe disability premium; ◆ they are a care leaver aged under 22 (para. 6.12 cases (d) and (e)).	Shared room rate
(b) couple or single claimant aged at least 25 or single claimant aged under 25 who falls within the exceptions above and the dwelling in which they live does not provide them with either: ◆ the exclusive use of at least two living rooms; or ◆ exclusive use of one room, a bathroom, toilet and either a kitchen or cooking facilities.	Shared room rate
(c) Any couple or single person to whom (b) applies but who lives in accommodation which provides them with the exclusive use of at least two rooms; or the exclusive use of one room, a bathroom, toilet and either a kitchen or cooking facilities.	Two room rate
(d) Any household entitled to three living rooms (including bedrooms) as defined by the size criteria (table 6.5).	Three room rate
(e) Any household entitled to four living rooms (including bedrooms) as defined by the size criteria (table 6.5).	Four room rate
(f) Any household entitled to five living rooms (including bedrooms) as defined by the size criteria (table 6.5).	Five room rate
(g) Any household entitled to six living rooms (including bedrooms) as defined by the size criteria (table 6.5).	Six room rate
(h) Any household entitled to seven or more living rooms as defined by the size criteria (table 6.5)	The appropriate rate already determined for that sized household or determined following an application to the rent officer (para. 22.46)

APPROPRIATE CATEGORY OF DWELLING FOR EACH HOUSEHOLD TYPE

22.42 The appropriate category of dwelling is determined by the rent officer size criteria (table 6.5) except where: HBR 11A(3)

a. the claimant is a 'young individual' (para. 6.12) to whom cases c, d, e and f only in paragraph 6.12 of this Guide do not apply (non-dependant, severe disability premium, care leaver);

b. the claimant is part of a couple without dependent children, or is single and aged at least 25, or is single and aged under 25 but falls within one of the four exceptions in (a) above.

In the case of (a): the category of dwelling will be the standard allowance for a room in 'shared accommodation'. In the case of (b) the category of dwelling will be the allowance for a two-roomed property except where the property in which they have chosen to live is shared accommodation (para. 22.45). A summary of the household type, appropriate category of dwelling and rate of LHA is provided in table 22.2.

COUNTING OCCUPIERS

22.43 In deciding the appropriate rate of LHA (other than the shared rate) the same rules apply as for counting the number of occupiers when applying the size criteria in a non-pathfinder authority (paras. 6.25-26 and table 6.5) except that the rules make it expressly clear that 'occupier' includes anyone who the authority 'is satisfied occupy as their home the dwelling to which the claim relates' but does not include 'any joint tenant who is not a member of the claimant's household'. HBR 11A(3)(b)(iii),(9)

RATE OF LOCAL HOUSING ALLOWANCE AND ITS PUBLICATION

22.44 The rates of the local housing allowance for each category of dwelling in a specific broad rental market area (paras. 22.20 and 22.48) are set by the rent officer each month. Each local housing allowance will apply for the month following the month in which it is set. Normally only allowances up to six roomed accommodation will be set unless the rent officer and authority agree that allowances for larger properties are regularly needed. Where the household requires accommodation of seven rooms or more and no LHA exists a special procedure applies (para. 22.46). The authority is required to take 'such steps as appropriate' to ensure that the rates of the LHA for any broad rental market area(s) in its boundary are 'brought to the attention' of potential claimants. ROO 4B(1), HBR 11B

HOUSEHOLDS NORMALLY ENTITLED TO THE TWO ROOM RATE BUT WHO LIVE IN ACCOMMODATION WHICH ONLY QUALIFIES FOR THE SHARED RATE

HBR 11A(3)(b) **22.45** A household in case (b) in paragraph 22.42 above is entitled to receive the two room rate of the local housing allowance, however if they choose to occupy certain smaller accommodation then they may not be entitled to the two room rate. The type of accommodation that will qualify them for the two room rate will be one which provides them with:

- the exclusive use of at least two living rooms; or
- the exclusive use of one living room, a bathroom and toilet and either a kitchen or cooking facilities.

In any other case they will only be entitled to the LHA rate for shared accommodation. Official DWP guidance states that accommodation will qualify the claimant for the two room rate if it is 'a one-bedroom flat or studio or other kind of self-contained accommodation' but that the accommodation will not qualify if it is 'a property where all or some of the facilities are shared' (GLHA paras. 2.40-41). Note that the descriptive terms 'shared accommodation', 'studio' and 'self-contained accommodation' are not terms which appear in the legislation. In deciding which rooms count as a living room, see paragraph 22.77.

RATE OF LHA FOR SEVEN ROOMED OR LARGER PROPERTIES

HBR 11A(4),(5) **22.46** Each month the rent officer will determine the LHA for each category of dwelling up to six roomed accommodation for each broad rental market area (or part of) within the pathfinder authority. They will only normally set the LHA for larger dwellings if they agree with the authority that the rates for larger dwellings are regularly required (para. 22.44). The rent officer will also set the LHA for larger dwellings if it relates to a specific claim and no LHA exists – a process which is initiated by the authority applying to the rent officer for one to be set. Similarly the authority must also apply for a determination where it receives a request on an approved form from a prospective tenant who is likely to claim housing benefit – in effect a type of pre-tenancy determination (para. 6.52) but one which does not require the consent of the landlord. In both cases the rent officer will be required to supply the LHA for the appropriate category of dwelling for each broad rental market area within the authority boundary. If a 'one off' LHA is set it will apply to any other similar claims made later in the same month.

COUNTING ROOMS

HBR 11A(9), ROO sch 3A para 1(2) **22.47** In counting the number of rooms in the dwelling for any category of dwelling other than the shared rate (table 22.2) 'room' means a bedroom or 'a room suitable for living in' except a room which is shared with any other person unless that person is:

- a member of the tenant's household;
- a non-dependant;
- a person who pays rent to the tenant.

The rent officer's determinations

LOCAL HOUSING ALLOWANCE DETERMINATIONS

22.48 Local housing allowance determinations for each category of dwelling are broadly modelled on the local reference rent (para 6.28) and single room rent (para. 6.31) determinations and the formula for setting them is similar (para. 22.20) but with certain modifications to the valuation assumptions. These are:

ROO 4B(1)-(5), sch 3A paras 2-4

- The hypothetical dwelling on which LHA determination is based is assumed to be situated within the 'broad rental market area' as the claimant's dwelling rather than being in the same locality (paras. 6.19 and 22.20).
- Unlike a locality which is centred on the claimant's dwelling a broad rental market area has a defined geographical boundary and so will not overlap with any other broad rental market area. Any boundary should be co-terminous with postcodes.
- Since the boundary of the broad rental market area is fixed, the LHA determination for each category of dwelling within it will be the same for any dwelling within that category.
- Unlike localities which comprise two or more neighbourhoods (para. 6.19) a broad rental market area is comprised of 'two or more distinct areas of residential accommodation' and there is no requirement that the facilities in paragraph 6.19 are '[...] in or accessible from the neighbourhood of the dwelling'.
- Instead of a single room rent for 'young individuals', a determination based on shared accommodation is set which is applicable to a wider group of claimants (para. 22.42) and is based on the rents of dwellings that have modestly more generous facilities than the single room rent (paras. 6.32 and 22.45).
- In setting the LHA (all categories of dwelling) the rent officer must exclude rental evidence attributable to 'services', 'facilities (including the use of furniture) provided for the tenant' and 'rights made available to the tenant', if any of these are ineligible to be met by housing benefit. Since the LHA is set with this assumption the authority should not

deduct any amount from the LHA in determining the eligible rent even if the tenancy includes ineligible services (para. 22.25).

- The LHA determinations for two roomed or larger dwellings will be based on evidence of dwellings in the same category. Therefore there is no need for the assumption that they match the appropriate size criteria (para. 6.29). The claimant's eligible rent will simply be the LHA for the category of dwelling which is applicable to them.
- A complete set of LHA determinations for each category of dwelling (up to six rooms) is made at the end of each month and will be in force on the first working day of the next month. The rent officer must also make determinations for any category of larger dwellings which they 'believe are likely to be required for the purpose of calculating housing benefit'. In practice this will be after discussion with the authority (para. 22.46). Any other determinations for larger dwellings are made as and when requested or a claim needs to be determined (paras. 22.44) and take effect for the remainder of that month and apply to any similar claim.
- The limits of each broad rental market area (or part of) which falls within the authority's boundary are determined when the pathfinder goes live (strictly speaking the rent officer determines these in the month before) and are changed when, in the rent officer's opinion, it is necessary. The postcodes within any broad rental market area that fall within authority's boundary must be notified.

In all other aspects the assumptions in paragraphs 6.19, 6.29, 6.30 and 6.32 apply.

BOARD AND ATTENDANCE DETERMINATIONS

HBR 11A(6), (7) ROO 4C

22.49 Where the authority receives a claim from a private sector tenant and it appears that a substantial part of the rent is attributable to board and attendance, it must refer the claim to the rent officer stating that it believes that to be the case. The referral should be made within the same time limits and accompanied by the same information as if a referral was being made in a non-pathfinder area (paras. 6.14-15).

SI 2003 No. 2399 reg 15

22.50 Where such a referral has been made, the rent officer will decide whether a substantial part of the rent is attributable to board and attendance. Where the rent officer decides that this is the case he/she will make a determination on the same basis as if the claim had been referred to them in a non-pathfinder authority except that if the claim was previously an old scheme case (paras. 10.7 and 10.51-66) it will treated as a new scheme case (paras. 10.7 and 10.33-50).

22.51 Where the rent officer determines that a substantial part of the rent is not attributable to board and attendance then he/she will notify the authority which will be obliged to treat the claim as it would any other pathfinder case (i.e. apply the appropriate LHA or the protected rate if that is higher).

22.52 Since the decision as to whether or not a substantial part of the rent is attributable to board and attendance is made by the rent officer this cannot be appealed to a tribunal (table 19.1) but the authority can ask for this decision, or any decisions where there is a board and attendance determination, to be redetermined. These 'appeal' procedures are described in paragraphs 22.63-67. CSPSSA Sch 7 para 6(2)(c)

Payment of benefit in pathfinder areas

22.53 In pathfinder areas the authority will no longer have discretion to make direct payments purely on the grounds that the claimant has consented to them (para.16.38) if the claim is one to which the pathfinder scheme applies (para. 22.22). Instead direct payments will only be permissible in certain set circumstances when the claimant is considered to be at risk or for purely transitional purposes during the early months of the pathfinder (para. 22.55). In both cases these conditions are subject to the landlord being a 'fit and proper person' (para. 16.31-33) and to any maximum payment (para. 22.56). These rules apply even if benefit is payable at the protected rate. HBR 94(1C)(a), (b)(ii),(iii)

22.54 The circumstances when claimants can be considered to be at risk are limited to the following cases:

- the claim is one to which mandatory direct payments would apply if was not in a pathfinder area (paras. 16.30-31);
- the first payment of the claim is yet to be made and the authority considers that the first payment should be made to the landlord (para.16.29);
- the claimant has moved owing rent (para.16.38);
- the authority considers that the claimant 'is likely to have difficulty managing his/her affairs' (para 22.57) – in the language of DWP guidance the claimant is 'vulnerable' (GLHA para. 4.00-63);
- the authority considers that it 'is improbable that the claimant will pay his/her rent' (para. 22.62).

For DWP guidance on the last two cases see paragraphs 22.57-61.

22.55 In addition, for transitional purposes during the start of the pathfinder, the authority will be able to make direct payments to a landlord where: HBR 94(1C)(b)(i),

- in 'big bang' pathfinders (para. 22.21 and table 22.1) the authority may continue to make direct payments for up to six months from the start of the pathfinder or until the next (i.e. second) LHA determination, whichever is the sooner, provided they have been continuously in receipt of HB since the start of the pathfinder;

- in 'phased' pathfinders (para. 22.21 and table 22.1) where direct payments were already being made on an award which was in force at the start of the pathfinder (table 22.1). In this case payments can continue until the first LHA determination is made (including any case where the claim is protected).

MAXIMUM AMOUNT OF HB WHICH CAN BE PAID TO A LANDLORD

HBR 93(2A) **22.56** Under the LHA scheme it is possible for the amount of HB to be greater than the claimant's actual rent. Where direct payments are being made to a landlord the maximum amount of benefit which can be paid to the landlord where the tenant is not in rent arrears is limited to the rent due. If the tenant has arrears, the authority can decide whether to pay any excess towards the arrears, but only up to the level of those arrears.

GUIDANCE ON VULNERABLE CLAIMANTS

22.57 In DWP guidance claimants who 'are likely to have difficulty in managing their affairs' are referred to as vulnerable. The guidance stresses the importance of grounding a decision on evidence although it states that authorities are not expected to be proactive in identifying potential cases (GLHA, 4.22, 4.30-37).

22.58 The guidance suggests that the sources of evidence will often be the typical causes or effects of vulnerability. Potential causes include: people with learning difficulties; people with poor literacy skills or unable to speak English; people addicted to drugs, alcohol or gambling; women fleeing domestic violence; single homeless care leavers; and people leaving prison. The guidance also suggests that the risk that a person is likely to be vulnerable will increase where the claimant lives alone and has no support (GLHA para. 4.41). Potential effects include: severe debt problems, DWP direct payments to utilities, the person is in receipt of support from a homeless charity, the person is receiving help through Supporting People, the person is unable to obtain a bank account or even that the person is incapable of providing evidence to support their claim of vulnerability (GLHA para. 4.42). In the last case, it stresses that this could provide a convenient excuse for lazy decision making.

22.59 The guidance suggests that the authority should always seek to interview the claimant and obtain written evidence from any relevant person (GLHA para. 4.31-32). All evidence should be weighed but any evidence from social services, a doctor, the DWP, the courts or a 'reputable financial institution' should be accepted without question (GLHA para. 4.33-44). Evidence can also be accepted from families, friends and landlords but should be treated with caution (GLHA 4.36-37). Other sources of evidence include: welfare groups, Citizens Advice Bureaux and homeless charities involved in assisting the claimant (GLHA paras. 4.35 and 4.42).

22.60 Somewhat controversially perhaps, the guidance stresses that payment should not be delayed pending the outcome of a decision and that 'how the claimant handles [any] payments may, in fact help [the authority] reach its decision' (GLHA para. 4.51).

22.61 The guidance suggests that someone who acts on behalf of the claimant as an appointee or agent (paras. 5.6 and 16.56-7) should not be considered vulnerable (GLHA para. 4.20).

22.62 Little guidance is given on the rule which allows benefit to be paid to the landlord 'if it is improbable that they will pay their rent' except that it could be used where the authority is aware 'that the tenant has consistently failed to pay their rent on past occasions without good reason [...]' (GLHA para. 5.10).

Appeals and errors

22.63 As in non-pathfinder areas there is no right of appeal against a decision which adopts a rent officer determination (para. 6.40). In addition, in pathfinder authorities there is also no right to seek a redetermination about the level of the LHA or the broad rental market area on which it is based. This is because, unlike non-pathfinder authorities where the rent officer's determinations relate to individual properties, a LHA determination in a pathfinder area relates to all claims within that category of dwelling and would trigger a review of all other claims. However, there are special procedures to allow for: HBR 12CA(1)(b),(5) CSPSSA sch 7 para 6(2)(c)

- authorities to ask for a redetermination of the rent officer's decision that a claim is a board and attendance case and any subsequent board and attendance determinations (para. 22.65). All exempted cases (para. 22.22) can have redeterminations;
- correction of accidental errors made by the rent officer (such as a typing mistake) which are not errors of professional judgment in the determination of an LHA or of a broad rental market area (para. 22.48). An example might be that the rent officer notified the authority of a broad rental market area but notified the authority of the wrong postcode districts to which it applies. Errors as to whether a particular claim is a board and attendance case can also be included in this type of appeal.

22.64 As in non-pathfinder areas, claimants can appeal decisions (chapter 17) made by the authority which are not made as a direct consequence of adopting a rent officer's determination. This may happen for example where:

- the household size has been incorrectly assessed resulting in the wrong category of LHA being applied (note that, unlike non-pathfinder authorities, the authority applies the size criteria, not the rent officer, who simply sets the rates of the LHA each month);

- the authority has incorrectly decided that the claimant is a 'young individual';
- the authority has incorrectly assessed the use of facilities resulting in the shared rate of LHA being applied instead of the two room rate (this is also a decision of the authority and not the rent officer);
- the authority has failed to apply the protected rate when the claimant is entitled to it;
- the decision as to whether the claim is exempt from the LHA (para. 22.22) is wrong (except where this is a direct consequence of a rent officer's determination that it is a board and attendance determination);
- any decision about the payment of benefit for pathfinder claims (paras. 22.53-62).

BOARD AND ATTENDANCE REDETERMINATIONS

HBR 12B, ROO 4D **22.65** The authority may apply to the rent officer for a redetermination as to their determination that a particular case is a board and attendance case; the procedure mirrors the procedure in paragraphs 6.44-46 of this guide.

ERRORS

HBR 12CA ROO 4E, 7A(2)-(3) **22.66** Where there has been an accidental error as described in paragraph 22.63 above a similar procedure as in paragraphs 6.48-50 of this guide applies for substitute determinations.

DATE ON WHICH CHANGES TAKE EFFECT FOLLOWING REVISIONS

HBR 12CA, 12E **22.67** In the limited circumstances where the rent officer is able to correct their error (i.e. where it is not an error of professional judgment) and their determination has been amended as a result, the rules in paragraph 17.42 apply.

23 Subsidy

23.1 This chapter provides an overview of the various subsidies that are available to meet local authority HB and CTB related expenditure in 2004-05. It applies to Great Britain only.

23.2 The special subsidy arrangements that apply to administering authorities other than local authorities are not described in this chapter.

The importance of subsidy

LOST INCOME

23.3 Authorities have sometimes overlooked the importance of central government HB and CTB related subsidies and have lost income as a consequence. This may be because they:

- failed to claim their full subsidy entitlement;
- were unable to substantiate their subsidy claims; or
- had followed incorrect procedures.

23.4 Where it appears that subsidy has been overpaid to an authority, or that there had been a breach of subsidy rules, the Secretary of State has the discretion to recover amounts under s 140C(3) of the Social Security Contributions and Benefits Act 1992. The criteria that the Secretary of State considers when exercising this power are set out in DWP Circular S1/2002 (para. 3). In *Isle of Anglesey County Council (R on the application of) v Secretary of State for Work and Pensions* the authority sought to challenge the Secretary of State's decision to recover subsidy of £444,461 due to the authority's failure to refer appropriate cases to the rent officer. The application was dismissed.

THE TENSION BETWEEN SUBSIDY RULES AND THE PROPER ADJUDICATION OF CLAIMS

23.5 Not only do subsidy payments form a significant proportion of most authorities' total income, they are also a vital factor in determining the quality, effectiveness and style of HB and CTB administration. Over the years studies of HB and CCB/CTB administration have highlighted the tension between proper decision-making and some of the perverse penalties and incentives built into the subsidy arrangements (see, for example, *Remote-Control: The National Administration of Housing Benefit,* Audit Commission, HMSO, 1993). While the changes to subsidy rules from 2004-2005 have removed some of these tensions, such as the rules on backdated claims (paras. 23.31-32), others, such as applying the appropriate category to overpayments, remain (paras. 23.34-39 and table 23.1).

Legislation and guidance

23.6 The Social Security Administration Act 1992 (sections 140A-140G) provides the outline legal framework relating to the payment of subsidies to authorities. The detailed legal rules are set out in the Income-related Benefits (Subsidy to Authorities) Order 1998 (SI 1998 No 562) as amended. The rules and rates relating to 2004-05 will be incorporated in an amendment to this order. This will be made, in accordance with established practice, after the end of the 2004–05 year.

23.7 The DWP issues guidance on the subsidy arrangements in the form of the *Subsidy Guidance Manual.* This is reissued each year to reflect the subsidy arrangements applicable for that year. The DWP also issues the S series of circulars with the aim of keeping authorities up to date with subsidy-related proposals and developments. Both sets of guidance are available on-line at *www.dwp.gov.uk/housingbenefit/*

23.8 For financial years prior to 2004-05 the outline legal framework relating to the payment of HRA rent rebate subsidy in England and Wales is set out in the Local Government and Housing Act, 1989. The detailed legal rules are contained in separate HRA Subsidy Determinations issued by the Office of the Deputy Prime Minister (ODPM) and National Assembly for Wales (NAW).

April 2004 revision of the subsidy arrangements

23.9 The Local Government Act 2003 makes provision for rent rebates to be taken out of the housing authority's housing revenue account (HRA). As a result responsibility for payment of rent rebate subsidy has been transferred from the Office of the Deputy Prime Minister (ODPM) and National Assembly for Wales to the DWP from 2004-05. The DWP has taken the opportunity to make wide-ranging changes to the way authorities are subsidised from April 2004 and to the rates and rules that apply to benefit subsidy (DWP Circular S9-2003).

Authority expenditure

23.10 An authority's expenditure on different aspects of the HB and CTB schemes may be categorised under the following headings:

- benefit payment costs, i.e. the money paid out in the form of HB or CTB;

- ongoing administrative costs, which includes salaries, accommodation costs, postage and computer running costs;
- additional administrative costs incurred as a result of changes to related benefit schemes, for example, the introduction of the new tax credit and pension credit arrangements; and
- the setup and operating costs associated with specific arrangements such as those incurred as a result of the adoption of the Verification Framework.

23.11 Money to meet these costs comes from either:

- central government subsidies; or
- the authority's own general fund, or in Wales the council fund.

23.12 A housing authority's housing revenue account (HRA) records income and expenditure relating primarily to council housing. Prior to April 2004, in England and Wales, housing revenue account (HRA) rent rebate expenditure (essentially council tenants' rent rebates) fell as a cost to the authority's housing revenue account. From April 2004 this falls as a cost to the general fund or in Wales the council fund. To the extent that this expenditure fails to attract subsidy, e.g. certain local authority error overpayments, this is a new cost to fall on the general fund or council fund. ODPM ministers have agreed that in England, authorities have the option of phasing this change in over two years. (Full details of the proposed transitional arrangements are in the consultation package for England accompanying the draft HRA subsidy determination 2004-05.) At the time of writing, NAW was considering the position for Wales.

Central government subsidies

23.13 From 2004-05 all central government subsidies relating to HB/CTB are under the control of the DWP.

BENEFIT EXPENDITURE SUBSIDY

23.14 Benefit subsidy is available to meet 100% (subject to the transitional protection arrangements described in para. 23.27 and specific exceptions identified in the rest of this chapter and summarised in table 23.1) of an authority's expenditure on:

- rent rebates;
- rent allowances; and
- council tax benefit.

23.15 Prior to 2004-05:

- expenditure on HRA rent rebates in England and Wales (but not Scotland) did not attract DWP benefit subsidy but did count in the calculation of HRA subsidy administered by the ODPM and NAW;
- the basic rate of DWP benefit subsidy was 95% (subject to specific exceptions);
- the ODPM, NAW and Scottish Executive paid a 5.5% residual rent allowance/CTB subsidy to authorities through Revenue Support Grant/ Grant Aided Expenditure.

ADDITIONAL SUBSIDIES

23.16 In addition to benefit subsidy, additional DWP subsidies are available to:

- assist with authorities' HB/CTB administration costs (administration subsidy);
- assist with the increased administrative costs associated with the new tax credit and pension credit schemes;
- set up and operate the Verification Framework;
- introduce data-matching and reviews from April 2004;
- encourage authorities to identify specific categories of overpayment and error – the Weekly Incorrect Benefit (WIB) (paras. 23.67-68) element of the Security Against Fraud and Error Scheme (SAFE);
- encourage authorities to apply sanctions and prosecute fraudsters (the sanctions and prosecutions reward scheme under the SAFE arrangements); and
- help authorities tackle the barriers to improved performance (Performance Standards Fund).

Qualifying expenditure

23.17 Benefit expenditure that counts for subsidy purposes is known as qualifying expenditure.

Table 23.1: Summary of benefit expenditure subsidy arrangements 2003-05

	Arrangements 03/04		Arrangements 04/05	
Basic rate	Rent allowance Non-HRA rent rebate CTB Rent rebate (Scotland)	95%	HB/CTB	100%
	HRA rent rebate England Wales	 101.7% 102.2%		
	(Amount taken into account where LA's rent increase kept to Gov guidelines)			
Backdated awards	Rent allowance Non-HRA rent rebate CTB Rent rebate (Scotland)	50%	HB/CTB	100%
	HRA rent rebate	Nil		
LA error OPs	Rent allowance Non-HRA rent rebate CTB Rent rebate (Scotland)	Nil	Determined by thresholds	100% 40% Nil
	HRA rent rebate	Nil		
OPs caused by fraud	Rent allowance Non-HRA rent rebate CTB Rent rebate (Scotland)	40%	HB/CTB	40%
	HRA rent rebate	Nil		
Rebate credited in advance of entitlement	Rent allowance Non-HRA rent rebate CTB Rent rebate (Scotland)	Nil	HB/CTB	Nil
	HRA rent rebate	Nil		

Local office Error	Rent allowance Non-HRA rent rebate CTB Rent rebate (Scotland) HRA rent rebate	95% 100%	HB/CTB	100%
OP due to delayed award of transitional relief/ budget substitution	CTB	Nil	CTB	Nil
Claimant error/other OPs	Rent allowance Non-HRA rent rebate CTB Rent rebate (Scotland) HRA rent rebate	40% Nil	HB/CTB	40%
Duplicate payments alleged to have been lost/stolen/not received & later found to be cashed	Rent allowance	25%	Rent allowance	25%
Disproportionate increase in LA rents	Scotland and New Towns Rent Rebate HRA rent rebates	Nil Nil		Nil
Unreasonable high rents – regulated private sector tenancies	Rent allowances (Subsidy on HB attributable to rent above threshold)	25%	Thresholds abolished	
Unreasonable rents – deregulated private sector tenancies (cases not affected by Jan 96 changes only)	Rent Allowances (subsidy on HB attributable to rent above rent officer determination)	60% or Nil	Rent Allowances (subsidy on HB attributable to rent above rent officer determination)	60% or Nil

Homeless people in board and lodging accommodation	Non-HRA rent rebates Subsidy on HB attributable to rent above rebate threshold up to level of cap	 10%	Rent rebates in Board & Lodge Subsidy on HB attributable to rent above rent rebate threshold up to level of cap	10%
	Above cap	Nil	Above cap	Nil
Homeless people in accommodation held on license by LAs	Subsidy on HB attributable to rent above rebate threshold up to level of cap	95%	Subsidy on HB attributable to rent above rent rebate threshold up to level of cap	100%
	Above cap	Nil	Above cap	Nil
Short term leased accommodation	Non-HRA rent rebates in England & Scotland (Subsidy on HB attributable to rent above rent rebate threshold up to level of cap)	95%	For short term leased accom in GB (Subsidy on HB attributable to rent above rent rebate threshold up to level of cap)	100%
	HRA rent rebates in Wales (Eligible rent above threshold excluded)	102.2%	Above cap	Nil
Modular Improvements Rule	HRA rent rebates in England and Wales	Nil		Nil

DISCRETIONARY LOCAL SCHEMES

23.18 Most authorities currently operate some form of discretionary local scheme for War Pensioners. This allows an authority to disregard some or all of any war disablement.

23.19 Any benefit expenditure attributable to a local scheme does not count as qualifying expenditure and is therefore not eligible for HB or CTB subsidy.

23.20 An authority's discretionary expenditure on modified schemes to enhance the mandatory disregards of Navy and Army war widows' pensions should be contained within the relevant permitted total.

23.21 From April 2004 an authority operating a discretionary local scheme receives an addition of 0.2% to its annual subsidy up to the value of 75% of the cost of the scheme to the authority.

RENT REBATE SUBSIDY LIMITATION SCHEME (ENGLAND AND WALES)

23.22 Subsidy is not paid on any additional rent rebate expenditure that results from an authority increasing its average actual rents by more than its central government guideline rent increase. From April 2004 the DWP is responsible for this Rent Rebate Subsidy Limitation Scheme. Deductions are calculated following the rules as previously set out by ODPM/NAW and remain a charge on the HRA. This necessitates a transfer from the HRA to the General Fund. ODPM is consulting on an accounting direction to bring about these transfers. NAW is currently considering the position for Wales. An authority may, however, apply for special determinations to disapply the rule where it can show that it faces exceptional circumstances outside its control. The details of the rules are described in *Rent Rebate Subsidy Limitation: Derogations in 2004-2005,* England (ODPM December 2003) *(www.odpm.gov.uk/stellent/groups/odpm_housing/documents/page/odpm_house_026326.pdf.)*

MODULAR IMPROVEMENT SCHEMES

23.23 Modular Improvement Schemes are schemes where council tenants choose to pay increased rents in return for additional rights, services or facilities such as a door entry system or improved heating. For the purpose of rent rebate subsidy, rent rebate expenditure attributable to modular or menu improvement schemes is not eligible for subsidy.

23.24 Authorities are exempt from the reduction, however, where the rights, services or facilities:

- were made available with the sole purpose either of improving the physical condition of the dwellings or of meeting the needs of tenants or both; and

- were available for tenants to choose regardless of whether the tenants were or were not in receipt of rebates; and
- were not an influence on the authorities' letting policies and practices in the current and two proceeding financial years in relation to tenants eligible to receive rebates; and
- were made available at reasonable cost.

CERTAIN CASH PAYMENTS AND PAYMENTS IN KIND

23.25 Qualifying rent rebate expenditure is also reduced by the amount of any cash payments or payments in kind made to a local authority tenant by the authority except:

- payments made that are unrelated to the fact that the claimant is a tenant of the local authority, e.g. educational bursaries;
- awards required by law;
- discretionary payments made under section 137 of the Local Government Act 1972;
- reasonable compensation for repairs or redecorating carried out by the tenant which would normally have been carried out by the landlord; and
- one-off compensation payments for the loss, damage or inconvenience caused because the tenant occupies a particular property. This provision catches, for example, certain rent payment incentive schemes.

Subsidy on qualifying HB/CTB benefit expenditure

23.26 In 2004-05 the normal subsidy rate on benefit expenditure is 100%. A lower rate is payable in specific circumstances.

TRANSITIONAL PROTECTION

23.27 The introduction of the new subsidy rates and rules across the whole HB system will result in subsidy 'winners and losers'. To minimise and cushion the effects of the new subsidy regime on authorities, any subsidy losses are limited to 0.5% in 2004-05, then to 1% in 2005-06 and to 2% in 2006-07 (DWP S2-2004). Authorities that are subsidy winners under the new arrangements will have to meet some of the costs from the increased subsidy they would otherwise receive.

Penalised benefit expenditure

23.28 To provide authorities with a firm incentive to monitor and control costs, the following areas of benefit expenditure are penalised in 2004-05.

- identified overpayments (para. 23.33);
- disproportionately high increases in rents for local authority tenants (para. 23.46);
- rent allowances claims subject to rent officer referral that have not been referred in the appropriate year;
- rent allowances claims subject to rent officer referral that are exempt from a maximum rent calculation but where the rent used in the calculation of HB is above the rent officer's claim related rent; and
- rent rebates paid for certain homeless families in bed and breakfast accommodation and occupants of certain short-term leased accommodation where the rent payment is above a certain level (para. 23.47).

23.29 In preceding years the following areas of expenditure were also penalised:

- the backdating of claims (para. 23.32);
- rent allowances paid in respect of unreasonably high rents on most pre-1988 Housing Act tenancies without a registered or reasonable rent (paras. 23.56-57); and
- cases that have overrun the maximum benefit period without a review taking place (benefit period overruns).

23.30 Authorities must apply the benefit rules fairly, objectively and impartially. They must not allow the subsidy penalties to interfere with this duty, though where the authority has a discretion one factor it may take into account is its own financial position *(R v Brent LBC HBRB ex parte Connery).*

Backdating of claims

23.31 From April 2004 the subsidy rate for HB/CTB awards that have been backdated where the claimant has 'continuous good cause' for a late claim (para. 5.76) is 100%. All subsidy on backdated benefit is subject to the external auditor's certification that good cause has been established (para. 13, S9-2003).

23.32 Prior to 2004-05:

- nil subsidy was payable on backdated HRA rent rebates in England and Wales, that had been backdated where the claimant had good cause for a late claim (para. 5.77);
- a fixed allowance allowed in the calculation of each English and Welsh authority's HRA subsidy entitlement partially reflected notional expenditure on backdating;

- 50% subsidy was payable on other amounts of backdated HB/CTB that had been backdated where the claimant has good cause for a late claim.

Overpayments/excess CTB

23.33 The subsidy payable on benefit overpayments/(excess CTB) varies with the category of the overpayment as shown in Table 23.1.

CATEGORIES

23.34 An 'authority error overpayment' means an overpayment caused by a mistake made, whether in the form of an act or omission, by an authority. It does not apply, however, where the claimant, a person acting on the claimant's behalf or any other person to whom the payment is made, caused or materially contributes to that mistake. This category also excludes any mistake of law that is shown to have been an error only by virtue of a subsequent decision of a court.

23.35 A 'fraudulent overpayment' means an overpayment in respect of a period falling wholly or partly after 31st March 1993 that:

- is classified as such by an officer of the authority, whom the authority has designated for the purpose, after that date; and
- occurs as a result of the payment of benefit arising in consequence of:
    - dishonest or false representations for the purpose of obtaining benefit (i.e. a breach of section 111A or 112(1) of the Social Security Administration Act 1992);
    - someone knowingly failing to report a relevant change of circumstances, (contrary to the requirements of reg. 75 of the HB Regulations, or of regulation 65 of the CTB Regulations) with the intention to obtain or retain the benefit for themselves or another.

23.36 A 'technical overpayment' means that part of an overpayment which occurs as a result of a rent rebate or CTB being awarded in advance of the payment when:

- a change of circumstances, which occurs subsequent to that award, reduces or eliminates entitlement to that rebate or benefit; or
- the authority identifies, subsequent to that award, a recoverable overpayment which does not arise from a change in circumstances.

23.37 It does not include, however, any part of that overpayment occurring before the benefit week following the week in which the change is disclosed to the authority or it identifies that overpayment.

23.38 A 'departmental error' overpayment means an overpayment caused by a mistake made, whether in the form of an act or omission

- by an officer of the DWP or of the Inland Revenue, acting as such, or a person providing services to that Department or to the Inland Revenue; or
- in a decision of an appeal tribunal or a Commissioner,

23.39 The category of 'departmental error' does not apply, however, where the claimant, a person acting on the claimant's behalf or any other person to whom the payment is made caused or materially contributes to that mistake. The definition also excludes any mistake of law that is shown to have been an error only by virtue of a subsequent decision of a Commissioner or a court.

SUBSIDY ON OVERPAYMENTS

23.40 In the case of overpayments the subsidy arrangement acts, at least in part, as an incentive to authorities. Subsidy is paid on the identified overpayments. Amounts recovered, except in the case of 'departmental error' overpayments, are not deducted from the authority's subsidy entitlement. For example, if the authority recovers a fraudulent overpayment or claimant error overpayment it receives 40% subsidy and keeps the money it has recovered.

LOCAL AUTHORITY ERROR OVERPAYMENTS

23.41 Prior to April 2004 the authority received nil subsidy on overpayments categorised as 'authority error'. From April 2004 the authority receives subsidy for 'authority error' overpayments in a way that rewards the authority for reducing the creation of such overpayments against the DWP's estimate of the authority's 'authority error' overpayments. This is done via a threshold system.

23.42 For 2004-05 the thresholds – expressed as a percentage of the council's correct payments – are 0.48% (the lower threshold) and 0.55% (the upper threshold). The council receives:

- 100% subsidy on all local authority error overpayments – if the level of error does not exceed the lower threshold;
- 40% subsidy on all local authority error overpayments – if the level of error is greater than the lower threshold but does not exceed the upper threshold; and
- nil subsidy on all local authority error overpayments – if the level of error is greater than the upper threshold.

23.43 Where the 'authority error' overpayment is recoverable the authority keeps any amount actually recovered without any loss of subsidy.

23.44 The reduced rate of subsidy on 'authority error' overpayments above the 0.48% threshold acts as a penalty on the authority and as an unintended 'incentive' to misclassification.

INDICATIVE RENT LEVELS

23.45 Rent officers supply authorities with indicative rent levels (IRLs). These are supplied on the first working day of each month for eight types of property. As the authority is unable to determine rent allowance entitlement under the January 1996 rules until the rent officer has made a full determination, IRLs can be used by the authority in working out the amount of a payment on account. Where the authority is unable to recover all or part of an overpaid payment on account caused by the difference between the final determination (and consequent maximum rent) and the IRL, full subsidy is payable on the unrecovered amount providing the IRL used was the correct one and provided the authority applies the final determination in the HB assessment by the Monday following the date it was received.

Disproportionate rent increase rule

23.46 The disproportionate rent increase rule is intended to discourage authorities from loading rent increases onto council tenants to unfairly generate increased subsidy income. An authority can gain exemption if it can convince its auditors that the authority has not deliberately targeted rent increases at tenants getting HB and that its rents during the year in question have increased by a common percentage with no subsidy deduction having been incurred in the previous year.

Homeless people in B & B, licensed and short-term leased accommodation outside the HRA

23.47 Reduced subsidy applies to rent rebates paid to people in:

- board and lodging (including bed and breakfast) accommodation where the liability arises under the relevant homeless persons' legislation (i.e. section 206(2)(b) of the Housing Act 1996 or section 35(2)(b) of the Housing (Scotland) Act 1987);
- accommodation held by the authority on license (e.g. hotel annexes) where the liability arises under the relevant homeless persons' legislation; and
- accommodation held by the authority on a lease not exceeding ten years, i.e. short-term leased (STL) accommodation.

23.48 Each authority is notified of:

- a cap; and
- a threshold.

For 2004-05 these caps and thresholds are shown in Annex B of S10-2003. The equivalent figures for 2003-04 are set out in Annex B of S4-2003.

23.49 Benefit attributable to that part of the eligible rent that exceeds the authority's cap attracts nil subsidy entitlement. In licensed and short-term leased accommodation, the remainder attracts 100% subsidy. This increased from 95% in 2003-04. However, in the case of board and lodging accommodation, benefit attributable to that part of eligible rent between the threshold and the cap attracts only 10% subsidy in both 2003-04 and 2004-05 – with the aim of making the use of such accommodation by housing authorities less attractive. The Government's stated policy intention is that no family with children should remain in bed and breakfast accommodation – except in an emergency – after March 2004 (para. 12, S4-2003).

Example of reduced subsidy available on rent rebates awarded on bed and breakfast accommodation (2004-05)

Using an illustrative threshold and cap as follows:

Threshold = £100

Cap = £140

(The difference is £40.)

The application of the threshold and cap is as follows:

Weekly eligible rent used to calculate HB is £200.

Since the weekly eligible rent exceeds the cap by £60 the first £60 of any HB paid would not attract subsidy.

If claimant's HB entitlement were £150, subsidy would be:

- nil on £60;
- 10% on £40; and
- 100% on £50.

If claimant's HB entitlement were £110, subsidy would be:

- nil on £60;
- 10% on £40; and
- 100% on £10

Subsidy and rent allowance awards

23.50 The basic rate of subsidy payable on rent allowance expenditure is 100% from April 2004.

23.51 Prior to April 2004 rent allowance threshold arrangements applied to HB awarded in respect of certain 'regulated tenancies' entered into before the deregulation of private renting (January 1989). These were abolished from April 2004.

23.52 Rent officer arrangements apply to HB awarded in respect of deregulated tenancies. Where the authority is required under regulations to apply for a Rent Officer determination during the relevant year but fails to do so the relevant rent allowance expenditure attracts nil subsidy.

23.53 Where a rent allowance claim falls within the Rent Officer referral arrangements but is not subject to a maximum rent calculation (i.e. referred to as old scheme cases – pre-January 1996) then in general no subsidy is payable on the rent allowance attributable to the rent above the Rent Officer's claim related rent determination, but there are exceptions to this general rule (para. 23.59).

23.54 Where Rent Officer's determinations are used directly to calculate the maximum rent on which a rent allowance can be assessed, full subsidy is normally payable. This entitlement to maximum subsidy includes those cases where the authority cannot restrict the rent because there has been bereavement in the household or where the rent could be afforded when the tenancy was taken up and the claimant has not been in receipt of HB for 52 weeks prior to the current claim (paras. 10.38-42).

23.55 Discretionary Housing Payments (paras. 22.2-9) do not count as qualifying expenditure for HB subsidy purposes and must be contained within the permitted totals figure.

REGULATED RENT ALLOWANCE THRESHOLDS

23.56 Regulated tenancies are lettings by individual private landlords or companies that are not Housing Associations, entered into before 15th January 1989 (England and Wales) or 2nd January 1989 (Scotland) and still in existence.

23.57 Prior to April 2004, when a rent allowance was paid in a regulated tenancy case and the rent had never been registered, a threshold controlled the subsidy available to the authority in most cases. Rent allowance expenditure attributable to rents above the threshold attracted 25% subsidy while rent allowance expenditure attributable to rents up to and including the threshold attracted the then basic rate of 95% subsidy. From April 2004 the threshold penalty system is abolished.

OLD SCHEME CASES – PRE JANUARY 1996

23.58 In most cases falling under the pre-January 1996 rules, no subsidy is payable on any rent allowance equal to or less than the amount by which the eligible rent exceeds the Rent Officer's significantly high rent figure or exceptionally high rent determination.

23.59 The exception to the general rule is where the authority is unable to treat a claimant's eligible rent as reduced. In certain cases falling under the pre-January 1996 rules, the authority is unable to restrict the claimant's eligible rent, or a rent increase. This applies, for example, where the claimant falls into a 'protected' category, e.g. the claimant is 60 or over and there is no suitable alternative accommodation available. In such cases, subsidy at the rate of 60 per cent is payable on any rent allowance equal to or less than the amount by which the eligible rent exceeds the Rent Officer's determination.

Specific grant for administration costs

23.60 Authorities are partially reimbursed their administrative expenditure via a cash limited specific grant. Since 2003-04, DWP has had the sole responsibility for distribution of this funding. It was previously funded 50% by DWP, the remaining 50% being funded by ODPM and NAW through the Revenue Support Grant and the Scottish Executive SE through Grant Aided Expenditure, using their own formulae.

23.61 In 2004-05 additional grant has been awarded for the increased administrative costs associated with the new tax credit and pension credit schemes.

23.62 The specific amounts awarded to each authority for 2004-05 are set out in Annex A of DWP circular S10/2003. This circular also explains the factors that determined each authority's share of the total amounts available to the DWP to assist with administration costs (i.e. the distribution methodology). DWP allocates administration subsidy among authorities on the basis of assumed workload rather than actual expenditure.

23.63 This unit cost subsidy fails to take account of 'quality of service' objectives such as the percentage of claims processed within the 14-day time period and error rates. As well as penalising inefficient authorities, a unit cost subsidy penalises those authorities that have sought to administer HB in a positive manner, for example by providing home visits to maximise take-up or by making their offices more accessible.

DWP funding for setting up and operating the Verification Framework

23.64 An authority may claim DWP funding for setting up and operating the Verification Framework. The sums available in 2003-04 and 2004-05 are set out in DWP circulars F25-2002 and F25-2003 (para. 4) (also issued as A29-2003).

23.65 A further additional sum is available in 2004-05 to help authorities with the cost of making the transition to the new Verification Framework that operates from April 2004 as a result of the abolition of benefit periods for all claimants from that date (DWP A39/2003).

Sanctions and prosecutions rewards scheme

23.66 The rewards available under the sanction and prosecution rewards scheme (S3/2004, paras. 1523-1533) are the same in 2004-05 as in 2003-04, i.e.

- £1,200 – for each administration penalty/formal caution issued and accepted;
- £1,200 – where information is laid with a court and the court issues a summons; and
- £2,000 – for a successful prosecution where the defendant has been found guilty.

Weekly incorrect benefit (WIBs)

23.67 Under the revised SAFE scheme that applies from April 2004 authorities are rewarded for identifying specific categories of overpayments (e.g. claimant error/fraud) found by authority initiative (including any attempt to contact the claimant such as under the VF review module). Rewards are not available for the actioning of changes of circumstances reported, unprompted, by claimants or Jobcentre Plus or the Pension Service. However, where an overpayment is identified by a claimant report made within 28 days of a contact made by the authority to that claimant, the overpayment is eligible for a reward. Overpayments categorised as authority error/technical are not be eligible for a reward.

23.68 Reward payments will be made by the DWP in two tranches. Initially, eligible overpayments amounting to between £5-£20 in the last week they were paid earn a reward of £10 and those over £20 earn a reward of £40. Any remaining funding not distributed as outlined will then be distributed pro-rata according to performance at the end of the year. The details of the WIB reward arrangements can be found in the DWP's VF/SAFE Manual 2004/05.

Performance standard fund

23.69 The DWP is making available £70m in 2004-05 and £90m for 2005-06 in a Performance Standards Fund. This is to help authorities tackle the barriers to improved performance. HB/CTB circular S6/2003 sets out detailed guidance on applying for the funding.

23.70 The Performance Standard Fund superseded The Help Fund that was set up in 2001 to provide support to authority initiatives for improving core administration of benefit.

Appendix 1: Main and recent regulations, orders and rules

Here we list the main statutory instruments for England, Wales and Scotland (also known as regulations and orders) that contain the detailed rules of the HB and CTB schemes, followed by the main statutory rules and orders in council governing the HB scheme in Northern Ireland.

MAIN REGULATIONS AND ORDERS: ENGLAND, WALES AND SCOTLAND

SI 1987 No. 1971	The Housing Benefit (General) Regulations
SI 1988 No. 662	The Housing Benefit (Supply of Information) Regulations
SI 1992 No. 1814	The Council Tax Benefit (General) Regulations
SI 1995 No. 1644	The Housing Benefit (General) Amendment Regulations
SI 1997 No. 1984	The Rent Officers (Housing Benefit Functions) Order
SI 1997 No. 1995	The Rent Officers (Housing Benefit Functions)(Scotland) Order
SI 1997 No. 2435	The Housing Benefit (Recovery of Overpayments) Regulations
SI 1997 No. 2436	The Housing Benefit (Information from Landlords and Agents) Regulations
SI 1997 No. 2813	The Social Security (Penalty Notice) Regulations
SI 1998 No. 562	The Income-related Benefits (Subsidy to Authorities) Order
SI 2001 No. 1002	The Housing Benefit and Council Tax Benefit (Decisions and Appeals) Regulations

RECENT REGULATIONS AND ORDERS: ENGLAND, WALES AND SCOTLAND

SI 2003 No. 325	The Housing Benefit and Council Tax Benefit (State Pension Credit) Regulations 2003
SI 2003 No. 973	The Administration of the Rent Officer Service (Wales) Order 2003

SI 2003 No.1050	The Social Security and Child Support (Miscellaneous Amendments) Regulations 2003
SI 2003 No. 1195	The Social Security (Hospital In-Patients and Miscellaneous Amendments) Regulations 2003
SI 2003 No. 1338	The Housing Benefit and Council Tax Benefit (State Pension Credit) (Abolition of Benefit Periods) Amendment Regulations 2003
SI 2003 No. 1589	The Social Security (Back to Work Bonus and Lone Parent Run-on) (Amendment and Revocation) Regulations 2003
SI 2003 No. 1632	The Social Security (Claims and Payments and Miscellaneous Amendments) Regulations 2003
SI 2003 No. 1701	The Social Security Amendment (Students and Income-related Benefits) Regulations 2003
SI 2003 No. 1731	The Social Security (Working Tax Credit and Child Tax Credit) (Consequential Amendments) (No. 3) Regulations 2003
SI 2003 No. 1914	The Social Security Amendment (Students and Income-related Benefits)(No. 2) Regulations 2003
SI 2003 No.2275	The Housing Benefit and Council Tax Benefit (State Pension Credit and Miscellaneous Amendments) Regulations 2003
SI 2003 No. 2279	The Social Security (Miscellaneous Amendments) (No.2) Regulations 2003
SI 2003 No. 2398	The Rent Officers (Housing Benefit Functions) (Local Housing Allowance) Amendment Order 2003
SI 2003 No. 2439	The Social Security (Incapacity Benefit Work-focused Interviews) Regulations 2003
SI 2003 No. 2399	The Housing Benefit (General) (Local Housing Allowance) Amendment Regulations 2003
SI 2003 No. 2526	The Housing Benefit and Council Tax Benefit (State Pension Credit and Miscellaneous Amendments) (Amendment) Regulations 2003
SI 2003 No.2634	The Housing Benefit and Council Tax Benefit (Miscellaneous Amendments) Regulations 2003
SI 2004 No. 14	The Housing Benefit and Council Tax Benefit (Abolition of Benefit Periods) Amendment Regulations 2004

SI 2004 No.154	The Council Tax Benefit (Abolition of Restrictions) Regulations 2004
SI 2004 No. 290	The Housing Benefit and Council Tax Benefit (State Pension Credit and Miscellaneous Amendments) Regulations 2004
SI 2004 No. 319	The Housing Benefit and Council Tax Benefit (Extended Payments (Severe Disablement Allowance and Incapacity Benefit)) Amendment Regulations 2004
SI 2004 No. 552	The Social Security Benefits Up-rating Order 2004
SI 2004 No. 565	The Social Security (Miscellaneous Amendments) Regulations 2004
SI 2004 No. 574	The Housing Benefit and Council Tax Benefit (Supply of Information) Amendment Regulations 2004
SI 2004 No. 747	The Children (Leaving Care) Social Security Benefits (Scotland) Regulations 2004
SI 2004 No. 781	The Housing Benefit and Council Tax Benefit (Miscellaneous Amendments) Regulations 2004
SI 2004 No. 1232	The Social Security (Habitual Residence) Amendment Regulations 2004

MAIN REGULATIONS: NORTHERN IRELAND

SR 1987 No. 461	The Housing Benefit (General) Regulations (Northern Ireland)(as amended)
SR 1988 No. 118	The Housing Benefit (Supply of Information) Regulations (Northern Ireland)
SR 1996 No. 111	The Housing Benefit (General)(Amendment No.2) Regulations (Northern Ireland)
SR 1997 No. 453	The Housing Benefit (Information from Landlords and Agents) Regulations (Northern Ireland)
SR 1997 No. 454	The Housing Benefit (Recovery of Overpayments) Regulations (Northern Ireland)
SR 1997 No. 514	The Social Security (Penalty Notice) Regulations (Northern Ireland)
SR 1999 No. 162	The Social Security and Child Support (Decisions and Appeals) Regulations (Northern Ireland)
SR 1999 No. 225	The Social Security Commissioners (Procedure) Regulations (Northern Ireland)

SR 2000 No. 71	The Social Security (Immigration and Asylum) Consequential Amendments Regulations (Northern Ireland)
SR 2001 No. 176	The Social Security (Work-focused Interviews) Regulations (Northern Ireland)
SR 2001 No. 213	The Housing Benefit (Decisions and Appeals) Regulations (Northern Ireland)
SR 2001 No. 216	The Discretionary Financial Assistance Regulations (Northern Ireland)

RECENT REGULATIONS AND ORDERS: NORTHERN IRELAND

SR 2003 No. 197	The Housing Benefit (State Pension Credit) Regulations (Northern Ireland) 2003
SR 2003 No. 224	The Social Security and Child Support (Miscellaneous Amendments) Regulations (Northern Ireland) 2003
SR 2003 No. 261	The Social Security (Hospital In-Patients and Miscellaneous Amendments) Regulations (Northern Ireland) 2003
SR 2003 No. 274	The Social Security (Work-focused Interviews) Regulations (Northern Ireland) 2003
SR 2003 No. 294	The Housing Benefit (State Pension Credit) (Abolition of Benefit Periods Amendment) Regulations (Northern Ireland) 2003
SR 2003 No. 317	The Social Security (Claims and Payments and Miscellaneous Amendments) Regulations (Northern Ireland) 2003
SR 2003 No. 329	The Social Security (Students and Income-Related Benefits Amendment) Regulations (Northern Ireland) 2003
SR 2003 No. 338	The Social Security (Working Tax Credit and Child Tax Credit Consequential Amendments No. 3) Regulations (Northern Ireland) 2003
SR 2003 No. 351	The Social Security (Students and Income-Related Benefits Amendment No. 2) Regulations (Northern Ireland) 2003
SR 2003 No. 367	The Social Security (Back to Work Bonus and Lone Parent Run-on Amendment and Revocation) Regulations (Northern Ireland) 2003

SR 2003 No. 417	The Social Security (Miscellaneous Amendments No. 2) Regulations (Northern Ireland) 2003
SR 2003 No. 418	The Housing Benefit (State Pension Credit and Miscellaneous Amendments) Regulations (Northern Ireland) 2003
SR 2003 No. 421	The State Pension Credit (Transitional and Miscellaneous Provisions) (Amendment) Regulations (Northern Ireland) 2003
SR 2003 No. 432	The Housing Benefit (State Pension Credit and Miscellaneous Amendments) (Amendment) Regulations (Northern Ireland) 2003
SR 2004 No. 45	The Social Security (Miscellaneous Amendments) Regulations (Northern Ireland) 2004
SR 2004 No. 46	The Housing Benefit (State Pension Credit and Miscellaneous Amendments) Regulations (Northern Ireland) 2004
SR 2004 No. 47	The Housing Benefit (Miscellaneous Amendments) Regulations (Northern Ireland) 2004
SR 2004 No. 82	The Social Security Benefits Up-rating Order (Northern Ireland) 2004
SR 2004 No. 143	The Social Security (Miscellaneous Amendments No. 2) Regulations (Northern Ireland) 2004
SR 2004 No. 144	The Housing Benefit (Abolition of Benefit Periods Amendment) Regulations (Northern Ireland) 2004
SR 2004 No. 145	The Housing Benefit (Extended payments (Severe Disablement Allowance and Incapacity Benefit) Amendment) Regulations (Northern Ireland) 2004
SR 2004 No. 163	The Social Security (Income-Related Benefits Self-Employment Route Amendment) Regulations (Northern Ireland) 2004
SI 2004 No. 197	The Social Security (Habitual Residence) Amendment Regulations (Northern Ireland) 2004

Appendix 2: Table of cases cited in guide

The following table lists all cases cited in the guide in the order they appear. Where possible the table indicates where a free on-line case transcript can be accessed. Where none is available both free and on-line the table provides a reference for a recognised published law report.

Social Security Commissioners' decisions cited in this guide are not included in this table. For further details on the status of Commissioners' decisions, see paras. 1.51-52. Hard copies of reported Commissioners' decisions (i.e. those prefixed by 'R') are available from Print Solutions, Room B0202, Benton Park Road, Longbenton, Newcastle upon Tyne, NE98 1YX (Tel: 0191 225 5422, Fax: 0191 225 7179). Reported decisions from 1991 are available on-line at *www.dwp.gov.uk/advisers/index.asp#commdecs*. All unreported Commissioners' decisions from 2002 and selected decisions from 2001 are available on-line at *www.osscsc.gov.uk/pages/des.htm*. Earlier unreported decisions in print are available from the Office of the Social Security Commissioners (para. 19.79). For Northern Ireland Commissioners' decisions see paragraph 1.52.

Para	Case *Neutral Citation/European Case Reference* *Full online transcript*	Date *Published report*	Court
1.61	**R v Maidstone BC ex p Bunce**	**23/06/94** *27 HLR 375*	**QBD**
2.27	**R v Birmingham CC HBRB ex p Ellery and Weir**	**04/04/89** *21 HLR 398*	**QBD**
2.34	**R v Poole BC HBRB ex p Ross**	**05/05/95** *28 HLR 351*	**QBD**
2.44	**R v Sheffield C C HBRB ex p Smith**	**08/12/94** *28 HLR 36*	**QBD**
2.34	**R v Sutton BC HBRB ex p Partridge**	**04/11/94** *28 HLR 315*	**QBD**
2.44	**R v Poole BC HBRB ex p Ross**	*See 2.34 above*	
2.47	**R v Solihull MBC HBRB ex p Simpson**	**03/12/93** *26 HLR 370*	**QBD**

Para	Case	Date	Court
	Neutral Citation/European Case Reference *Full online transcript*	*Published report*	
2.47	**R v Sutton LBC ex p Keegan**	**15/05/92**	**QBD**
		27 HLR 92	
2.50	**R v Manchester CC ex p Baragrove Properties**	**15/03/91**	**QBD**
		23 HLR 337	
2.54	**R (on the application of Painter) v Carmarthenshire CC HBRB**	**04/05/01**	**QBD**
	[2001] EWHC Admin 308	*Times 16/05/01*	
	www.casetrack.co.uk Subscriber site Case reference CO/3011/2000		
2.56	**Secretary of State for Social Security v Tucker**	**08/11/01**	**CA**
	[2001] EWCA Civ 1646	*[2002] HLR 27*	
	www.casetrack.co.uk Subscriber site Case reference CO/01/1222		
2.66	**The Governors of Peabody Donation Fund v Higgins**	**20/06/83**	**CA**
	[1983]	*1 WLR 1091*	
3.25	**Secretary of State for Work and Pensions v Miah**	**25/07/03**	**CA**
	[2003] EWCA Civ 1111		
	http://www.bailii.org/ew/cases/EWCA/Civ/2003/1111.html		
3.35	**R v Penwith DC HBRB ex p Burt**	**26/02/90**	**QBD**
		22 HLR 292	
4.8	**Crake and Butterworth v Supplementary Benefit Commission**	**21/07/80**	**QBD**
	[1982] 1 All ER 498		
4.9	**R v Penwith DC ex p Menear**	**11/10/91**	**QBD**
		24 HLR 115	
4.9	**R v South Ribble BC HBRB ex p Hamilton**	**24/01/00**	**CA**
	www.casetrack.co.uk Subscriber site Case reference: QBCOF/1999/1021/C		
5.19	**R v Penwith DC ex p Menear**		
		See 4.9 above	
5.36	**R v Liverpool CC ex p Johnson (No 2)**	**31/10/94**	**QBD**
		[1995] COD 200	

Para	Case *Neutral Citation/European Case Reference* *Full online transcript*	Date *Published report*	Court
5.36	**R v Winston** *[1998] EWCA Crim 2256* *http://www.bailii.org/ew/cases/EWCA/Crim/1998/2256.html*	**07/07/98**	**CA**
5.72	**Secretary of State for Work and Pensions v Robinson and Another** *[2004] EWCA Civ 342* *http://www.bailii.org/ew/cases/EWCA/civ/342.html*	**11/02/04**	
6.1	**R (on the application of Cumpsty) v The Rent Service**	**05/12/02** *Times 05/12/02*	**CA**
6.18	**R (on the application of Saadat and Others) v The Rent Service** *[2001] EWCA Civ 1559* *http://www.bailii.org/ew/cases/EWCA/Civ/2001/1559.html*	**26/10/01**	**CA**
6.26	**R v Swale BC HBRB ex p Marchant** *www.casetrack.co.uk Subscriber site Case reference: QBCOF/1999/0071/C*	**09/11/99** *32 HLR 856*	**CA**
6.40	**R (on the application of Cumpsty v The Rent Service**	*See 6.1 above*	
10.6	**R (on the application of Naghshbandi) v Camden LBC HBRB** *[2002] EWCA Civ 1038* *http://www.bailii.org/ew/cases/EWCA/Civ/2002/1038.html*	**19/07/02**	**CA**
10.48	**R (on the application of Laali) v Westminster CC HBRB** *www.casetrack.co.uk Subscriber site Case reference: CO/1845/2000*	**08/12/00**	**QBD**
10.54	**R v Swale BC HBRB ex p Marchant**	*See 6.26 above*	
10.56	**R v Beverley DC HBRB ex p Hare**	**21/02/95** *27 HLR 637*	**QBD**

Para	Case *Neutral Citation/European Case Reference* *Full online transcript*	Date *Published report*	Court
10.56	**Malcolm v Tweedale HBRB**	**06/08/91** *1994 SLT 1212*	**CS**
10.57	**Malcolm v Tweedale HBRB**	*See 10.56 above*	
10.60	**R v East Devon DC HBRB ex p Gibson**	**10/03/93** *25 HLR 487*	**CA**
10.61	**R v Sefton MBC ex p Cunningham**	**22/05/91** *23 HLR 534*	**QBD**
10.62	**R v Westminster CC HBRB ex p Mehanne** *[2001] UKHL 11* *http://www.publications.parliament.uk/pa/ld200001/ldjudgmt/jd010308/mehann-1.htm*	**08/03/01** *33 HLR 46*	**HL**
10.62	**R v Beverley DC HBRB ex p Hare**	*See 10.56 above*	
10.62	**R v Brent LBC ex p Connery**	**20/10/89** *22 HLR 40*	**QBD**
10.64	**R v Brent LBC ex p Connery**	*See 10.62 above*	
13.20	**Hourigan v Secretary of State for Work and Pensions** *[2002] EWCA Civ 1890* *http://www2.bailii.org/ew/cases/EWCA/Civ/2002/1890.html*	**19/12/02**	**CA**
16.6	**R v Liverpool CC ex p Johnson (No 1)**	**23/06/94** *unreported*	**QBD**
16.17	**R v Haringey LBC ex p Ayub**	**13/04/92** *25 HLR 566*	**QBD**
16.34	**R v Haringey LBC ex p Ayub**	*See 16.17 above*	
18.11	**R v Cambridge CC HBRB ex p Sier** *[2001] EWCA Civ 1523* *www.casetrack.co.uk Subscriber site Case reference C/01/0694*	**08/10/01**	**CA**

Para	Case	Date	Court
	Neutral Citation/European Case Reference *Full online transcript*	*Published report*	
18.12	**R v Liverpool CC ex p Griffiths**	**14/03/90** *22 HLR 312*	**QBD**
18.15	**Adan v Hounslow LBC** *[2004] EWCA Civ 101* *http://www.bailii.org/ew/cases/EWCA/Civ/2004/101.html*	**19/02/04**	**CA**
18.30	**Warwick DC v Freeman**	**31/10/94** *27 HLR 616*	**CA**
18.30	**Secretary of State for Work and Pensions v Chiltern DC and Warden Housing Association** *[2003] EWCA Civ 508* *http://www.bailii.org/ew/cases/EWCA/Civ/2003/508.html*	**26/03/03**	**CA**
18.57	**R v Haringey ex p Ayub**	*See 16.17 above*	
18.68	**R v Thanet DC ex p Warren Court Hotels Ltd** *www.casetrack.co.uk Subscriber site Case reference C/523/1999*	**06/04/00** *33 HLR 32*	**QBD**
18.68	**Warwick DC v Freeman**	*See XX.yy above*	
18.69	**Haringey LBC v Awaritefe** *[1999] EWCA Civ 1491* *http://www.bailii.org/ew/cases/EWCA/Civ/1999/1491.html*	**26/05/99**	**CA**
18.70	**Waveney DC v Jones** *www.casetrack.co.uk Subscriber site Case reference CCRTF/1998/1482/B2*	**01/12/99** *33 HLR 3*	**CA**
18.70	**Norwich CC v Stringer** *www.casetrack.co.uk Subscriber site Case reference FC2 99/7400/B2*	**03/05/00** *33 HLR 15*	**CA**
20.26	**Yildiz v Secretary of State for Social Security** *[2001] EWCA Civ 309* *www.casetrack.co.uk Subscriber site Case reference C/2000/3093*	**01/03/01**	**CA**

Para	Case	Date	Court
	Neutral Citation/European Case Reference *Full online transcript*	*Published report*	
20.42	**Angenjeux v Hakenberg**	**12/07/73**	**ECJ**
13/73 *http://europa.eu.int/smartapi/cgi/sga_doc?smartapi!celexplus!prod!CELEXnumdoc&numdoc=61973J0013&lg=EN*			
20.42	**Di Paolo v Office National de L'Emploi**	**17/02/77**	**ECJ**
76/76 *http://europa.eu.int/smartapi/cgi/sga_doc?smartapi!celexplus!prod!CELEXnumdoc&lg=en&numdoc=61976J0076*			
20.45	**Re J (A Minor) (Abduction)**	**17/05/90**	**HL**
		[1990] 2 AC 562	
20.48	**Nessa v Chief Adjudication Officer**	**21/10/99**	**HL**
http://www.publications.parliament.uk/pa/ld199899/ldjudgmt/jd991021/nessa.htm			
20.48	**Swaddling v Chief Adjudication Officer**	**25/02/99**	**ECJ**
C-90/97 *http://europa.eu.int/smartapi/cgi/sga_doc?smartapi!celexplus!prod!CELEXnumdoc&lg=en&numdoc=61997J0090*			
21.8	**O'Connor v Chief Adjudication Officer**	**03/03/99**	**CA**
[1999] EWCA 884 *http://www.bailii.org/ew/cases/EWCA/Civ/1999/884.html*			
23.4	**Isle of Angelsey County Council (R on the application of) v Secretary of State for Work and Pensions**	**30/10/03**	**QBD**
[2003] EWHC 2518 Admin *http://www.bailii.org//ew/cases/EWHC/Admin/2003/2518.html*			
23.20	**R v Brent LBC ex p Connery**	*See 10.62 above*	

ABBREVIATIONS USED IN THIS APPENDIX

AC	Appeal Cases, published by The Incorporated Council of Law Reporting for England and Wales, London
All ER	All England Law Reports, published by Butterworths
BC	Borough Council
CA	Court of Appeal for England and Wales
CC	City Council
COD	Crown Office Digest, published by Sweet & Maxwell
CS	Court of Session, Scotland
DC	District Council
ECJ	European Court of Justice
EWCA Civ	Court of Appeal Civil Division for England & Wales (neutral citation)
EWCA Crim	Court of Appeal Criminal Division for England & Wales (neutral citation)
EWHC Admin	High Court for England & Wales, Administrative Court (neutral citation)
HBRB	Housing Benefit Review Board
HL	House of Lords
HLR	Housing Law Reports, published by Sweet & Maxwell
LBC	London Borough Council
MBC	Metropolitan Borough Council
QBD	High Court (England & Wales) Queens Bench Division
SLT	Scots Law Times, published by W. Green, Edinburgh
UKHL	House of Lords, UK case (neutral citation)
WLR	Weekly Law Reports, published by The Incorporated Council of Law Reporting for England and Wales, London

Appendix 3: Recent HB and CTB circulars

This appendix lists:

- all DWP circulars in the 'A' (adjudication and operations) series which remain current following the issue of amendment 3 (February 2004) to the DWP's Housing Benefit and Council Tax Benefit Guidance Manual, the list being extrapolated from circular HB/CTB A9/2004; and
- all DWP circulars in the 'S'(subsidy) series since the beginning of 2003.

ADJUDICATION AND OPERATION CIRCULARS

HB/CTB A31/2002 (November 2002)

1 Proforma LA17
2 Benefit Fraud Inspectorate revised model claim form
3 Claimants from Zimbabwe
4 Amendment to HB/CTB A28/2002

HB/CTB A9/2003 (March 2003)

Sangatte arrivals

HB/CTB A11/2003 (April 2003)

Replacement of Exceptional Leave To Remain with Humanitarian Protection

HB/CTB A15/2003 (April 2003)

1 Pension Credit Update
2 Correction to HB/CTB Circular A2/2003

HB/CTB A16/2003 (April 2003)

Background to Pension Credit

HB/CTB A21/2003 (August 2003)

Update on the replacement for benefit periods

HB/CTB A22/2003 (August 2003)

Performance indicator:
Speed of processing renewal claims and quartile target for 2003-04

HB/CTB A23/2003 (September 2003)

Update on Pension Credit and HB/CTB issues

HB/CTB A25/2003 (September 2003)

Update on Pension Credit and HB/CTB issues

HB/CTB A26/2003 (September 2003)

Update (2) on the replacement regime for the abolition of benefit periods

HB/CTB A27/2003 (September 2003, revised October 2003)
Employment Retention and Advancement (ERA) Scheme

HB/CTB A28/2003 (October 2003)
Guidance on the application of the requirements of Section 1(1A) and 1(1B) of the Social Security (Administration) Act 1992 (commonly referred to as Section 19) for HB and CTB claims association with certain Department for Work and Pensions (DWP) administered benefits

HB/CTB A29/2003 (October 2003)
Verification Framework – funding arrangements for 2004/2005

HB/CTB A30/2003 (October 2003)
1 Return to Work Credit: Introduction in pilot areas from 27 October 2003 and 5 April 2004
2 Addendum to HB/CTB Guidance Manual Amendment 2

HB/CTB A31/2003 (October 2003)
HB/CTB Performance Standards

HB/CTB A32/2003 (October 2003)
The processes and procedures for the new HBMS regime from October 2003

HB/CTB A33/2003 (November 2003)
Uprating of benefits for 2003/2004: deductions from eligible rent

HB/CTB A35/2003 (November 2003)
Decision Making and Appeals

HB/CTB A36/2003 (November 2003)
Extended Access to Departmental Data for Local Authorities (EAD-DLA) project

HB/CTB A37/2003 (November 2003)
Rent Officer referral arrangements from 6 October 2003 following abolition of benefit periods for pensioners

HB/CTB A38/2003 (November 2003)
Changes to the Verification Framework (VF) and Security Against Fraud and Error (SAFE) schemes from April 2004

HB/CTB A39/2003 (December 2003)
Funding for introducing data-matching and reviews from April 2004

HB/CTB A40/2003 (December 2003)
New Immigration Status Letters for Grant of asylum, Discretionary grant of leave to enter/remain, Grant of Humanitarian Protections, Sponsorship agreements, NASS35

HB/CTB A1/2004 (January 2004)
Abolition of the Council Tax Benefit restriction

HB/CTB A2/2004 (January 2004, with revision January 2004)
2004 Uprating

HB/CTB A3/2004 (January 2004)
1 Amendment to Circular A31/2003
2 Amendment to HB/CTB Performance Standards
3 Additional earnings disregard in HB/CTB

HB/CTB A4/2004 (January 2004)
1 Providing photocopied or scanned evidence to the Pension Service
2 Best Value Performance Indicators – effects of abolition of benefit periods and the introduction of Pension Credit
3 Transitional Housing Benefit Scheme

HB/CTB A5/2004 (February 2004)
Impact of the Customer Management System in HB/CTB

HB/CTB A6/2004 (February 2004)
1 The Social Security (Income and Capital Disregards) Amendment Regulations 2004
2 Abolition of the Council Tax Benefit (CTB) restriction

HB/CTB A7/2004 (February 2004)
Extended payments for those in receipt of Income Support and Income-based Jobseeker's Allowance

HB/CTB A8/2004 (February 2004)
2004 uprating of savings credit only cases and the assessed income figure

HB/CTB A9/2004 (February 2004)
1 Disregard of Lone Parent Work Search Premium and Lone Parent In Work Credit
2 Current HB/CTB A Circulars list

HB/CTB A10/2004 (February 2004)
Families given extended leave to remain in UK, granted exceptional leave outside Immigration Rules, as a result of Home Secretary's announcement of 24 October 2003

HB/CTB A11/2004 (February 2004)
1 Uprating non state second pensions
2 Multiple Changes of Circumstances
3 2004 Uprating of savings credit only cases and the Assessed Income Figure
4 Reason for delay in processing

5 Unconverted cases

6 Mis-match of data between that held by DWP and that held on LA IT systems

7 Single point of contact for AIF queries

HB/CTB A12/2004 (March 2004)

Children (Leaving Care) Act 2000 – Introduction of Local Authority support arrangements in Scotland from 1 April 2004

HB/CTB A13/2004 (March 2004)

1 Uprating 2004 – Frequently Asked Questions

2 The Pension Service Partnership Fund

HB/CTB A14/2004 (March 2004)

Extended payments for Incapacity Benefit and Severe Disablement Allowance (EP – IB/SDA) claimants

HB/CTB A15/2004 (March 2004)

Housing Benefit Matching Service (HBMS) Data Take on and Processing Schedule (DTOPS)

HB/CTB A16/2004

Update on the Verification Framework (VF) and Security Against Friends and Enemies (SAFE) schemes from April 2004

HB/CTB A17/2004 (March 2004)

The Housing Benefit and Council Tax Benefit (Abolition of Benefit Periods) Amendment Regulations 2003

HB/CTB A18/2004 (March 2004)

1 The HCTB1(PC) claim form and supplementary forms

2 When is a person treated as occupying a dwelling as a home – dual liability

3 Assessing weekly income from Tax Credits

HB/CTB A19/2004 (March 2004)

Further guidance on the Verification Framework (VF) and Security Against Fraud and Error (SAFE) schemes from April 2004

HB/CTB A20/2004 (April 2004)

1 Treatment of HB/CTB overpayments arising from a problem with the electronic transmission to Local Authorities of Pension Credit uprating details for savings credit only cases

2 Tax credits renewals

SUBSIDY CIRCULARS

HB/CTB S1/2003 (February 2003)

Housing Benefit and Council Tax Benefit subsidy 2003/2004: details of the specific grant for administration costs in Scotland

HB/CTB S2/2003 (March 2003)

Details of the distribution of the government contribution and overall DHPs for 2003/2004

HB/CTB S3/2003 (April 2003)

Additional administration subsidy and special subsidy provision for the implementation of new tax credits

HB/CTB S4/2003 (April 2003)

HB and CTB subsidy arrangements 2003/2004: details of the benefit subsidy arrangements and the specific grant for administration costs

HB/CTB S5/2003 (May 2003)

2002/03 HB/CTB Subsidy Guidance Manual

HB/CTB S6/2003 (August 2003)

To invite further applications to the Performance Standards Fund for 2004/05 and 2005/06

HB/CTB S7/2003 (August 2003)

Guidance on completion of progress reports on projects with Performance Standards Funding

HB/CTB S8/2003 (August 2003)

Adjustment to the Security Against Fraud and Error scheme for 2003/04 to take account of the impact of Pension Credit

HB/CTB S9/2003 (December 2003)

HB/CTB Subsidy review – 2004/05 changes

HB/CTB S10/2003 (December 2003)

1 Details of the Department for Work and Pensions (DWP) specific grant for Local Authorities' (LA) administration costs in 2004/05

2 Non-Housing Revenue Account (HRA) thresholds and caps for 2004/05

HB/CTB S11/2003 (December 2003)

1 To notify Local Authorities [LAs] of the amounts of indirect Rent Allowance and CTB subsidy paid through the Revenue Support Grant, which will be transferred to Department for Work and Pensions for payment by direct grant from 2004/05

2 To provide further advice on the new transitional protection system by way of a Question and Answer brief at Annex A which reflects frequently asked questions as a result of HB/CTB Circular S9/2003 sent out to authorities on 1 December 2003.

HB/CTB S1/2004 (January 2004)

Adjustment to the Security Against Fraud and Error (SAFE) scheme for 2003/04 to take account of the impact of Pension Credit

HB/CTB S2/2004 (February 2004)

To notify Local Authorities (LAs) of the change to the Transitional Protection Scheme announced in circular S9/2003

HB/CTB S3/2004 (February 2004)

2003/04 HB/CTB Subsidy Guidance Manual

HB/CTB S4/2004 (March 2004)

HB/CTB subsidy arrangements 2004/05: details of the benefit subsidy arrangements and the specific grant for administration costs

HB/CTB S5/2005 (March 2004, revised March 2004)

Details of the distribution of the government contribution and overall DHPs for 2004/05

Appendix 4: HB and CTB rates and allowances (from April 2004)

Personal Allowances

SINGLE CLAIMANT	
Aged 16-24	£44.05
Aged 25-59	£55.65
Aged 60-64	£105.45
Aged 65 or over	£121.00
LONE PARENT	
Under 18	£44.05
Aged 18 or over	£55.65
COUPLE	
Both under 18	£66.50
At least one 18-59	£ 87.30
Both aged 60-64	£160.95
At least one aged 65	£181.20
DEPENDENT CHILDREN/YOUNG PERSONS	
All ages under 19	£42.27

Premiums

Family*	normal rate	£15.95
	'baby' rate	£26.45
Severe disability	single	£44.15
	couple (lower rate)	£44.15
	couple (higher rate)	£88.30
Carer	claimant or partner or each	£25.55
Disabled child	each child/young person	£42.49
Enhanced disability	each child/young person	£17.08
Enhanced disability	single/lone parent	£11.60
	couple (one or both qualifying)	£16.75

PLUS IF AGED UNDER 60 HIGHEST ONLY OF:

Bereavement		£23.95
Disability	single	£23.70
	couple	£33.85

* there is a higher rate of family premium in certain cases (para. 12.9)

Earned income disregards

STANDARD DISREGARD (HIGHEST ONE ONLY)

Lone parent	£25.00
Certain people who are: disabled, carers or in select occupations	£20.00
Couple	£10.00
All others (single)	£ 5.00

ADDITIONAL 16/30 HOUR WORK DISREGARD (ONE ONLY)

Any claimant awarded working tax credit 30 hour work element	£12.32
Lone parents & certain single people who work at least 30 hours	£12.32
Couple with child, one member works at least 30 hours	£12.32
Certain couples where combined work is at least 30 hours	£12.32

ADDITIONAL CHILDCARE DISREGARD (HIGHEST ONE ONLY)

Qualifying childcare charges for 1 child (actual costs up to)	£135.00
Qualifying childcare charges for 2 or more children (actual costs up to)	£200.00

Non dependant deductions in HB

AGE 18 OR OVER AND WORKING AT LEAST 16 HOURS: GROSS INCOME

£308.00 or more	£47.75
£247.00 - £307.99	£43.50
£186.00 - £246.99	£38.20
£144.00 - £185.99	£23.35
£97.00 - £143.99	£17.00
Under £97.00	£7.40

OTHERS NOT IN WORK OR WORKING UNDER 16 HOURS

Under 25 on IS or JSA(IB)	£0.00
Most others	£7.40

Meals deductions (HB)

FULL BOARD

Each person aged 16+	£19.85
Each child under 16	£10.05

HALF BOARD

Each person aged 16+	£13.20
Each child under 16	£6.65

BREAKFAST ONLY

Each person (inc. children)	£2.45

Fuel charge deductions (HB)

PEOPLE OCCUPYING MORE THAN ONE ROOM

All fuel	£13.00
Heating	£9.80
Hot water	£1.20
Lighting	£0.80
Cooking	£1.20

PEOPLE OCCUPYING ONE ROOM ONLY

All fuel except cooking	£5.90
Cooking	£1.20

Non dependant deductions in CTB

AGE 18 OR OVER AND WORKING AT LEAST 16 HOURS: GROSS INCOME

£308.00 or more	£6.95
£247.00 - £307.99	£5.80
£144.00 - £246.99	£4.60
Under £144.00	£2.30

ALL OTHERS NOT IN WORK OR WORKING UNDER 16 HOURS)

On IS or JSA/IB or guarantee credit	£0.00
Most others	£2.30

Second adult rebates

CIRCUMSTANCES	AMOUNT OF REBATE
All second adults on IS or JSA(IB) or pension credit	25% of council tax
Second adults gross income under £144.00	25% of council tax
Second adults gross income £144.00 - £185.99	7.5% of council tax
Second adults gross income £186.00 or more	Nil

Non dependant deductions in rates

AGE 18 OR OVER AND WORKING AT LEAST 16 HOURS: GROSS INCOME

£308.00 or more	£6.95
£247.00 - £307.99	£5.80
£144.00 - £246.99	£4.60
Under £144.00	£2.30

ALL OTHERS NOT IN WORK OR WORKING UNDER 16 HOURS

On IS or JSA(IB) or guarantee credit	£0.00
Most others	£2.30

Appendix 5: Other benefit rates (from April 2004)

CONTRIBUTION-BASED JOBSEEKER'S ALLOWANCE

claimant aged under 18	£33.50
claimant aged 18 to 24	£44.05
claimant aged 25 or more	£55.65

CHILD BENEFIT

only or older/oldest child (general rate)	£16.50
only or older/oldest child (protected lone parent rate)	£17.55
each other child (couple or lone parent)	£11.05

INCAPACITY BENEFIT

Long-term rate	
single person	£74.15
couple	£118.50
Short-term higher rate	
single person	£66.15
couple	£100.75
Short-term lower rate	
single person	£55.90
couple	£90.50

RETIREMENT PENSION STANDARD RATE

single person	£79.60
couple	£127.25

DISABILITY LIVING ALLOWANCE

Care component	
highest rate	£58.80
middle rate	£39.35
lowest rate	£15.55

MOBILITY COMPONENT

higher rate	£41.05
lower rate	£15.55

SPECIAL PAYMENT

for pre-1973 war widows/widowers	£62.68

Appendix 6: Categories of people for non-dependant deduction and second adult rebate purposes

There are many categories of people relevant for non-dependant deductions in HB, for non-dependant deductions in main CTB, and for second adult rebate. The categories are not always the same for these three purposes.

This appendix defines all the categories relevant for these purposes, and answers the following questions for each category:

- Is there a non-dependant deduction for them in HB (including, in Northern Ireland, HB in respect of rates) and main CTB (paras. 7.19, 7.26)?
- Are they 'disregarded persons' for second adult rebate purposes?

The second question is relevant because a 'disregarded person' cannot be a second adult (para. 8.8); and because the rules about whether couples and joint occupiers can qualify for second adult rebate refer to 'disregarded persons' (paras. 8.17-18). It is also relevant to the rules about council tax discounts (para. 9.16).

People may fall into more than one category. If a particular category (e.g. category 1) indicates that a non-dependant deduction applies (or that they are not 'disregarded persons'), this is over-ridden if they fall into another category (e.g. category 13) where no non-dependant deduction applies (or where they are 'disregarded persons').

The category numbers have no significance except to aid cross-referencing.

1. PEOPLE ON JSA(IB), IS OR GUARANTEE CREDIT

HB	No non-dependant deduction if aged under 25. Otherwise a non-dependant deduction applies.
Main CTB	No non-dependant deduction.
Second adult rebate	Not 'disregarded persons'.

This means anyone in receipt of income-based jobseeker's allowance, income support or guarantee credit. This includes people receiving JSA(IB) or IS while on government training schemes, and people who would get JSA(IB) except that they are currently subject to a sanction.

2. PEOPLE UNDER 18

HB and main CTB	No non-dependant deduction.
Second adult rebate	'Disregarded persons' (because they do not count as 'residents').

This means anyone under 18 whether a member of the claimant's family or not.

3. 18-YEAR-OLDS FOR WHOM CHILD BENEFIT IS PAYABLE

HB and main CTB	No non-dependant deduction.
Second adult rebate	'Disregarded persons'.

This means 18-year-olds for whom someone receives or could receive child benefit – e.g. at school and shortly after leaving school (see also category 4).

4. EDUCATION LEAVERS UNDER 20

HB	A non-dependant deduction applies unless they fall within categories 2 or 3.
Main CTB	No non-dependant deduction.
Second adult rebate	'Disregarded persons'.

This only applies from 1st May to 31st October inclusive each year. It means anyone who leaves the type of education described in category 5 or 6 within that period. It lasts until that person reaches 20 or until 31st October, whichever comes first.

5. STUDENTS UNDER 20 AT SCHOOL OR COLLEGE

HB and main CTB	Whether there is a non-dependant deduction depends on whether they fall within category 2, 3 or 10.
Second adult rebate	'Disregarded persons'.

The full definition is not given here. Its main elements are that the person:

- is under 20; and
- is studying up to (but not above) A level, ONC, OND or equivalent; and
- is on a course of at least 3 months' duration; and
- is normally required to study at least 12 hours per week in term times; and
- does not fall within categories 6 to 8.

6. FULL-TIME STUDENTS IN FURTHER OR HIGHER EDUCATION

HB and main CTB	Whether there is a non-dependant deduction depends on whether they fall within category 10.
Second adult rebate	'Disregarded persons'.

The full definition is not given here. Its main elements are that the person:

- is attending a course of further or higher education (e.g. university); and
- is on a course of at least one academic or calendar year's duration; and
- is normally required to study at least 21 hours per week for at least 24 weeks per year.

7. FOREIGN LANGUAGE ASSISTANTS

HB and main CTB	Whether there is a non-dependant deduction depends on whether they fall within category 10.
Second adult rebate	'Disregarded persons'.

They must be registered with the Central Bureau for Educational Visits and Exchanges.

8. STUDENTS ON NURSING AND RELATED COURSES

HB and main CTB	Whether there is a non-dependant deduction depends on whether they fall within category 10.
Second adult rebate	'Disregarded persons'.

This means anyone studying for a first inclusion in Parts 1 to 6 or 8 of the nursing register.

9. STUDENT NURSES STUDYING FOR THEIR FIRST NURSING REGISTRATION

HB and main CTB	Whether there is a non-dependant deduction depends on whether they fall within category 10.
Second adult rebate	'Disregarded persons'.

This means anyone studying for a first inclusion in Parts 1 to 6 or 8 of the nursing register.

10. FULL-TIME STUDENTS

HB	No non-dependant deduction except during any period they take up remunerative work (16 hours per week or more) in a summer vacation.
Main CTB	No non-dependant deduction.
Second adult rebate	'Disregarded persons'.

A student at a further education college counts as 'full-time' if he or she is normally expected to undertake more than 16 guided learning hours per week. All students on sandwich courses count as 'full-time'. Otherwise 'full-time' is not defined.

11. WORK BASED TRAINING ALLOWANCE TRAINEES

HB and main CTB	No non-dependant deduction.
Second adult rebate	'Disregarded persons' only if under 25.

This means people in receipt of a Work Based Training Allowance as a trainee.

12. APPRENTICES ON NCVQ/SVEC COURSES

HB	A non-dependant deduction applies.
Main CTB	No non-dependant deduction.
Second adult rebate	'Disregarded persons'.

This means someone who:

- is in employment; and
- is studying for a qualification accredited by the National Council for Vocational Qualifications (England and Wales) or Scottish Vocational Education Council (Scotland); and
- receives a reduced rate of pay because of being an apprentice; and
- receives gross pay which does not exceed £160 per week.

13. PEOPLE WHO ARE 'SEVERELY MENTALLY IMPAIRED'

HB	A non-dependant deduction applies.
Main CTB	No non-dependant deduction.
Second adult rebate	'Disregarded persons'.

This means someone who has 'a severe impairment of intelligence and social functioning (however caused) which appears to be permanent'; and has a medical certificate confirming this; and is receiving one or more of the following (or would do so apart from the fact that he or she has reached pension age):

- the highest or middle rate of the care component of disability living allowance (DLA), or
- attendance allowance, constant attendance allowance or certain equivalent additions to industrial injuries and war pensions, or
- incapacity benefit (IB), or severe disablement allowance (SDA), or
- income support or JSA(IB) (or his or her partner is) – but only if it includes a disability premium awarded because of the person's incapacity for work.

14. CARERS OF PEOPLE RECEIVING CERTAIN BENEFITS

HB	A non-dependant deduction applies unless they fall within category 17.
Main CTB	No non-dependant deduction.
Second adult rebate	'Disregarded persons'.

This applies to someone if:

- he or she is providing care or support for at least 35 hours a week; and
- he or she resides with the person receiving the care or support; and
- that person is not a child of his or hers under 18, nor his or her partner; and
- that person is entitled to the highest rate of the care component of disability living allowance, or a higher rate attendance allowance, or certain equivalent additions to industrial injuries and war pensions.

15. CARERS INTRODUCED BY AN OFFICIAL OR CHARITABLE BODY

HB	A non-dependant deduction applies unless they fall within category 17.
Main CTB	No non-dependant deduction.
Second adult rebate	'Disregarded persons'.

This means someone who:

- is engaged or employed to provide care or support for at least 24 hours a week for no more than £36 per week; and
- is resident (for the better performance of this work) in premises provided by or on behalf of the person receiving the care or support; and
- is employed by that person; and
- was introduced to that person by a local authority, government department or charitable body.

16. CARERS RESIDENT IN OFFICIAL OR CHARITABLE PREMISES

HB	A non-dependant deduction applies unless they fall within category 17.
Main CTB	No non-dependant deduction.
Second adult rebate	'Disregarded persons'.

This means someone who:

- is engaged or employed to provide care or support for at least 24 hours a week for no more than £36 per week; and
- is resident (for the better performance of this work) in premises provided by or on behalf of a local authority, government department or charitable body, on whose behalf the care or support is provided.

17. CARERS FOR WHOM THE CLAIMANT OR PARTNER IS CHARGED

HB and main CTB	No non-dependant deduction.
Second adult rebate	'Disregarded persons' only if they fall within categories 14 to 16.

This means carers caring for the claimant or partner, who are provided by a charitable or voluntary body which charges the claimant or partner for this.

18. PEOPLE IN PRISON OR OTHER FORMS OF DETENTION

HB	No non-dependant deduction.
Main CTB	No non-dependant deduction unless detained only for non-payment of a fine or (in England and Wales) council tax.
Second adult rebate	'Disregarded persons' unless detained only for non-payment of a fine or (in England and Wales) council tax.

The full definition is not given here, but this includes people in almost any kind of detention.

19. PEOPLE WHO HAVE BEEN IN AN NHS HOSPITAL FOR MORE THAN 52 WEEKS

HB and main CTB	No non-dependant deduction.
Second adult rebate	'Disregarded persons' only if they fall within category 20.

This means someone who is in hospital and has been for more than 52 weeks – but only in the case of NHS hospitals (including NHS Trust hospitals) and not for wholly private patients. Two or more stays in hospital are added together if the break between them is four weeks or less.

20. PEOPLE ACTUALLY RESIDENT ELSEWHERE

HB and main CTB	No non-dependant deduction.
Second adult rebate	'Disregarded persons' (because they are not 'residents').

A person is 'resident' in his or her 'sole or main residence'. It does not matter what type of accommodation this is: it could be an ordinary home, a hospital, a care home, a hostel, or any other type of accommodation. This category could apply to a visitor or to a student returning just for the holidays.

21. PEOPLE NORMALLY RESIDENT ELSEWHERE

HB and main CTB	No non-dependant deduction.
Second adult rebate	Not 'disregarded persons' unless they fall within category 20.

The concept is not defined. In practice, it is very difficult to distinguish it from category 20.

22. RESIDENTS IN HOSPITALS, CARE HOMES AND CERTAIN HOSTELS

'Disregarded persons'.

Although a claim for HB is possible in some of these types of accommodation (and in rare cases a claim for CTB might be possible), it is unlikely that any claimant would have a non-dependant/second adult. This category is included because it affects council tax discounts in such accommodation. It applies to any of the following:

- patients with sole or main residence in an NHS hospital, military hospital, residential care home, nursing home or mental nursing home;
- people with sole or main residence in non-self-contained accommodation which provides them with personal care for old age, disablement, or past or present alcohol or drug dependence or mental disorder;
- people with sole or main residence in non-self-contained accommodation which provides licences (not tenancies) for people of no fixed abode and no settled way of life;
- people with sole or main residence in a bail hostel or probation hostel.

23. MEMBERS OF RELIGIOUS COMMUNITIES

HB	A non-dependant deduction applies.
Main CTB	No non-dependant deduction.
Second adult rebate	'Disregarded persons'.

This means someone who:

- is a member of a religious community whose principal occupation is prayer, contemplation, education, the relief of suffering, or any combination of those; and
- has no income (other than an occupational pension) or capital; and
- is dependent on the community for his or her material needs.

24. (a) MEMBERS OF CERTAIN INTERNATIONAL BODIES OR OF VISITING FORCES, (b) THEIR NON-BRITISH SPOUSES, AND (c) CERTAIN NON-BRITISH SPOUSES OF STUDENTS

HB	A non-dependant deduction applies.
Main CTB	No non-dependant deduction.
Second adult rebate	'Disregarded persons'.

The full definitions are not given here. Group (a) includes members of certain international headquarters and defence organisations and certain visiting forces (and in some cases their dependents). For groups (b) and (c), in broad terms, the spouse must be prevented from working or claiming. For group (c), 'student' means someone in category 4, 5 or 6.

25. ANYONE ELSE

HB and main CTB	A non-dependant deduction applies.
Second adult rebate	Not 'disregarded persons'.

This means anyone who does not fall into any of the previous categories.

Index

References in the index are to paragraph numbers (not page numbers), except that 'A' refers to appendices, 'T' refers to tables in the text and 'Ch' refers to a chapter.

J

L

M

Q

R

U

V

W

Y